Justifying Judgment

Justifying Judgment

Practicing Law and Philosophy

Vincent J. Samar

University Press of Kansas

Published by the University Press of Kansas (Lawrence, Kansas 66049), which was organized by the Kansas Board of Regents and is operated and funded by Emporia State University, Fort Hays State University, Kansas State University, Pittsburg State University, the University of Kansas, and Wichita State University

I want to acknowledge the following presses who graciously granted me permission to reprint various extracts from works they have published: BETWEEN FACTS AND NORMS by Jürgen Habermas. © 1996 by MIT Press. Extracts from pages 58, 65–66, 115, 128–29, 150. Reprinted by permission of MIT Press and Blackwell Publishers. This work originally appeared in German under the title *Faktizität und Geltung: Beiträge zur Diskurstheorie des Rechts und des demokratischen Rechtssaat,* © 1992 Suhrkamp Verlag, Frankfurt am Main, Germany. THE CONCEPT OF LAW by H. L. A. Hart. © 1961, 1994, by Oxford University Press. Extracts from 1st edition on pages 13–14, 57, 80, 86–88, 105–6, 246n98. Extract from 2d edition on page 252. Reprinted by permission of Oxford University Press. LAW AS A MORAL JUDGMENT by Deryck Beyleveld and Roger Brownsword. Extracts from pages 2, 32–33, 147n26, 149–50, 159. © 1986 by Sweet & Maxwell. Reprinted by permission of Sweet & Maxwell. "Law, Morality, and Sexual Orientation" by John Finnis, Volume 69, Issue 5, *Notre Dame Law Review* (1994): 1049, 1067, 1069. Reprinted with permission. © 1994 by *Notre Dame Law Review,* University of Notre Dame. A MATTER OF PRINCIPLE by Ronald Dworkin. Extracts from pages 119, 134–36, 143–44, 161–62, 172, 174. © 1985 by Ronald Dworkin. Reprinted by permission of Harvard University Press. PARTIAL CONSTITUTION by Cass Sunstein. Extracts from pages 4, 42–45, 55, 61, 67, 76, 101–2, 114, 146, 235–38, 363n33. © 1993 by the Presidents and Fellows of Harvard College. Reprinted by permission of Harvard University Press. PHILOSOPHICAL INVESTIGATIONS, 3/E by Anscombe, Translator (Wittgenst), © 1953. Drawing from page 194e. Reprinted by permission of Prentice-Hall, Inc., Upper Saddle River, NJ. REASON AND MORALITY by Alan Gewirth. © 1978 by the University of Chicago Press. All rights reserved. Published 1978. Phoenix edition 1981. Printed in the United States of America. Extracts from pages 6, 20, 23, 32, 55, 67–68, 108, 119, 121, 142–44, 159–61, 168, 172–76, 188–89, 205, 242, 292, 294, 208–9, 312–13, 332, 361–63. Reprinted by permission of the University of Chicago Press. WE THE PEOPLE, FOUNDATIONS, volume 1, by Bruce Ackerman. © 1991 by the Presidents and Fellows of Harvard College. Extracts from pages 58, 65–66, 115, 128–29, 150. Reprinted by permission of Harvard University Press.

Library of Congress Cataloging-in-Publication Data

Samar, Vincent Joseph, 1953–
Justifying judgment : practicing law and philosophy / Vincent J. Samar.
p. cm.
Includes bibliographical references and index.
ISBN 0-7006-0854-0 (alk. paper)
1. Justice. 2. Law and politics. 3. Law and ethics. 4. Judicial process. I. Title.
K240.S36 1998
340'.11—dc21 97-18323

British Library Cataloguing in Publication Data is available.

Printed in the United States of America

10 9 8 7 6 5 4 3 2 1

The paper used in this publication meets the minimum requirements of the American National Standard for Permanence of Paper for Printed Library Materials Z39.48-1984.

To Alan Gewirth

CONTENTS

Preface *ix*

Introduction *1*

1. Sources of Law 7
   Legal Philosophy 8
   Shortcomings of Legal Philosophy 26

2. The Duty to Obey Law 30
   Political Philosophy 36
   The Doctrine of Political Responsibility 47

3. Metatheory 61
   Justice as an End of Political Responsibility 62
   Analyzing Metatheory 67
   Substantive Principles and the Question of Objectivity 82

4. Virtual Law 90
   Skepticism: External and Internal 91
   Theoretical Reason 99
   Practical Reason 107

5. Real Law 110
   Two Understandings of Truth 110
   From the Internal Point of View to Political Morality 115
   From Political Morality to Law 126

6. Difficult Cases 138
   Privacy, Sodomy, and Society's Political Morality 140
   Slavery and Natural Law 147
   Abortion and the Internal Point of View 152

Lochner and the Court's Failure to Do Justice 162
Plessy, Brown, and the Social Construction of the "Natural" 171

7. Legal Education 179
   A Brief Word About Terminology 181
   Traditionalism 183
   Legal Constructivism 193
   Threshing, Not Trashing 207

Conclusion 220

Notes 233

Selected Bibliography 279

Index 293

PREFACE

Ever since the publication of Ronald Dworkin's *Taking Rights Seriously* in 1977 lawyers have been discussing "hard cases."[1] The precedents in hard cases go in both directions, and no clear legal rules apply. One suggestion for deciding these cases has appealed to broader substantive principles of society's political morality. By political morality, I mean the application of morality to the operations and justification of political institutions. The problem with this suggestion, however, is that it presupposes that a judge is not faced with having to decide a case in which the society's political morality is internally inconsistent or under serious attack from some alternative political morality. The alternative political morality may be the position of some substantial portion of the society, or it may be some ideal that seems to the judge to be more persuasive. Either way, when the alternative occurs, the judge is faced with a very hard case. The phrase very hard is not meant to generate an attack from composition mavens concerned with the boundary conditions of the word "very." It is to suggest that as one moves up the ladder of normative discourses from the traditionally legal to the society's morality to universal morality to decide a case, the uncertainties of interpretation and justification become more rather than less difficult. This situation is different from that of the hard case in which a judge merely has no fixed legal rule to apply. With the hard case, the judge could at least rely on the society's political morality to provide a basis of well-recognized, even if abstract, legal principles to decide the case. With the very hard case, legal principles are of no help because they are either internally inconsistent or offend some deeper concern about justice.

Philosophers disagree about how to resolve very hard cases, usually without any attempt to distinguish them from hard cases. Some, for example, think that in any well-developed legal system there will be available enough legal principles and prior precedents to decide almost any case that comes along.[2] Others think that very hard cases are unresolvable by any rational means, because law is a patchwork of unconnected political compromises.[3] (The word "rational" references here a *type* of argument that would instantiate each case decision as a *token* rather than treating each such decision as unrelated to every other one except, possibly, for the fact that each one secures the interest of some dominant political force in society.) Since the latter view can lead to the possibility of contradictory decisions, the label of the critical legal studies (CLS) movement in calling such case decisions—when undertaken as a group—a patchwork quilt of unconnected political compromises seems apropos. Naturally, if the former view of how to decide very hard cases is correct, there will be few unresolvable cases; if the latter view is correct, resolutions will reduce to politics, that is, to bowing to the greatest political force at the moment.

Of course, the latter view is not self-evident. For even if one adopts the point of view that politics dominates the legislative function, as it no doubt does, it still does not follow that the people who are appointed to the federal bench will not develop more than simply political concerns. For one thing, they must at least appear to justify the decisions they make in terms of protecting some set of important social interests. Thus, to show the latter view to be true, one must demonstrate that any attempt to derive a consistent set of legal principles will fail. A weaker and I believe less adequate attempt would be to show what everyone already knows: that competing forces run through private law.[4] I say "less adequate" because the mere fact that a particular solution may benefit some set of interests and disadvantage others does not mean it is unprincipled from a moral point of view. Rather, it merely reflects the fact that given the limitations of our nature, logic, and moral reasonings, law cannot be truly neutral. Perhaps the beneficiaries are the poor, and morality requires giving assistance to the poor. On the other hand, if one contends that the latter view is incorrect, one faces the opposite challenge. The goal then would be to develop a means for providing a consistent set of just legal principles. As I believe that law can be made consistent and just, this must be my goal, too.

Such a demonstration may not be possible if one has to work only with the prevailing political morality of the society, however, since any attempt to demonstrate the internal consistency of legal principles would beg the question of the internal consistency of the society's political morality. If the society's political morality is just a patchwork of conflicting, not merely competing, doctrines, then, of course, it will not be possible to obtain a consistent set of legal principles. If it is not a patchwork, what is the deep principle that makes it consistent, and why that principle over some other? The question thus becomes, why must the society's political morality, especially if it is inconsistent, be our starting point? Very hard cases show us the need for a different starting point. They show us the need for a more general political morality that can provide a consistent and determinative set of just legal principles upon which judges can decide cases.

Solving the problem of very hard cases requires, then, finding a political morality from which to derive a consistent set of just legal principles. This means finding a point of view that takes both the principles of law and the *society's* political morality as its objects. Such a point of view is necessarily external to the traditional legal system since it calls into question the system itself and the political morality of which it is a part.[5] This point of view is that of the political philosopher.[6] It is broader than that of the legal philosopher. It aims to answer deep questions about the role of justice in law and the nature of legal obligations, as opposed to what constitutes legitimate sources of law from within the legal point of view. It also tries to justify the duty to obey law or—in its more particular form as applied to the judiciary—the judge's institutional responsibility to decide a case according to the law.[7] This duty cannot be justified strictly from the internal point of view without begging the question. Moreover, the external point of view regards the duty to obey law as independent of law itself in the same way that the duty to be a good parent is independent of parenting. The duty to obey law is more properly a token of a general type of duty that citizens in a democracy owe to their political institutions. In this, it is more properly a subject of political philosophy than of legal philosophy.[8]

The claim that a system of law is either totally internally coherent or totally internally incoherent does not affect the analysis I have been suggesting. To the contrary, the former fails to preempt the question because even if the legal system is truly coherent, there is still the possibility of unjust decisions arising. The latter fails to preempt the issue because if the legal system is truly incoherent, a fortiori it is necessary to provide the judge with a means to decide all types of cases and a reason for doing so. Of course, the question of justification is only likely to arise in a context where the society's political morality is itself being challenged. Still, the implications of even this proposition are startling.

If the possibility of rationally resolving very hard cases provides the only key to unlocking the duty to obey law, then in easy cases the duty is being presumed. But that means that in easy cases we must be uncertain whether our obedience to law has any rational basis. We have only our presumption that the system is just. Failing to recognize this explains why some scholars commit a methodological error when they attempt to resolve very hard cases from within the legal point of view. The problem is that these cases are calling into question the very system that is being relied upon to resolve them. Positivists, for example, who banally hold that a developed legal system will always include a metarule—in the sense of an internally accepted algorithm—to be used in deciding very hard cases, fail to appreciate that such rules cannot be justified from within the legal system.[9] A similar problem befalls scholars who seek to resolve very hard cases by employing a combination of substantive and interpretative *legal* principles as if these principles were not in need of independent justification.

Very hard cases, then, pose the problem of requiring the judge to look outside the framework of a traditional system of laws to fulfill the court's institutional responsibility to decide the case. When this happens, the judge needs to justify stepping outside the traditional law by appealing to a metatheory that makes available a more comprehensive set of sources. The metatheory must be able to reference the sources as well as the appropriate priority rules that determine how the sources are ranked relative to each other. A political morality that is merely internal to the legal system will not be general enough to provide this. Such a political theory will be just too close to the existing sources of law, having itself arisen in the context of those sources, to be able to see them in any broader context.

Most natural law scholars who have approached the issue of very hard cases have treated it as an issue of what law is.[10] This viewpoint has created a confusion from the beginning, for legal philosophy and political philosophy operate at different levels of abstraction: legal philosophy is concerned with what law means and how it is justified within a political—possibly moral— perspective; political philosophy is concerned with justifying the institutional duties, rights, and obligations defining *that* perspective. The latter encompasses the former but only because there is a duty to obey law that is itself not a part of law. The problem of formulating a metatheory to assist judges in deciding very hard cases is that one must take simultaneous account of the duty to obey law along with providing a criterion for deciding what the law is. This dual task means treating the institution of law itself as requiring a justification under a more general doctrine of political morality than would be the case if we had merely to justify our determination of what the law is. Consequently, grounding a metatheory of law is a step removed from grounding a theory of law because the duty to obey law must also be justified. In both instances, political morality is involved, but only in the latter is it viewed at its maximum generality.

This raises an epistemological question: such an inquiry suggests the demise of an idea that has become widespread in discussions about social political moralities.[11] The idea is implied by the phrase "internal point of view." It is the notion that a point of view references a distinct conceptual scheme or worldview. There are thus no overlapping concepts with any other conceptual scheme since the very idea that there might be overlap is logically inconsistent with the notion of a distinct worldview. Indeed, I contend that the correct interpretation of the internal point of view is not that of a conceptual scheme because I do not take discussions about internal and external as the incommensurable totalities that some scholars have suggested. Instead, I view such frameworks as a means progressively to compare wider ranges of concepts.[12] Sometimes this approach takes the perspective of seeing a lesser framework included within a broader one, as, for example, when one stops a game of chess to discuss the social significance of chess. Other times it takes the perspective of searching for a common framework to allow discussion to proceed about two narrowly distinct frameworks. For example, law and personal morality may not share any overlapping set of concepts though both may be part of a broader conceptual framework concerned with regulating and enabling human behavior.[13]

By focusing on sets of concepts rather than on incommensurable conceptual schemes, the door is open to two distinct types of justifications. The first selects the most coherent interpretation within a conceptual framework. The second corresponds the interpretation selected to the best interpretation within a broader conceptual framework. Interestingly, the second type of justification collapses into the first when the scope of the conceptual framework is the whole of one's discourse language, including its principles of interpretation.

Except where very hard cases are being considered, different sets of concepts will constitute the internal point of view of the judge and the external point of view of the political philosopher. Where very hard cases are involved, we discover that certain concepts—say, those that make up the ethical positions of Alan Gewirth and John Rawls—mesh much better with the concepts held by most judges in advanced capitalistic democracies than, say, the ideas of Karl Marx. For this reason, different justifications must apply to the political philosopher's metatheories and the judge's legal theories. In the typically easy case, where one thinks that the legal questions are not hard, judges justify their decisions almost exclusively from a point of view internal to the legal system based on traditional sources of law, and the political philosopher says nothing. No broader ethical justification guarantees the decision, nor do political philosophers necessarily feel any need to provide one. Consequently, when deciding easy cases judges do no more than presuppose that the law they are applying is the law that some metatheory would say they ought to be applying. The concern, of course, is that a judge might make a mistake. But this will not manifest itself unless the outcome is an egregious violation of justice or of the prevailing political morality. It becomes a problem only if, after a judge decides a very hard case, the decision leads other judges to reconsider cases previously thought to be easy. At that point, the judges who currently make up the legal system face the fact that the courts previously committed serious errors that need to be corrected.

Virtual law is a good description of the body of laws one follows in easy cases in which questions of moral justification do not arise. The term virtual implies that the laws one is obeying may or may not be the laws one ought to be obeying. Modifying "law" and not "legality" is analogous to what the physicist does when using the term virtual particle as opposed to virtual reality. Postulating virtual particles, for example, in black-hole physics allows physicists to maintain the belief that they are operating within the conservation laws that normally govern the universe.[14] Yet if they spoke of the periphery of a black hole as a virtual reality, they would either have to give up thinking of such bodies as part of the universe or give up their conservation rules. The former is not possible if they are to think of such bodies as physically existing and especially as having a causal influence on other bodies. The latter seems too restrictive if there is no way to see beyond the event horizon to what might lie inside a black hole. Similarly, virtual laws are laws that we postulate on some ground to be morally justified so that we have a reason to be bound by them. Virtual legality, were we to adopt that term, would imply that we are not bound by laws regardless of how at first things might appear. This implication has been lurking behind the question of very hard cases and is the reason that such cases may be the most important ones for courts to decide. In the context of such cases, judges have a strong reason to question what the law is. At all other times, judges may feel comfortable with following the law as it appears. Consequently, my real challenge is to develop a metatheory of law that would afford guidelines to judges deciding very hard cases. Such a theory would treat the connection between legitimate sources of law and the duty to obey law as a problem of normative political philosophy or what I have called a general political morality.

In attempting to meet this challenge, in chapter 1 I shall focus on sources for law. In particular, I will consider the views of several schools of jurisprudential thought to determine what law is and how it comes about. In chapter 2 I treat the derivation of the duty to obey the law and focus on broader theories of political philosophy to set a foundation for the duty to obey law. In chapter 3 I present a metatheory for how a judge should decide difficult—both hard and very hard—cases. In chapter 4 I take up the issue of what we mean by the internal point of view, showing that scholars often misunderstand the issue and that a better understanding could lead only to a *presumption* of the existing legal system's legitimacy. In chapter 5 I provide a natural law justification for a legal system containing morally just laws. In chapter 6 I apply the metatheory developed in chapter 3 to resolve two hard and three very hard historically significant constitutional cases. Then I take up the implications of what has been going on in legal education between traditionalists and (post)modernists in chapter 7 and offer a suggestion based on the metatheory I have developed for how legal education might proceed in the future. In the conclusion I offer a comment about the inherent incompleteness of law and how the law might be understood.

This book presents a bridge for crossing two important jurisprudential divides. The first occurs at the high theory level in which the separation between natural law theory and socially based legal theories becomes prominent. This can be seen most clearly in the metaethical theory of Alan Gewirth, which, when treated as a kind of natural law philosophy, stands in contrast to the social morality presupposed by the legal philosophy of Ronald Dworkin. In order to span these two grounds, I focus on the boundary where the two theories meet, the external and internal points of view. But the book goes beyond each theory in the way it accommodates both to enhance their mutual strengths. It goes beyond the Gewirthian view in that it allows for the possibility of virtual law with no prior moral justification; it goes beyond Dworkin's position by recognizing as legitimate the external point of view.[15] The only theoretical limit the book runs into when expanding to these higher grounds is what Donald Davidson calls the scheme/content distinction. If the book is successful, it should advance our understanding of the relationship of law to morality and legal to political philosophy.

The second divide is found in the distinction between traditional legal reasoning or reasoning by analogy and the more comprehensive approaches that several legal thinkers have advocated courts to adopt before undertaking legal decisions. Here the separation is between incompletely theorized jurisprudence, as described in the writings of Cass Sunstein, and the more fully theorized approaches of such authors as Ronald Dworkin, Jürgen Habermas, and Richard Posner and others in the school of law and economics. The point is to show that each side has something important to contribute to judicial decisionmaking without treating either as providing the sole approach to legal resolutions. Thus, only when judges disagree about the possible outcomes for a particular case should they appeal to more highly ordered political moralities, initially from within the legal system. And only when that political morality is itself in question will the judge, then, be warranted in appealing to an external moral theory that would also justify the legal system as a whole. The latter encompasses the foundation for natural law jurisprudence.

In this book I describe the relation between legal and political philosophy. While I focus on responsibilities of the judiciary, aspects of my general thesis may be applicable to other institutional actors, such as legislators and executives, who make or carry out law. These people too affect how very hard cases are resolved by the statutes, administrative decisions, and executive orders they create. Moreover, although the examples in the book are drawn from the American judicial system—as the system with which I am most familiar—the theory is not bound to any particular nation-state but should be broad enough to apply to any legal system in which the primary function of the courts is to do justice. In this regard, there may be a need to adjust to different institutional settings in which courts operate with different sets of guidelines. Still, this should pose no permanent problem for the general theory being presented here. The book should be of interest not only to legal scholars and philosophers but also to political scientists, legal practitioners, people concerned with the direction of legal education, and to everyone involved in or concerned with the making and interpretation of law.

As with any project of this sort, one is indebted to the kindness of others. I wish to thank Barry Breitung, Steve Burton, Theodore Grippo Jr., David Ingram, Christopher Lane, David Malament, and Donald Whitfield for their helpful comments regarding several ideas raised herein. Especially, I want to thank Alan Gewirth, Douglas Litowitz, and Raymond Belliotti for thoroughly evaluating an earlier draft of this book and making many helpful criticisms and suggestions concerning its clarity and interpretation. Sarah Geis did some very careful proofreading. I also wish to acknowledge my Philosophy of Law students at Loyola University of Chicago and my Jurisprudence students at the Illinois Institute of Technology, Chicago/Kent College of Law. Through their own critical questions, these students have supported this work and encouraged my search for the answers contained herein. Of course, any confusions or misunderstandings are strictly my own. I want to thank the library staffs of Loyola University of Chicago, Northwestern University School of Law, and IIT-Chicago/Kent for their invaluable resource help, along with the staff of Loyola's Academic Technologies for giving me countless and perhaps thankless hours of computer assistance. And I want to thank Cynthia Rudolph, the Loyola Water Tower philosophy secretary, for taking care of my classroom typing needs, thus freeing me up to work on this book, and Greg Hamill, assistant dean of the College of Arts and Sciences, for providing me regular office facilities. This book is dedicated to Alan Gewirth—teacher, mentor, and friend—whose own writings prove the importance of reason to the most fundamental of human concerns.

INTRODUCTION

One of the first facts that every student of law learns is the difference between primary and secondary sources of law. Primary sources include constitutional texts, treaties, statutes, and cases. These sources have the authority of rules, an arranged hierarchy of one to the other, and a binding control over the cases or controversies to which they apply.[1] Secondary sources include legislative histories and debates, scholarly comments on legislation and cases, and to varying lesser extent discussions about the justice and social policy functions of political institutions.[2] Secondary sources are not binding, only instructive as to the meaning and validity of primary sources.

In this book, I contend that the distinction between primary and secondary sources is more a product of a certain legal philosophy than an actual state of the law. Notwithstanding the importance of stare decisis to our ability to know and predict legal results, I also contend that recognizing this distinction has created an artificial separation between legal and political philosophy that has impeded the ability of judges to seek the most just—as opposed to the most formally correct—solutions in very hard cases. By very hard cases, I mean cases in which the principles of law either are internally inconsistent or offend the political morality of the law.[3] Very hard cases stand in contrast to hard cases, in which a judge merely has no clear rule to apply and must therefore resort to using a combination of substantive and interpretative legal principles.[4]

I suggest that we abandon the distinction between primary and secondary sources and that in its place we develop metalegal criteria for deciding when any purported source of law becomes a source of law. In this respect, I hope to improve the practice of legal decisionmaking generally. I also hope to deconstruct—if I may borrow that term—the apparent barrier between political morality, which attempts to justify a legal system externally, and legal philosophy, which provides internal hierarchies of rules and principles.[5] Finally, I hope to support the idea that justice is best served in a legal system justified under a broader theory of political morality.

One caveat should be noted. The argument to be presented here applies to legal systems in which the judges are expected to apply the law justly. In a legal system where doing justice is not even a minimal expectation, the "obligation to obey the law" will be either incoherent, as having no moral foundation, or sui generis and sometimes in conflict with moral duties.[6]

The thesis being presented here clearly reopens many old questions about the nature and validity of law, when law is properly given effect, and what the relationship is between law and morality. The practice of law, if not the academic study of law, has ignored many of these issues by restricting the question of what law is either to the positivist view that it is what the legislature says it is or to the legal realist view that it is what courts will do when deciding cases. The former of these approaches is illustrated by court deference to legislative authorities when deciding cases. The latter is shown by the amount of time and effort lawyers spend in trying to anticipate future court decisions on behalf of their clients. The net effect of this seeming lack of interest with more philosophical issues of law, at least in the practice of law, has been to focus the intellectual energies of lawyers toward the development of legal strategies and away from the development of any sort of critique on the nature of law and its function in society. That the practice of law has become so dominated by mundane substantive questions and that the intellectual energies of lawyers are primarily devoted to questions of prediction and strategy reflect the fact that our society sees the use of these skills as what lawyers do.

In academic circles, where issues of law and morality are still considered, a serious debate has ensued. Some scholars argue desperately on behalf of various theoretical approaches to the development of a consistent legal doctrine to explain the actions of judges.[7] Other scholars adamantly deny the existence of any such doctrine.[8] The result is a seemingly intractable battle over the legitimacy of law itself.

What has caused the academic community to feel so much uncertainty about the legitimacy of law and the legal profession to place so much emphasis on prediction and strategy over substance? Scholars for a long time have sought answers to the difficult questions of living in society. No doubt, they hoped that the rationality of the modern period would provide the answers. Unfortunately, the atrocities of the second half of the twentieth century and the decline of socialism left them profoundly disappointed. For lawyers, there is the need to provide clear and precise rules in a highly technical, highly urban society where time to decide cases is short and the number of cases is large.[9] Beyond this, there may be a not-so-hidden design to preserve the existing power structure of society, be it economically, socially, or gender-based, in which lawyers have a material role to play.[10] (I will not seek here to decide among these possibilities or even to suggest that only one motive is involved.) Certainly, whatever the motives, having a set, determined way for deciding what the laws are preserves the power status quo in society. It also allows society to undergo more rapid technological advance than would be the case if the rules governing behavior were less certain. Ironically, justice may be served by limiting the behaviors that are to be protected or proscribed only to those that can be precisely described because foreknowledge gives rise to the possibility of more meaningful choices among alternative courses of action. A problem arises, however, when the rules that govern the practice are found in very hard cases to be either inconsistent or contrary to justice.

Here the solution may be quite complex and will no doubt vary with the ideological bent of the individuals doing the assessment: Marxism on the political/economic side, feminism on the gender side, and various libertarian theories on the side of wealth maximization compete for dominance in determining the academic outlook on law.[11] Yet these theories fail to provide more than a surface political morality for the types of duties people are thought to have in society. Theory determines what a legitimate source of law is and what it is not, but what makes one theory better than another cannot depend on theoretical determinations called into question. Thus, in a pluralistic society the possibility exists that no one theory will dominate, and this, in turn, can lead to inconsistent approaches making up the political morality of the society. When this happens, a still deeper philosophical critique is necessary to unmask, if unmasking is even possible, which theory best describes what the law is. This is the problem of very hard cases.

I propose, therefore, to construct a metatheory for law. Such a theory would adjudicate among various competing schools of jurisprudence by saying when and under what circumstances a theory associated with a particular legal school ought to be followed by a court. More important, from a practical standpoint, such a metatheory would determine appropriate sources of law by providing a ground for deciding very hard cases. This latter aspect reflects the reality that courts have to decide very hard cases in which the disputes are as much about broad theoretical issues of law as they are about the specific controversies raised by the parties involved.

Two fundamental questions arise with the development of any metatheory for law. The first concerns how one makes the bridge between an internal—society-centered—point of view on the political morality of law and an external point of view, whatever that may be. If one has only the internal point of view, on what basis could one ever assess the legitimacy of the other perspective?[12] The second question concerns whether any determinate external theory of political morality can be regarded as nonarbitrary in the sense of being based on some criterion other than the idiosyncratic preferences of the people relying on it.[13] Such a criterion rules out selection of a theory solely to manufacture the results I want.

The latter issue is well known to moral theorists, even though a positive answer to it is often disputed. Still, there is no reason to think that a nonarbitrary, determinate theory of political morality cannot be found. Moreover, given that the internal point of view may be incapable of presenting a satisfactory set of consistent legal principles to justify the decisions in very hard cases, finding an external point of view appears desirable. Another question also arises: Will some of the law taken as settled need to be rethought, should an adequate external theory be found? This issue will occur only where the external metatheory fails to reproduce a law previously thought to be both settled and just. In that instance, courts may have to face the possibility that some previous decisions were mistaken, but at least their decisions will be principled and not just the arbitrary results of some inconsistent set of political compromises currently in vogue.

Ronald Dworkin has attempted to sidestep appealing to an external point of view by refusing to consider any theory of law as justified unless its range of principles harmonizes closely with those generally defining the constitutional law of the community.[14] This he calls "law as integrity." I contend that this is a mistake because the standards of the legal community need be neither internally consistent nor morally correct. Consequently, any legal system that one perceives as morally justified cannot so narrowly restrict what constitutes its operative principles. Further, I will argue that a workable metatheory grounded in an external political morality is not barred by viewing law as an internal normative system. Indeed, to the contrary, I will show that even in easy cases the internal piggybacks on the external, as is demonstrated by the fact that the institution of law presupposes fidelity to law, or, correspondingly, fidelity to the judge's duty to follow the law. More generally, the external view serves two functions. First, it provides legitimacy for the legal system when viewed from outside, that is, from a moral point of view. By legitimacy, I mean that the language of the external moral theory is sufficiently broad to encompass within its own logic a justification for the internal system. Second, the external point of view justifies the duty to obey law by determining which laws are morally worthy of obedience. From the internal point of view, such decisions could be seen only as pragmatic choices, given a prevailing presumption that the laws are just. Pragmatism plays the role from the internal point of view of explaining why a judge may need to appeal to a broader theory of political morality than what the society provides. This occurs when the judge's duty to decide a case based on the law cannot be satisfied solely from the devices—rules and principles—that the legal system puts at the court's disposal. The judge recognizes that this situation exists when the available principles are themselves inconsistent or contrary to well-thought-out critiques of social justice.

In sum, I expect to show that from the internal point of view the duty to obey the law and the courts' duty to follow the law both follow from a pretense of doing justice. Judges assume, when they render their decisions, that their actions are morally justified, at least from within the point of view of the prevailing political morality. This assumption, however, will not always hold up when very hard cases have to be decided. Such cases call into question the adequacy, if not the legitimacy, of the prevailing political morality itself. Consequently, if courts are going to both preserve their legitimacy and decide very hard cases in a morally satisfactory way, judges must be able to show, at least when necessary, that their decisions are ultimately supported by an external theory of reasonable—in the sense of nonarbitrary and determinate—political morality. Judges thus have a duty to consider as potential sources of law broader and broader frameworks of political morality that clearly go beyond a source of law that a positivist would consider legitimate but that a natural law theorist might adopt.

CHAPTER ONE

Sources of Law

Perhaps the best-known jurisprudential puzzle is figuring out how to distinguish law from other social norms. Lawyers and judges concern themselves with this problem when they have to render an opinion on a case where the facts do not accord with an existing statute or with prior case precedent. Their motive in considering this question is to determine what the law is so that all parties would know their legal obligations and judges could decide cases nonarbitrarily. However, the problem is not as easily solved as it is identified. As H. L. A. Hart has noted,

> The same predicament was expressed by some famous words of St. Augustine about the notion of time. "What then is time? If no one asks me I know: if I wish to explain it to one who asks I know not." It is in this way that even skilled lawyers have felt that, though they know the law, there is much about law and its relations to other things that they cannot explain and do not fully understand. Like a person who can get from one point to another in a familiar town but cannot explain or show others how to do it, those who press for a definition need a map exhibiting clearly the relationships dimly felt to exist between the law they know and other things.[1]

The analogy with a map is more telling of the difficulty of this problem than Hart surely had in mind. For on the one hand, some ground or criterion for determining what constitutes a source of law is needed. But like a map, the route makes no sense unless it is presented against a background context of fixed reference points. Moreover, the farther one travels, the wider must be the scope of the reference points one needs to rely on. In short, the map itself must change to meet the needs of the trip. This notion of changing to broader maps to find reference points for consecutively wider travels is analogous to what some judges or lawyers, for example, former U.S. Supreme Court Justice William Brennan, do when trying to figure out progressively harder cases, that is, cases in which the facts do not obviously reference existing law. These judges or lawyers in this situation appeal to a broader conceptual framework that can encompass both the particular difficulty the case poses and the theory of law capable of resolving it. The idea of judges or lawyers changing maps, however, has never taken hold in jurisprudential theory. This may be a reflection of the desire for certainty in law, which change is often thought to undercut. Consequently, the approaches of scholars who have considered the question of how difficult cases should be decided have tended toward static as opposed to dynamic models of law, although not exclusively.

Legal Philosophy

Historically, scholars did not always see law as distinguishable from morality. An earlier and still sometimes fashionable account of the nature of law places it much more centrally in the realm of moral thinking. Plato clearly thought that the law of the good city must be set up to do justice.[2] Aristotle thought that universal justice encompassed conformity to law as a means of promoting the social virtues.[3] And Thomas Aquinas saw the morality of law as discernible from the natural order of things. But more recent attempts to explain law have sought to separate it from morality on the assumption that a social directive could be a law even if it were immoral.

NATURAL LAW

Aquinas's argument about the nature of law is fourfold. First, Aquinas contended that "law was a rule and measure of acts." It induces people to act, or it restrains them from acting.[4] Here reason directs the end; the rule and measure of human acts is a kind of reason. Thus, "law is something pertaining to reason."[5] Second, following Aristotle, Aquinas believed that "the last end of human life was happiness or beatitude."[6] The happiness or beatitude of the perfect community is universal happiness or the common good. Thus, Aquinas saw that "every law [must be] ordained to the common good."[7]

Third, to order anything to the common good concerns the one to whom the end belongs.[8] The common good belongs either to the people as a whole or to the one who has the care of the community.[9] Thus, only he, she, or they who have the care of the whole people must make every law.[10] Finally, since laws bind people, it is necessary that the people know the law.[11] To make a law known is the same as to promulgate it.[12] Thus, every law must be promulgated. From these four considerations, Aquinas derives the following definition of law. A rule is a law if and only if (a) it is an ordinance of reason, which means it conforms to natural law; (b) it is for the common good; (c) it is promulgated; (d) it is made by him, her, or them who have the care of the community.[13] Thus, one sees that for Aquinas the very idea of law must incorporate these four elements.

Of the various possibilities for the designation of law, Aquinas describes four rules that conform to the preceding definition. The first is eternal law, or God's law for the governance of the universe.[14] The second is divine law, or laws directing human beings to their supernatural end.[15] The third are natural laws, or laws directing human beings to their earthly goal of happiness.[16] Finally, there are human laws, or laws governing human beings as members of particular communities. According to Aquinas, human law must be in conformity with natural law, although it can specify more particular outcomes.[17] This latter requirement is necessary to guarantee consistency between the requirements of human law and those of natural law.

Implicit in Aquinas's thinking is a view of nature analogous to a view of manufactured objects. For example, if one wants to nail two boards together, one would not select a camera to drive the nails through the wood. The camera would drive the nails in crooked and be destroyed in the process because it is designed to serve a different and much more delicate purpose than driving nails into wood. On the other hand, a hammer, which is designed for this purpose, would be just the right tool for nailing the boards together. Analogously, Aquinas thought the whole of nature has an overall design-purpose. That purpose is discovered not from knowing the designer or what the designer intended, but from observing the ways in which the laws of nature appear to fit together. For instance, if one does not pay attention to the law of gravity, one is likely to suffer injury. If one does not pay attention to the laws of sanitation and nutrition, one is likely to suffer ill health. More generally, Aquinas thought human beings were designed with a purpose, that being to achieve, among other things, earthly happiness. (Here, Aquinas seems influenced by Aristotle's idea that the highest good for human beings is happiness.[18]) Aquinas's idea of natural law represents a claim to objective truth based on one's observations about the workings of nature. Of course, Aquinas did not know about areas of nature that are not deterministic but are probabilistic in a principled sense, such as quantum mechanics.[19] Thus, for Aquinas, one does not need to believe in the existence of a creator God with a planned purpose to figure out one's moral duties. One can discover these through inference, from the way in which other objects in the universe operate. This is the sense of rationality that Aquinas sees operating in the universe.

For Aquinas, "The whole community of the universe is governed by divine reason."[20] Laws share in this reason by governing the universe rationally—that is, according to his definition of rationality. Making up the universe are inanimate objects that obey these laws out of necessity, brutes that obey these laws out of instinct, and human beings who sometimes obey and sometimes disobey these laws out of choice. Thus, following nature's design is for Aquinas the principle of both nonhuman existence and human morality.[21]

Aquinas thought that "the order of the precepts of the natural law is according to the order of natural inclinations."[22] For human beings the greatest moral duty, and therefore a requirement for all law, is to keep their behavior in conformity with what is in common with all of nature, self-preservation.[23] Here is where we find the justification for laws against murder, abortion, assault, and battery. Second, human beings have a moral duty, which the law must recognize, to follow what is common to all other animal life, procreation and the education of offspring.[24] Under this requirement, the hierarchy of the Roman Catholic Church and some state legislatures find a justification for holding sodomy, especially homosexual sodomy, to be impermissible. Third, human beings have an inclination that is proper to them alone, and to which the law must pay heed, "to know the truth about God and to live in society."[25] It is this provision that some individuals believe provides a justification for religious tolerance, given the many different views of religions about the nature of God.

Not all modern natural law thinkers believe that for a rule to be law it must conform to morality.[26] Some believe that the courts do not have the authority to override a constitutional provision or a piece of legislation merely because it conflicts with some moral principle. Still, these thinkers hold that in applying the rule or principle a judge must decide whether "the law violates an important objective moral right."[27] If it does, the duty of the court would be to interpret the law so as to avoid the conflict by upholding the moral right. In short, these thinkers believe that it is the duty of the courts when applying a rule to a situation not anticipated by it to interpret it in conformity with a principle of natural law.[28] Ronald Dworkin has argued that U.S. Supreme Court Justice Clarence Thomas's writings before joining the Court indicate that he subscribes to this kind of natural law theory.[29] Another follower of this view is Michael Moore. Moore claims that "law requires interpretation and concedes that legal reasoning, much like literary criticism, theology and dream theory, depends on the antecedent existence of a text in need of such interpretation."[30] Surely it was the presence of arguments such as these against a background of some of history's worst atrocities that best explains the post–World War II reemergence of natural law as a tool first to try Nazi war criminals for acts against humanity and more recently to try former East German border guards who shot to death people trying to escape to the West. In both of these instances, and certainly with regard to recent concerns about war crimes in Bosnia and Cambodia, it is obvious that the institutions for enforcing the positive law of these societies and perhaps the law itself are inadequate to guarantee that justice will be done for the harms that the people of these societies actually suffered.

Still, natural law theories succumb to various objections. To begin with, theories such as Aquinas's that require conformity with morality as part of the definition of law are contrary to experience. People regularly speak of and treat a host of rules as law that have no recognizable conformity to morality. Consider the former apartheid statutes of South Africa, Nazi statutes, and the laws that regulated the American slave trade. Even from an interpretivist position, various constitutional provisions have been found legally to allow actions that later scholars and judges deeply regret, for example, the *Dred Scott* decision,[31] *Plessy v. Ferguson*,[32] and possibly *Bowers v. Hardwick*.[33]

Moreover, natural law theories and, in particular, Aquinas's version leave unclear the concept of the natural that does the heavy work of the theory. On the logical side, one might ask what meaning is to be assigned to the natural. If it is to be a substitute for the moral, does this not beg the question? If it is to be a justification for the moral, how does one bridge the gap between an is-statement of what is natural and an ought-statement of what should be done? On the normative side, one might ask of the Roman Catholic Church, for example, because it follows Aquinas's natural law, why is intercourse during an infertile period considered natural while intercourse using a contraceptive is unnatural? Human beings after all invented contraceptives as the natural outcome of their thinking on procreation. Why is heterosexuality natural while homosexuality is unnatural? Homosexuality is found among species of animals and may play an evolutionary role, by freeing parents in rural communities to farm while gay relatives take care of offspring, or vice versa.[34]

Also, in the Aquinian version, there is a problem of inconsistency. The natural law precept that one should not kill derives from the more general precept that one should do no harm.[35] Yet, it appears that for Aquinas human law may allow the death penalty as a specification of the natural law precept allowing punishment of wrongdoers. Since the principle that no one should harm another does not incorporate any limitation such as applying only where the other is an innocent, the Thomist interpretation allowing the death penalty is at least incomplete if not internally inconsistent.[36]

The significance of this point is not to accuse Aquinas of failing to generate a specific legal conclusion where one was needed. It is doubtful that he ever saw this as his task. Rather, as one scholar has noted, Aquinas may have undercut the task he did set for himself, "to validate the truth of objectivism by revealing the barest framework of the natural order he presumed exists in humans and the universe," by adopting a theory that was simultaneously, on the one hand, very general and, on the other hand, very specific.[37] Considering these various objections to natural law theory, it is no wonder that while natural law theories began to decline toward the end of the nineteenth century, positivism started to grow.

POSITIVISM

John Austin distinguished rules as constituting either positive law or positive morality. By "positive," Austin meant established by position—that is, by some social/political convention—as opposed to being established in the natural course of things. In the case of positive laws, these are set by a political superior. Thus Austin's views about laws start out with very different assumptions from those of Aquinas. For him, laws properly so-called were commands requiring conduct, and some, called positive law, issued from a sovereign to members of an independent political society over which the sovereign exercises sovereignty.[38] Here we see the distinction between rules that Austin denies calling law—like rules of morality—and rules that he properly calls law—namely, positive law. The former rules are not law because they do not come about by the action of any political superior. So-called laws of fashion or laws of honor fit this area of rules.[39] In contrast, for a rule to be truly part of positive law, it must meet certain definite considerations.

For Austin, three conditions obtain. First, there must be a command to the general populace. A command is a purpose backed up by a power to impose sanctions for disobedience.[40] A law is a command issued not to one person but to the members of the society generally. Second, there must be a sovereign who issues the command. A sovereign is a person or group who gives no habitual obedience to any greater superior but receives habitual obedience.[41] Third, there must be an independent political society. An independent political society is one in which the bulk of citizens habitually obey a sovereign.[42] If each of these three conditions is present, Austin says we can properly term the rules that come about as laws.

Positivism has its pitfalls, and, in particular, Austin's views succumb to a wide range of embarrassing questions. For instance, would a federal system like the United States fit Austin's model?[43] "Is the power dependent notion of a command adequate or would an authority dependent notion of a rule" prove more adequate?[44] For instance, people regularly stop at a red light when the way is clear and no police car is present. Has Austin taken penal laws to be the prototypes of all laws, distorting other types of law?[45] "Are the rules that govern the validity of laws to be taken as commands by the sovereign to himself or herself and, if so, does that account do justice to claims of invalidity" in modern society?[46] Are judicial decisions in those societies where they have precedential value really the commands of the sovereign?[47] Do not judges enjoy a great deal of discretion? "Does Austin's account of sovereignty distinguish legitimate exercise of political power through legislation from effective legislative exercise of political power?"[48]

LEGAL REALISM

A distinctively American response to the kind of objections raised against natural law and positive theories is legal realism. This school of thought includes such distinguished jurists as Justice Oliver Wendell Holmes and judges Jerome Frank, Karl Llewellyn, and John Chipman Gray. Its proponents believe that the "rules which constitute the Law of a community are distinguished from the other rules by which the members of the community govern their conduct by the fact that the former are laid down by the courts of the community in accordance with which they make their decrees."[49] Under this view, the function of a judge is not merely to declare the law but to maintain the peace by deciding controversies.[50] In short, the law is what the courts say the law is.

Central to the legal realist position is the problem of indeterminacy. The contention is that no one result need ultimately determine a court's holding in a particular case. The rationale has two parts. The first part is that in any given case there will always be a cluster of rules, as opposed to one rule, to use in the decision. For example, in contract cases, a judge has to be concerned about offer and acceptance, consideration, revocation, and so forth. Therefore, if any one rule is vague or ambiguous that can affect the outcome. The second part rejects the time-honored distinction between dictum and holding. Tradition had it that the grounds essential to a decision in a case were its holding; the dicta were everything else.

> Even when the judge writing an opinion characterizes part of it as "the holding," judges writing subsequent opinions were not bound by the original judge's perception of what was essential for the decision. Subsequent judges were indeed bound by the decision itself, that is, by the finding for or against the plaintiff, and very rarely was the decision in a precedent labeled as mistaken. But this apparently strict obligation to follow precedent was highly misleading, according to the realists. For latter judges had tremendous leeway in being able to redefine the holding and the dictum in the precedential cases. This leeway enabled judges, in effect, to rewrite the rules of law on which earlier cases had been decided. The upshot was that in almost any case which reached the state of litigation, a judge could find opinions which read relevant precedents as stating a contrary rule.[51]

Of course, this second part of the realist position offers the deepest and most pervasive challenge to there being right answers in the law. It was not that realists denied that they were bound by legal rules. As Llewellyn has noted, for any case a judge had to decide, there were available competing "authoritative premises."[52] No doubt, the present-day critical legal studies (CLS) movement is an outgrowth of this school of thought.[53] So too is the legal pragmatist movement of which Holmes would count as an early example[54] and Richard Posner as a more recent one. Holmes's famous statement, "Law is not logic but experience," can be seen to conform to the pragmatist, outcome-determinative view that law should be an instrument for the achievement of socially desirable results. The conformity is brought about with the realization that different experiences may lead to different understandings of socially desirable ends.

Some embarrassing questions are associated with legal realism. "Do we then have the purported injustice of ex post facto laws in novel cases?"[55] (In a sense, legal realists view all law as ex post facto due to indeterminacy.) Are we "at the mercy of the courts when we expect the best decision on principle?"[56] What is the function of precedent in this tradition? One recent variation on this tradition, the critical legal studies movement,[57] and some feminist[58] and Marxist[59] views have not been very successful in solving these problems because these movements disavow the use of principles[60] and assume that laws are but a patchwork of political compromises.[61] Consequently, they fall under the weight of their own critiques, which arguably force them to give up the idea of "*rationally* appealing human goods."[62] For example, any CLS follower who might want to question the wisdom of certain court decisions—such as those that favor big business—will find it difficult to explain why anyone else should adopt the criticism.

POSITIVISM REVISITED

To save positivism from the criticisms levied against Austin, H. L. A. Hart draws a distinction between an individual being obliged in the sense of being coerced—as when a gunman says "your money or your life"—and an individual having an obligation.[63] From an internal point of view, Hart contends that having an obligation means accepting the primary rules of the system as binding on oneself.[64] One may accept, for example, the rules laid down by a sovereign, but it would not be from fear of incurring a sanction that one accepts an obligation to follow the rules. Rather, it would be because one believed one was bound by what the sovereign says. Thus, in deciding if a given pronouncement is a law, the question is not the Austinian one: Is it the command of a sovereign backed by a sanction where the emphasis is clearly on power and fear? Rather, it is whether the rule has the right pedigree where the emphasis is on what the society recognizes to be an exercise of legitimate sovereign authority. For Hart, a primary rule of obligation is supposed to affect behavior. It is valid only if it arises from a process established by a recognized secondary rule for deciding what the primary rules are.[65] For example, in the United States, passage by both houses of Congress followed by the signature of the president is a secondary rule that produces most federal legislation.[66] It is not the only one since presidential vetoes can be overridden by a two-thirds vote of both houses and, under certain circumstances, a bill passed by both houses can become a law without presidential signature.[67] The only rule that has no pedigree because its claim to authority is by acceptance and not by validity is the basic constitutional order of the society—what Hart calls the Rule of Recognition.[68]

Although the Hartian view avoids some problems associated with the Austinian model, it fails to account for the obligation to obey the law except where the obligation happens to overlap specific moral, minimum content, duties.[69] These duties, Hart believes, come about because if a society failed to prevent certain sorts of crimes—for example, widespread murder or theft—it would cease to be a society. So the question remains: Can there be legal obligations that at least sometimes are wholly disparate from moral responsibilities? If the answer to this question is yes, then where do these amoral—perhaps in some situations immoral—obligations come from? And is there a moral limit to what can count as law? Lon Fuller argues in favor of making laws known, of not allowing them to be ex post facto, and of not punishing the sought-after behavior as providing such a moral limit internal to law itself.[70] Further, laws must come about in the context of a background legal system that is at least provisionally thought to be good.[71] Otherwise, how would the internal obligation of obedience to law ever arise?[72] If the answer to the question of whether legal obligations can exist without moral responsibility is no, then what should a court do when deciding a case in which the most formally correct legal solution is also the most unjust? Should it matter to a court if its decision will produce serious harm before there is any possibility of legislative correction or constitutional change? These problems relate to another question: Is there an obligation to obey law as such?

LEGAL IDEALISM

The failure of positivism, legal realism, and natural law theories to provide a coherent foundation for legal obligation caused Ronald Dworkin to set forth an interpretive approach that a judge could use from within a legal system to decide hard cases. The key distinction in Dworkin's system, sometimes called "legal idealism,"[73] is between rules and principles. Rules apply in an all-or-nothing fashion and are based on economic, political, or social policy goals or on previous decisions grounded on principle.[74] If a case falls squarely under a rule, the rule will decide the case, provided only that the rule is valid according to the standard that is the accepted criterion of validity. In contrast to rules, principles have the dimension of weight, which means that they appeal to one's motives to uphold obligations of justice, or fairness, or some other aspect of morality running through the community's institutions.[75] In this sense, principles are reasons for performing certain actions but are not necessarily determinative of the action to be performed. If no valid rule clearly applies to a case, a court will judge the case by principles that provide reasons for or against how the case should be decided.[76] Because they have the dimension of weight, principles can be set against one another to determine the outcome of a case.[77]

Thus in hard cases where no clear rule applies, judges do not have complete discretion to do as they want subject only to some general moral concern for fairness.[78] A legal community that expects its judges to perform their duties in light of relevant principles will expect cogent and complete responses on how these principles offset each other in particular cases.[79] Such a community will also not be afraid to debate the relative weight to be assigned to the various principles at stake.[80] Moreover, even when a rule seems to apply to a particular case, there will be an expectation for the judge to set forth the interpretive principles—such as stare decisis or deference to legislative authority—that determine the rule's application.[81]

Finally, because Dworkin treats principles as part of law and not as some extralegal basis for critiquing law, he opens the door—in a way that had not been done since the days when natural law philosophy dominated—to sources of law other than constitutional texts, statutes, and case determinations. This means that no longer is law or legal obligation to be considered as a realm independent of morality but that morality in the sense of the society's political morality is to be reflected in the very principles a judge is bound to take into account.[82] This does not mean that judges in deciding cases are free to choose or make up principles, however.

When deciding hard cases, judges are governed by a principle of political responsibility that requires that they make only such decisions as can be justified within a political theory that also justifies the other decisions that they will make.[83] Thus, there arises a concern for precedent and the consideration of hypothetical examples.[84] Also, most legal systems are not completely autonomous environments.[85] Often constitutional texts, statutes, and case law leave certain questions open for determination based on sources of law not traditionally recognized.[86] The rules or principles that apply when searching out these nontraditional sources must still preserve the institutional character of the legal system, especially its general purposes and function.[87]

In his early publications, Dworkin argues that judges deciding a hard case should choose their principles of determination first from what will fit—in the sense of conform—to the best scheme of law where the principles will be applied.[88] If a judge has to choose between two principles to decide a case and one would reproduce more of the settled law than the other, the judge should choose the principle that reproduces more of the law taken as settled. Only after deciding that two or more principles fit the settled law equally well should a judge further decide which principle is superior as a matter of political or moral theory, that is, which principle best reproduces the rights people actually have.[89] Thus judges are obligated to set forth in each case their own version of the soundest theory of the law for deciding the case that will also justify any other decisions they plan to make.[90] Because each judge is subject to so high a level of responsibility, Dworkin refers to each judge who succeeds as Hercules.[91]

More recently, Dworkin substitutes "law as integrity" for the "soundest theory of law." "According to law as integrity, propositions of law are true if they figure in or follow from the principles of justice, fairness, and procedural due process that provide the best constructive interpretation of the community's legal practice."[92] Thus, when lawyers disagree about what the law is, what they are disagreeing about is the best constructive interpretation of the legal community's practices. By constructive interpretation, Dworkin means collecting relevant precedents, constructing a theory of the purposes, goals, and principles in practice, and reforming the practice in light of deeper democratic principles of distributive justice, fairness, and due process.[93] Fit and political morality come into the analysis in the way that each succeeding author in a chain novel is supposed to add to the novel to continue the story's flow and coherence seamlessly, as if the story were written by one person.[94] The effect of this approach Dworkin believes is to allow Hercules in a hard case, where principles appear to conflict, to put together a coherent scheme of the law within the area where conflict exists or, if that is not possible, within a gradually broadening area that incorporates the conflict area.[95]

Like most of the theories already discussed, Dworkin's views have come under various criticisms. J. L. Mackie, for example, asks why we should not believe that many decisions will not fall into the realm of political morality.[96] Constitutional privacy, for example, is not specifically set out in the Constitution. Why must what the law is depend on the best moral explanation and justification of the settled law, which may be subjective?[97] Much of the current abortion debate provides a good illustration of this. Does not Dworkin's theory lead to greater indeterminacy by requiring judges to rely on subjective views about morality?[98] Joseph Raz argues that "the assumption that all law was promulgated in pursuit of one set of principles" is "false to the spirit of all the bodies which enjoy legal authority."[99] Moreover, the proponents of critical legal studies challenge the idea that there could be a coherent interpretation of law, since they see law as a patchwork of politics, class conflicts, and ideology that is inconsistent.[100]

Dworkin responds to some of these objections in *Law's Empire*.[101] Still, what should a judge do if the solution that seems best for resolving the case cannot be justified from recognized principles even when one takes into account the political morality of the society?[102] "Inclusive integrity stops short of rescinding the injustice inherent in the system as a whole; pure integrity, by contrast, seeks 'a single, coherent scheme of justice as fairness in the right relation' grounded in a shared communal ideal."[103] In very hard cases, it would appear that stopping short of questioning the justice of the system as a whole is exactly the problem. Here too a judge needs to do more than rely on the society's political morality. Ideally, the judge should assess that morality from a perspective that is at least not obviously internal to what the society already believes or takes as its operating values. If this is true, to what values should a judge look and how would any that the judge considered not be regarded as part of the society's political morality? At its narrowest point, the problem is conceptual: What do we mean by society's political morality? In its broader expanse, the problem is epistemological: What is there to be looked at that is not internal to the beliefs the society already holds? The two questions are related, but first we need to consider yet another, rather different, set of legal theories that question whether judges can ever break free from the spell of the society's dominant ideology.

CRITICAL THEORY

Here we come upon a wide range of theories that share at least three themes. First is the view that the current state of the law functions to preserve the political/social/economic status quo of the most dominant force(s) in society. Second is the conviction that the law of the state at any time in history is inherently contingent on the forces modeling the society at that time. Third is the notion that law has no inherent authority of its own. The types of theories of jurisprudence that represent these views are Marxism, some feminism, critical legal studies, and critical race theory.[104] As Raymond Belliotti describes them, these types of theories generally do not attempt to provide a self-sustaining jurisprudence but are each concerned with challenging in its own way the idea that our prevailing notions of rationality, morality, logic, and language can provide an "unproblematic starting point for our jurisprudential inquiries."[105] Moreover, each theory is connected to the others by its willingness to adopt certain notions that have their roots in classical Marxism: alienation, exploitation, superstructure, false consciousness, and dialectical method.

According to Belliotti, by alienation, Marx means that a worker in a capitalistic society acts on interests not truly his own.[106] The worker is alienated from the product because his labor power has been bought in advance, and therefore the worker has no share in the output of the product created. The worker is also alienated from the capitalist because the worker's interest is in higher wages and the capitalist's interest is in higher profits. The worker is alienated from other workers who vie for a position by offering to sell their labor power for increasingly lower wages until subsistence is reached, unless there is a minimum wage law in effect. Finally, the worker is alienated from himself by participating in a system that stifles the worker's creative species life by making the worker an instrument for the capitalist's greed. This greed also alienates the worker by forcing continued participation in the system as a necessary condition for the worker's biological survival.

By exploitation, Belliotti continues, Marx means that the worker does not control the surplus of his production, but the surplus is controlled by the people who own the means of production.[107] In short, one class of persons (workers) is being used for the benefit of another class of persons (owners) with little or no regard for the interests of the former. By the superstructure, Marx has in mind the sum total of our political, legal, religious, and moral institutions and rules that provide support for the society's particular mode of production, which in modern nation-states is capitalism:

> In the social production of their like, humans enter into definite relations that are indispensable and independent of their will, relations of production which correspond to a definite stage of development of their material productive forces. The sum total of these relations of production constitutes the economic structure of society, the real foundation, on which rises a legal and political superstructure and to which corresponds definite forms of social consciousness. The mode of production of material life conditions the social, political, and intellectual life processes in general.[108]

Related to the idea of superstructure is the idea of false consciousness. By that term, which Marx does not apparently use but clearly intends, is meant an "inverted representation of reality" brought about by a superstructure that "justifies, stabilizes, and reinforces the social and political status quo."[109] Having a false consciousness with regard to a particular position means that the person is unaware of the underlying motives that caused him to adopt that position. Finally, Belliotti notes that Marx uses a dialectical method to create "conflict, antagonism and contradictions" to achieve "social progress."[110] The latter comes about through the interplay of possibly partially true, although opposite, views that ultimately reveal a still larger truth. Here we see a hint of John Stuart Mill's argument for freedom of expression running through Marx, although obviously not from Mill's individualistic utilitarian perspective.[111]

Together these classical Marxist notions provide a basis for a profound set of critiques that critical theorists use to undercut any theory that claims to provide a foundation for law. Scholars have suggested that awareness of law's vulnerability to the influence of social ideology began to take hold with the rise of the legal realist movement, a precursor of the CLS movement. Judges such as Jerome Frank and Oliver Wendell Holmes came to realize that "although judges often took themselves to be deriving necessary conclusions from preexisting legal materials, they in fact were thinking and acting under the mystifying spell of the dominant ideology."[112] As Mort J. Horwitz explains:

> The 1950s search for "neutral principles" was just one more effort to separate law from politics in American culture, one more expression of the persistent yearning to find an Olympian position from which to objectively cushion the terrors of social choice. The search for neutral principles has always been the secular alternative in religiously pluralistic American society to a direct resort to religious authority. Yet it has served similar dogmatic and legitimating functions. One of its most important influences has been to encourage the production of abstract jurisprudential debate divorced from more particular (and inevitably controversial) political and moral visions. These abstract jurisprudential controversies have repeatedly served as snares and delusions to generations of legal thinkers, misled into believing that the previous generation's jurisprudential controversies necessarily continue to have the same political and moral significance.[113]

But Belliotti's point, as he himself describes it, encompasses much more than legal realism. His point captures the central theme of feminist jurisprudence, which, in the viewpoint of Catharine MacKinnon,

> claims that dominant legal analyses place women in a double bind: on the one hand, if the law uses a single standard and "neutrally" involves similar treatment for men and women, then women are measured according to their correspondence with men and to a standard whose default position registers male images; on the other hand, if the law uses a special protection rule for women, thereby making allowances for the real differences between men and women, then women are measured according to their lack of correspondence with men and by their distance from male standards.[114]

Belliotti's comment also captures a central theme of the CLS movement, which denies that there is any underlying rationale other than politics that supports the decisions courts reach or the statutes legislatures adopt. Here the points are (a) that no method of analysis can provide a single right answer to a legal problem; (b) that traditional legal theories create a false legitimation by making it appear that certain legal rules and standards are inevitable and do not reflect political choices; and (c) that law really acts to rationalize the actions embedded in the existing ideological assumptions of society.[115] Finally, the idea of law serving to protect the dominant ideology fits well a recent work in the area of critical race theory. In *Words that Wound*, Mari J. Matsuda et al. claim that existing "institutions and dominant normative discourses facilitate and systematize racial subordination."[116]

Understood in this way, these positions share a broad critique not just of particular laws or particular themes of jurisprudential thought but of legal institutions generally and of theories that attempt to rationally justify law. This approach challenges any view that claims to provide a self-sustaining theory of law to respond to this sort of criticism. To put the point another way, before a jurisprudential theory can be successful in providing a nonrelativist foundation for law, it must be able to overcome the challenge that it is merely an expression of the dominant ideology attempting to maintain the status quo. This a theory could do, if it exhibited a truly ahistorical foundation, but that is unlikely unless the theory can also take into account different levels of legal analyses. Most theories offered to account for law are underinclusive on some issues and overinclusive on others. Therefore, I suggest as a better approach a theory that could provide several stages of analysis, each representing a wider range of concepts than the one before. The strategy, then, would be to undermine the radical jurisprudential critique, not by showing it to be false at any given level of analysis, but by illustrating it as trivial because we can move to higher or more abstract levels.

ECONOMIC ANALYSIS

Before leaving this discussion of sources of law, some attention should be directed to the area known as economic analysis of law. This approach attempts to resolve hard cases by asking which rule will best promote economic efficiency.[117] Economic efficiency is its first principle. The approach is forward looking—teleological—in that it does not consider itself bound to any prior case decision if the economic result of the choice would prevent engaging in wealth maximization. This view is at variance with another view that economic principles are inherent in the common law so that judges tease out what would apply anyway. More than any other area, economic analysis seems to undercut our ordinary intuitions about law's exactitude, substituting instead a more systematic assessment of the economic consequences of legal decisions. In this respect, economic analysis revives and makes even more cutting Jeremy Bentham's famous utilitarian attack on the common law, that law must serve the common good.[118] Moreover, because economic approaches often anticipate the counterintuitive effects of legal decisions, they may have a profound impact on how these decisions ought to be made.

Still, one problem that economic analysis cannot resolve is a difficulty frequently associated with utilitarian theories.[119] Although economic analysis can compare how different people evaluate the various consequences of a legal decision, it cannot decide which outcome is better as such. It can say only that one is economically more efficient.[120] Thus economic analysis raises questions about the common good—in the sense of what would maximize general utility—without any consideration about what the good should be.

The failure of traditional economic analysis to uncover what the common good is may explain why some scholars in the field have abandoned the question altogether while others seem tied to finding an answer.[121] U.S. Supreme Court Justice Stephen Breyer offers one attempt to find an answer. According to him, in determining whether a legislative or a regulatory policy is for the common good one should ask if (a) the justification for the policy makes sense on the basis of either economic or noneconomic reasoning; (b) the policy corrects a market defect; or (c) the policy accomplishes some other worthwhile purpose for society.[122] If it does any of these, then it is for the common good. Otherwise, it is likely to be the result of self-interested (private) motives.[123] Justice Breyer's approach clearly illustrates the need for an analysis that takes into account a wider range of influences, including some noneconomic norms like justice and fairness.[124] His proposal for regulatory reform suggests that mismatches between regulatory methods and the problems these methods are supposed to cure are not simply reducible to regulatory politics.[125]

In contrast, adherents of public choice analyses claim that one can understand the outcomes of legislative and regulatory decisionmaking only by understanding the influence that powerful interests have in securing decisions favorable to themselves.[126] The difficulty with the public choice approach is that it leaves no place for the public interest if powerful enough private interests are against it. Consider, for example, when regulatory policies are viewed as

> market-like transactions between those who demand regulation (the buyers) and those who supply it (the sellers). The buyers are organized interests who support or oppose regulation according to the self-interest of their members. The sellers are public officials who make regulatory decisions according to their own self-interest. Legislators respond to buyers who offer support for reelection, while agency officials respond to buyers who can assist them to obtain additional power and prestige. When organized interests compete, the outcome depends on what group or groups offer the greatest rewards to legislators or administrators.[127]

An instance that may appear to some people as a policy failure to achieve a common good is to the public choice theorists but another example of a situation where politics ensures that private interests trump public interests.

The difference between public and private interests concerns who will benefit and not solely who supports the policy, although the latter may indicate whether it is in the public's interest. That interest manifests itself when we consider situations where the greater number of people in the public want a different outcome from that which is desired by some smaller group and have at least some interest in securing it. Stated more precisely, proponents of public choice theory, in contrast to the common good position of Justice Breyer and other scholars, believe that legislation and regulation are adopted only when the influence of the groups in favor of it is sufficiently great to offset the influence of the groups against it. This means that legislation that may be in the interests of a great many people will fail to achieve passage if the cost to each citizen of the legislation failing is less than the cost of participation in collective action. Of course, a problem arises in determining what makes a group sufficiently strong to have the required influence. It would seem, contrary to expectations, that it is not the number of members the group has. For instance, groups with large numbers of members may have less influence because the cost of an adverse law or regulation is small per member, the possibility of free ridership on what other groups do is large, and the expense associated with organizing for collective action is high.[128]

Still, public choice analysis may not be the final nail in the coffin of the common good for several reasons. First, it is inadequate to account for all influences that clearly affect policy decisions. For instance, public choice analyses cannot account for the influence of "ideological politicians like

Reagan and Thatcher."[129] Second, the approach cannot adequately describe why citizens vote when in most elections the costs in time and inconvenience to go to the polls far outweigh any chance that the individual's vote will affect the outcome.[130] These problems suggest that perhaps a common interest can be found even if not by means of combining preferences. Kenneth Arrow has showed that no way of combining preferences could ever achieve the minimum rationality necessary to ensure that the society would become better off.[131] But if this is the case, how is the common good to be determined? Perhaps the answer lies in building into the institutional structure norms that are both economic and noneconomic against which policies are determined. One problem with this approach, however, is what to do when the norms themselves conflict, for example, when considerations of justice and the common good suggest opposite outcomes.

The problem is that the logic behind the two issues is not the same. The latter involves aggregative criteria; the former is concerned with distributive criteria.[132] For this reason, both traditional economic analysis and public choice theory treat the problem of justice as an independent entity and possibly as opposed to utility. In the case of traditional economic analysis, the problem of justice is pushed aside in favor of the common good, which is itself left unspecified. As a result, traditional economic analysis falls prey to the challenge raised by critics of utilitarianism that it gives inadequate attention to the question of justice when the choice is between maximizing utility and effecting justice. The problem for proponents of economic analysis is that their answer to choose the option that will most maximize wealth begs the question.[133] This has left a gap regarding the relationship of these two concepts to decision theories. The gap is particularly acute in the context of economic decisions since so often these, more than other decisions, reflect competing views of the public interest.

In the case of public choice theory, questions about justice, like questions about the common good, are subordinated to the politics of groups. This raises an even broader issue of how questions concerning the common good, let alone questions concerning justice, can play any role in the development of public policy. Presumably, governmental institutions, as Justice Breyer suggests, should be able to deal with these issues, but how are they to operate, especially in light of the public choice critique?

Perhaps the problem can be thought of this way: neither a theory of the common good nor one of justice can resolve the choice between aggregation and distribution. Therefore, if the choice is to be made and the apparatus of government is set to do it, then it must be based on some independent consideration. In a democracy, courts operate to ensure individual justice; the legislature functions by passing statutes to promote the common good.[134] Together, the two institutions create the balance between considerations of justice and considerations of utility, provided neither one attempts to usurp the function of the other. Of course, whether either one does usurp the other will be a question of political philosophy; in particular, it will center on the legitimacy of the values that limit the power of each of these institutions. In this instance very hard cases become most critical, for they question the current balance of considerations and suggest the need for a more highly ordered theory to resolve the problem. *Lochner v. New York* is a good example.[135]

If it is true that the function of the courts is to do justice and the function of the legislature is to promote the common good, then the issue of choice between utility and justice may be resolved for a time by keeping the two functions separate. Accordingly, Dworkin contends that a court, when figuring out the application of a statute, may consider the underlying policy choices that influenced the legislature that passed the statute. But when making a choice of principle, a court should treat the issue as involving a question of justice. Of course, there is the problem of what justice requires and what one should do when principles and policies conflict.

Shortcomings of Legal Philosophy

Evidently, a connection between legal and political philosophy occurs at the point where, in a democracy, a judge's duty to decide a case cannot be fulfilled using strictly primary sources. Perhaps the primary sources are vague or would lead to a substantial injustice. At this point, either a judge must say that primary legal sources do not provide a basis for the claim and, therefore, the parties must look elsewhere, such as to the legislature, or the judge must consider other, secondary, sources of law. Otherwise, the judge may be in the position of applying a "law" that is immoral. I argue that where the issue is one of principle and not policy or where principle and policy conflict, a judge may very well have to appeal to the prevailing political morality of the society or, where that is unsatisfactory, to some more highly ordered political morality to avoid injustice. This is made manifest with the realization that the judge's duty to decide cases justly is a specific instantiation of a general doctrine of political responsibility. That doctrine requires all governmental actors to preserve order, protect the social welfare, promote justice, and support majority rule.

We have seen how various theories of law provide different answers to the question of what is law. For instance, natural law theories identify sources of law by positing some "moral" fact, which any law must conform to. (The question of whether there are any "moral" facts is one of the problems natural law theories often succumb to.) Positivist accounts follow similar lines, but instead of requiring conformity with a moral fact, they rely on conformity with an empirical fact recognized within the given society as delimiting what the law is. Legal realists, in contrast to both positivists and natural law thinkers, leave the determination solely in the hands of the courts. Ronald Dworkin treats the question as one of providing the best constructive interpretation from within the legal system of its own history and political morality. Finally, Marxists, feminists, and the proponents of critical legal studies question when power divides unequally in a society whether any source of law can be binding, especially on those not benefited by it.

These theories reflect the fact that the word "law" encompasses different uses appropriate to different purposes while maintaining a family resemblance.[136] Natural law, positivism, legal realism, legal idealism, and various critical and economic approaches constitute different senses of the term law. Each can provide guidance to judges who must decide cases of varying degrees of difficulty. They do so by setting out an area of abstraction wherein certain kinds of questions are answerable. But, like our analogy with the road map, no one theory has proved capable of doing the whole job adequately. Natural law theory, for example, may provide help if the issue is whether a particular legislative enactment is morally binding, but, like a world map, it may be inadequate for deciding how to get from Chicago to Peoria. Positivism, on the other hand, may be more helpful in deciding these mundane cases but be of almost no help in deciding whether the Constitution guarantees a right to privacy. The latter may be better served by a Dworkinian approach. Further, legal idealism may break down at points where the society's political morality is under serious attack, as witnessed by the abolitionist movement against slavery, in which case a natural law theory might be more helpful. Moreover, except for natural law, none of these partial theories explains why any political institution is justified in passing laws at all. Positivism, for example, requires political approval without providing a normative ground for that approval. This was the meaning of Hart's Rule of Recognition. Even Dworkin, although requiring a political morality, does not believe he needs to explain ultimately why democracy is more justified—if it is—than dictatorship. And even in a democracy, we need to explain when laws are justified and when they are not.

These views do have in common their concern with whether law is a uniquely distinct normative practice, distinct from morals in general, and, if so, what makes this known. Unfortunately, every one of these approaches has failed to produce a general theory of law capable of deciding in a determinative and nonarbitrary manner all the cases that have come before the courts because the nature of the problems posed by the different cases was not at the same level of abstraction. Consequently, they were not within the conceptual confines of any one theory. This is a criticism of the static nature of the traditional legal schools of jurisprudence such as natural law, positivism, and legal idealism. But it is also a criticism of the radical scholars who challenge these types of theories but offer little by way of a self-sustained approach of their own for the evaluation and understanding of legal decisions. Natural law theories, for instance, may be helpful where the issue is moral and there is not a lot of controversy about its requirements. But positivism probably better serves cases where the issue centers on what the recognized social authorities have commanded. Legal realism fits cases where legislative enactments are nonexistent or unclear, and legal idealism works best in situations where there exists a legal tradition that upholds a consistent set of deeply embedded principles even at the expense of individual rules. As a result of their failure to allow for movement among theories, legal scholars until recently have produced, under the guise of full theories, only partial theories or sets of reasons for how particularly difficult cases might be resolved. And legal critics have been able to assail these theories because one could always discover some kind of case or institutional arrangement for setting forth laws that did not meet the particular theory's assumptions. Finally, since some theories, such as positivism, legal realism, and legal idealism, begin their analyses from within an existing legal structure, and since natural law attempts to find a more neutral ground in morality, one difficulty that has been identified but not well understood concerns the relation between the internal perspective of the judge or lawyer and the external perspective of the political philosopher. I hope to show that it is in the latter perspective that the normative nature of law resides. For now, however, I hope that I have provided at least a little better understanding of what we mean by law and why the various theories that have sought to provide meaning have been only partially successful.

We are fast approaching that point where we will need to consider what judges should do if they have to choose among various theories of law. What will be needed is a determinative metatheory that will provide the meaning of and justification for the choice. Finding such a theory means, continuing our metaphor of the map, finding an approach to legal decisionmaking analogous to a theory of cartography that will explain the relationship among the various partial theories and relate these theories to any case that comes along. But first, I need to make even more clear why it is that positivism and legal idealism break down in providing complete theories of law. The answer cannot be fully understood just internally to the positivist or legal idealist model because both models simply will produce no answers to certain sorts of questions. Hence, we must consider looking for the answer in a political philosophy that is both broader and more encompassing than both of these theories. A good start is to ask what the duty to obey law is all about.

CHAPTER TWO

The Duty to Obey Law

I have suggested that the duty to obey law is a particular instantiation of a general doctrine of political responsibility that applies to all governmental actors.[1] Let us now consider the nature of that general doctrine—its scope and function—so that it can be used to provide a grounding for the duty to obey law.

To begin with, let us return to our map analogy. Only now let us consider it from the standpoint of two very different uses of maps. Again, if one wants to drive from Chicago to New York City, using a map of the world (or a globe) would be too crude a device, lacking detail sufficient to plan the trip. Yet if one is teaching geography, a world map or a globe might be just the right device to identify major land masses, routes of migration, and climatic conditions. The road and world maps are related, of course, in that one could imagine a very large globe or world map in which each section was made up of highly detailed regional maps. But such an extensive globe or world map would be too overwhelming for most purposes. No doubt the military uses electronic maps capable of expanding and contracting the scale of measurement to lead bombers and missiles to targets on the other side of the world; however, for most purposes, this need to vary scales is unnecessary. Similarly, political philosophy may provide a general doctrine of political responsibility that applies to all governmental actors. It may also be too crude a device to be instructive to courts in deciding particular cases. Even so, there may be some cases in which the courts need a broader perspective, either because at a certain level of generality the law is unclear or inconsistent principles seem to apply. In those situations, the ability to change scales of detail may be most helpful to courts having to decide hard and very hard cases.

I want to consider the globe map of political philosophy in part to show that the duty to obey law, if it exists at all, has its origin not in an analytical understanding of what the law is, but in a normative understanding of how the actions of political institutions are justified. Since I regard the two spheres—legal and political philosophy—less as independent categories and more as maps with different scales of detail, it is fair to say I see them as setting up a continuum in which more highly ordered questions of law are understood and dealt with as problems of political morality.[2] Further, treating questions of law, at least at the higher orders of generality, as problems of political morality will allow us to bridge the gap between internal and external perspectives.

In examining the various philosophical approaches to law, I have shown how overall each one seemed incomplete or only partial in its effort to provide an explanation of what law is. More specifically, positivism, legal realism, and various economic approaches to law fail at justifying a duty to obey law. Positivism fails because it cannot afford a legal reason to obey laws that are seriously immoral. The paradox in positivism is its claim to maintain the separateness of law and morality while—at least on Hart's account—maintaining the obligation to obey law.[3] The problem is what to do about very bad laws. Either the positivist separation thesis must be given up or positivism must disaffirm any duty to obey law. Some attempts to try to get around this paradox claim a prima facie duty to obey law that can be overridden in morally questionable contexts. However, the claim to a prima facie duty to obey law begs the question of why a very bad law should have even this much legitimacy.[4] One wonders with the legal realist why a court's prior determination should bear any weight on a current decision if the principle to be applied would create an injustice. The critical schools question even the use of moral language in such contexts as blinding us to the political realities of events. As for economic approaches, these theories fail by being too concerned with efficiency or interest group politics while having little or no concern about the ultimate ends to which the society is directed, or, if they are concerned with ends, it is more by act of fiat than on principle. For example, in discussing wealth maximization, economic theory fails to investigate why wealth is a good or whether there may be circumstances under which maximization should not be pursued. In discussing public choice, it fails to discern any important social difference among choices, focusing only on the amount of influence of the groups affected.

In contrast to these theories lie natural law and legal idealism. These two approaches are different from the others because of their ability to produce an argument for the duty to obey law. Natural law does so by appealing to a broader theory of morality that any law must accord with. The status of the "must" here is categorical, deriving from the idea that morality provides the ground for justified human action. This is true whether one's construction of the theory of natural law treats the implied ought as part of the definition of law or as a means for interpreting ambiguous laws. In the latter situation, where an unjust law appears clear, ambiguities might be sought to defeat most of the law's effect. From the standpoint of justifying a duty to obey law, the difficulties with natural law are threefold: First, how are we to define the natural? Second, how can one go from the claim that something is natural to the conclusion that it is just and ought to be followed? Third, what do we do with a law that appears just but would be unjust if applied?[5] Lon Fuller's attempt to discover morality in law does not run into these same three problems. Fuller sees the internal morality of law as defined by a procedural and not a substantive moral standard, such as not punishing sought-after behavior and not having secret or ex post facto laws.[6] This approach leaves him open to the charge that laws, which appear to meet the procedural requirements of justice—for example, laws that treat like cases alike—may, nevertheless, fail to do justice. *Lex injusta non est lex,* a good example being laws that invidiously discriminate against an entire class of persons but do so consistently.

In contrast, John Finnis defines law both procedurally and substantively as

> rules made, in accordance with regulative legal rules, by a determinative and effective authority . . . for a 'complete' community, and buttressed by sanctions in accordance with the rule-guided stipulations of adjudicative institutions, this ensemble of rules and institutions being directed to reasonably resolving any of the community's co-ordination problems . . . for the common good of that community, according to a manner and form itself adopted to that common good by features of specificity, minimization of arbitrariness, and maintenance of a quality of reciprocity between the subjects of the law both amongst themselves and in their relations with the law-making authorities.[7]

The definition presupposes the existence of "legal" rules and a conception of the common good as "a set of conditions which enables the members of a community to obtain for themselves reasonable objectives, or to realize reasonably for themselves the value(s), for the sake of which they have reason to collaborate with each other (positively or negatively) in a community."[8]

The problem with Finnis's approach is that it leaves too much to what a community is likely to consider a "reasonable objective" or a reasonable realization of its values. Finnis's approach works best where the disputes involve relatively narrow questions of application as opposed to fundamental disagreements over values.[9] It would not be of much help, for example, in solving the problem of whether a woman should have a right to choose abortion in late twentieth-century America.

Legal idealism, in contrast to natural law, attempts to establish the duty to obey law by requiring that all statutes and case determinations conform to the prevailing political morality of the society. The problem with legal idealism is that the society's political morality may be in flux, as it was on the question of slavery in America just before the Civil War. Thus, although the theories of traditional natural law and legal idealism both offer arguments about the duty to obey law, neither can provide an adequate foundation for the duty. Both theories do make clear, however, that the foundation for a duty to obey law cannot be found in law itself but must be sought in some wider notion of political morality if it is to be found at all. Exactly what that wider notion is and how it goes beyond the prevailing political morality of the society are questions we must begin to answer.

But first it might be helpful to consider the possibility that there is no moral duty to obey law. Russell Hardin, for instance, argues that "we cannot salvage a general claim to obey the law even for those who share the morality that might underlie the law."[10] His reason is that the same moral principles may put different demands on institutions. Consider, for example, a Nazi march in Skokie, Illinois, where survivors of the Holocaust live. Here it may be that the Nazis have a moral/legal right to march, but it may not be right for them to march. It may on some occasions be right to break the law and right for law to punish the breach. Putting the problem a different way, Joel Feinberg notes that the duty to obey law is not self-evident, nor does it seem derivable from basic prima facie moral duties like promise-keeping, gratitude, fairness, or justice.[11] The view that law is but the institutional creation of the people seeking to maintain the political status quo seems quite appealing insofar as it avoids the thorny problems associated with making sense of the common good or justifying law. It also seems to fit situations where a law seems to exist in the sense that some recognized legislative act has produced it even though large numbers of people believe that the law is morally quite reprehensible. Of course, the problem with this view is that it does not account for how people go about justifying their behavior in light of the law. After all, not all (and possibly not even most) instances of our obedience to law can be accounted for by prudential reasons or even as conditioned responses. For example, an automobile stops at a stop sign on a deserted highway on a perfectly clear moonlit night, even though it is obvious to the driver that no police car is present, no danger would exist to any person if the car did not stop, and the driver is in a hurry to get home. When asked to justify the behavior, the driver responds, quite surprised: "It is the law that I stop!" Under these circumstances, "It is the law that I stop" is not prudential. It is clear to the driver that no adverse effect will come about by not stopping. So the claim is moral—my *duty* is not to break the law—rather than prudential—it is *in my interests* not to break the law.[12]

This view, which is obviously held by one who accepts the law regarding stop signs as binding, cannot be explained without some appeal to moral obligation. The moral obligation might be general, in that it requires obedience to all laws created by democratic procedures, or specific to this particular traffic law, because it is thought to avoid harm to others. Obviously, the latter reason does not work to justify obedience under the circumstances posited because it was clear from the description that no harm was present. Perhaps one is trying to create in oneself a habit of obedience so as to avoid breaking laws in situations where a real danger might exist. That would provide some basis for the latter justification, but it also raises a broader criticism of whether we are ever free when making choices to obey or not. However, this broader challenge may not be difficult to meet if we perceive ourselves as free.[13] So from our own perspective, we need only to account for our obedience and not for our capacity for obedience.

Yet the former democratic justification may also be inadequate if, for instance, no allowance is made for breaches of law in situations where obedience would produce a morally unjustified result and there is too little time to effect a change in the law through democratic processes. In this situation, it seems clear that the question of whether to obey the law or not requires taking much more into account than whether the law is morally acceptable. One needs also to consider whether the issue truly involves a situation where great harm is going to occur and what democratic procedures are available. Indeed, the latter may be particularly valuable if allowing time for education of the public strengthens the public's respect for law by improving the likelihood that the law serves to create only good social order. These questions are not easily resolved and require a theory of civil disobedience for their resolution. A more complex problem arises when the law in question is meant to affect strictly private behavior. There the justification for disobedience may be less, and correspondingly, the state's burden to prove harm to third parties will be greater.

This is a good time to note a distinction in our use of the word law that is related to the meaning of affording obedience to law. That distinction is between laws that are descriptive and those that are prescriptive. Descriptive laws, like the law of gravity, describe causal phenomena that seems unchanging, given our previous experiences and our expectation that the future will be like the past. John Austin's use of law seems to fit into this category once we treat as a cause the influence of sanctions. Descriptive laws thus make predictions about future events based on our familiarity with past events and our understanding of consequences that may follow a legal breach.

Prescriptive laws, such as "thou shalt not kill," make claims as to what ought to be our behavior whether we follow the law or not. Prescriptive laws lay out obligations others expect us to follow because they are thought binding, even though we may not always follow the law. Prescriptive laws can be either civil, if they are the creations of governmental institutions assigned with the responsibility of making laws, or moral, if they are general categorical imperatives for correct human behavior. Natural law is the name we assign laws of morality arguably derived from certain purposive facts about human nature. Since my concern here is primarily with civil laws, I face the dual task of stating what it is that makes such laws civil as well as what it is that creates in the recipients a duty to obey such laws. The positivists are right in thinking that some sort of pedigree must be involved in distinguishing civil laws from other sorts of social obligations. But what the pedigree is, especially when court-created principles are treated as laws, may be controversial and in flux. At the very least, resolving this question will involve an appeal to a legal theory, if law is not to appear arbitrary. Still, there remains the problem of justice in our selection of a legal theory. If some of the laws that bear the right pedigree are unjust, we may have no duty to obey them. Even laws that initially appear to us to be just in terms of the prevailing political morality of the society may come to be thought of at some later point as unjust, if that morality is itself brought into question. This suggests that, as we search for a foundation for the duty to obey law, we not confine ourselves to the internal political morality of any legal theory we take as given. Instead, we must entertain the possibility of a broader, external perspective from which we can choose between various legal theories. Such a broader perspective I take to be sufficiently general to be labeled political philosophy.

Political Philosophy

The nature of the political institution is relevant to the way the justification for a duty to obey law bears out. As John Rawls has noted, the institution of the legislature differs from that of the court in that the former is forward-looking to provide for the common good, whereas the latter is backward-looking, to the facts of a particular case, to do justice.[14] In a democracy, one hopes the legislature will create laws that provide for the common good in the sense of maximizing overall utility. Thus legislative representatives are elected on either a geographic basis (as in the United States) or on a political/ideological one (as in much of Europe), and a majority of the representatives must vote in favor of any legislation before it becomes a law. In contrast, courts are set up to be fact finders to determine, in particular cases, who did what to whom. For this reason, judges are sometimes appointed rather than elected, and professional merit plays a relevant and material role in their selection.

It should be noted that the particular institutional structures I am referencing here cannot be conceived meaningfully without an understanding of the political theory that gives them shape. That theory may itself be the product of a struggle between several different political philosophies. For example, in the United States, different political philosophies—quasi-monarchal, federalist, classical republican, and so on—played a role in the compromises that resulted in setting up the American political institutions. One may hope that the result is an arrangement that can be justified by a rational moral argument, but that is a separate question. The process by which the institutions were formed is the result of a political struggle that involved a fair amount of conflict and compromise, including the issue of slavery, which the Founders provided for in the Constitution. In this sense, institutional facts are never outside the political philosophies that bring them about. A good example of this is separation of powers. Here the writings of the French philosopher Baron de Montesquieu, regarding how best to guarantee individual freedom, led to the idea that the powers of the state could be split among distinct institutions: the legislative assigned to making the laws, the executive assigned to enforcing the laws, and the judicial assigned to interpreting the laws.[15] A similar arrangement, federalism, is yet another example.[16] It exists in those societies, like the United States, that separate local and national powers. In the United States, separation of powers and federalism are believed to be necessary to ensure that no one branch, particularly the national government, becomes too powerful. Thus, the difference in outlook between U.S. legislatures and U.S. courts and the corresponding difference in outlook between state and national assemblies reflect their different political responsibilities under this theory.

Given this background, one does not have to take sides in justifying a legislative or a court action in arguing on behalf of justice or social utility. Both arguments play their roles in their institutional arenas. For instance, for the courts, the dominant concern is with punishing only the guilty or only those responsible for causing harm. For the legislature, it is with providing for the common good either in the sense of Bentham's famous phrase, "the greatest good for the greatest number," or on the basis of some wider, all-encompassing, corporatist notion. Here, an argument could be made for courts deferring to the legislature in the determination of economic and social policy. But even for the legislature, where social utility reigns, the importance of a general practice that emphasizes fairness in individual responsibility is essential, given that widespread disregard of this ideal would lessen the society's faith in its political institutions. As Rawls has noted, if "tellishment" were the punishing of the innocent—as in framing an innocent person for a crime—and one could not distinguish between instances of true punishment and instances of tellishment, the ability of our political institutions to ensure the common good would be substantially compromised.[17]

Thus, in democracies, notions like the separation of powers and federalism prevent courts and legislatures from making new laws merely because they believe the new laws would benefit society. That would be for one branch to overstep the function of the other or for the federal government to overstep the responsibilities of the states. But there is no prohibition on courts adjusting existing laws, including degrees of individual freedom, to accommodate justice. This is necessary to ensure that the society's faith in the fairness of its institutions is maintained. For example, a court could not decree a law creating a national bank or a law changing the economy from capitalism to socialism, but it could put limits on corporate freedom in areas where market distortions make it difficult to discover individual corporate responsibility. An example is the recent development of the notion of market share liability.[18]

How are notions such as separation of powers and federalism to be justified? Historically, the justification—here, I mean a causal explanation—may proceed from understanding the particular forces that confronted a people at some earlier period in their history. Analytically, it might proceed from understanding how power can be limited so as not to produce tyranny.[19] Both of these approaches may be important in the development of democratic theory, but neither is satisfactory for our needs. We are not concerned about the particular arrangements adopted within a society to ensure democracy but about why democracy is a valuable choice worth being pursued. The question of justification of any particular approach, therefore, is subordinate to a deeper question that cannot be answered from the perspective of the prevailing political ideology alone. For such ideologies presuppose facts about human nature and social history and do not say enough about the underlying moral principles that give them rise or even identify these principles. Although such elaborations may be enlightening at the level of democratic theory, they fail to provide the deeper normative analysis needed here. Consequently, I shall explain how we arrive at prescriptive principles in political philosophy first and then how to justify a general doctrine of political morality that can be a foundation for democratic theory.[20]

Alan Gewirth has noted that the central task of political philosophy "is the moral evaluation of political power."[21] If so, then the question of whether a state can justifiably use its laws and regulations to coerce individual behavior must itself be a question of political philosophy. This is consistent with the idea that the meaning and efficacy of law is often determined in the context of other political institutions such as a legislature, an executive, and a judiciary. Gewirth's comment also raises the point that political philosophy differs from moral philosophy only in that the latter concerns "the most general considerations of moral values and obligations."[22] In this regard, political philosophy realizes justified state coercion only through the institutional application of moral values and obligations. Marxism notwithstanding, political philosophy differs from ideology unless the latter presents "general principles at the level of truth, validity [and] justification and not merely at the level of propaganda, persuasion or rhetorical victory."[23] This latter point affirms a long tradition in Greek thought, beginning at least as early as Plato, that the primary task of philosophy is to seek out and unravel the truth.

But it also opens the door to the contemporary question of whether morality has a foundation outside its historical and social/political context. As C. G. Prado, citing Michael Foucault, points out:

> We have to investigate "the historical conditions which motivate our conceptualization. We need a historical awareness of our present circumstance." That awareness problematizes current truths both by tracing

> their descent and emergence and by uncovering alternatives. We gain this awareness by asking questions like Foucault's—whether "the critical discourse that addresses itself to repression" of sexuality really does "act as a roadblock to a power mechanism" or rather is in fact a mechanism integral to what it supposedly opposes.[24]

The point can also be found in Nietzsche:

> What the philosophers called "a rational foundation for morality" and tried to supply was, seen in the right light, merely a scholarly variation of the common *faith* in the prevalent morality; a means of *expression* for this faith; and thus just another fact within a particular morality; indeed in the last analysis a kind of denial that this morality might ever be considered problematic—certainly the very opposite of an examination, analysis, questioning, and vivisection of this very faith.[25]

These issues are particularly troubling because in their broadest construction, they erase even the attempt to lay a foundation for morality as a product of our ideological (Judeo-Christian) heritage. Still, the question of whether morality has a foundation is not resolved by these criticisms that are aimed at prompting us to question our prevailing views. For it may be that in the process of our own questioning, we arrive at baseline conclusions we need not take further. If so, then the question of whether we have discovered a foundation for morality is, for all important purposes, the question of whether we have taken our moral reflections as far as we needed to resolve the moral issues currently before us. This internal sense of expanding our moral considerations to wider ranges of concepts allows us to decide moral questions. We need not consider any external metaphysical claims to fundamental moral rightness to provide us with a foundation for our moral determinations. Nor need we do it to say we have a foundation. That is ultimately determined by whether we have taken our inquiry far enough to decide the issues before us. In this sense, moral inquiry is similar to scientific inquiry: both begin with a process of induction and only after they reach a certain level of abstraction is the process reversed and the method of deduction brought forth. Of course, how far up the scale of abstraction we need go to pursue answers to our questions and whether our inquiry will ultimately arrive at a dead end at some final intersubjective first principle of moral knowledge is another issue (see chapter 5).

Returning to our immediate task of unraveling the central questions of political philosophy, we continue, following Gewirth, by asking:

1. Why should human beings form societies?
2. Why should they obey any government and who should have political power over whom?
3. What are the criteria for determining who has political power?
4. What limits should there be on political power and do these limits include specific rights or freedoms?
5. What should be the ends of political power and how are these ends to be determined?[26]

Of course, there may be other questions not included on the list, but given the general nature of these questions, it is likely that any others would fall under them. Let us consider these questions from the standpoint of developing an understanding of when a state may justifiably use its laws to restrict the freedoms of its own people.

Two approaches philosophers have used to evaluate political actions morally are deontological and teleological.[27] Under the deontological approach (*deon*, from the Greek, duty or obligation), political actions are evaluated in terms of whether they are inherently fair or right, or whether they conform to some more general moral principle.[28] Immanuel Kant's theory of morality as based in rationality alone is a good example of a deontological approach. Under the teleological approach (*telos*, from the Greek, end), political actions are evaluated in terms of their relative ability to do the most good.[29] A few philosophers—Hobbes, for example—have relied on egoistic criteria as opposed to criteria that seek out the good of society treated as an organic whole.[30]

Still, there is a problem in treating either of these two approaches as providing the exclusive and exhaustive evaluation of normative political theories. It arises because morality encompasses concerns from both approaches without either being held to the exclusion of the other. For instance, one could imagine a situation in which a violent rape had been committed by a member of one social group against a member of another social group. If the two groups are sufficiently hostile to one another, especially if one of the two groups exhibits some form of irrational prejudice toward the other, the potential for a riot may develop. In that instance, a sheriff, who is concerned to keep the peace, may face the choice of framing an innocent person or being unable to avoid the riot. From a utilitarian or teleological perspective, framing the innocent person might produce the greatest happiness and the least pain.[31] But from a deontological approach, such an action would be clearly unjust. Similarly, fulfilling an earlier promise to return to your friend a weapon after you discover she has become unstable may satisfy a deontological criterion of promise-keeping but it is unlikely to produce more happiness than pain.[32] Attempts to circumvent this difficulty by creating impartial general rules that are justified by the good they achieve—also called rule utilitarianism—may prove no better in resolving the problem. For example, under this analysis, slavery could be justified if it provided a sufficiently high standard of living for a great enough number of nonslave, free citizens. Even the legal enslavement of a large number of innocent persons could be justified if some general benefit could be shown to a large enough group of persons. A different attempt to resolve this difficulty has been to encompass both approaches within a single theoretical framework. Natural law theories have evolved in just this direction.

Early natural law theories represented these approaches separately depending on whether they relied on consent (Locke), in which case they were deontological, or provided that "good must be done and pursued, and evil avoided" (Aquinas), in which case they were teleological.[33] Because the two approaches applied to the same actions, the possibility of inconsistent results was recognized. Some scholars (Gewirth and Rawls, for example) sought to remedy this tension by producing rules that seek out some good or avoidance of some evil that also take into account the "equal dignity" of all persons. A good example of this compromise is a rule recognizing all people's "equal opportunity to produce goods for themselves and others," and "their unequal actual contribution toward such production."[34] Rules directed toward assessing merit performance to govern promotion decisions also fit into this category. In this regard, we begin to see how the two approaches play a vital role in the justification of a state's coercive authority through laws.

Returning to Gewirth's five questions, the first asks why human beings should live in society. The point here is not to ask a historical question but to describe what good living in society serves.[35] The most widely accepted answers have been egoistic or utilitarian.[36] That is, people "should live in society because of the obvious advantages derived from it."[37] The advantages may be individualistic in the sense of satisfying individual needs and desires—such as the need for security in one's person and property—or organic or corporatist in the sense of satisfying some general interest of society treated as a whole.[38] Historically, Hobbes, Hume, Bentham, James Mill, and J. S. Mill fall under the former; Plato, Rousseau, Hegel, and Marx fall under the latter.

Concerning why human beings should obey any government, a utilitarian interpretation of the question differs from a deontological one. For the organic utilitarian, the ends that justify some people having political power over others are the needs of society.[39] For the individualist utilitarian (Bentham, James Mill, and J. S. Mill), correspondence of society's needs to those of the individual creates an incentive for individual acquiescence in the public good.[40] Individualist utilitarians, of course, reach an impasse when some people in society can satisfy their individual needs by not having the laws that apply to others fall on them.[41] Plato took up this problem in the Second Book of the *Republic*, as did Rousseau, who followed him from an organic utilitarian point of view.[42] Certainly, if everyone adopted this view, then no one's interests would be satisfied, at least not to the same degree were everyone to cooperate and follow the law.[43] Clearly, the justification offered by the individualist utilitarian may justify too little state coercion, and the justification offered by the organic utilitarian may justify too much. This has produced a conceptual space midway between the two views occupied by the "natural rights deontologists"—philosophers such as Locke and Kant.[44] They say that though the self will aim at its own interests, it still can recognize the equal rights of others.[45] Thus, it can be subject to a set of interpersonal rules that do not directly appeal to self-interest.

Together, these three points of view afford different answers for why some people should have political power over others. All agree that government is under a duty to do justice. However, each theoretical approach affords a different answer to what justice requires and to why government is under this duty.[46] For the natural rights deontologists, justice and reason are purely formal, negative, and attached to an impartial and minimalist set of rules.[47] For the organic utilitarian, justice and reason are substantive, affirmative, and maximal.[48] With the individualist utilitarian, justice and reason involve a means/ends calculation that seeks to maximize utility but is largely negative.[49]

As for the question of who should have political power, the history of political thought has offered three different deontological answers.[50] In modern times, natural rights deontologists have suggested that no one should have political power over another without the latter's consent.[51] Usually this doctrine is taught along with the concept of the "state of nature," a hypothetical state in which human beings exist prior to the existence of any government.[52] It is a state of conflict insofar as each person tries to protect what he has by war and the forming of alliances. Eventually, people living in the state of nature may form a government to provide for their own preservation. From this idea emerges the notion that human beings are naturally free and equal.[53] Hobbes thought this was because of their relative similarity in physical strength.[54] With the forming of a government come laws against assault, which are justified, given the approximate equality of strength among human beings. Locke believed the doctrine of natural freedom and equality was justified by a moral "fact," namely, that all human beings were "equally endowed with certain basic rights to life, liberty and the fruits of their labors."[55] Thus, for Locke, the state of nature was not a state of hostility or war but a state of natural rights. No doubt he would agree with the basic civil liberties protections enshrined in the American Bill of Rights.[56] Locke and especially Kant emphasized that the doctrine presupposes people's ability to recognize the moral law and to conform their behavior to it.[57] Thus did these philosophers recognize the metaphor of consent as conjoined with that of a social contract.[58]

In Hobbes and Locke, the contract creates the political society, but the allocation of power to a ruler is for Hobbes a gift and for Locke a trust.[59] In contrast, Rousseau relies on the contract both to establish the society and to allocate the power to the general will.[60] Utilitarians, both individualists, like Hume, and organicists, like Hegel, have criticized the unhistorical, fictional character of the contract.[61] No one really claims a true historical event. All are appealing to the voluntary, consensual, purposive nature of society.[62] These critics are challenging the very idea of a voluntary purposive subject prior to society. Moreover, most people "are born into a political society and cannot 'contract out' of it."[63] Consent-deontologists try to get around this objection by asserting that it is not the individual's consent that is important but that of the majority.[64] This raises the question of why anyone should have to go along with the majority. At this point, the deontologists' reliance on consent may become fused with the utilitarian answer that majority rule produces the best consequences, thus making the requirement of consent contingent on producing good consequences.[65] But, of course, here we run into the problem of determining what a good consequence is.

In the Middle Ages, the deontological justification appealed to the province of God as establishing the divine right of kings.[66] In the ancient world, Plato appealed to the natural status of certain people to become "philosopher-kings."[67] The idea was that certain people were more suited in temperament and intellectual ability to be rulers while others were more suited by virtue of their passions for military or commercial pursuits. Corresponding with this hierarchical view, and in contrast to more egalitarian positions that seek to provide equal opportunity for all persons, is the belief that government should promote the maximal development of the moral virtues over providing political equality.[68]

In contrast to the deontological views is the utilitarian answer to who should have political power. "Merit utilitarians" such as Aristotle and John Stuart Mill thought that political power should be distributed according to one's contribution in producing or maximizing goods.[69] Here, the deontological criterion of distributive justice is subsumed under the utilitarian criterion of maximizing goods.[70] Bonuses to workers who produce more or who try harder reflect a contemporary corporate-management example of this philosophy. Nationally, what constitutes appropriate merit to make political decisions depends on whether the society one lives in is an aristocracy, in which case it is virtue; oligarchy, wealth; or democracy, free birth.[71] Result-utilitarians, on the other hand, thought that the distribution of political power should be based strictly on what would most maximize goods, with no regard to contributing merits.[72] Lowering the corporate tax rate and providing job incentives are examples of how government applies this philosophy to industry. Indeed, most utilitarians—both individualist and organic—are result-utilitarians. Individualists such as Hobbes emphasized self-preservation; Locke, who had a utilitarian side, thought tyranny was worse than civil war.[73] Bentham and James Mill emphasized maximizing general utility, and J. S. Mill sought to foster the moral and intellectual development of society's members.[74] On the organic side, the concern is with a corporate good, that is, a good for the whole society. Signing a nuclear nonproliferation treaty or establishing a nationwide system of public schools fits this approach. Here Rousseau sought to find an ideal common interest represented by the "general will," which could usually be achieved by majority vote.[75] And Hegel sought the common good "in the spirit of the nation as reflected in its historical development."[76]

Regarding what should be the limits of political power, "the *procedures* and *operations* of government" and "the range of *objects* and *acts* controlled by government" must receive consideration.[77] Deontologists with a formalist bent wanted to set procedures limiting political power by the "rule of law" (Aristotle) or the "essence of the general will" (Rousseau).[78] This desire ties in with their concern to protect consent. It also raises our problem of duty when one has to deal with the possibility of unjust laws. Formal-deontologists also wanted to limit the range of objects controlled by government by imposing a principle of "equal freedom," which would ensure that government provides the same rights to all persons.[79] But even here a problem arises when one has to make sense of "equal freedom." Should a person be free to do anything to another that he is willing to have done back (Hobbes, Hume, Rousseau)? Should she be free to do anything to another that leaves the other in a position to return the act (Herbert Spencer)? Or should a person be able to act so that the "other's general freedom of action" is undiminished (Kant)?[80] Clearly, the first and second interpretations open the door to social disorder, the third to behavior that may not limit another's freedoms but that still is socially undesirable, for example, throwing garbage out of one's window.[81] This, then, raises a separate question of whether the assignment of rights must also comport with a principle requiring a compatible liberty for others.

The utilitarian approach to this problem would allow the person to act, provided the action does not harm anyone else.[82] However, there may be serious disagreements over whether another is harmed, as is seen in the current dispute over pornography, not to mention abortion, and debates over antidiscrimination legislation for gays and lesbians.[83] Even when no one is harmed, sometimes the public interest outweighs private interests, as in having to pay taxes to support public schools.[84]

Concerning what should be the end of political power, both individual and organic utilitarians answer the question in terms of maximizing either individual or collective goods.[85] The organicist, of course, conceives the goods in terms of the social whole (national defense); the individualist conceives them in terms of aggregates of individuals (lowering the individual income tax rate to increase the gross national product [GNP]).[86] Both differ from the natural rights deontologists, who view the end of government largely in terms of maintaining a legal framework that ensures a just distribution (for example, not depriving one of life, liberty, or property without due process of law).[87] Another deontological position, somewhat more related to the organicist view, sees individuals as so closely related to their social context that one cannot consider what is just for these individuals independent of the social forces making up the environment. Here the result may lead to laws against discrimination for the physically and mentally challenged and to the provision of welfare for those unable to find work.[88] As a result, an end of government must be to remove evils such as physical disease and economic privation and to foster equality of opportunity for everyone.[89] Clearly, in these last two examples, one sees the contemporary debate between libertarians, who measure freedom in terms of property rights, and liberals, who measure it in terms of equal opportunity.

Libertarians, who are also referred to as classical liberals or liberals of the nineteenth century, believe individuals have a natural right to property that can be interfered with only for the sake of protecting liberty. Often they will attempt to justify their position based on a Lockean interpretation of property rights.[90] Recall, Locke thought persons had a property right in the labor of their own bodies; therefore, what they produced with their own hands from the unowned earth they received a property right in.[91] By way of convention, through the recognition of some form of currency, the society can agree to maintain these property rights over time.[92] Thus, government needs to limit the kinds of transactions that might arise in the market place—for example, theft—to ensure that individual choices are not frustrated. But government may not do what the egalitarian liberal might hope, which is to limit an individual's economic freedom, to impose some ideal notion of equality on society. For the libertarian, government must be minimalist, imposing no additional rules on the market other than those the participants agree to.[93] This perspective contrasts with the views of the egalitarian liberal, who sees government as having a responsibility to provide at least a social safety net to ensure individual welfare. Still, most libertarians would agree that government should provide police, fire, and national defense since these measures cannot be efficiently supported privately, and they affect everyone alike. The strongest disagreements arise over redistribution of wealth through taxation for purposes of achieving economic parity.

Of course, the deontological and utilitarian criteria raise the possibility of substantial conflicts with respect to these issues.[94] If the goal is to create government "that is at once democratic, constitutionally liberal, and concerned with equality of opportunity for individual development and social welfare"—that is, a government that attempts to merge deontological and utilitarian concerns together—these criteria should be interpreted to avoid most potential conflicts.[95] Gewirth has argued that such a goal is obligatory if the full range of moral considerations is to be maintained. Still, one is inclined to ask exactly how the goal is to be met in the context of justifying a general social duty to obey law and, in particular, a judicial duty to follow the law. The answer requires finding a balance between the two approaches, theoretically as well as practically. It is not enough to say courts perform one function, legislatures perform another. One must have a reason for why this should be the case. Such a reason will be political in that it will justify relationships among institutions of government. It will also be moral in that it will set limits on the nature of these relationships in light of deontological and teleological moral considerations.

The Doctrine of Political Responsibility

Here I will focus on two different types of normative political theory: hypothetical consent and ethical rationalism. Most of the political arguments that historically have been offered to justify a general moral duty of political responsibility fall under one of these two types. For example, the theories of Hobbes, Locke, and Rousseau fall under hypothetical consent, Kant's under ethical rationalism. For each type, I will consider a contemporary version that is particularly illustrative of and influential in its area.

It should be noted that my focus is on theories that have both deontological and teleological components. Such theories are better-suited to unraveling the multiple moral considerations that justify law than are theories that operate only with a single component. If the legislature is primarily concerned with utilitarian considerations—either organic or individual—the courts must be concerned with doing justice. Since justice concerns fair treatment of persons who have preexisting duties, deontological theories—or, at least, theories with a strong deontological component—are appropriate. On the other hand, the courts cannot figure out what one's preexisting duties are without some sense of the purposes or goals to which the laws are directed. In this sense, the choice to focus on deontological theories when thinking about courts also allows for the merger of utilitarian considerations as I have suggested. In allowing legislatures to make the law and courts to interpret it, both considerations are brought into balance. An obvious problem occurs, however, when a court's interpretation of a statute is contrary to the legislature's intent or when a court's interpretation of the common or constitutional law creates a new area of rights and responsibilities. Here the answer must be to appeal to a determinative moral principle that not only takes into account deontological and teleological considerations but that also can adjudicate between them. Such a principle will be foundational for a theory of political morality.

HYPOTHETICAL CONSENT

Judges and lawyers sometimes appeal to the notion of hypothetical consent—an outcome the parties would have agreed to if only they had had the opportunity—to decide certain types of hard cases.[96] Daniel Brudney has noted that, even in instances where particular self-interests do not dominate, appeals of this sort lack moral force.[97] They are not like the use of hypothetical consent in political philosophy to justify general principles of justice.

For hypothetical consent to work, it must involve an *idealized* choice position in which self-interest does not dominate, and the interests at stake must themselves be moral. Thus hypothetical consent requires both a gap and a match between agents inside and agents outside the choice situation, a match because the choice in the idealized position is supposed to apply to those outside. It is in virtue of some feature or features shared by those inside and outside that the choice in the idealized position must not be a mere stand-in for an identifiable individual's (hypothetical) choice at some specified time.[98] It is not sufficient that the idealized choice position limits the information available to the parties about how their own choices will affect their interests, however.

> The point is simple enough. The impartiality generated by information constraints may be necessary to keep the agents in the choice position from being mapped onto any specified agent outside, and so to keep the agent in the choice position from rigging matters in favor of some specifiable individual. But if there is to be moral force to a choice from an idealized position, the description of the agent's interest is equally critical.[99]

That description, Brudney contends, must above all provide an independent foundation for showing that the interests the agent operates from are themselves moral interests independently determined.[100]

In his book *Political Liberalism*, John Rawls relies on the idea of a hypothetical, "original" position to give *content* to principles of justice. In this position, representative agents choose principles of justice to govern their society behind a veil of ignorance, which limits the information the representatives have about themselves and the specifics of their society.[101] The point of the original position is to illustrate how in a democratic society citizens with very different comprehensive philosophical, religious, or moral doctrines—after engaging in reflective equilibrium, that is, after juxtaposing possible principles of justice against their considered moral judgments—could choose principles solely because they are just. As Brudney notes, Rawls does not use the original position as a way to establish a *duty* of justice, which he contends is "a fundamental natural duty."[102] Rawls's notion presupposes that the representative agents in the original position start with a dual power: a sense of justice and a *capacity* for a conception of the good—that is, for ends that are worthwhile obtaining independently of how they might affect the particular individual making the choice. In this sense, built into the original position is the possibility of recognizing interests that are themselves moral. The representatives share these interests with agents outside the original position, although as agents in the original position, they do not affirm any particular conception of the good.[103] Brudney notes that this blind sense of justice and capacity for an unspecified conception of the good is morally relevant because it is abstracted from specific ends that may or may not have worthiness. Thus, Rawls's original position meets Brudney's requirements for determining the content of some moral duties, given that "(a) those in the choice position are choosing on behalf of beings who are like the agent in the morally relevant respects (i.e., their interests and capacities), and (b) the particular choice position is the proper procedure to determine the content of some particular duty of the agent."[104] Here, (b) follows from the fact that Rawls's original position clears out morally irrelevant information, as would go to self-interest, that would deflect the agents from seeing their true moral duties within a pluralistic democratic society.

The original position provides for recognizing a general doctrine of political responsibility applicable to democratic institutions, including the judiciary. Through the use of the veil of ignorance, recognition is gained for two principles of justice. The first recognizes equality of basic political rights, such as freedom of speech, travel, privacy, and voting. The second provides for social and economic inequalities, provided they work to the benefit of the least advantaged and are attached to positions and offices open to all.[105] The former applies to constitutional interpretation of fundamental rights, due process, and equal protection of the laws, the latter to the economic and social policy choices of the legislature. The manner in which the principles apply to governmental institutions is first to create a constitutional order and, then, with information that order provides, to create laws and policies to serve and promote the common good. Here common good refers to the results that arise when persons with *reasonable* comprehensive doctrines—that is, doctrines that accept the principles of justice as a means of ordering society—develop an overlapping consensus on questions of social and economic policy. Since the principles of justice apply to all institutions of society, the legal order that results should reflect James Madison's idea of deliberative democracy. That is, it should reflect the balance between majority rule and protection of minority rights, especially in respect to opportunities for deliberation and debate.[106] Given the institutional role of the courts to ensure that justice is done, the latter are just the sorts of principles one would expect the judiciary to protect. Thus, the general doctrine of political responsibility that results from Rawls's original position is that all participants in governmental institutions are obligated to apply the principles of justice, first, to justify the constitutional order and, second, considering that order, to justify individual constitutional and legislative decisions. The result is a political morality that meliorates both the deontological and utilitarian roles of the different branches of government, while at the same time justifying democratic forms of government. It is also one that brings together a theory of individual rights "with the civic republican virtue of participation in political life," without "the civic humanist view that such participation is necessarily a 'privileged focus of the good life.'"[107]

Rawls's theory meliorates the deontological function of the courts to do justice by allowing for a consensus to develop, first, as to what the basic constitutional goods are—for example, free speech, right to travel, right to privacy, and so on—and, second, as to more particular matters regarding social and economic policy. The theory also limits the utilitarian function of the legislature by ensuring that no law will be held constitutional if it undermines the basic constitutional order as defined by the principles of justice. This would include prohibiting punishing the innocent to avoid a still greater harm to a larger segment of society.

Here I would note an important difference between *Political Liberalism* and Rawls's earlier work, *A Theory of Justice*.[108] Because the claims in *Political Liberalism* are more modest, not engaging a metaethical justification for a theory of justice but instead assuming the desire for reasonable comprehensive doctrines from which to start, Rawls avoids some of the more obvious objections that have been raised against *Theory*. For one thing, he avoids the problem that the veil of ignorance is counterintuitive.[109] This he does by claiming that the "parties are like actors playing the role of being impartial to various particular comprehensive doctrines."[110] He also avoids the concern that individuals who stand to be better off with the status quo would never put themselves behind the veil of ignorance. Since the theory as it originally appeared seemed to invoke a means/ends rationality, this point made it also seem counterrational.[111] Because the original position is merely a representational device, the parties can rationally "agree to principles they believe will most benefit those they represent" by ensuring fair terms of cooperation, "development and full exercise of the two moral powers," and the ability of citizens to advance their own "determinative reasonable conceptions of the good."[112] Moreover, *Political Liberalism* avoids the circularity criticism that *Theory*, in its construction of the original position, assumed the very equality it attempted to justify.[113] In *Political Liberalism*, Rawls is not claiming "that a 'well-ordered society' need be stable, relatively homogeneous in its basic moral beliefs, and have broad agreement on what constitutes the good life."[114] And he avoids the claim of abstracting the essential nature of the person from her particular conception of the good.[115] Instead, Rawls treats the conception of the person politically, not metaphysically.[116]

Still, there may be times when even *Political Liberalism* runs into problems. Such a situation would arise if incompatible comprehensive doctrines prevent one from engaging in the kind of social cooperation presupposed by Rawls's social constructivism. The theory is necessarily limited to situations where the comprehensive doctrines are reasonable in the sense that they do not prohibit the possibility of overlapping consensus and social cooperation. Consensus will not be possible where the ideas over which it is to range are abhorrent. According to Alan Gewirth:

> Permissiveness and tolerance are indeed possible and desirable in . . . religion, despite, or perhaps because of, the variety of religions; and it is important to differentiate religious statements from scientific ones. But what of the conflicts within morality, law and other such [fields]? Must the morality of apartheid be accepted equally with the morality of racial nondiscrimination, and the law of totalitarian repression equally with the law of civil liberties? Unless "morality" and "law" are question-beggingly confined to certain favored alternatives, critical justificatory questions arise in these [fields]; and these questions cannot be answered simply by reiterating the principles or criteria of each [field].[117]

And as I have pointed out:

> Rawls believes that Kantianism, utilitarianism and a pluralist account of the realm of values should be able to exist under the political conception of justice. But is this possible? The above quotation [referring to Gewirth] suggests that the sense of reasonable in reasonable comprehensive doctrines might be too liberal. But what if it is too conservative? For example, many people today are debating whether one has a basic right not to be discriminated against on the basis of sexual orientation. All sides agree that a basic liberty is involved—although they disagree about whose liberty it is. Is an overlapping consensus possible on the issue? Has it been possible on the abortion question? Is this not the problem that necessitated the Court stepping in on the issue? To put the point succinctly: How reasonable must reasonable comprehensive doctrines be to have a well-ordered democratic society?[118]

Or, to put the point still one other way, Jürgen Habermas has noted that the "abstract conditions that make impartial *judgment* of practical questions possible" for Rawls

> do not coincide with the conditions under which we are disposed to *act* on moral insight. This leads Rawls to seek out the motivational thrust of an accommodating political culture, which he finds at the privileged site of a continuous constitutional tradition that stretches back over two hundred years. Though certainly challenged again and again by conflicts of class and race, this tradition has consistently been renewed and revitalized by new interpretations. If one takes this relation to tradition literally, though, the theory's *politically* convincing force is limited to a few responsive contexts.[119]

ETHICAL RATIONALISM

Alan Gewirth contends that there are certain rights that every rational agent logically must accept on pain of contradiction. His view starts with two features of human action: voluntariness and purposiveness. By voluntariness, Gewirth means that the action is "under the agent's control in that he unforcedly chooses to act as he does."[120] By purposiveness, he means that the agent acts for some end or purpose. Together, these two features are necessary for the performance of any act that can be subject to moral evaluation. Gewirth believes that in these two features he has found an independent, nonarbitrary, noncontingent, starting point for any moral theory qua moral theory. Based solely on these two features, he sets up an argument that *all* agents could make from their own internal connotative standpoints—as indicated by the quotation marks—to decide what rights they have. (An internal connotative standpoint is what the agent understands his own reasonings to imply.) The argument proceeds deductively:

(1) "I do X for purpose E."[121] The sentence focuses on the fact that the action is voluntary and purposive, despite the object to which it is directed. The quotes show that the agent asserts the claim from his own internal connotative standpoint. (2) "E is good."[122] Here the agent affirms a reason for why he chooses to act. The good is not necessarily a moral good but any specific criterion that explains why a person acts. It may be merely that the agent thinks it is worth doing according to whatever criterion he follows in deciding. (3) "My freedom and well-being are necessary goods."[123] The idea of freedom comes in with voluntariness. The idea of well-being comes in

with purposiveness. The agent affirms both as necessary to achieve the purposes for which he acts. Thus, freedom is the procedural generic feature of action. Well-being is the substantive generic feature of action. (4) "I have rights to freedom and well-being."[124] At this point, some people might want to object to introducing the word "right," so Gewirth considers what happens if (4) were to be denied.

Beginning with (3) "My freedom and well-being are necessary goods," we can rewrite the statement without alteration of its meaning as (3a) "I must have freedom and well-being."[125] We want to deny (4) "I have rights to freedom and well-being." Call this denial (4') "It is not the case that I have rights to freedom and well-being." This means (5') "I have to deny that all other persons ought (at least) to refrain from removing or interfering with my freedom and well-being."[126] This follows from the fact that the rights denied by (4') are claim rights, that is, rights that have correlative duties.[127] Next, follows (6') "I have to accept that I may not—that is, it is permissible that I not—have freedom and well-being."[128] (The point here is not to justify contingent beliefs that an agent may hold from his own idiosyncratic point of view but to show the logical relation between a set of nonmoral premises and a moral conclusion. Thus, we have a ground for a later response to someone who might want to challenge the theory on the ground that it would allow for a lower-caste Indian villager to starve, while the upper caste eats well, because the villager does not perceive the arrangement to destroy her freedom and well-being. The ground is that the institutional arrangement may itself be violative of the villager's freedom and well-being because it prevents the very perception that would expose the immoral consequence.[129]) Now (6') contradicts (3a). But (3a) was derived from the noncontroversial (3), and (6') was derived from the controversy over (4). Therefore, (4) as originally written must have been correct.[130] What we have been given here is a proof by negation: if the opposite of a conclusion proves false, the conclusion as originally written must have been true.

Going back to (4) "I have rights to freedom and well-being," Gewirth notes that we have proved so far only a *prudential* rights claim—what the agent must claim to be consistent with wanting to do X for purpose E. To make this a moral claim, I must recognize the principle of sufficient reason that (5) "My need for freedom and well-being was the sole basis upon which I made my rights claim."[131] But this means that I recognize as a principle of universality that (6) "All other persons similarly situated—that is, who want to do X for purpose E—could make the same rights claim."[132] From these considerations follows (7) "Act in accord with the generic rights—that is, rights to freedom and well-being—of your recipients as well as yourself."[133] To deny (7) while affirming (5) and (6) would be to contradict oneself. One would be in the position of saying that one had rights that on the same foundation others did not have.

This final step, which Gewirth calls the "Principle of Generic Consistency" (PGC) stands on its own assertorically, that is, outside the dialectical approach, since presumably anyone could have gone through the dialectically necessary procedure that gives it rise. Therefore, we no longer need the quotes. Thus, the principle is truly a universal principle of morality because it derives from no other contents than the canons of deductive and inductive logic and the fact that human beings act voluntarily for their own purposes, a necessary feature of any moral theory we can conceive.

At this point, one might want to ask why we need to reify rights and, in particular, why the generic rights delineated here. Gewirth's probable answer to the first question would seem to follow from the central point of the PGC, to determine those "strict" duties that are at the heart of morality and are correlative with rights.[134] Thus, the PGC takes account of rights as categorical in the way that a dependent variable presumes an independent variable. It does it as a priori within the structure of purposive action. As for the second question, freedom and well-being are the generic rights because together they guarantee the one quality all moral theories must presuppose: the possibility of voluntary purposive behavior. But even looking beyond the pure moral claim to the legal/political one, we reify rights to find the balance between "private and public autonomy."[135] Habermas has noted that this is necessary if citizens are going to be able to "regulate their lives together by means of positive law."[136]

Gewirth's theory produces a justification for a doctrine of political responsibility that can be seen by considering the ways the PGC justifies both human actions and the actions of society's institutions generally. The PGC provides a moral ground for maximizing both human freedom and, with it, the possibility of purpose-fulfillment. It does so by protecting three types of goods in an order of importance, which is determined by the degree to which the goods are necessary to purpose-fulfillment. At the level of *basic* well-being, the PGC requires the protection of life, physical integrity, as in not being assaulted or maimed, and mental equilibrium, as in not being subject to thought control or mind-altering drugs. These are conditions essential to the very possibility of agency. Additionally, the PGC protects *nonsubtractive* rights, rights that prevent having one's level of purpose-fulfillment decreased, as occurs when one is lied to or made the victim of broken promises. Finally, the PGC supports *additive* rights, rights that add to one's level of purpose-fulfillment, such as the right to an education and to obtaining adequate health care. Because these goods are usually better secured through institutional rather than by self-help methods, the PGC justifies democratic institutions that protect rights generally. Democratic institutions are justified because by protecting consent not only is the freedom component of the PGC met, but the well-being component is more strongly guaranteed.

In terms of political institutions, the PGC justifies under its freedom component institutions that protect rights to freedom of speech, autonomy, and privacy and to consent by majority rule as is manifested in the right to vote for legislative representatives.[137] This is the deontological side of the PGC, and a fundamental responsibility of the courts. Under its well-being component, the PGC justifies institutions that protect the rights of all people to live and, wherever possible, to pursue their own happiness—what legislatures are supposed to guarantee.[138] This is the teleological side. Concerns for due process and equal protection play a necessary instrumental role in ensuring that only guilty parties are punished and that no one is treated as a second-class citizen.[139] Hence, the PGC recognizes restrictions on majority rule to preserve order and to do justice. But it also gives a fair amount of differential authority to legislatures, especially in the area of additive rights, to develop means for ensuring the general welfare.

This justification for democratic institutions to protect freedom and to advance purpose-fulfillment is the foundation of a Gewirthian doctrine of political responsibility. That doctrine obliges participants in democratic institutions to use their institutional positions to ensure that everyone's rights are protected and their possibility of purpose-fulfillment is maximized. Here agency as a foundation for moral rights and duties can be limited only where it would otherwise result in a contradiction. The political structure of the society will specify the means by which this responsibility is carried out. That is, how institutions meet the responsibilities of the PGC will depend on their specific role in that structure. The judiciary in the United States, for example, plays the crucial role of checking the legislative and executive branches of government so that, in the name of majoritarian democracy, these branches do not trade off basic rights. It does not engage in policy decisions over how best to provide for the common good. That is the function of the legislature and may take on a number of different institutional forms—national health care, a right to work, welfare, and so on—for the sake of protecting basic rights.[140] Of course, all necessary roles—legislative, executive, and judicial—must be in existence if freedom and well-being are to be maintained. Not to provide in some manner for any one of these roles would seriously undermine the political responsibility of government as mandated by the PGC.

Since the necessary conditions of human agency ground the PGC, the principle provides a deeper foundation for morally evaluating action than Rawls's hypothetical consent, which presupposes "reasonable" comprehensive doctrines that may not always hold true. Rawls's conception operates within a pluralistic democratic society when there exists an overlapping consensus, despite incompatible religious, moral, or philosophical doctrines. Such a consensus comes about provided the citizens share a sense of justice and a capacity for a conception of the good. In contrast, Gewirth's approach is metaethical in that it attempts to adjudicate among different fundamental political/moral conceptions to arrive at a justification for the rights all people have. Thus, Gewirth's approach can resolve conflicts between different conceptions that Rawls cannot solve.

Both theories provide a basis for a general duty to obey law and for a particular duty of courts to decide cases justly. Only Gewirth's, however, provides it at a sufficient level of generality to be able to resolve a conflict that may exist in the society's political morality. Under both theories, the obligations are clearly moral and the institutions to which they apply include the political. Therefore, following Dworkin, I will continue to refer to the obligations created as "political morality," although later I will also treat Gewirth's theory as a kind of natural law theory that presides over the highest level of legal reasoning. For now, I intend my emphasis to be on morality's association to political institutions rather than to particular instances of legal reasoning. However, it should be noted that Gewirth's theory is not a theory that Dworkin would look to, at least not directly, since the theory decides the legitimacy of judicial decisionmaking from *outside* the internal point of view. That is, the theory is not confined to the prevailing political morality of any society as Dworkin's view would have it. More important, the theory is able to provide a critique of the prevailing political morality by pushing one to a level of abstraction where the society's political morality itself can be called into question. In this sense, the theory responds to the external skeptic who wants to question the foundation of the legal order that the judge takes as given. The theory provides a moral justification for choosing among the various theories of law—positivism, legal idealism, natural law—depending on the generality of the question involved and the moral issues that are at stake. Dworkin also has problems with Rawls's reflective equilibrium, although not the same problems he would have with Gewirth, since reflective equilibrium is not restricted by the fit requirement to the settled law that Dworkin wants to hold to.[141]

CRITICISM: ANALOGICAL REASONING

Practitioners will read my argument as an attack on the sometimes tenuous, sometimes strong distinction between primary and secondary sources of law. No doubt they will see it as interposing a new level of uncertainty by introducing a form of analysis that is not typically brought to bear on legal problems by individuals engaged in the practice of law. If, on the other hand, lawyers see what I have done as laying a foundation in political morality for the general obligation to obey law and the corresponding judicial obligation to follow the law, perhaps they will find in that disclosure a means for handling legal problems when more traditional approaches break down. I shall give an account here of the actual practice of lawyers and judges and how that practice might be advanced by the development of a more general theory.

My purpose is not an attempt to discredit the method of reasoning, known as "reasoning by analogy," relied on by the legal profession. I doubt it could be discredited, but I want to show that the reasons for preferring that method to more holistic accounts are inadequate, at least in very hard cases. In short, although the judge and practicing lawyers may find it helpful to rely on reasoning by analogy to resolve hard cases where the society's political morality is consistent, they are likely to find it unhelpful when dealing with very hard cases where the society's political morality is inconsistent. This latter point is at the heart of the question: Are there right answers in very hard cases?

Let us consider this question in terms of Cass Sunstein's criticism that the holistic theories of Dworkin, economic analysts, and other scholars do not provide an adequate place for the traditionally important role of analogical reasoning in legal decisionmaking. According to Sunstein, holistic

> theories are produced largely on the basis of abstract moral theory. These theories are then brought to bear on particular problems. But this is not how lawyers proceed. In deciding whether a restriction on cross-burning offends the First Amendment, lawyers do not really ask which interpretation will make the amendment the best it can be. They do not begin with a high-level conception of value promoted by the Amendment. To develop such a conception they would have to ask questions that are too broad and abstract—too hard, large, and open-ended for legal actors to handle. Such questions call for responses that are too deeply theorized.[142]

On the contrary, "In thinking about free speech issues, lawyers instead ask what particular sorts of practices seem to violate the First Amendment, or the principle of free expression, and then whether a restriction on—for example—cross-burning is relevantly similar or relevantly different."[143] This use of reasoning by analogy, Sunstein argues, has certain definite advantages over holistic theories. First, it better recognizes the limits in time and capacity of judges than, for example, Dworkin's view of law as integrity.[144] Recall, Dworkin's view requires a judge to make coherent a substantial portion of the relevantly situated settled law prior to rendering any decision. Second, reasoning by analogy may allow for agreement on the conclusion of a particular case even by people who disagree about what principles are relevant.[145] Third, analogical reasoning may aid a moral evolution of values by showing how values may set new directions when applied to novel cases.[146] Finally, analogical reasoning can take account of precedents even where there is disagreement about the results embodied in those precedents.[147] For these reasons, Sunstein claims that law, which develops along discrete lines, is better served by analogical reasoning than by the reasonings associated with broader approaches.

As far as it goes, I have no difficulty with Sunstein's argument and would even support it with two further reasons. Allowing law to develop by discrete moves rather than by holistic change protects democracy by ensuring that judges, who often are appointed, do not overstep the institutional function of elected legislatures. Moreover, discrete moves may allow for easier-to-effectuate change in the law, especially where the change is in relation to a previously decided case later thought to be a mistake.

A problem arises, however, in contexts where the meaning of the law is unclear or the justification for a particular rule or principle is disputed. In such contexts, there may be no agreed-upon basis for determining whether a particular analogy is even relevant. Consider, for example, three cases that trace an unexpected yet major development in an area of tort law. The first, *Winterbottom v. Wright*,[148] an English case, held that an injured party could not sue the ultimate manufacturer of a wagon for injuries sustained when the wagon broke down because there was no privity of contract between the parties. The injured party could sue the retailer who had sold him the wagon but who probably did not have a very deep pocket. In the second case, *Thomas v. Winchester*,[149] husband buys wife a mislabeled bottle of poison marked as a medicine. The wife consumes the poison and almost dies. Though there was no privity of contract between the husband and wife and the ultimate manufacturer of the drug, the New York Court of Appeals, through Justice Benjamin Cardozo, carved out an exception to the no privity rule when applied to inherently dangerous items. The court reasoned that a local druggist would not know that the item had been mislabeled, and so there was a special duty on the individuals manufacturing inherently dangerous items such as drugs to see to it that they were properly labeled. In the third case, *MacPherson v. Buick Motor Company*,[150] a court again faced the question of whom one can sue when injuries were sustained, this time because of a defective motor car. Although from one point of view an automobile is more like a wagon than a bottle of mislabeled medicine, the court, nevertheless, applied the exception marked out in *Thomas*. After noting that automobiles had become a necessity of life and were so complex that a retailer might not notice a defect, the court held that a manufacturer had a special duty to see to it that they were safe and fit for their intended use before placing them in the marketplace.[151] These examples are meant to suggest that the determination of relevance between situations will often depend on the background theoretical framework against which the situations are being assessed. Consequently, where the background theoretical framework is itself in dispute, reasoning by analogy may be of no help in solving the problem.

It is in contexts such as these that a broader approach is needed. But what should such an approach consider? Should it consider the purposes of the individuals who articulated the rule or principle? Should it attempt an elaboration of the concepts making it up? What about possible justifications? Are there any that should carry more weight than others? This last question is especially important where more fundamental matters may be in dispute and the principles or rules are on opposite sides of the society's political morality. For it is in just this situation that secondary sources, including appeals to natural law theory, prove to be an important source of law and do not provide merely an external critique of law. It is also in this area that these nontraditional sources may provide an important interpretative means in which to understand the law and, thus, to draw the analogies that one needs to decide very hard cases.

Why does this situation come about? Why are we not content with saying that in this area the law is simply unclear or nonexistent? The answer lies in the political responsibility that every judge has to decide cases in a way that promotes the deeper purposes of the legal system to preserve order, do justice, and protect individual rights. It is in the context of just these deeper considerations that a judge will seek to determine an appropriate background political morality to decide very hard cases.[152] Deciding a case by appeal to political morality is a vertical move in the way that deciding a case by drawing an analogy is a horizontal move. The vertical move results when the judge, after following a narrow set of traditionally legal concepts, adopts a broad set of moral ones as befits the case at hand. The resulting theory will also provide a judge with a wider basis of knowledge with which to decide other cases. For these reasons, I will call this internal vertical move by the judge "epistemic pragmatism." The name is meant to reflect the fact that from the judge's point of view, to fulfill the responsibility to decide very hard cases it has become necessary to go beyond traditional legal sources.

CHAPTER THREE

Metatheory

Having examined differences among possible sources of law and how generally judges ought to decide cases, let us now see what these differences reveal when applied to judicial decisionmaking. I shall begin by stating what it means for justice to be an end of political responsibility and by developing a classification for the various approaches judges take to legal decisionmaking in terms of the two variables: source of law and duty to obey law. Next I shall consider whether there should be any flexibility in the way judges go about deciding cases—whether, for example, there may be reasons for a judge who normally follows one approach to shift to a different approach. Then I shall comment on how objective a judge's approach to a legal decision really is. What I am about to describe is the internal side of the relationship between legal and political philosophy, that is, the relationship between sources of law and conceptions about the duty to obey the law from the point of view of the judge. By using the phrase "conceptions about the duty to obey law" I recognize that even if there is general agreement as to what the doctrine of political responsibility requires of judges, there may still be disagreement over how best to apply that doctrine in deciding particular cases. One judge, for example, may believe that the best way to decide a case is to follow the intent of the framers where applicable. Another may believe that the best approach is to interpret the law so as to provide the greatest degree of justice as that term is understood in contemporary society. Since I plan to say which approach a judge ought to adopt under which set of circumstances, it is proper to label the discussion here metatheory. The prefix "meta" denotes the fact that I shall not be confined to a single theory of law—positivism, legal idealism, or natural law. Instead, I shall consider a number of different theories and the various reasons that might determine a choice of one theory over another in the context of judicial decisionmaking.

Justice as an End of Political Responsibility

I have pointed out that the political responsibility of the courts in a democracy is to do justice. This responsibility manifests itself in the court's obligation to look backward from the case before it to find the relevant principle that determines legal responsibility. Sometimes courts do this by asking if the law conforms to constitutional requirements of due process and equal protection, if it does not violate any fundamental rights either on its face or as applied, and if it is not vague in its meaning. More important, courts are justified in deciding if the laws are unjust since there is no duty to obey an unjust law and certainly not for the courts to follow one. The latter result follows from our general doctrine of political responsibility, which requires courts, among other things, to do justice. Of course, this raises the question of the meaning of justice.

Consider, for example, how a translator of a foreign language would determine whether a particular word or phrase translates into English as the word "justice." Surely, if the word or phrase in the foreign language describes treating like cases alike or, to use one of Plato's definitions, "rendering to each person that which is their due," the translator will want to use the English word "justice."[1] More specifically, following Aristotle, the translator may want to use "rectificatory" or "corrective" justice if the issue is one of paying someone back for a contract breached or a tort committed. The translator will most likely use "distributive" justice if it concerns the allocation of benefits or detriments among many people.[2] The former is arithmetical, reflecting the one-to-one relationship of the remedy to the violation. Although in Aristotle's time there were only civil lawsuits, the contemporary notion of having the punishment fit the crime is an example in the public sphere of rectificatory justice.[3] Distributive justice, in contrast, concerns the relationship between some qualifying characteristic and the goods or services one receives. Twice the pay for twice the work would be an example of this relationship. This form of justice is geometric, reflecting the proportionality that exists between the justifying characteristic and the distribution. Here concerns arise when some irrelevant factor impedes the proper distribution. The presence of class, race, ancestry, sexual orientation, or gender-based discrimination within a society often gives rise to questions of distributive justice.[4] Aristotle thought that the justifying characteristic depended on the society in which one lived: aristocracy, possession of the virtues; oligarchy, possession of wealth; democracy, free birth.[5] Within democratic societies, questions of distributive justice often produce legislation establishing equal pay for equal work to avoid discrimination, minimum wages to counter market distortions, and limitations on the number of hours one can work and conditions affecting the safety of the workplace to protect basic well-being. Sometimes distributive questions arise when the legislature bails out one company within an industry from going bankrupt because of the number of workers it employs or its general effect on the economy. In such cases, appeals to distributive justice provide little support, so the legislation would probably be justified on grounds that it promotes some utilitarian notion of the common good.[6]

These several examples suggest that questions about justice are more complex than one might think when only the concept of justice was under consideration. For instance, if the courts are bound to treat like cases alike, under what circumstances are two cases alike? If a court believes it made an error in the way it decided the earlier case, must it still decide a latter case in the same way in order to treat like cases alike? Should the court enforce a legislative or a constitutional provision requiring that all persons of a certain race be bound to servitude? What is a person's due under conditions where there were unequal bargaining advantages at the time of negotiation? Should individuals have the right to discriminate in matters of housing, public accommodations, and employment where the basis of the discrimination is either irrational or irrelevant to the matter at hand? Questions such as these led John Rawls to distinguish the concept of justice from the particular conception of justice under consideration.[7]

The latter concerned the particular rights and duties that political institutions can or should enforce by law. It is usually with respect to various conceptions of justice that the most difficult and troubling cases of justice arise. Consider, for example, that Rawls's egalitarian pattern of justice would disavow social and economic inequalities except where they benefit the least advantaged. What would be the import of Rawls's view in today's United States? Is this an issue for the courts to decide, the legislature to decide, or the people to decide by way of constitutional change? Compare Rawls's view with the way Robert Nozick would allow any resulting distribution of property provided only that the original acquisition was a product of mixing one's labor with something previously unowned (according to John Locke) and that all subsequent transfers were by gift, bequest, or purchase and sale.[8] Would Nozick's libertarian view create too limited a control over property rights?[9] What should one's rights be regarding selling life-sustaining drugs at whatever price the market will bear? What rights have those people who simply cannot afford the drugs? Would government be under any duty to provide them financial support? If so, where would this money come from—taxation? What these questions point to is the need to adjudicate among the different conceptions of justice in contexts where the choice affects the outcome, as is typical in very hard cases. How should one undertake this adjudication? Which institution of government should be responsible?

According to Alan Gewirth,

> Traditionally, the main concern of justice has been the relation or proportion of the distribution of goods or rights among persons. It is false that the concept of distributive justice necessarily implies a social or distributing authority; what is essential is the distributive relation itself. The PGC shows how this relation is central to all morality, and it also shows how the agent, in acting toward his recipients, ought to distribute goods and rights in a certain relation as between himself and them.[10]

The relation is central to all morality because all agents qua agent, prospective or actual, must claim rights at least implicitly if they are to do any action for any purpose.[11] The focus on agents and their needs for action reflects the fact that morality is centrally concerned with voluntary purposive behavior. The notion of an agent identifies individuals who can engage in such action at least prospectively. Any other standard, either more or less inclusive, would run the risk of injecting into morality a judgment not necessarily contained within all moral theories. It is this sense of an agent as defined by the ability to engage in voluntary purposive behavior that serves as a neutral starting point from which to derive a moral theory.

How, then, is agency relevant in the context of scarce resources? The relevance to law is to determine, especially in reference to legislation, what the law should be so as to best take into account the common good. Of course, whose good constitutes the common good needs to be addressed. Although the principle of morality as determined by agency identifies who has moral claims on various resources such as food, health care, and so forth, it does not say how these resources should actually be distributed if, through no one's fault, there is an inadequate supply.[12] A good example might be too few respirators to serve the people who need them. One solution would be to distribute the resources randomly without taking into account such facts as age, survivability, and so on.[13] Another solution would be to distribute the resources according to the principle of doing the most good or avoiding the greatest pain.[14] Clearly, the choice here raises serious moral questions that any theory that is to operate in the real world must take into account. From Gewirth's standpoint, the best solution would be to set up morally just institutions that aim to protect agency in the long run. Anything less may result in an immoral outcome because it violates important rights. Here the point is to distribute resources not just according to how well they satisfy immediate needs but also according to how well they are likely to meet fundamental needs tomorrow.[15] The latter approach suggests that at least some of our investment should go to scientific research and some to meeting the needs of starving people both at home and abroad. It also leaves to other theoretical frameworks such as economics the best way to satisfy these two ends. Related to this issue will also be a duty to assist all countries to the best we are able to develop their own economic, medical, and political institutions to solve their problems. These are moral considerations that relate to, are justified by, but are not strictly about agency, since they consider future agents. Nevertheless, a theory of morality, including one based on agency, must take these considerations into account.

The distribution is one of initial equality because affirming any other distribution would lead to a contradiction. For example, if one were to affirm a distribution based on race, religion, gender, sexual orientation, even merit, one would be implying that some criterion *in addition* to being an agent—a person who unforcedly acts for purposes she takes to be good with knowledge of relevant circumstances—is essential to the claim of having rights. But the only basis Gewirth recognizes for deriving rights is that the person is an agent. Thus, to require more than mere agency, within Gewirth's framework, would put the claimer of rights in the position of both affirming and denying that agency is the sole basis for the moral justification of rights. This is a contradiction. Even so, there will be times when deviations occur in the distribution of basic rights either because of the intentional actions of some actors or because, within events, persons are left without basic goods and services through no fault of their own. In such situations, the PGC justifies laws to reestablish basic rights:

> In a broad sense, then, both retributive and redistributive justice are corrective and distributive in that both undertake, at least in part, to correct situations that are morally wrong (in that they violate the equality of generic rights) either by distributing penalties to persons who deserve them because of their criminal actions or by redistributing components

> of well-being. The morally wrong situation that retributive justice corrects, however, carries a connotation of personal guilt in that some particular person (or persons) has intentionally inflicted an occurrent disruption of an antecedent, narrowly circumscribed equality of generic rights; retributive justice as static seeks to restore this equality. The situation corrected by redistributive justice, on the other hand, although it too is morally wrong in that it dispositionally violates the equality of generic rights, does not carry a connotation of personal guilt because the situation is a social, dispositional one involving multitudes of persons whose comparative possession of well-being has, at least in part, a much broader historical and institutional base. Redistributive justice, as dynamic, seeks to move toward a previously nonexistent equality.[16]

Gewirth's view is consistent with the distinction between legislative and judicial functions in democratic societies that separate the two. In this regard, deciding questions of retributive justice is appropriate to the backward-looking role of the courts in determining who did what to whom. Deciding questions of redistributive justice is appropriate to the forward-looking function of the legislature to establish the common good. Where the legislature fails to take into account distributive effects and considers only aggregation, the courts have an obligation in protecting individual rights to limit the legislature's actions to do justice. In a nearly just society, one would hope that the constitution recognizes this all-important function for the courts. The courts do not, however, have a right, given their institutional role, to decide what additive goods and services—above protecting basic and nonsubtractive well-being—the legislature should provide for. Similarly, if the courts fail in their duty to do justice by being too lenient in their interpretations of the law, for example, the legislature should be able to change the jurisdiction of the courts to correct this situation, provided it does not overstep its own constitutional authority.[17] This reflects the fact that the PGC protects not only well-being but also freedom. The latter can be overridden where the impact of the harm to others cannot be overcome or overcome in time by engaging the normal democratic procedures of the state. It can also be overridden when the conditions necessary to an effective democratic process, such as freedom of speech and press, right of assembly, and right to vote, are in serious jeopardy of being enfeebled or destroyed by particular legislation. In such situations, the courts, in the interests of preserving basic rights and democratic processes, should be able to set standards that the other branches have to follow. But in all other situations, where immediate action is not necessary to protect basic rights and where the voting public would presumably gain understanding by a lively and spirited debate on an issue, the courts must leave to the legislature the choice of which policies to adopt. This latter point also reflects the fact that because dispositional, long-term harms are potentially more damaging to a democratic society than occurrent short-term harms, their resolution requires more direct participation by the citizenry.

Sometimes an occurrent denial of individual freedom and well-being is accompanied by a dispositional denial of society's political freedom. Here, I mean not only to set occurrent against dispositional but also individual against society. The latter reflects the common interests of a large group of people in their capacity as citizens.[18] This is the situation in cases where a poll tax exists that effectively excludes poor people from voting, where minorities, including blacks, women, and gays, are denied the equal protection of the laws and equal access to the same employment opportunities and other benefits as enjoyed by their straight, white, male counterparts. But it is also the case where the political institutions of the society cannot operate for the common good in the sense of protecting the freedom and well-being of all persons. The problem may be that there is no legal provision for representative—direct is not reasonable in a large, complex society—participation in the political process. Alternatively, even if there is such a provision, it may be enfeebled by a failure to require more than a simple majority vote on issues that affect the most basic relationship of the state to its citizens, such as which liberties are to be legally protected and which economic structure is to be provided.[19] The first kind of harm is substantive, in that the harm at stake directly affects the ability of individuals to effect their own interests. The second is procedural, reflecting a lack of adequate access to the institutions that could prevent substantive harm from occurring. In these cases, the PGC's freedom component is threatened and with it the possibility of morally collective justified political actions. Hence, to avoid these problems, the PGC allows establishment of written and unwritten constitutions and traditions, including provisions that require supermajority votes, to protect basic rights in the long run.

Analyzing Metatheory

Now I am ready to present a metatheory that will resolve the problem of very hard cases and explain how partial theories such as Dworkin's fit into the legal landscape. In presenting this theory, I do not disaffirm the possibility of alternative approaches. I only hope that they would meet as many of the concerns as this theory does. Especially important is uniting a duty to obey law with what the law is. In this regard, the cogency of the theory will be its suitability as a model for legal decisionmaking given the profound needs of judges and others who engage the difficult moral and legal problems that currently confront society. The presentation consists of two parts, reflecting dual views about how such a theory explains what judges do as well as prescribes what they ought to do.

DESCRIPTIVE VIEW

I shall describe the relationship between a judge's political philosophy about the duty to follow law and her legal philosophy regarding appropriate sources of law, but to make this relationship clear, the judicial role will be somewhat simplified (see Fig. 1).[20] Let S_p be political morality as a source of law and S_t be more traditional legal materials, such as a constitution, statute, regulation, or past case precedent, as a source of law. Here political morality may refer to the society's political morality to the extent that it provides clear, coherent, moral criteria for deciding cases. It may also encompass a theory of natural law/natural rights. Also, let D_p be a judge's political responsibility to do justice and D_t be a judge's legal responsibility, under a certain traditional theory of legal responsibility, to decide a case based only on traditional sources of law. Cross-referencing both sets of criteria on a single matrix, we have four classes of judicial decisionmaking.

Box one (D_pS_p) classifies the political activist, a judge who views law as an open system and her duty as primarily to preserve background, political rights. Such a judge is likely to be a follower of natural law/natural rights theories. Note that a political activist judge will not necessarily be a political liberal, depending upon what she views to be the background political morality. Box two (D_pS_t) classifies the judicial activist, a judge who views law as a closed system but still maintains that her duty is primarily to preserve background political rights. Such a judge is likely to be an interpretativist, that is, one who interprets traditional legal principles to accord with society's background morality. A Dworkinian analysis is appropriate here. Again, such a judge can be liberal or conservative. Box three (D_tS_p) classifies the judicial conservative, a judge who views law as an open system but her duty as primarily to preserve legislative prerogatives over judicial ones. Such a judge will also be an interpretativist but in the narrow sense of protecting majoritarian democracy as society's background political morality. She may subscribe to an economic analysis of the law. Box four (D_tS_t) clas-

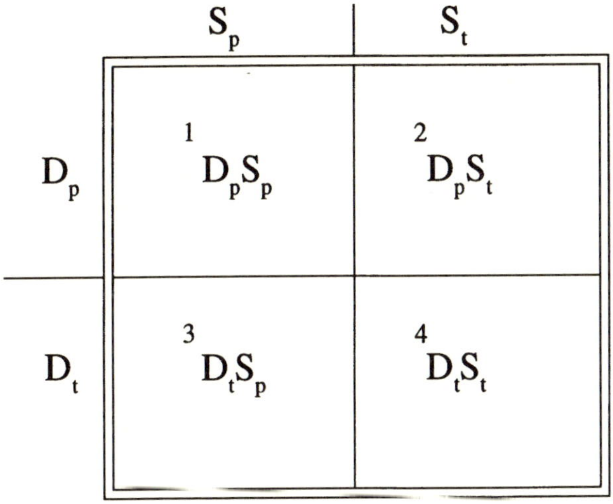

Figure 1. Sources of law versus judicial duty.

sifies the political conservative, a judge who views law as a closed system and her duty as primarily to preserve institutional rights and prerogatives. Such a judge is likely to be a noninterpretativist and a legal positivist. In practice, such a judge may afford a great deal of deference to other institutional authorities. Notice that a judge's "right" to engage in interpretation distinguishes boxes two and three from boxes one and four. Absent from this discussion is any unique doctrinal role for the legal realist judge because such a judge is unlikely to situate herself within the mainframe of any dogmatic theory. Also absent is a representation for persons who consider themselves members of the critical legal studies movement, feminist jurisprudence, and critical race theory. People from these movements fit better the role of outside critics of legal doctrine than the role of judges operating within a legal system.

The four classes of judicial behavior describe a particular system of law (see Fig. 2). Let us, following Dworkin, draw a distinction between issues of principle and issues of policy.[21] Further, let this distinction correspond to the distinction between deontological and teleological approaches to law. A judicial activist judge will be inclined to see a hard or very hard case deontologically, as involving principles of justice; a judicially conservative judge would more likely see the case teleologically, as involving a policy to be determined by a legislative majority. If the judge is a judicial activist, she will feel an obligation to decide the case in light of the principles of justice

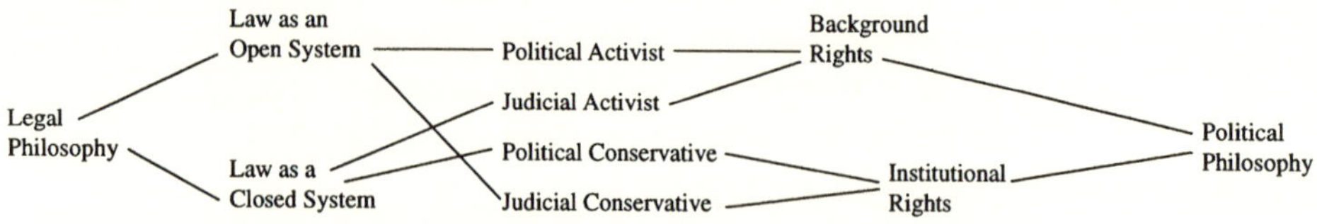

Figure 2. The judge's internal perspective of the relationship between legal and political philosophy.

underlying society's background political morality. If the judge is a judicial conservative, she will be inclined to decide the case to preserve such institutional rights as that of the legislature to decide questions of policy or of the executive to carry out the law. Obviously, a judicial conservative's view about the legitimacy of a particular law, say, a national health care statute, could run contrary to her personal ideological view about the constitutional order or the nature of society. Similarly, a judicial activist judge may have difficulty striking down a hate crimes statute as unconstitutional if doing so would be likely to continue the marginalization of a substantial segment of society. In the former case, one may want to question why the judge's own political view should play no role. In the latter case, one may want to ask which political morality—one that provides overriding deference to free speech or one that guarantees equality of opportunity—a judge should follow. Both questions raise a deep issue about the appropriate political philosophy, deontological and teleological, a court should adopt. Since one can argue on grounds of justice both for free speech and equality of opportunity, the need for another argument to adjudicate between the two becomes paramount. But is it appropriate for a court to make this argument where the legislature has not yet spoken and the constitution is silent?

In contrast to these two positions are those of the political activist and the political conservative. Here the relevant distinction, which is also Dworkin's, is between seeing law as involving principles and law as involving rules.[22] The former sees law as lacking doctrine, that is, as a kind of unschematized data within a broader nonlegal interpretative framework. The latter sees it as involving particular rules that a court is obligated to follow. Deontological and teleological differences are buried under the analytic distinction between a principle and a rule. To the political activist, a judge is obligated to provide the law with meaning and direction. A judge does so by appealing to some deep conception of political morality. For the political conservative, a judge must confine her decisionmaking to the set of rules recognized to constitute the law of the society. Here also there may come times when a political activist or a political conservative may find it difficult to maintain her position. Normative considerations break through the analytic cover of principle versus rule when the judge cannot morally defend the conclusions that would otherwise follow in terms of the duty to obey law. For instance, what is the political conservative to do, when deciding, for example, a case involving an area of business law, if the precedents she receives so vastly misunderstand the economic climate as to be effectively incoherent? How can a political activist justify the trial of a war criminal who claims that his actions were not violative of the law then in force?

The matrix—because it assumes that judges will confine themselves to only one legal approach: natural law, legal idealism, legal realism, positivism—may be too static to account for necessary paradigm changes to resolve very hard cases. Moreover, there is the problem of what a court should do when the prevailing political morality of the society is itself inconsistent. We need a theory of law that can move among theories of judicial decisionmaking and one that can encompass a broader conception of morality than that which may constitute the prevailing political morality of the society. Such a metatheory will be different from metatheories previously raised in legal literature.[23]

For one thing, such a metatheory would have to recognize that judicial decisionmaking is a composite of two aspects: a judge's legal philosophy, about whether law is an open or closed system, and her political philosophy, as to the source of the obligation to obey and follow the law (see Fig. 2).[24] In this regard, the theory would have to keep separate the two components that make up any legal decision, the law and the duty to obey the law. Regarding the latter component, the theory would also have to allow consideration of outside critiques of law such as might arise from a Marxist critique of capitalism or a feminist critique of gender roles. (For example, a court, under a constitution, may question a law that promoted capitalism at the expense of individual rights; a legislature might ask whether, in the workplace, the existence of a wage or a promotion advantage to males over females can be overcome by a statute.) It would also have to overcome the claim that legal doctrine is just a patchwork quilt of political compromises. If the theory is to succeed, it has to account for the inherent connection between the legitimacy of a rule or principle and the justification of a legal system. Thus it must respond to the criticisms against the various schools already presented, including the criticisms raised by the critical theorists. In this sense, a good theory must incorporate a broader ethical scheme. Further, a good theory will have to avoid the incommensurability problem that

Dworkin suggests arises when one distinguishes between the internal (the judge's) and the external (the political philosopher's) perspectives in resolving the problem of very hard cases.[25]

A PRESCRIPTIVE VIEW

The relationship between traditional legal and political philosophy just described is static. It becomes dynamic at the point where one can move between the various theories of legal decisionmaking.

Let us now ask whether a dynamic metatheoretical approach to legal decisionmaking is preferable to an ardent following of any one traditional theory making up the static approach. Let us also begin by noting certain institutional facts: first, the presence of a system of rules and principles for deciding cases, whatever the rules and principles may be; second, a widespread belief that everyone has a duty to obey the law and that judges must follow the law when deciding cases (this second criterion is no doubt subject to moral qualifications, but what exactly those are may not be too clear in the public's mind); and third, a judgment as to what the source of law is. For our purposes, these three facts constitute the internal view of the law.[26]

Within this view, theories of interpretation incorporate canons for determining legislative or constitutional intent and criteria for finding relevant analogies to provide the basis for the judicial resolution of most cases.[27] Outside this view, theories of political philosophy provide a basis for choosing appropriate sources of law and discovering one's legal obligations. The former perspective is internal to an established legal system that, if highly complete, will provide all the principles of interpretation and relevance needed for deciding most cases. The latter perspective is external to any such set of rules or principles but is free to derive rules and principles as may seem appropriate to the operation of a legal system along with other democratic institutions.

In essence, the external point of view provides a justification *ratio essendi* for a legal system from very basic premises.[28] The internal perspective attempts to discover what the laws are *ratio cognoscendi* from the existing set of recognized principles of discovery and interpretation.[29] This distinction between external and internal does not mean that judges begin with no political philosophy about what role—political or judicial, activist or conservative—they should play in deciding cases. Indeed, they often do have such a view, including a view about appropriate sources of law. It is necessary that they should have such a view if they are to maintain consistency in the issuance of decisions. The distinction does show, however, that a perspective which from the internal point of view appears as a most strongly held political philosophy is from the external perspective, at most, a tentatively fixed position, pending a reason to change it. This is the inherent incompleteness of the internal point of view. What the nature of such an external reason might be is an issue to which we will soon turn. First, however, we must consider the judge's internal perspective regarding her role in deciding cases.

In a society that views itself as nearly just—that is, with a political morality capable of providing just principles—there is only the internal point of view.[30] The internal perspective unites the judicial obligation to follow the law, along with the general obligation to obey law, with the principles or rules recognized by the society as law. This it does by treating every so-called law as arising from a corresponding moral obligation that the society accepts.[31] The law may treat the same object as morality, as with laws against murder, or it may treat a different nonmoral object, such as which side of the street to drive on. The latter connects to morality by way of a principle of consistency, the duty being to avoid accidents and the fear of accidents. Consequently, in a nearly just society, Dworkin's view and even the positivist view of law have an initial appeal.[32] Dworkin's view argues against the possibility of any meaningful separation of the internal and external.[33] Still, the mere fact that something is a law is not a reason for obedience. The law could be gravely immoral. In such a case, the question would not be whether a moral principle overrides a legal one; it would be whether there is even a prima facie moral obligation to obey the law.[34] Consequently, in a society that views itself as less nearly just, the duty to obey the law—or the judge's duty to follow the law—may have no foundation in any deeper principle of political morality. The Nazi war crimes trials at Nuremberg and, more recently, the trials of the former East German border guards illustrate this outcome. In both of these cases the duty to obey the law, upon which the defendants relied, was questionable if not unsupportable. Consequently, it was not particularly persuasive to the courts as a defense argument, although it does raise troubling questions for us. Unless some broader moral theory has piggybacked the duty to obey law onto a different source not traditionally thought to be a source of law, no moral justification exists. Natural law is an example of a theory that attempts this piggyback.

The relationship between the external and the internal points of view manifests itself in just this latter situation. What I have called very hard cases are those instances where a court cannot resolve an issue under the prevailing political morality without causing injustice. Usually this is the situation when the legal firmament provides no rule or principle that most capable judges would view as just, or if such a principle exists, its scope is too narrow or its justification too insecure to warrant its application. If either of these problems exists, the nature of the difficulty is not one of finding the best analogy to some previous case or precedent—for, as yet, there is no criterion upon which to draw the analogy—but of deriving a just principle for deciding the case.

This problem does not arise in a society that views itself, even wrongly, as nearly just, provided the cases being dealt with do not challenge the prevailing political morality. In such a society, Dworkin's ideas of fit and political morality are apropos. The notion of fit secures a connection to existing rules and principles, thus encouraging predictability and the view of treating like cases alike. The notion of political morality provides the connection to the society's values. However, if a substantial segment of the society realizes an important part of its law is unjust, the issue of deciding very hard cases will require finding a justification before selecting and applying any legal rules or principles. This situation will become apparent when the rules or principles of law are either inconsistent or incapable of leading to a just result. The latter may occur when a controversy has arisen over the values that determine the prevailing political morality. The abolitionist movement just prior to the American Civil War exemplifies the kind of controversy I have in mind.[35] Here appeals to theories such as to natural law or natural rights become essential as external guideposts to the kind of decision one might render. In the former society the appropriate method of reasoning is *ratio cognoscendi*, but in the latter it is *ratio essendi*. Both appeals look at structural features of the institutions involved and normative considerations, both deontological and teleological, about rights, but only in the latter are these matters thought to be questions in need of independent justification. Notice that even in the nearly just society, if the coverage of the rules is not sufficient to subsume a case, we need to appeal to sources of law that will not be traditionally legal. That is, we need to appeal to other than primary sources, and this too may mean appealing to more general considerations of political morality.

I have not yet said anything specific about the distinction between "a society that views itself as morally just" and "a society that is nearly just." It is time to correct that situation by looking more closely at the word "society" in this context. By society, I mean the group of people who live within a closed political boundary; share some set of common interests, at least when viewed from the perspective of their membership in the group; and who, at least occasionally, voluntarily act either passively, by obeying the laws and paying taxes, or actively, by voting and performing other kinds of community services, to promote the collective welfare of the group. Examples of such societies would include a village, town, city, state or province, or nation. It would not include the world community, although sometimes one hears that phrase. The latter would be included only if there were a binding international agreement, perhaps through the United Nations, to regard the world as under a single political authority, however that authority might be constituted. From this definition of society, we see the possibility of mutually collective action directed toward some set of ends believed to be in the joint interests of the members involved.

Society in this sense need not be bounded by a fully worked-out ideology, and indeed, the membership may reflect a variety of different ideological positions, provided only that they are willing to accept the possibility of mutual cooperation with respect to the interests that would benefit them as members of the group. In this, I follow Rawls, who treats society as a "fair system of social cooperation."[36] But unlike Rawls, I do not end the matter at this point. Although the notion of a fair system of social cooperation may provide some clue as to whether, for example, the laws are just, it does not actually decide the question once one has challenged the justice of the laws. And it is not reasonable to leave the question unanswered because that could undermine the society's ability to hold together, especially in the long run. One has to remember only the way that American society became divided in the nineteenth century over the question of slavery to see how this might happen. Nor can the question of whether the laws are just be resolved internally by appeal to the political morality that created them. My idea of society must value the possibility of a reconsideration of its own values, especially when fundamentally different ideologies are at stake. A good example of this actually occurred with the nonviolent revolutionary change that brought an end to communism in the former Soviet Union. Thus, I differ from Rawls in that I am unwilling to separate ideological disagreement from cooperative political action. Rather, my treatment of society allows for the possibility that a wider range of social norms may be needed and adopted to resolve basic differences that arise from fundamentally different ideological viewpoints. Thus, unlike Dworkin's idea of a community as a distinctly constituted group with a particular set of social attitudes,[37] my notion of society is more flexible in that, like the surface of a balloon, it can expand or contract the norms it adopts to meet the moral challenges it confronts.

Herein lies my distinction between a society that views itself as nearly just and a society that is nearly just. The former references the actual perception of the membership at a particular time. The latter compares that perception with a later perception by allowing for the possibility that moral reflection might open new and more abstract levels of moral inquiry not previously imagined. These higher orders of moral inquiry may, in turn, provide answers to questions not previously thought answerable or that previously were answered in different ways. Thus, I show that the actual justice of a society is determined when each move to a more highly ordered moral principle justifies the decision at the previous level.

I am now ready to provide criteria from the internal point of view for determining when a judge should decide a case based on traditional legal materials and society's political morality and when she should appeal to a broader theory of natural law/natural rights. The criteria stem from the belief that in a nearly just society, courts are on their strongest footing, that is, have the greatest likelihood of engendering integrity and respect, when they decide cases on clearly delimited legal rules and principles than when they do not. But the criteria also provide for when a judge should exit the internal point of view and thus when a court should make an external evaluation of the rights people have, to decide very hard cases. In this latter regard, nothing turns on the judge's idiosyncratic view of whether the society is just or not. For if the challenge to the law is too broad, it will fail when the court determines that the best arguments—best in the sense that they are consistent with a more highly ordered political morality—favor the current system even if not the specific rule or principle. Similarly, if the challenge is too narrow, it will be incapable of directing a court to an adequate set of principles capable of resolving the dispute. There are five criteria:

1. When the traditional sources of law are clear and on point, a judge should rely on these sources if the society views itself as nearly just, despite her own views as to the most just result. In effect, the judge should follow the political conservative (positivist) position.
2. If the traditional sources of law include past case precedents, then, if the society is nearly just, a judge should analogize the case to bring it under the particular precedent that would provide the most just result. In effect, the judge should follow the traditional legal approach of reasoning by analogy.
3. If the traditional sources of law are not clear or on point and the case involves a question of policy, then, if the society is nearly just, the court

should follow an economic analysis or appropriate policy approach to deciding what would best serve the common good. In effect, the judge should be a judicial conservative.

4. When the traditional sources of law are not clear or on point and the case involves a fundamental question of justice, then if the society is nearly just, a judge should interpret the traditional legal sources, considering the society's prevailing political morality to produce the most just result. Here considerations of fit and political morality should aid in the determination of the case. The judge should be a judicial activist.
5. In cases where the society is not nearly just or where the particular issue is so controversial as not to be resolvable within the society's political morality, because the society's political morality is itself in question, then, despite whether the law is clear or on point, a judge has no political responsibility to follow the law. In such a case, the judge's responsibility is to act upon the best political theory the court can find to do justice and, if possible, to create along the way democratic procedures that will be constitutionally liberal and concerned for the equal opportunity of all individuals. Here, the judge should opt out of the internal point of view, which is to say she should adopt an external natural law/natural rights resolution of the problem. In effect, the judge should become a political activist.

I note that this view, although it involves some of Dworkin's most important elements—such as the distinctions between principles and policies, and principles and rules—is not strictly speaking a Dworkinian view. It does not require a judge to decide issues of fit and political morality in each case to provide for the general integrity of, or the best constructive approach to, the legal system. Sometimes the legal system may be too corrupt to allow for such a construction. Other times, the legal system may be sufficiently just and the legal issues in the case sufficiently clear to render unnecessary and, perhaps, undesirable any broader constructive approach.[38] (Imagine the burden on the legal system if Dworkin's process of interpreting a major chunk of the law were imposed in every traffic case.) The latter occurs when the approach would undermine institutional distinctions between legislative and judicial functions for no apparent moral purpose. Here, the judge chooses the theoretical framework that best resolves the case before the court, using one of the five criteria. In this way, every judge does not have to be Hercules in every case, only in cases where being Hercules matters. Moreover, as indicated in criterion five, there may be very hard cases that require going outside the prevailing political morality, a move Dworkin would not allow. If the society is nearly just, one hopes that these will be few. However, where they do exist, a judge has to be more than a Hercules; she must become a philosopher-king.

One comment should be made with respect to the choice of criteria when dealing with evil institutions in a society that wrongly views itself as nearly just. In a Nazi society, for example, should a judge follow criterion one or should the judge rely on criterion five when deciding whether to uphold a particularly heinous law? The former would imply that as long as the society—rightly or wrongly—views itself as nearly just and the law is clear, "a judge must be politically conservative and uphold the law."[39] The latter would suggest the exact opposite. The problem with this example is that it conflates what the metatheory is doing with what a moral theory of politics ought to do. The metatheory is not performing any substantive role. It is not claiming that one who must decide this matter must do so by a newspaper poll of the citizens to see whether they view the society as just or not. Nor is it claiming that a judge should be free to pick and choose to uphold only those laws she likes. Indeed, it is not offering any substantive basis for how the decision should actually be made. The metatheory simply is giving the judge who decides the issue the opportunity to appeal to the best ethical theory of politics available, assuming the judge even recognizes that there is a moral issue. (Obviously, if the judge does not, we never reach this question.) That ethical theory of politics, in turn, provides the substantive basis for the decision. If a law is challenged and a judge relying on the best ethical theory finds no reason to attack it, then, of course, the judge should follow criterion one and uphold the law. It is doubtful, however, that a judge in such a situation as the Nazi example, who was honestly looking, would not find a compelling ethical argument against upholding the law. Thus, the example appeared to present a real challenge to the metatheory only because it failed to recognize the different roles for the metalegal theory and the background moral theory on which the decision must ultimately be grounded.

A critic of my position might question why a court should seek to do justice if the effect is to require it to reach beyond traditional legal materials and to usurp a legislative function. The answer to this is a variation of the idea that the duty to obey the law—or in the judge's case, to follow the law—must be founded either in the society's political morality if the system is just, or, as is often the case in very hard cases, in the positive rights of all persons to the necessary conditions of human agency because they cannot obtain them for themselves.[40] More particularly, it is that a judge has no duty to obey an immoral law. In a democracy, the political responsibility of the courts is to do justice, as with the legislature it is to serve the common good.[41] This follows from the fact that government is morally obligated to fulfill deontological and teleological functions, and these functions are often, in democracies, divided between courts and legislature. Thus, if the issue before the court involves a dispute over policy, it is appropriate for the court to ask what the legislature meant when it drafted a particular statute, not whether the statute is just as a matter of principle. The court should interpret the statute to advance the policy purpose of the legislature, be it wealth maximization, economic efficiency, or other kinds of socially or economically related concerns. The only proviso here is that the policy not conflict with either the prevailing political morality of the society or, when that is in dispute, with the best—in the sense of most coherent and complete—interpretation of natural law.

Another objection is the argument that considering political morality as a possible outcome of law opens the door to courts imposing upon society their own beliefs about what is just. The previous objection addressed the way I formulate the judicial duty to follow the law, but this objection addresses how we identify what the law is. In response to this objection, I note, following Dworkin, that the appeal to political morality must be limited, at least within a society that is nearly just, to theories that justify most of the law taken as settled. This itself follows a principle of justice: providing predictability of result as an element of fairness. Hence, we find my discussion of the judicial activist focusing primarily on interpretation. In those few very hard cases where the existing law is inconsistent or unjust, a court should adopt a natural law/natural rights view that would reproduce the political rights people have.[42] Even here the court is not free to make any choice because it must justify whatever choice it makes using the analytical tools, such as conceptual and normative analyses, of the philosopher.

Still, we might want to push the challenge a step further. A Marxist judge, for example, would most likely view my application of a rule adopted in a capitalist society as unjust per se. Does this mean that the Marxist judge can refuse to apply capitalist law? Clearly, the answer cannot be reduced to whether the judge took an oath to obey the capitalist law, for such a promise, if found to conflict with a higher principle of morality, would lose its prescriptive force. Indeed, the judge may have converted to Marxism after becoming a judge or may uphold a view of Marxism that encourages subversion of the capitalistic order through infiltration of political and judicial positions. Still, even under these circumstances, it seems clear that the judge should not give up wholesale the system of laws that capitalism might produce.[43] The duty to obey law, established by the oath, is at least a prima facie obligation, which, when overridden, does not drop out of the equation but takes a back seat, acting as a kind of regulatory device for just how far the judge can go in refusing to obey the law. Put another way, the reason the judge cannot give up the legal system wholesale is not because the internal point of view imposes a duty on the judge to obey law, regardless of any other principles that may be at stake. Rather, the answer lies in the fact that, from the external point of view, a sound theory of political morality may appear to justify at least some of the capitalist system of laws that protects private property within certain definite parameters. If so, that external theory is on a par with the external theory of the Marxist judge and, therefore, must be evaluated along with the Marxist position in terms of a deeper set of moral values. Both the judge's justification and her parameters for neglecting the law must thus be determined by what the best ethical theory of politics provides.

If Gewirth's view of these matters is correct, then the answer must be that which would promote voluntarily purposive behavior and generally successful action for all people.[44] It will not help to claim that human beings cannot engage in voluntary purposive behavior because the pervasive ideology of capitalism has in fact rendered them incapable of free choice. Putting aside for the moment deep questions concerning whether individual choices are ever truly free,[45] it is at least the case that people from their own point of view make choices to follow or not to follow a given ideology in light of various concerns for self-interest and the interests of others. Moreover, people can change ideological commitments, as witnessed throughout history and more recently in Eastern Europe. Such changes in direction reflect the fact that human beings are capable of engaging in external evaluations of their social conditions where external is understood to mean using a wider conceptual framework to evaluate a narrower one.

A related objection would ask what a judge should do if the system of law—the political way laws come about and the judicial manner in which they are interpreted—is corrupt but particular laws are just. No doubt a few of the laws pertaining to routine matters followed by Nazi courts met this situation. In this case, since the system of law is unjust, a court should determine what laws it will follow by how well they conform to a justified scheme of natural law/natural rights. Similarly, if the problem is that a just law is attenuated by being made to apply unjustly in some situations, such as Nazi marriage laws that prohibited interracial marriage, a court should interpret the law, again in keeping with natural law, so as to eliminate the unjust consequences.

Why might this result appear startling? The answer has to do with the controls one wants to place on a judge's evaluation of competing theories of political morality. The problem, as raised by Douglas Litowitz, specifically about Dworkin's theory, is that internally imposed controls beg the question.[46] For instance, the reason a judge is appealing to a theory of natural law/natural rights may be because the legal system as a whole is unjust or the particular case cannot be resolved, given the prevailing political morality. If so, a judge must turn away from the narrower internal and move to a broader internal framework of concepts and decide the very hard case in a way that comports with the best theory of political morality she can find.[47] In the comparatively easier hard-case situations, a judge can decide the matter by appealing to the prevailing political morality. But even there, she must reverse course to avoid appearing arbitrary once the appeal is made to justify the decision at hand. There is simply no way to circumvent going outside traditional law when deciding hard and very hard cases, outside in this context meaning appealing to a more highly ordered conceptual framework for legal decisionmaking. The only exception is when one reaches the level of natural law, and that is because there is no place to go after that within the modality of normative principles. At the level of natural law, the notion of incompleteness is ill defined. I conclude, therefore, that at every level of generality, no matter how well defined, the internal perspective will be incomplete. This will become most apparent when the issues in the case before the court question the very laws and legal theory that define that perspective.

Still, the fact that a judge may have to move higher within the internal point of view and evaluate the theories of political morality at the lower level externally, by way of deduction from the wider framework, does not mean that her decision process is unconstrained. Both theory and practice provide constraint that judges are not free to ignore. The theoretical constraints on the judge include the principles of deductive and inductive logic, and most important that the theory adopted accord with a justifiable theory of natural law/natural rights. The practical constraints, at a minimum, are that the theory adopted neither overdetermine nor underdetermine the problems it is to confront. The theory must not allow the courts either to alter aspects of the law that have nothing to do with the issue at hand or render itself unable to deal adequately with real issues because the principles of law make classifications and distinctions irrelevant to the actual lives of people.[48] Further, the court would need to provide for its own legitimacy against a background in which even Supreme Court justices are not completely immune from the political process.[49]

Substantive Principles and the Question of Objectivity

The theory I have offered makes use of substantive principles as opposed to semantic principles. The distinction is well described by Cass Sunstein in *The Partial Constitution*.[50] According to Sunstein, two types of interpretative principles exist:

> Semantic principles are those whose acceptance counts as part of what it means to speak the relevant language in a simple, dictionary sense. People who reject semantic principles reveal that they do not understand what certain words mean. . . . [T]he constitutional provisions requiring that constitutional amendments be ratified by three-quarters of the states, and that the President be at least thirty-five years of age, have clear meanings simply because the governing semantic principles are well-known to those who read English. . . . Substantive principles are different. Such principles require not a language lesson or a dictionary, but a substantive political justification. The idea that the original understanding is (or is not) binding falls within the category of substantive principles. So too with the idea that constitutional provisions should always be read to promote the functioning of democratic processes. These ideas are contested not because one side does not understand English, but because there is a dispute over the best way to make sense of the Constitution.[51]

Sunstein argues that substantive principles apply in hard, and presumably in very hard, cases and must be justified in terms of moral and political arguments. Claims like those of Robert Bork, who argues for a framers' interpretation of the Constitution,[52] or of John Hart Ely, who argues for a strictly procedural, democratic-reinforcing approach,[53] require for their justification an appeal to political morality. (Ely argues that judicial interpretation of the Constitution should aim at protecting the democratic process rather than at enforcing substantive value choices that the justices may share.[54]) In contrast, Frederick Shauer argues that even the so-called easy cases may not be clear, depending on the adjudicated context.[55] It is true that certain specific language can narrow the scope of what is litigated. Does the requirement that the president be at least thirty-five mean "thirty-five" or "mature" or "thirty-five, given a life expectancy of fifty?" The point is that language creates boundaries on the range of possible outcomes instead of attempting a unique right answer in the abstract. Whether one associates this limitation with a semantic principle or a substantive one is related more to the vagueness that the language embodies. Perhaps it is possible for language to bring us to a unique solution, but it is more likely such a solution will arise, if at all, as a consequence of a deeper theoretical approach. For this reason, any attempt at justification must take into account the relevant history of the Constitution, including the Court opinions that have interpreted it. This is not because history will always be relevant to the issues at stake but because judges should not do anything they want. In this sense, Sunstein's approach is close to Dworkin's fit and political morality requirements and to my position, that judges must start from a narrow conceptual framework about what the law is before expanding to broader theories of political morality. The latter, of course, does not mean that a judge should never consider broader theories. Since the court has a duty to decide the case justly, the judge can justify choosing a broader theory by the irrelevance or injustice of existing precedent.

Having said that substantive principles should play a role in legal decisionmaking, I need to comment on what that role should be. Connecting different legal theories to decide a case is the role of metatheory. In interpreting, for example, the equal protection and due process clauses of the Bill of Rights and the Fourteenth Amendment, substantive principles play the role of providing a background political theory—what the Constitution is, or should be, aiming at. In this sense, substantive principles give meaning to important legal texts, which in turn allow the courts to know how to apply the text to particular cases and controversies. In the particular metadiscussion I have been engaged in, substantive principles provide a court with choices among formalistic concerns about what the rules of law are (positivism) to deep commitments about how the rules should be interpreted (Dworkin) to still deeper understandings about whether the rules fall under a duty of obedience at all (natural law). At each succeeding level, the questions become more abstract and theoretical. Still, not all legal controversies will be at the same level. Some controversies will be at higher levels; others are at lower levels. Consequently, it would help for courts to move between levels of abstraction—to higher or lower orders of generalization—to meet the controversy where it lies. The metatheory of law allows movement among competing legal theories.

Of course, this raises another question: Have we just substituted a fancy description for what will inevitably be the individual predilections of the judges? The question arises against a background postmodern/poststructuralist critique that has become popular in certain philosophical and literary arenas. That critique attempts to discount reason as anything other than just another kind of belief that members of a society might hold and "realism" as anything real at all. According to Richard Rorty, a self-proclaimed follower of this view,[56]

> The distinction between "rationality" and something else has traditionally been drawn so as to coincide roughly with the distinction between inference and imagination. We are being rational, so the story goes, insofar as we stick to the logical space given at the beginning of the inquiry and so long as we can offer an argument for the beliefs held at the end of the inquiry by referring back to the beliefs held at the beginning.[57]

Rorty defines realism as supporting "the idea that inquiry is a matter of finding out the nature of something which lies outside the web of beliefs and desires."[58] He argues that rationality is situated; there is no rationality as such. Realism he attacks and claims that works by Donald Davidson and postmodernist/poststructuralists support his position. I discuss the works of Davidson as they apply to my metatheory in chapter 4, but I do want to comment here on the impact of views such as Rorty's on the legal culture.

Cass Sunstein points out that in the debate over formalism in the law that a law should meet some formal set of criteria, two positions manifest the antiformalist stance. The first, conventionalism, holds that legal meanings are "settled by people with power to do the settling."[59] The second, deconstructionism, argues that "the meaning of texts is indeterminate, undecidable, or irreducibly 'political' or 'subjective.' . . . On this view, meaning is created rather than found. . . . Perspectives and creations differ along ideological lines. In the face of conflicting perspectives, often operating across such divides as race, class, and gender, the imposition of one meaning rather than another is a product of arbitrariness, or power, or whim."[60] Both views challenge reason's role as providing a foundation for law, the first because it makes law—as the Critical Legal Studies people would have it—a patchwork quilt of political compromises and the second because it undercuts any justification for improving the state of law—making it better than what it currently is.

Conventionalism implies that the duty to obey law is sui generis, that is, independent of whether the law is just. I have argued that the duty to obey law arises from a doctrine of political responsibility that requires the judiciary to do justice and the legislature to ensure the common good. I also argued, following Gewirth and Rawls, that doing justice meant protecting fundamental rights fairly. The duty to obey law, though independent of conceptions about what law is, is not unrelated to the particular law's content or its application. Nor is it unrelated to the functioning of institutions that have to apply it. The duty to obey law applies both to institutions and to individuals. It applies to the former by requiring that they prescribe only those laws that will protect the generic rights to freedom and well-being of all persons. It also applies by requiring institutions to allow for considerations of due process and equal protection. It applies to individuals by supplying them with a moral reason for showing obedience to just laws. That is, the duty to obey law is the duty to obey just laws, democratically created and justly applied. This raises the question of justifiable civil disobedience to combat unjust laws. As Rawls has noted, however, if an unjust law will not cause immediate harm and internal appeals are possible, there is no justification for disobedience. Thus unnecessary disorder or the rise of a general disrespect for law is avoided.[61] Only if the appeals fail is there a justification for disobedience.

Deconstruction undermines the very possibility of a social critique of law. With respect to this line of criticism, it is important to note just how far the social constructionist is pushing his thesis. He is not claiming merely that ideology constructs the world we see, nor even denying the possibility of a meaningful world independent of ideology. The thesis goes much further, denying the possibility of a social critique, and therefore it undercuts itself as a particular form of a social critique. In a particularly revealing but high-handed passage, Richard Posner identifies how this self-contradiction comes about:

> Philosophical postmodernism, which has its roots in Nietzsche and Wittgenstein and of which its best-known exemplars are Foucault and Derrida in France and in this country Rorty and Fish, is the use of logic, rhetoric, historical and sociological investigation, and other methods of argument or analysis to debunk the philosophical tenets of the enlightenment—objectivity, observer independence, and the rest. Philosophical postmodernism denies both the givenness of the object and the freedom of the subject, and depending on which denial is emphasized can thus be either Utopian or quietistic. When the contingent, constructed character of social and in some versions even physical reality is emphasized, the

> radical transformation of the world and society is seen as possible and desirable. Much radical feminism is of this character; likewise the social constructionist view of sexuality. But when the ethnocentric, embedded, socially constructed character of the self is emphasized, social criticism becomes an oxymoron; it presupposes an external standpoint that postmodernism denies. So we have both politically radical postmodernism, and political radicals' criticism of postmodernism as a roadblock to social critique.[62]

The critique is high-handed in that it conflates and dismisses many diverse postmodern critics, without taking into account their more subtle distinctions. These distinctions include differences between neopragmatism and poststructuralism,[63] differences in political attitudes,[64] and differences in interpretations of leading philosophical works, such as Hilary Putman's objectivist interpretation of Wittgenstein's private-language argument.[65] Although Posner's conclusion is generally correct, he unfortunately fails to provide detailed arguments to support it.

In particular, one can identify several separate and distinct postmodern strains. On the question of meaning, for instance, there are hermeneutical philosophy's experiential approach,[66] Wittgenstein's language games,[67] deconstructionism,[68] and interpretative theory.[69] Moreover, very little unites these different approaches except, perhaps, their explicit denial of metaphysical foundations and sometimes objective truth.[70] Yet even on the question of objective truth, there are different viewpoints, as witnessed by Rorty's adoption of what he calls "Davidson's pragmatism,"[71] which I argue is objective (see chapter 4). In short, there is probably no single critique that does justice to the variant accounts of postmodernism. For instance, an unusual account regards postmodernism as modernism's critique of itself.[72] Still, this does not mean that certain directions in postmodernism—particularly, those that critique reason's ability to provide a moral connection to law—are beyond criticism. As Gewirth has noted, some scholars argue "that reason itself in turn pass various justificatory tests set by religious faith, aesthetic rapture, and so forth. But the very scrutiny to determine whether these tests are passed must itself make use of reason. . . . Thus any attack on reason or any claim to supersede it by some other human power or criterion must rely on reason to justify its claims."[73]

Even within the so-called postmodernist vantage point, one can distinguish poststructuralist/deconstructionist approaches[74] from postmodernist/neopragmatic approaches.[75] The former adopts the view that a text has no one correct meaning but can be found to have different opposite meanings. Some of these meanings are privileged, as when we privilege cause over effect, conscious over unconscious, masculine over feminine, speech over writing, presence over absence, and construction over destruction, which is the specific opposition that the term deconstruction tries both to contain and subvert, and so on.[76] This follows Jacques Derrida's idea "that we tend to think and express our thoughts in terms of opposites" and that culture expresses a preference for one of the two opposites as superior in status over the other as inferior.[77] Nevertheless, nothing binds us to maintaining this hierarchy of opposites. We could just as easily turn them around and privilege effect over cause, writing over speech, and absence over presence. In its broadest sense, deconstruction seeks to critique Western idealism, which would include the theories of Kant, Rousseau, and others, along with logic and language. Thus, deconstruction can be said to be without boundaries on just what can and cannot be deconstructed. The latter postmodernist/neopragmatists attempt to reconstruct law by, among other things, paying close attention to the contextual details of everyday living.[78] For instance, less radical feminists have made great strides in pointing out the influence of gender in the workings of laws involving rape,[79] privacy,[80] and pornography.[81] Sometimes these approaches operate beside poststructuralist/deconstructionist approaches,[82] sometimes not.[83]

Any success these reconstructionist approaches might have, however, falls on its face when the subject/thinker critic is deconstructed.[84] This outcome is what is most revealing about Posner's explanation. It is the postmodern view that one can never leave one's position as an object in the world to make any assessment of that relation because one is always a part of the world and its influences. One might achieve some relatively neutral position for a time, but never to the point of reaching human essence or reason as such.[85] Thus, any assault on a view of the world must presuppose the influence of the world on the subject making the attack. This suggests that one can never adopt any position other than the third-person perspective that treats the subject as an object in the world. Any attempt to try to break this influence is doomed to failure. The status of the subject, when making these determinations, is always situated in a social context.

This criticism "is a form of self-referential paradox: applying the 'postmodernist' deconstruction to herself, she is disabled from critical commentary as well as from constructive rejoinder."[86] But unlike some self-referential paradoxes that can be resolved by appeals to higher orders of language—such as "whether the statement 'all morals are relative' is itself a moral statement"—

this one cannot be, because deconstruction allows no broader theory to contain it.[87] The "disabling" causes the view to implode when applied to the self. For on the one hand, we have the claim that all our concepts and understandings are constructions; on the other hand, we find ourselves—the persons who we are—to be constructed by these concepts. We have no place to go in critically assessing the world or our place in it.[88] Deconstruction, when applied to the self, simply fails as a tool of social commentary.

The point might thus be made: if deconstruction is a viable means for producing social commentary, then, when applied to the self, it undermines the possibility of such commentary. But if deconstruction fails as a viable means of producing social commentary when applied to the self, then deconstruction is not a means of producing social commentary at all. This follows from the observation that there is no reason inside deconstruction to treat the self, when taken as an object of deconstruction, any differently from any other object. If deconstruction does not work when applied to the self as an object, then there is no reason for believing it works when applied to any other object. In short, deconstruction, when it attempts to deconstruct the self, deconstructs itself and with it any useful role it might play in the development of social commentary.

Cast in this way, the paradox of deconstruction is apparent, but so is a possible solution. Simply put, deconstruction must be constrained from being the all-encompassing epistemic theory that some scholars have claimed. Instead, it must be applied only to situations in which the self as subject stands aside from the self as object.[89] In this role, deconstruction must buy into some broader framework outside of what it seeks to dismantle. Because deconstruction "is forced to use the very concepts it sees as being unsustainable in terms of the claims made for them, it must (at least provisionally) sustain these claims."[90] To the extent postmodernists are willing to interpret deconstruction in this way, it might become a valuable tool of social science.

One such broader framework is provided by Kant's theory of morality.[91] According to this view, the distinction between the self as subject and the self as object provides a basis for a social critique that deconstruction is unable to provide. Only the former, by virtue of its first-person perspective, contains a truly necessary autonomy independent of any causal constraints imposed by the world of experience. This is made manifest where one critiques one's own views, where one even critiques the critique. At some point, because the object-self is always present to the subject-self but not the reverse, one reaches the conclusion that further investigation is no longer useful. Usually, this is at the point where the nature of the issue has changed from what the question was originally, let us say from a question of empirical psychology to a priori epistemology. At that point, the subject-self can reasonably believe it has reached an answer to the question posed. If the answer later turns out to be only provisional in light of some further questioning, nothing is lost to the logic of what had been done by then moving on to answer that further question. Even if the later answer gives a surprising result that contradicts the earlier answer, provided the earlier answer was based on the best information then known, one can reasonably claim that one did one's best with the information available.

A different but equally powerful response to the deconstructionist attack on objectivism that also brings out the point of acting from the best information available follows Davidson's discussion of what it means to recognize error. "For every 'alien' thought or belief the interpreter claims to identify, he or she must also mark out an area of wider agreement and familiarity, since . . . what the thought or belief is about ('alien' or no) can only be fixed by supposing other shared, surrounding truths."[92] The agreement must be material in that what is being agreed to affects the issues at stake, and, of course, it must be relevant in that it raises the possibility of affecting these issues. In other words, before we can have disagreement, we must have agreement and a lot of it. Agreement implies a kind of objectivity, at least at the level of possessing a shared set of beliefs. Davidson is suggesting only this intersubjective sense of objectivity here, but it would seem to be enough. Since disagreement over law and morality and their applications exists, so must agreement. Hence, objectivity also must exist in the sense described.

I shall mention one further concern. Throughout this discussion, I have had in mind that everyone in society can support the criteria for legal decisionmaking, but, most particularly, members of the legal profession. In this way, there would be a kind of professional opinion check monitoring how a court judges the justice of society's laws and institutions and the corresponding duties that follow such a determination. Such a check does not mean tying a court's hands to the majority's sentiments on any given issue. The problem here is one of justice, not of majority. To admit that opinions as to particular outcomes may vary should itself be a reason for judges to consider various points of view and to investigate relevant and material philosophical discussions regarding the matters before them. The check from the professional community ensures only that as a judge moves away from relying on traditional legal sources, she provides a strong justification for that movement. The level of generality of the issues raised in the particular case will determine whether the grounds of that justification should be more abstract or concrete.

CHAPTER FOUR

Virtual Law

What should a court do if it comes to believe that the prevailing political morality is wrong in treating as just a law that appears unjust? What would be its moral obligation with respect to following the law? If the answer is that courts have no moral obligation to follow immoral laws, what does this suggest regarding laws the courts are uncertain about? More important, how is a disagreement about society's political morality to be resolved?

The problem arises because of the outlook courts have by believing they are in a nearly just society. Typically, one holds such a belief because the prevailing political morality provides at least provisionally acceptable answers to most political/moral questions.[1] In such a society, the duty to obey law, or the judge's duty to follow the law, merges with what the law is to form the internal point of view. From this vantage point, there will be simply no way to distinguish when one should not obey a law from when one should obey it. Here is another example of the incompleteness of the internal point of view. At most, a judge will find an inconsistency among applicable principles or an argument appealing to some external moral position, which the court may feel obliged to reject. Internally, then, any law that conforms to the prevailing political morality appears morally justified. This is a presumption that the internal point of view forces on the courts. It is only a presumption, however, unless one also accepts the argument that no other point of view is possible. So the question remains: Does the internal point of view identify a real incommensurability, or does it merely define an artificial line between two different levels of moral evaluation: the level of the society's particular set of political/moral beliefs and political morality in general? If the internal point of view merely defines an artificial line, by what reasoning can the courts cross over to the external perspective, and what would it mean for a court to do so? Must not the possibility also exist that there may be laws the prevailing political morality upholds that are unjust? What, then, is the real nature of the internal and external perspectives?

Skepticism: External and Internal

H. L. A. Hart was, perhaps, the first to recognize the significance of the internal and external perspectives to our understanding of the nature of legal obligation. For Hart, the internal point of view defines the perspective of persons within a given society who accept the rules of that society as a binding obligation. The external point of view defines the perspective of an outsider to the society, who may seek to understand the society but who does not accept as binding the rules of the society.[2] For such a person, the rules may help in predicting the consequences of engaging in certain forms of behavior but are not in themselves duties requiring obedience.

> Statements made from the external point of view may themselves be of different kinds. For the observer may, without accepting the rules himself, assert that the group accepts the rules, and thus may from outside refer to the way in which *they* are concerned with them from the internal point of view. . . . Such an observer is content merely to record the regularities of observable behaviour in which conformity with the rules partly consists and those further regularities, in the form of hostile reaction, reproofs, or punishments, with which deviations from the rules are met. After a time the external observer may, on the basis of the regularities observed, correlate deviation from hostile reaction, and be able to predict with a fair measure of success, and to assess the chances that deviation from the group's normal behaviour will meet with hostile reaction or punishment. Such knowledge may not only reveal much about the group, but might enable him to live among them without unpleasant consequences which would attend one who attempted to do so without such knowledge.
>
> If, however, the observer really keeps austerely to his extreme external point of view and does not give any account of the manner in which members of the group who accept the rules view their own regular behaviour, his description of their life cannot be in terms of rules at all, and so not in the terms of the rule-dependent notions of obligation and duty.

> Instead, it will be in terms of observable regularities of conduct, predictions, possibilities, and signs. For such an observer, deviations by a member of the group from normal conduct will be a sign that hostile reaction is likely to follow, and nothing more. His view will be like the view of one who, having observed the working of a traffic signal in a busy street for some time, limits himself to saying that when the light turns red there is a high probability that the traffic will stop. He treats the light merely as a natural *sign that* people will behave in certain ways, as clouds are a *sign that* rain will come. In so doing, he will miss out a whole dimension of the social life of those whom he is watching, since for them the red light is not merely a sign that others will stop: they look upon it as a *signal for* them to stop, and so a reason for stopping in conformity to the rules which make stopping when the light is red a standard of behaviour and an obligation. To mention this is to bring into the account the way in which the group regards its own behaviour. It is to refer to the internal aspect of rules seen from the internal point of view.[3]

Hart's view clearly establishes a dichotomy between questions of prescription and those of description. Accordingly, only the former is appropriate to our understanding of the sense of binding obligation that laws seem to entail. Hart believes that the question of obligation is directly related to how members of the society "view their own regular behavior." Recall that earlier positivists such as John Austin viewed law solely from a descriptive, external point of view. Hart distinguishes himself from Austin in that law is no longer seen simply as a command backed by a sanction—what Hart calls "being obliged"—but as creating obligations citizens accept as their own. Still, this does not mean Hart believes law and morality logically conjoin. As he says to those American legal realists who suggest a juncture between law and morals at the point where a statute needs interpretation, "It does not follow that, because the opposite of a decision reached blindly in the formalist or literalist manner is a decision intelligently reached by reference to some conception of what ought to be, we have a juncture of law and morals."[4] For example, in a Nazi society, judges might interpret the law to force conformity and block dissent. Thus, Hart also joins issue with those natural law/natural rights thinkers, such as Lon Fuller, who observe that a strictly positivist approach to law cannot account for the duty to obey law or, as I would also note, the judge's duty to follow the law. For Hart, the obligation is a product of being within the internal point of view. It is the result of having accepted a secondary rule to determine what the primary rules are.

To the extent that Hart sees law and morality as connected at all, the connection is logically contingent.

> Rules forbidding free use of violence and rules constituting the minimum form of property . . . are so fundamental that if the legal system did not have them, there would be no point in having any other rules at all. Such rules overlap the basic moral principles vetoing murder, violence and theft; and so we can add to the factual statement that all legal systems in fact coincide with morality at such vital points, the statement that this is, in this sense, necessarily so. And why not call it a "natural necessity"?[5]

So although Hart views all legal obligations as internal to a normative system regulating human actions, he does not necessarily view them as moral. To the extent that he views them as internal, however, he and Ronald Dworkin agree. For even though Dworkin finds a necessary connection between law and morality, he does so without appeal to any external metaphysical argument. Quite to the contrary, he is quick to reject all such arguments. Instead, Dworkin finds the connection between law and morality in the best constructive interpretation of the community's legal practice. Here one finds a similarity to Rawls's political constructivism, which he uses to derive the principles of justice.[6]

In effect, Dworkin contends that from the internal point of view there are no arguments other than internal arguments. So the point is not to choose between internal and external, as if this were possible. The internal point of view *is* simply the point of view:

> I have yet been given no reason to think that any skeptical argument about morality can be other than a moral argument, or skeptical argument about law other than a legal argument, or skeptical argument about interpretation other than an interpretative argument. I think that the problem of objectivity, as it is usually posed, is a fake because the distinction that might give it meaning, the distinction between substantive arguments within and skeptical arguments about social practices, is itself a fake.[7]

That Dworkin views the obligation to obey the law as internal to a legal system is evident from another response he makes, this time to the skeptic who wants to deny the possibility of any logical connection, other than a contingent one, between law and morality. Dworkin distinguishes external skepticism from internal skepticism:

> Internal skepticism . . . relies on the soundness of a general interpretive attitude to call into question all possible interpretations of a particular object of interpretation. One can be skeptical in this way not just about a particular [object] but more generally about an enterprise. . . . External skepticism is a metaphysical theory, not an interpretive or moral one. The external critic does not challenge any particular moral or interpretive claim. . . . His theory is rather a second-level theory about the philosophical standing or classification of these claims. He insists they are not descriptions that can be proved or tested like physics: he denies that aesthetic or moral values can be part of what he calls . . . the "fabric" of the universe. His skepticism is external because disengaged: it claims to leave the actual conduct of interpretation untouched by its conclusions. . . . He only insists that all these opinions are projected upon, not discovered in, "reality."[8]

Here it may be questioned whether an external skeptic truly believes that his conclusions have no effect on the conduct of interpretation. But that is a point for another day.

Under Dworkin's view, external skepticism is "silly and wasteful. . . . The only skepticism worth anything is skepticism of the internal kind, and this must be earned by arguments of the same contested character as the arguments it opposes, not claimed in advance by some pretense at hardhitting empirical metaphysics."[9] Dworkin believes his view overcomes internal skepticism by requiring any interpretation of law first to fit the settled law. If after that the law is still unclear, the judge must seek a further interpretation to conform to the prevailing political morality of the society. By doing this, Dworkin believes, one exposes a fundamental connection between law and morality. I have already suggested some problems with this view; for now, however, we see that what originally was Hart's distinction between the internal and the external points of view in Dworkin's hands becomes a barrier to foundationalist—natural law—arguments for assessing the validity of one's legal obligations. The issue, of course, is whether Dworkin is correct.

Alan Gewirth contends that one can provide an external metaethical justification for a supreme principle of morality, the Principle of Generic Consistency, based on premises that any moral theory must start from (see chapter 2). Although my own metatheory is not contingent on Gewirth's being right, since it derives out of the duty to obey law and not agency as such, it certainly would be consistent with his system if he is right, because it affords no contrary normative assertions. My system establishes different levels of normative evaluation for legal decisionmaking. At the highest level, one hopes for a kind of theory of natural law/natural rights to plug into. Gewirth's system provides that receptacle (see chapter 5). Still, as my theory requires only that there be a system in place at that high level and not that the system be either Gewirth's or anyone else's, it should be treated independently of the system chosen. Having said this, let us consider a necessary outcome of Gewirth's PGC claim, that once derived, the principle provides an external normative foundation for a morally just legal system.

In *Reason and Morality*, Gewirth makes this connection between the normative status of the principle and its foundation in metaethics.

> Consider the following statement, which I shall call "J": "A certain moral principle, the PGC is rationally justifiable." Is J a statement in "metaethics" or "normative ethics"? It seems to be both. It is metaethical because it says something about the logical status and structure of the moral principle. It is also normatively ethical because it says that the content of the principle is morally right or correct by virtue of being rationally justifiable. Thus the argument for the PGC shows that in important (though not in all) respects there is no valid distinction between metaethics and normative ethics because metaethical statements have specific normative ethical implications, and normative ethical statements, when traced back to their ultimate grounds, rest on specific metaethical doctrines about the meanings of moral terms and the methods of supporting moral judgments.[10]

If Gewirth is correct, his view demolishes Dworkin's claim that all discussions about ethics must occur from within an internal point of view. Because we can conceive the possibility of metaethical statements—we can talk about them and debate their relative merits—we cannot be conceptually bound against such conceptions. This is a transcendental argument that shows Dworkin's narrow interpretation is simply wrong. Moreover, that normative ethical statements must necessarily presuppose metaethical ones undercuts the idea of a barrier. To the extent that we accept any normative ethical statements at all, we presume their justification. Of course, this does not mean one actually has an external justification for a particular theory of morality, only that one cannot rule out such proofs *eo ipso*. Thus, by the very fact of conceiving what it would mean to have a metaethical justification, the possibility of an external point of view existing becomes plausible.

Let me stress the significance of this claim. If Gewirth is correct, it is plausible that one can develop a metaethical system to evaluate the norms that make up the internal point of view itself. Thus, we open the door to the possibility of developing natural law/natural rights theories. For the plausibility consideration resurrects the possibility that one can assess the justice of laws and legal decisions external to the legal system, possibly, even to the society, of which they are a part. Moreover, any failure to make this assessment, as happens where no one raises questions about external justice, would simply mean that one's duty to obey law *may* be unjustified. In other words, in a nearly just society, we rely on the positivist notion of identification as a law to say that there exists a duty to obey law. Since some laws may be immoral and we do not question which laws those are, all laws, to the extent they are taken to imply a duty of obedience, are virtual. Virtual law is the most that the internal point of view produces.

Dworkin seems to recognize this problem by allowing the best constructive interpretation of the society's legal practice to meet the issue of justification. To be successful in the way he wants, however, he needs further to show that this is the only possible justification. He needs to show that appeals to the external point of view are not available because one cannot ("should not" already implies an external point of view) step outside one's own normative position. When making a legal argument one can hope only to show that its conclusion is superior either as a matter of consistency with other cases taken as settled or as essential to the best constructive interpretation of the community's legal practice. Clearly, if Dworkin is right in his claim, the possibility of very hard cases should never present a problem. Persons should be able to rely on principles of deductive and inductive reason and noncontroversial statements about the society's political morality to resolve every case that comes along. If he is wrong, very hard cases will present problems. Such cases will resist resolution because the principles or rules that would resolve them are the ones the case is calling into question. In the United States, during the nineteenth century, the legal/moral problems raised by the institution of slavery, along with its libertarian aftermath during the period of Reconstruction, provide a number of such examples. So let us consider the theoretical foundation of Dworkin's claim. In particular, what does Dworkin mean when he says that one can never step outside the internal point of view, remembering that, for Dworkin, the internal point of view includes the prevailing political morality of the society?

I propose two interpretations: one "strong" and the other "weak." No doubt there are many interpretations in between, but I think that these can be fleshed out by the reader from my analysis of the two pillars to which they are attached. The two interpretations I shall offer are at the extremes of what Dworkin has in mind. The strong interpretation is an analogue of certain positions that suggest the impossibility of understanding other religions, cultures, and societies, which have become fashionable in some areas of religious studies, anthropology, and history. So-called social constructionists in these fields often make these arguments by focusing on conceptual schemes as ways to organize the world. In particular, in religious studies,

> The claim is that religious traditions typically represent alternative conceptual frameworks, or ways of looking at the world. Frameworks may coincide, differing only over, perhaps, the advisability of infant baptism. Or they may be as wildly divergent as, say, those of the conservative Congregationalist and the Brazilian Bororo, who, in certain ritual settings, will claim to be a parrot. But whether their differences are innocuous or exceptional, religious conceptual frameworks supply a set of categories through which experience is organized and the world known.[11]

According to the strong interpretation, there is a schematic limitation on what we can know, that is, on what we can take as objective. This is the result of thinking that one's conceptual framework alone can provide unity and organization to what would otherwise be widespread and deep-rooted conceptual differences among its adherents. The idea that religion explains physical phenomena better than science may for the ardent believer be such an example.[12] Truth is always about a scheme, and thus "reality" for one scheme may be illusion for another.[13] Consequently, for followers of the strong interpretation, it is not possible to step outside one's own scheme, for to do so would only present us with unschematized content, which tells us nothing either about our own experiences or the world.

If Dworkin's position embodies this interpretation, one concludes that he sees human beings as barred from being able independently to assess the validity of their own moral/legal positions. He would be holding that moral truth is always about one's society's own internal political morality. Dworkin might be legitimately considered as holding this strong interpretation:

> I have no interest in trying to compose a general defense of the objectivity of my interpretive or legal opinions. In fact, I think that the whole

> issue of objectivity, which so dominates contemporary theory in these areas, is a kind of fake. We should stick to knitting. We should account to ourselves for our convictions as best we can, standing ready to abandon those that do not survive reflective inspection. We should make such arguments to others who do not share our opinions, as we can make in good faith and break off arguing when no further argument is appropriate. I do not mean that this is all we can do because we are creatures with limited access to true reality or with necessarily parochial viewpoints. I mean that we can give no sense to the idea that there is anything else we could do in deciding whether our judgments are "really" true.[14]

In contrast to the strong interpretation, the weak interpretation holds that (at least) for the judge, there is a duty not to look beyond those sources of law recognized by the society even if some broad theory of morality might suggest doing so. This duty is often associated with the view that judges, being unelected, have no standing to undermine the collective judgment of society's representatives unless it clearly violates constitutional provisions.[15] The view is an outgrowth of combining the positivist insistence that in areas where the law is unclear a judge has discretion with contractarian theories about who should have political power over others. Consequently, under the weak interpretation, a judge has a duty to limit—as opposed to an epistemological limit on—what he recognizes to constitute the law. Dworkin's position does not seem to rely on this weak interpretation, however. He is not claiming that our parochial viewpoints create a duty of confinement but that they confine our understanding. Thus I will consider this interpretation more as a position he might want to adopt if the strong interpretation proves untenable.

I expect to prove that Dworkin's position fails under either interpretative strategy and that this means a judge can look beyond traditional sources of law when deciding very hard cases. In doing so, a judge will not succumb to either objection that the two interpretations represent. The judge will not succumb to the first objection of incoherence because a well-constructed epistemological view of law will allow the possibility of a metaethical justification for the court's decisions. Nor will the judge succumb to the second objection of violating a duty to follow only traditional sources because once alternate political moralities are admitted, the duty is to decide a case based on principles that the best alternative provides. That alternative may set forth different understandings of what the law is as, for example, would occur in a choice between natural law and positivism. Consequently, a judge under these circumstances may find himself consulting sources that, under one interpretation, are taken to be law but under a different interpretation are not law. Regarding this last point, I contend that the best alternative is the one that has the strongest reasons behind it as viewed from the next highest level of normative abstraction. Exactly why we appeal only one level up from the level where the two alternatives reside is determined by pragmatic considerations, which I identify as likely to gain a society's support (see chapter 5).

One additional point: I have been discussing a problem that is simultaneously practical and theoretical. The practical part is to account for the judge's duty to look beyond traditional legal sources. The theoretical part is to explain how this is possible, especially in light of Dworkin's strong interpretative criticism. Because these two different issues themselves require two different approaches, I shall treat them in reverse order, reflecting the a priori standing in this context of the theoretical over the practical.

Theoretical Reason

To refute the external skeptic's position, Dworkin must first explain it: "External skepticism is a metaphysical theory, not an interpretative or moral one. . . . [It is] a second-level theory about the philosophical standing or classification [of moral or aesthetic] claims."[16] More important, Dworkin must explain what he means by the external point of view: it is the belief that aesthetic or moral claims "can be proved or tested like physics"; that aesthetic or moral values "can be part of . . . the fabric of the universe."[17] Notice that in both descriptions, Dworkin is describing a position he takes to be "silly and wasteful," which some other scholars, in variant ways, clearly believe.[18] I do not mean to be making too much out of this particular phrase, but insofar as it seems connected to certain important epistemological claims, I need to address it through a related question: What could Dworkin mean by saying that such beliefs are "silly and wasteful"? Dworkin avoids answering this external question in keeping with his hermeneutic turn toward coherence theory.

Earlier, I commented that Dworkin believes an epistemological barrier prevents us from even engaging in such discussions: "I have yet given no reason to think that any skeptical argument about morality can be other than a moral argument, or skeptical argument about law other than a legal argument, or skeptical argument about interpretation other than an interpretative argument."[19] If this is true, we cannot talk about the external point of view. We cannot classify it as "silly and wasteful." According to Donald Davidson, we could not interpret a community's beliefs, if we presumed most of those beliefs were false.

> The meaning of a sentence, the content of a belief or desire, is not an item that can be attached to it in isolation from its fellows. We cannot intelligibly attribute the thought that a piece of ice is melting to someone who does not have many true beliefs about the nature of ice, its physical properties connected with water, cold, solidity, and so forth. The one attribution rests on the supposition of more—endlessly more. And among the beliefs we suppose a man to have, many must be true (in our view) if any are to be understood by us. The clarity and cogency of our attributions of attitude, motive and belief are proportionate, then, to the extent to which we find others consistent and correct. We often, and justifiably, find others irrational and wrong; but such judgments are most firmly based when there is most agreement. We understand someone best when we hold him to be rational and sage, and this understanding is what gives our disputes with him a keen edge.[20]

This is Davidson's Agreement thesis, or Principle of Charity. It is the view that particular error is commensurable only against a background of true beliefs. In other words, error makes sense only where one can assess what is said because many, if not all, of the language statements are true to the listener. Consider Socrates' argument with Thrasymachus in Book 1 of *The Republic*. The alleged error Socrates points out in Thrasymachus's view of justice can be made sense of only if both parties understand the notions of power and influence, as well as self-interest, that are at stake. Moreover, Socrates can persuade Thrasymachus of the error of his view only if they both find common ground in their premises. Such common ground is what Davidson means by saying that we must assume a person to have many true beliefs before we can make sense of his error. Jürgen Habermas makes a similar claim from a related standpoint. Concerned with how language affects social coordination and drawing on the writings of "American pragmatism and the speech-act theories of John L. Austin and John Searle, Habermas considers a 'formal-pragmatic' approach to language as the most adequate for social theory."[21] According to William Rehg, the translator of his work,

> Conflict resolution will be rendered easier the more the members of the group can limit their discursive efforts to a few problematic validity claims.

For example, if they are at odds over how best to manage a particular environmental threat—one might imagine a city council debating over how to deal with an imminent flood—they have a better chance of reaching agreement if they only have to resolve an empirical question about the effectiveness of two competing strategies, and do not also have to argue over fairness criteria, or what would count as a successful outcome.[22]

About the relationship between our thoughts and our expressions, Davidson writes:

> Someone who can interpret an utterance of the English sentence "The gun is loaded" must have many beliefs, and those beliefs must be much like the beliefs someone must have if he entertains the thought that the gun is loaded. The interpreter must, we may suppose, believe that a gun is a weapon, and that it is a more or less enduring physical object. There is probably no definite list of things that must be believed by someone who understands the English sentence "The gun is loaded," but it is necessary that there be endless interlocked beliefs.[23]

Dworkin wants to refute the external point of view not because it does not exist, but because it is incoherent as a point of view. My references to Davidson make the point that for Dworkin to succeed in this endeavor, he must presuppose the plausibility of the very thing he wants to deny, for he must presuppose a great deal of agreement between what he believes and what those who espouse the external position believe: "It isn't that any false belief necessarily destroys our ability to identify further beliefs, but that the intelligibility of such identification must depend on a background of largely unmentioned and unquestioned true beliefs. To put it another way: the more things a believer is right about, the sharper his errors are. Too much mistake simply blurs the focus."[24] This is a transcendental argument that shows a priori the possibility of an external point of view as a means to discuss legal and ethical questions. It shows that the possibility of such a point of view is not necessarily incoherent, though particular claims about it may be wrong. Therefore, if Dworkin is to discount as "silly and wasteful" discussions about the external perspective, it should be for either of two reasons unrelated to the epistemological question: that there exists a moral duty, resembling the weak interpretation, not to pursue such avenues of inquiry, or that the internal point of view is the only one that provides determinative answers to the questions we want to ask regarding legal decisionmaking.

At this point, I need to say something about a criticism that has been lurking in the background of the present discussion. It concerns the general nature of reasoning itself. Thus far I have assumed, and will assume again, a rationalistic view of the self that privileges (using a postmodern term) ego-centered reasoning. By ego-centered, I mean "that all claims or arguments about the nature of law or the world are addressed to the rational ego itself."[25] It differs from a prerational view that takes as fixed, and therefore not subject to debate, our commitment to follow some intuition, craft, convention, tradition, or other text. It also differs from a "modernist" account, as presented in some critical theory literature, which denies ego-centered reason its privileged center in our epistemological examinations. Instead, it assigns reason to the status of being a construction brought about by "a contradiction between the means and relations of production (Marx), the advent of bureaucratic organization (Weber), the unconscious (Freud), will to power (Nietzsche), [or] cultural practice (Wittgenstein)."[26] The ego-centered approach also differs from a poststructuralistic critique that denies "totalizations" and holds to the view that what we lack can never be presented but "must be experienced negatively."[27] Given these very different and sometimes contradictory approaches, what privileges my method over any of these others? Put another way, have I not in taking my approach begged the question that this criticism is putting forth?

The answer to this challenge is twofold. Admittedly, my answer is not going to impress the dyed-in-the-wool poststructuralist. The first part of the answer is that from my own point of view, within ego-centered reason, there is no place else to go. That is to say, there is no outside to the "subject I" to which everything else is object. This is the totality of the ego-centered approach. This is the sense of Gewirth's response to the critics who claim reason must pass some further justificatory test as "set by religious faith, aesthetic rapture and so forth." The Gewirthian reponse is out of court here, but was not where he originally offered it, because the nature of the question has changed. In that earlier case, it was the rationalist who was being invited to question reason. Here the question being posed is why be a rationalist. In other words, the problem as presented here is not being posed from inside the internal point of view of ego-centered reason; rather, it is being solicited *about* an ego-centered approach.[28] Consequently, argument in the usual sense has no place in its resolution since that is what is being called into question. But neither does it have any place when offered by the other side, for then we would be inside reason and the Gewirthian counterresponse would apply. It may be that the ego-centered approach should not have to respond to this sort of criticism, given its epistemically separate foundation in the "subject I." That is a strong response since it says that from the first-person point of view, everything else is necessarily object or fits the a priori conditions of our having any knowledge of objects. Still, I should not offer this as my response since I have not really joined issue on the criticism with the postmodernist, assuming that such a joining is even possible. One might, however, try to understand the criticism and engage it without the use of argument.[29]

This brings me to the second part of my answer. Here I rely on the fact that by establishing a metatheory for law, I have allowed various approaches to the defining and critique of law to be adopted to the needs of a particular case. Moreover, I have implicitly accepted the idea that the metatheory itself, like the legal theories it encompasses, might be contained in some super metatheory. (That is, after all, what this book is about, presenting and justifying a metatheory of law.) But if this is true, I face the question of where to stop the meta-analyses? Perhaps a pragmatic answer should be tried. Is there anything to be gained, either deontologically or teleologically, by continuing to push the postmodernist critique? At least at the point where a serious metatheory of law is available, it would seem that I should give up any need for further pretension that I might more fully lay to rest the challenge that has been presented. At least, that would seem to be the most I can do from a third-person perspective.

Earlier, I argued that Davidson's position is directly opposite to the conceptual relativism suggested by Dworkin. Let me now make the point explicitly. "Given the underlying methodology of interpretation, we could not be in a position to judge that others had concepts or beliefs radically different from our own."[30] Nor can we intelligibly say that all speakers of a language share a common conceptual scheme. "For if we cannot intelligibly say that schemes are different, neither can we intelligibly say that they are one."[31] What we can say is that different conceptual frameworks (not schemes) are just that. They are means for organizing large chunks of our concepts according to some principles of connection.[32] The connections may be resemblance, contiguity, or cause and effect, as David Hume thought,[33] or the various pure concepts of the understanding mentioned by Immanuel Kant,[34] or something else. Whatever the connections are, they provide an account of the relationships between at least some of our ideas. They do not necessarily organize all our ideas. In any event, we could not know if this were the case. We conclude, therefore, that it is probably more useful to construe various conceptual frameworks as organized sets of concepts, sometimes competing with other sets—as, for example, in religious frameworks versus scientific frameworks—sometimes not. Viewed in this way, conceptual frameworks may stand sometimes, though not always, in hierarchical relationships to each other. Moral frameworks, for example, stand in hierarchical relationship to frameworks like law and etiquette.

I have not set forth any grounds for determining the legitimacy of any particular metaethical approach, only that an honest inquiry into such questions need not be incoherent. Now I would like to make the claim a bit stronger. For based on the same kind of transcendental argument that Davidson advances for the possibility of interpreting what I call "conceptual frameworks" (although not schemes), he also argues for the possibility of there being truth in metaphysics.

> It may seem that the argument so far shows only that good interpretation breeds concurrence, while leaving quite open the question whether what is agreed upon is true. And certainly agreement, no matter how widespread, does not guarantee truth. This observation misses the point of the argument, however. The basic claim is that much community of belief is needed to provide a basis for communication or understanding; the extended claim should then be that objective error can occur only in a setting of largely true belief. Agreement does not make for truth, but much of what is agreed must be true if some of what is agreed is false.[35]

In effect, Davidson discredits a certain claim that has been associated with Nietzsche, "namely, that truth is only another name for illusion, for lie."[36] By shifting down the analysis of what we can know to our agreed intersubjective beliefs, as witnessed by our language, Davidson is able to avoid further inquiry into whether those beliefs correspond to some "unknowable" thing in itself that is prior to all experience. Of course, the shutdown cannot be arbitrary, and it is not. Davidson is not shutting down the inquiry to avoid the problem of explaining how our beliefs correspond to the noumenal thing in itself. He is shutting it down because there is no longer a meaningful problem to be unraveled. Of course, Davidson's comments here do not imply that we know "where the truth lies,"[37] only that "massive error about the world is simply unintelligible."[38]

One hears the objection that "we presuppose the world is intelligible (or maybe we necessarily make it so through the categories of our minds) but whether the world is inherently unintelligible (a Heraclitean flux, as it were) we cannot know. Thus, in a trivial sense, 'massive error about the world is simply unintelligible' [is true] but that does not necessarily show anything about truth, our beliefs, or the inherent nature of the world."[39] The problem with this criticism is that it fails to take Davidson where he stands. Again, like Kant before him, Davidson is saying we cannot know the thing in itself (noumenon). We can know only what our intersubjective understanding of the world provides. But that also means that we can have only collective agreement from which to begin our inquiries. The agreement may be on method as well as substance, on form as well as content, on particulars as well as universals, even on contexts as well as absolutes. Nevertheless, it is still agreement. That we may eventually reach a point in our inquiries beyond which we cannot go will not alter our achievement if we have obtained a sufficiently wide set of interrelated concepts to provide coherent solutions to most of the problems that confront us. And is not this just what we mean by truth? (For the relevance to this argument of the distinction between coherence truth and correspondence truth, see chapter 5.)

Now I want to be especially cautious. Although Davidson's view prohibits the possibility of massive error, it does not imply that only minor and insignificant error is possible. Especially on questions that are highly theoretical, the degree of agreement needed about background beliefs is less than would be the case on more practical questions. Still, there must be some agreement to make even theoretical error intelligible.

> With increasing theoreticity, error becomes, for purposes of interpretation, increasingly tolerable (and probable). Especially at the non-observational level, we can interpret error noncharitably—perhaps by noticing the workings of some causal factor of which the subject seems to be unaware. . . . At the same time, considerations of charity assert themselves even at the level of theory, for we want to make our attribution of belief (true or false) as precise and intelligible as we can. For this reason, we cannot attribute a belief, say in ghosts (false by our lights) unless we attribute beliefs, say in persons and death (true by our lights). Without some such latter beliefs that are shared, we would put into doubt that the initial belief attributed was one about *ghosts*.[40]

This raises a different challenge. In response to a notion implicit in Davidson's view—that we keep in mind the perspective of the outside field linguist to make sense of our linguistic behavior—Hilary Putman argues:

> If the cause-effect description [of our linguistic behavior qua production of noises] is complete from a philosophical as well as from a behavioral-

> scientific point of view; if all there is to say about language is that it consists in the production of noises (and subvocalizations) according to a certain causal pattern; *if the causal story is not to be and need not be supplemented by a normative story* . . . then there is no way in which the noises we utter . . . are more than mere expressions of our subjectivity.[41]

In response to this criticism, Richard Rorty argues, "Putman's insistence that there is more to truth than disquotationalism can offer is not based on having looked at 'true,' or at the language games we play, and having seen more than Davidson saw. Rather, it is based on the hope [à la Plato] that there is more to the notion of a 'philosophical account' than Dewey or Davidson think there can be."[42]

On the one hand, Rorty is contending that Davidson's approach undermines the possibility of backing up our understanding by a metaphysical or scientific account of what exists. This seems true if by "backing up" one means to find truth in correspondence to some unschematized matter in the universe.[43] On the other hand, Davidson himself does not mean to deny the possibility of metaethical truth, provided only that the appeal is intersubjective to what we believe as speakers of a common language, including our principles of translation.

> In giving up dependence on the concept of an unprincipled reality, something outside all schemes and science, we do not relinquish the notion of objective truth—quite the contrary. Given the dogma of a dualism of scheme and reality, we get conceptual relativity, and truth relative to a scheme. Of course, truth of sentences remains relative to a language, but that is as objective as it can be. In giving up the dualism of scheme and world, we do not give up the world, but re-establish unmediated touch with the familiar objects whose antics make our sentences true and false.[44]

What can we conclude from this discussion? We conclude, assuming Davidson is correct, that no metaphysical foundation for a scheme of political morality is discoverable outside our own intersubjective understanding of the world in which we live. The total set of beliefs we have about the world, including our beliefs about relevant and material evidence, and our principles of translation, constitute that understanding. In saying this, I do not mean to imply that at any given point in time our understanding of the world is complete or true, only that at all points in time our understanding of the world will depend on the total set of beliefs we hold. In this regard, when framing particular solutions to specific problems, we need to discover within our understanding of the world applications of the rules of logic and consistency that allow us to uphold most of the beliefs we take to be true.[45] In the case of moral theory, this means we need to find the theory that best preserves our understanding of what morality is, who are moral agents, and why morality creates rights and duties. The point, then, is not the metaphysical one that at any given moment the world is such. The point is epistemological: that at any given moment, we can make claims about the truth of some proposition based on our best understanding of the world in which we live. Dworkin had it right in thinking that the external skeptic position ultimately leads to incoherence, although it was not the external point of view that was incoherent. It was thinking that we could talk about unschematized matter as something independent of our beliefs about the world. There is no bridge here between epistemology and metaphysics. There is only epistemology with a healthy dose of philosophy of language thrown in, and that may be all that is needed.

Practical Reason

I have been arguing that the strong interpretation of Dworkin's account of the internal and external points of view is untenable, that the minute one says anything about these two perspectives, even just to distinguish them, one engages a conceptual framework that can encompass them both. Why not, at this point, start with the narrower framework of the "internal point of view," and show how the pragmatic reasons presented in chapter 3 explain why a judge might wish to move to the external position? The answer is that I have not yet shown that the external point of view could be of any help to the judge. Cass Sunstein offers three reasons to question this:

> First, lawyers may misunderstand philosophers (as they sometimes misunderstand economists).... Second, and more interestingly, lawyers may fail to understand the difficulties in bringing philosophical arguments to bear on concrete legal problems. The application may seem mechanical, but it usually requires an act of translation, and one that involves a large element of construction.
>
> There is a third problem, having to do with the need for legal solutions to operate in a world with distinctive limitations.... Even if wealth

> maximization is not in the end a good approach to justice, it might be shown that greater social wealth is at least roughly connected with the achievement of important known values.[46]

Sunstein's concerns make a great deal of sense if one has only to choose between top-down theories of law and bottom-up approaches. The latter I hesitate to call theories of law since they are much less thorough than what that phrase usually references. Top-down theories are theories that provide a canon of general norms that the law is supposed to incorporate. Dworkin and Rawls serve as good examples of persons who hold top-down theories. In contrast, bottom-up approaches allow a judge to tinker with the way a case fits a norm in the hope of achieving an overall better understanding of the law. An example of a bottom-up approach that Sunstein approves is reasoning by analogy.

I have already expressed some reservations about reasoning by analogy when applied too broadly, so I will take Sunstein's critique of top-down theories as providing a reason for why a judge should always begin his analysis of a case from the bottom-up approach. That is to say, a judge who believes the legal system is nearly just should start the analysis by asking if there is a valid rule that governs the case directly or if the case is similar enough to another previously decided case such that an analogy might be drawn. If such a rule exists or the case is analogizable, the judge should decide the case accordingly, provided only that the result would not be unjust. If there is no clearly applicable rule of law or case precedent, however, the judge should ask if the issue here is one of principle or of policy. Does the issue concern an economic or political goal of the society, or does it raise a concern about justice or morality? If the answer is that the issue raises a question of principle, a judge must decide which principle in the prevailing political morality it is. Here the judge's concern would be to decide the case justly according to the prevailing principles of morality. If no principle can be found either because the applicable principles are inconsistent or because the institutional norms seem out of step with concerns for justice, then the judge must look elsewhere to find a principle to decide the case. The latter occurs when the prevailing political morality is itself in dispute.

In effect, what I have been describing here—earlier I designated it as the prescriptive side of a metatheory of law—is pragmatism.[47] It is not the pragmatism whose name identifies a certain legal tradition beginning with Oliver Wendell Holmes[48] and continuing with Richard Posner.[49] The sense of pragmatism I have in mind does not approach the world from a particular teleological point of view, whether it is wealth maximization[50] or some communitarian premise.[51] Nor does it disaffirm the possibility of getting at the truth of legal propositions,[52] in Davidsonian terms.[53] My sense of pragmatism is instrumental only in that it provides reasons for a judge who approaches deciding a case from the internal point of view to move up a hierarchy of progressively broader conceptual frameworks. The judge begins with the traditionally legal and moves to the politically moral to natural law. Here, pragmatism may involve in its application the use of reasoning by analogy, induction, observation, common sense, intuition, and, of course, deduction. Still, its root is a deep, deontological understanding of the judge's institutional duty to decide cases by applying just laws. The fact that the law itself may reflect the legislature's view as to the common good of society does not alter this conclusion. To the contrary, it supports it, given that courts are obligated, where questions of policy arise and no deontological moral principle is at stake, to defer to the legislature. I call this view "epistemic pragmatism," reflecting in the word pragmatism the court's need to find principled solutions to difficult cases. The addition of the word epistemic reflects the search for a principled foundation based on concentrically wider conceptual frameworks, which I could not have discovered had I been relying only on traditional legal sources.

CHAPTER FIVE

Real Law

It should now be plain why I called the previous chapter "Virtual Law." From the internal point of view, law exists without moral justification. That is, what appears to us in the first instance to be law—traditional legal sources—does so only by virtue of a presumption we make believing we live in a nearly just society. Of course, without moral justification, we can never be certain that the presumption is valid and, therefore, that we have a duty to obey law.

A second way in which law turns out to be virtual has to do with our language, including the ability to recognize and translate other languages. If Donald Davidson is correct, we cannot provide a coherent notion of a foundation for law any deeper than what our total set of beliefs about the world as described by our language would allow. Still, this does not mean that political morality is not external to legal theory or even that political morality in general is not external to a narrowly constructed social view of it. The point is only that the traditional metaphysical approaches to this question, which try to ground political morality in some unschematized matter making up the universe, are not very useful. In examining the implications of these two contentions for developing "real" justifications for law, I want in particular to show that the metaethical approach of Alan Gewirth, properly interpreted, can justify a fair system of law without confronting the incommensurability problem that Davidson warns us against.

Two Understandings of Truth

Two understandings of the idea of truth are of particular significance to the discussion.[1] The first is as an expression of coherence among several ideas.

The second is as an expression of correspondence between a sentence—the distinction between sentences and propositions need not concern us here—and its reference.

COHERENCE TRUTH

Truth is an expression of the coherence among several ideas. The ideas might be about physical bodies, including written documents, or events, or nonphysical objects such as depict the underlying narrative of a story, "It was a beautiful summer day." The concern for coherence arises where there is a question about meaning. Unlike correspondence truth, however, here there is a need for a third criterion besides the idea and its reference. That criterion is the notion of ground rules governing what interpretations should count as interpretations of the given object. For example, in *A Matter of Principle*, Ronald Dworkin takes up the question, "Is there no right answer in hard cases?"[2] His solution is to draw an analogy between the way a literary critic sets out to find an answer to a question about a piece of literature and how a judge finds an answer in a hard case. He begins his discussion by explaining the task of the literary critic.

> Suppose a group of Dickens scholars proposes to discuss David Copperfield as if David were a real person. They propose to say, for example, that David attended Salem House, that he was industrious, and so forth. They might well develop the following ground rules governing these various assertions:
>
> (1) Any proposition about David may be asserted as "true" if Dickens said it, or said something else such that it would have been inconsistent had Dickens denied it.
>
> (2) Any proposition may be denied as "false" if Dickens denied it, or said something else such that it would have been inconsistent had Dickens denied it. . . .
>
> If it is true that Dickens attended Salem House, then it must be false, under the rules, that he did not, and vice versa. If it is true that David had an affair with Steerforth there, then it must be false, under the rules, that he did not, and vice versa. . . .
>
> We can even say, of David as of real people, that for any property it is true that either David had that property or not, because the law of the excluded middle is a necessary truth that it would have been inconsistent for Dickens to deny once he had said anything at all about David.

> But the . . . no-right-answer thesis would hold in the literary enterprise, for there would be many propositions about David that the participants would know were neither assertable as true nor deniable as false. . . .
>
> The participants in the literary game . . . might easily have chosen less ascetic ground rules for themselves. . . . The second form of the exercise might provide, for example, that further propositions about David are assertable as true (or deniable as false) if it would be very likely indeed (or very unlikely indeed) that a real person having the properties true of David under the standard game would also have the properties asserted in the further proposition. The . . . no-right-answer thesis would still hold for the second form of the literary exercise, but there would be many fewer cases of questions that might have no right answer in the second form than in the first, not because the raw data of what Dickens said have changed, but because the ground rules now warrant the assertion or denial of much more. We can imagine a third form of the exercise in which the number of such questions would be reduced to very boring questions no one would wish to ask. The rules of this third form provide that a further proposition about David is assertable as true (or deniable as false) if that further proposition provides a better (or worse) fit than its negation with propositions already established because it explains in a more satisfactory way why David was what he was, or said what he said, or did what he did, according to those already established propositions. In fact, literary criticism often takes the form of an exercise much closer to this third form of the exercise than to either of the other two.[3]

Having set forth the task of the literary critic, Dworkin next suggests that a similar approach should obtain about what a judge does in deciding a hard case. If the legal enterprise in which the judge operates is like the first form of the literary enterprise, then certain legal questions will have no right answers. This would be consistent with the positivist position that only rules that have a certain pedigree count as law. Everything else is a matter of judicial discretion. If the legal enterprise is more like the third form, then few, if any, questions will be without right answers. Here a judge can determine the truth of a proposition of law depending on whether it offers a better or worse fit with the best constructive interpretation of the society's legal practice. If two or more propositions would fit the settled law equally well, the judge chooses the proposition that as a matter of political morality provides the best justification for propositions of law already established. In any event, it becomes a question of fact whether our legal system is directly analogous to the first or the third form only after the judge decides what ground rules to follow. Which ground rules are chosen, on the other hand, is a matter of political philosophy.

CORRESPONDENCE TRUTH

Truth is the correspondence of an idea with the object to which the idea refers. Sometimes the object is in existence, as suggested by the sentence, "The automobile is red." Other times, it may be an event, as suggested by the sentence, "Yesterday, I celebrated my forty-second birthday." Sometimes it is an essence, such as "Three straight lines joined at their ends are the essence of a triangle." (Whether essence implies existence or not, or what essence means in this context, need not concern us here.) What the nature of correspondence is and what kinds of sentences it attaches to do concern us.

Traditionally, if we can decide the truth value of the sentence independently of any *experience* about its reference, we have a priori truth. The sentence, "Tomorrow, it will rain at a particular time and place, or it will not," is an example of a priori truth. Here, we decide the sentence's truth without any experience about what tomorrow brings at the place in question. If we cannot decide the truth value of the sentence independently of experience of the things the sentence is about, we have an a posteriori truth. "The automobile is red" is an example of an a posteriori truth. A priori and a posteriori are epistemic categories. They refer to the different ways in which we obtain knowledge of the world.

If we decide the truth of a sentence solely from understanding the sentence's meaning, we have an analytic truth. "All bachelors are unmarried men" is an example of an analytic truth since the idea of a bachelor—the subject of the sentence—contains the idea of being an unmarried man—the predicate of the sentence. Analytically true sentences can be either syntactic or semantic. They are syntactic if the form and the meanings of their logical terms alone determine their truth value. "All bachelors are bachelors" is an example of a syntactically true analytic sentence. Its form and the meanings of its logical terms ("All —— are ——") determines its truth value. (Note that the "——" after "All" is the same as the "——" after "are.") "All bachelors are unmarried" is an example of a semantically true analytic sentence since to determine its truth value one needs to know more than just the form and meaning of its logical terms: "All —— are . . ."; we must also know the meaning of its nonlogical term "bachelor." In contrast, if we cannot decide the truth of a sentence from its meaning alone, either syntactic or semantic, we have a synthetic truth.[4] "There are five people in this room" is an example of a synthetic truth since we cannot decide the truth of the sentence merely by understanding its meaning. Analytic and synthetic are logical categories. They refer to the scope and limits of our understanding of meaning.

Cross-referencing a priori and a posteriori with analytic and synthetic, four possible judgments present themselves. A judgment such as "All bachelors are unmarried men" is a priori, analytic. A judgment such as "There are five people in this room" is a posteriori, synthetic. It is debated whether there are judgments that are a posteriori and analytic. G. W. Leibniz and Saul Kripke think that there are.[5] Whether there are judgments that are a priori and synthetic is also problematic.[6] Sentences such as "If something is red all over, it is not green," "Seven plus five equals twelve," and "A cube has twelve edges" led Kant and others to believe that synthetic a priori judgments are possible.

Unfortunately, this view of truth has had a long and problematic history in philosophy. A key problem with the relation of correspondence is that we have no nonquestion-begging way to define the facts. This is necessary if truth is to be understood as correspondence to facts. Donald Davidson's solution to the problem is to adopt Alfred Tarski's notion of satisfaction. "The solution depends on first characterizing a relation called *satisfaction* and then defining truth by means of it. The entities that are satisfied are sentences both open and closed; the satisfiers are functions that map the variables of the object language on to the entities over which they range—almost everything if the language is English."[7]

Richard Rorty interprets Davidson as suggesting that we give up "sentence-world" for "word-world" mappings.[8] "Going around this circle means not attempting (in the manner of building block theories of reference) to start with some 'secure' links, but rather going back and forth between guesses at translations of occasion-sentences [whose truth depends on place and time] and of standing-sentences [believed true or false after observation] until something like Rawlsian 'reflective equilibrium' emerges."[9] In the end we are left with no separation between conceptual scheme and unschematized content in the world, only with language and beliefs.

> Davidson's favorite characterization of the picture which the skeptic should abjure is "the dualism of scheme and content." A common feature of all the forms of this dualism which Davidson lists is that the relations between the two sides of the dualism are non-causal. Such *tertia* as a

> "conceptual framework" or an "intended interpretation" are non-causally related to the things which they organize or intend. They vary independently of the rest of the universe, just as do the skeptic's relations of "correspondence" or "representation." The moral is that if we have no such *tertia*, then we have no suitable items to serve as representations, and thus no need to ask whether our beliefs represent the world accurately. We still have beliefs, but they will seem from the outside as the field linguist sees them (as causal interactions with the environment) or from the inside as the preepistemological native sees them (as rules for action).[10]

Thus, we give up the idea of thinking "of a language as something which may or may not (how could one ever tell?) 'fit the world.'"[11]

In the law, judgments involving three of these four forms have application. Courts use analytic, a priori judgments to determine the application of statutes and regulations where the meanings are clear. For example, if some court needs to decide whether a city ordinance that prohibits vehicles in the park applies to mopeds, it must consult the ordinance's legislative history to decide whether the legislature intended the word "vehicle" in the statute to encompass mopeds. (The fact that this involves a factual element in terms of looking at legislative histories is not a problem, provided the legislative histories are construed as part of the law.) Findings of fact by a court based on what the testimony and hard evidence revealed are examples of a posteriori synthetic judgments. (Note that the way testimony and hard evidence serve to support a court's findings of fact illustrates the satisfaction relationship.) A court might find that the assailant used a certain knife in the commission of the crime based on eye witness testimony or a DNA analysis of the blood on the knife. What is less obvious but will become clear is that a priori synthetic judgments also have a place in the law. It is in resolving the theoretical question of whether a law can create a binding obligation if it is unjust.

From the Internal Point of View to Political Morality

With an understanding of truth as coherence and correspondence, one can account for how a judge might justify a particular interpretation of the law in hard cases. Given that the judge believes that he lives in a nearly just society, the justification needed would fit the coherence view of truth. That is to say, the judge would want to interpret the rules and principles of law to ensure "the best constructive interpretation of the community's legal practice."[12] The judge would follow Dworkin in that, depending upon whether the issue was one of principle or policy, the court would seek the interpretation that most clearly cohered with the society's prevailing political morality. Here, principles of stare decisis and deference to legislative authority become relevant.[13] The judge would be very much like the participant in the creation of a chain novel whose duty it is to advance the story so that it coheres with what had been set forth earlier either in other statutes or case precedents.[14] Of course, there may be a great deal of subtlety and nuancing involved in how a statute or prior set of cases is interpreted. For now it is enough to say that in a nearly just society, the judge should resolve these broader questions within the internal point of view of the prevailing political morality.

When should judges consider broader questions, such as whether the society's political morality is itself justified? They should do so when they cannot reconcile the prevailing set of policies or principles without appealing to their own idiosyncratic views about a case. Such cases are likely to arise when an area of legislative policymaking or judicial precedent-setting has become inconsistent due to changes in the political makeup of the legislature or the courts. It is just in these situations, when policies and principles are most incoherent, that the challenges to coherence theories like Dworkin's are most strong. How are we to account for the possibility of such situations arising? Why does not a broad-based ideological consensus, say, at the constitutional level, constrain or at least render consistent ideological disputes at the level of legislative or judicial decisionmaking?[15]

Surely, the answer to this problem depends on how pervasive the ideological disputes are across the authoritative levels of decisionmaking. For example, in the United States, the president, with the advice and consent of the Senate, appoints federal judges and Supreme Court justices to life tenure.[16] Since it is unlikely that any one president will appoint all the members of the Supreme Court, the chances are very high that different presidents from different ideological bents will appoint justices who share their ideologies. Since it is reasonable to assume that in deciding cases, these different justices will in turn reflect the ideological bents of those who appointed them, it is equally likely that the constitutional and statutory interpretations of these justices will be inconsistent on matters over which there might exist strong ideological disagreement. Moreover, the variety of these justices' different ideological bents may reflect not only differences in political opinions on substantive topics but also differences in how to interpret the Constitution and the proper role of a judiciary in a democracy.

Together, these different areas of ideological dispute create a matrix of decisions that may defy rational interpretation or construction—at least, if one's hope is to discover a principled political morality. The proponents of critical legal studies have been claiming this persistently. It may be why, at an earlier time, legal realists pronounced that law is what the courts say law is. Even if there were, let us say, a consensus on the question of deference to legislative authority, there would be nothing to unify the area of law that would result other than the power plays that come about when a few groups assume dominance over the decisionmaking functions of government. The only exception would be if the new dominant ideology were to change the interpretations and prior substantive policies and principles to reflect the views of the time. Even then, though there might be rational unity, there would be no claim to its justification, only the mere fact of agreement, which is no justification at all.

What is the significance of this CLS challenge? It is to show a limitation on Dworkin's distinction between principles and rules. Recall that for Dworkin, principles have the dimension of weight; rules apply in an all-or-nothing fashion. This suggests that we might weigh different groupings of principles against each other to resolve ideological disputes. The problem with this approach is that there may be nothing even close to a consensus about how to find the weight of very different principles. How, for example, are the principles adopted by a prolife judge to be squared with the principles followed by a prochoice judge? One wants to discover some common denominator upon which to assess the conflicting principles. What could this common denominator be? The problem is especially acute where the society has no consensus at the level of its political morality for how to weigh and rank various conflicting principles. Clearly, under these circumstances, a judge who had to decide a very hard case would have no choice but to appeal to principles broader than the political morality of the society. The level of the dispute will determine how high up the ladder of political theory a judge will have to go to decide the question. Otherwise, if the judge were merely to adopt the viewpoint of one side of the dispute, say, on the ground that he favored a constitutional interpretation that affirms individual autonomy, the decision would be unprincipled in light of the real question being asked: Does the court have a moral *obligation* to interpret the Constitution to support individual autonomy? Here the idea of correspondence truth becomes applicable.

In the situation of a very hard case where the society's political morality is unable to provide a determinate answer to a conflict of principles, a judge should consider adopting a set of still more general principles of political morality that can decide the case. The way the court would arrive at this broader political morality would be by considering secondary sources of law. Crossing between the different conceptual frameworks of traditional sources of law, the political morality of one's society, and political morality in general is the satisfaction notion of correspondence truth. A court will need to make use of this idea when it shifts from the confines of traditional sources to each of these consecutively more highly ordered frameworks because it will need to justify its upward shift on the basis of the possibilities each of these succeeding levels creates for rendering just decisions.

Still, one might want to raise a challenge here of a different sort. One may claim, for example, to understand how pragmatism may lead a judge to a higher level of normative evaluation and how correspondence truth allows a judge then to justify a decision in terms of principles from that high level. But this assumes that the way a judge starts out interpreting a case—whether it involves a principle or policy, a rule or a principle, and so forth—can be fixed. That is, all distinctions are bright lines; there are no important areas of gray. But is it true that judges never have to interpret how a case is to be understood? Is it true that a judge knows early in a case just where on the hierarchy of levels it is to be placed? Often a judge does not know. Even in easy cases, a judge must interpret what is going on. The difference between the easy and the hard cases is that there is not likely to be a lot of disagreement as to what the cases stand for. But if this is true, so the challenge goes, do we not need criteria for how a judge should interpret a hard or very hard case in the same way we have provided criteria for when a judge should move up the ladder of levels? And what should that criteria be?

A qualification is needed here. What I am talking about is not how to interpret disputes about facts in a case. Arguably, they are resolved by way of the rules of evidence applicable in a trial. To the contrary, I am talking about disputes over what set of principles or policies should apply when the facts in the case are not yet in dispute. This issue is raised every time a plaintiff's complaint or a defendant's answer is attacked by a motion to dismiss, even where no evidence that would support a motion for summary judgment is provided. In effect, what needs to be asked in these situations is whether there is a justifiable basis for the claim and, if so, what is it? There may be close calls in which an interpretation can go either way. Is an argument for allowing the death penalty, for example, a matter of policy or principle? (This may need to be answered before the argument on the other side is considered.) If the issue is protecting society from serious threats to the physical well-being of its citizens, is that a matter of policy, or is it a matter of principle if the issue is whether and under what circumstances the state has the right to take a life? Do the two interpretations collapse into one, cancel each other out, or have nothing to say to each other?

Before we can answer that question, we need to make use of the idea of coherence truth in the development of a narrative that provides the greatest fit to the feature in the case that is significant. The idea of significance here is to provide for as many features of the case as possible in relation to the issue being raised. What constitutes whether a feature is material is whether it adds to the resolution of the issue at hand. Resolution is determined vertically by appeal up the ladder of normative abstractions; interpretation works horizontally by making the features in the case fit the issues involved. In practice, the two work together to provide the best understanding of what the case is really about and how it should be resolved. If an important feature is overlooked—perhaps because the participants in the process are uncertain of the feature's application or because they have been inadequately sensitized to the issue (as is often argued in sexual harassment disputes)—then the party who stands to benefit from the presentation has the burden to explain why the court should take this feature into consideration when rendering its decision. No other person has as much to lose if the relevant considerations are not taken into account. Depending on the issue involved, then, this may mean presenting a normative argument, or it may involve presenting psychological, social, economic, or scientific reasons. Whatever the reasons are, however, the party in whose favor the presentment would serve should have the burden to move it forward.

For example, let us say that a judge has to decide whether in the United States the Fourteenth Amendment's equal protection clause prohibits discrimination against gays and lesbians in the military. If we interpret the Fourteenth Amendment to protect all persons who, through no fault of their own, fall into a politically powerless class because of an immutable trait that has made them the objects of historical discrimination, then obviously the Fourteenth Amendment would prohibit the discrimination. On the other hand, if we view the primary purpose of the Fourteenth Amendment as preventing race discrimination, which was a motivating factor in its adoption, the result is less certain. This uncertainty is particularly true, given the Supreme Court's historical deference to military authorities on questions involving the armed forces. In recent years, the Court has expanded the coverage of the amendment beyond the confines of race to include national origin, illegitimacy, and to a lesser extent gender-based discrimination.[17]

What makes the matter complicated is that so much depends on the test the Court applies to determine whether the discrimination violates the Constitution. If the Court applies the "suspect classification" test, it will most likely reach a very different result than if it applies either the "intermediate" or "rationality" tests. The suspect classification test makes it almost impossible for the state to justify discrimination. The state would have to show that the discrimination was necessary to protect a compelling interest that was essential to the well-being of the society and could not be protected by any less stringent means. On the other hand, if the Court applies the intermediate test or, especially, if it applies the rationality test, justification is almost ensured, in the latter instance because the state can almost always find some rational basis for its discrimination.[18] Again, we are back to the question: Should the description of being politically powerless because of an immutable trait that has had a long history of discrimination associated with it be a reason, by itself, for deciding the case in a certain way? Should the fact that when the country adopted the amendment the principal problem was to end all vestiges of slavery influence the court's decision? If so, does this mean courts should not include, within the amendment's coverage, sexual-orientation discrimination? Clearly, the problem is one of substantive interpretation. It is also a problem of generality, since not all theories of political morality are equally general. This example suggests the need for judges to consider sources of law broader than traditional legal materials might provide to fulfill their political responsibility to decide hard cases justly. When they do so, they will be employing a notion of correspondence between their decisions and the sources they are considering. They will be searching in the broader theory for principles of interpretation that can make consistent and just the legal sources they need to rely on to decide the case. In the preceding example, the legal source is the Fourteenth Amendment to the Constitution. Once having found those interpretative principles, they can then rely on them to justify the decision at hand.

One further question should be considered. Throughout this book, I have made use of bright-line distinctions between power/reason, politics/principles, and the like. One may want to question the assumptions that underlie these distinctions and if they are tenable. For example, one might want to say that a measure the legislature enacted was morally justified even though the legislators who voted for it did so for purely political reasons. At stake in situations like these is not how to interpret the result but how to interpret what was done. In other words, is there anything that distinguishes power from reason, politics from principles, such that an interpretation in terms of one of these concepts is somehow better or at least different from an interpretation in terms of the other? That is, could not the same interpretation serve equally well two or more concepts?

Surely, it would seem not in all cases, given that lawyers spend so very much time and resources trying to interpret a case because they think it will produce the result they want. But this, of course, is an empirical answer, and the question is really whether or not anything deeper lies behind it. If one interprets the concepts in terms of their relation to some background framework, which is what we do when we say a particular fact is relevant in a particular case, then distinctions between concepts become tenable. For example, in the distinction between politics and principles, one may appeal to a framework that includes criteria for deciding between the two as a way of choosing which to apply. Such a framework might be morality as opposed to one that maximizes individual self-interest. Notably, Gewirth's appeal to an internal point of view on agency was a way to provide a ground for his supreme principle of morality. Thus the answer to the question of whether we can draw bright-line distinctions depends on the background framework against which we are attempting to make these distinctions and why we should find one framework more useful than another.

Which sources beyond traditional legal sources should a judge consider? Which political moralities are relevant? If the society is nearly just, a judge should consider the prevailing political morality. If the prevailing political morality is inadequate, the court should consider philosophical sources, especially the writings of Alan Gewirth, if they can be interpreted to provide a morally sound natural law approach to resolving very hard cases. Here again I would note that it is not necessary that Gewirth's ethical theory be correct to provide the ultimate-decision approach I seek. His theory, however, seems to be the best candidate for the job. Therefore, I will spend a fair amount of space working it into my system. If some future theory proves more adequate to performing this task, then a future reader will have an analogy from which to draw to incorporate that new theory.

Recall that Gewirth shows how a supreme principle of morality—the PGC—can be derived solely from what an agent qua agent necessarily must admit on pain of contradiction. The agent must first admit, from her own internal conative standpoint, the necessity of freedom and well-being to the performance of any action. Next, the agent must claim rights to freedom and well-being to be consistent with the desire to act. Once this is done, the agent sees that the need for freedom and well-being was the only base upon which she claimed rights. This means that logically any agent who wants to perform any action could have made this same claim. Consequently, the agent is obligated to recognize the similar claims of other agents as well as her own.

What does this mean in a context where a fellow agent wants to carry out an action that conflicts with one's own freedom and well-being? Assuming the parties have not agreed to perform the action, the analysis takes one of two directions. If the right that one agent is asserting conflicts at the same level with the right of another agent, such as when one wants to kill an innocent person, a court can justify, in the name of protecting against transactional inconsistency, removing that inconsistency by punishing the violator. On the other hand, rights sometimes conflict at different levels, such as when a person violates a requirements contract to deliver airline brakes by a certain date because he discovers a defect in the manufacturing process that renders the brakes unsafe. Here a court must consider which right—the right of a person to contract or the right to life—is the more important to the preservation of purposive-fulfillment. The court may also want to consider whether the defect could have been discovered earlier by reasonable inspection, and whether the manufacturer should bear the responsibility for such inspections as a way of ensuring everyone's safety.

I need now to explain how Gewirth's theory fits into our earlier analysis of conceptual frameworks that a judge can appeal to. I have cited Davidson as saying that the truth of sentences is relative to one's language, including its principles of translation and one's beliefs.[19] Thus I must ask how can I hold to the view that the truth of a sentence is relative to one's language writ large and still believe in the *objective* truth of Gewirth's theory? The answer to this question comes from Gewirth himself. It occurs in the context of a discussion of how morals constitute only one modality—one form of discourse (although the ultimate one in setting forth obligations)—inside a broader language scheme. In that form of discourse, one can draw a parallel to what goes on in scientific discourse. There an independent variable, observation, becomes a foundation for what we take the world to be like. Here, the generic features of action provide a similarly independent foundation for determining what our moral rights are.

According to Gewirth:

> Although the practical precepts and behaviors from which my inquiry began also involve many complexities, the resulting concept of action or agency can be given a definition that is kept fixed within the context of the ensuing argument while reflecting the empirical realities upon which it is based. For the kinds of phenomena in question are held to be

sufficiently understood for the purposes of the inquiry, although if the inquiry were of a different sort (such as metaphysical or psychological), its conclusions would be severely limited in modality by the large penumbra of insufficiently understood features of action. . . . The PGC and the moral judgments that follow from it are true in that they correspond to the concept of a rational agent as this is involved in the normative structure of action. For they indicate both what obligations must logically be admitted by every agent, on pain of contradicting himself, and hence what obligations necessarily pertain to every agent. . . .

This correspondence, when more fully developed, indicates a somewhat more complex way in which the PGC and its entailed moral judgments may be held to be true not only analytically but also by virtue of correspondence. . . . The whole of my argument for the PGC, however, has undertaken to establish that the generic features of action provide objective, ineluctable contents for testing the truth or correspondence of moral judgments, parallel to the objectivity and ineluctability of the contents that observable facts provide for testing empirical and scientific propositions. . . . In this way, action or agency provide the objective content or subject matter that deductively tests the truth or correctness of moral judgments.[20]

Gewirth is not claiming some metaphysical truth as a thing independent of the language and beliefs that make up our intersubjective understanding of the world. To the contrary, Gewirth provides an epistemological account for a theory of morality based on what it means to be an agent and to participate in action. So long as we who share this normative conceptual framework believe ourselves to be agents, we must affirm the PGC on pain of contradiction. If this is a limitation on Gewirth's theory, it is a limitation not because of conceptual relativism. There is nothing relative about the concept of action as necessarily implicated in any theory of morality. Therefore, if Gewirth's system does admit of a limitation, it is the limitation that follows any good inquiry: it leaves us open to yet another set of questions, this time regarding theories of action. In this, Gewirth's view is consistent with another feature of the metatheory I have presented, namely, to allow for a separation in our conceptual frameworks to include more than just moral discourse and thus for an enhancement in our understanding of who we are and the world in which we live.

Here one may wish to query the application of Gewirth's system to persons whose normative conceptual framework is different from one's own.

Obviously, if the differences are so vast that there is not even the possibility of common assertions, including use of the concepts of right, duty, good, or having a pro-attitude toward the taking of some action, then Gewirth's theory would not apply. The concept of action in the sense essential to launching the theory would be out of the question, and there would be no metaethical claim that could be asserted. In such a world, there would be no persons. Hence, there would be no moral expectations that the inhabitants of this world would act in any moral way. Even if we as outsiders wanted to treat the inhabitants as we ourselves would want to be treated, we could not in any sense guarantee, except possibly by force or operant conditioning, that they would act as we would wish them to. Of course, in our world the concept of action is not lacking and manifests itself even in very different moral traditions. Consequently, no serious change befalls Gewirth's theory as a result of this objection.

Since I have focused on the descriptive truth of Gewirth's argument, I need to address the prescriptive side. What makes the theory prescriptive? Surely, the "prescriptiveness stems ultimately from the conativeness of the purposive action. Because of this conativeness, agents regard their purposes as good and claim rights to the necessary conditions of their fulfillment. Thus both the rights claims and the correlative 'ought'-judgments have prescriptive force for agents who advocate or endorse the actions to which the 'oughts' are attached."[21] Gewirth is saying here that his argument operates within a conceptual framework that (a) presupposes the internal conative standpoint of an agent and (b) takes action itself to have the normative properties of voluntariness and purposiveness. The inferences to be drawn from such a framework will be very different from what would follow if the agent's advocation or endorsement of her own actions was not presupposed. In that case, there would be no way to bridge the logical gap between an is-statement about action and purposes and the ought-statement about how I should act. Gewirth has not failed in his task to find a supreme principle of morality by not finding a moral ought inside such a purely descriptive framework because inside a purely descriptive framework there are no deontic concepts to be found. That is not to say that one could not describe normative terms in such a framework, only that one could not show them to be prescriptive. The point is similar to Lon Fuller's recognition that H. L. A. Hart had joined issue on the question of the morality of law by admitting, over the positions of previous positivists, that law requires fidelity.[22] With morality, too, we start, if Gewirth is correct, inside a conceptual framework that preserves our own advocacy, at least for what we have a pro-attitude about, be it a moral or not.

Taking this, then, as the starting point, each person can affirm within his own standpoint, as indicated by the quotations, that "if I am a prospective purposive agent, I *must* consider that all other prospective purposive agents ought to refrain from interfering with my freedom and well-being." This follows from the fact that "I view my freedom and well-being as necessary conditions for purposive action, and I view myself as an agent who may want to engage in such action." This follows a line similar to Kant, who said that each person must presuppose his own freedom to offer reasons for choices made within his own standpoint, regardless of whether to a third party those same choices may appear to have outside causes. But this also means "I accept as a valid inference within my own conative standpoint that being a prospective purposive agent is a ground for others not to interfere with my freedom and well-being." Universalizing the former claim, and still staying within my own point of view, I infer that "if another is a prospective purposive agent, then all prospective purposive agents including myself ought to refrain from interfering with the other's freedom and well-being." This follows because agency alone was the sole basis upon which, from the internal point of view, I asserted my rights claim. Thus I ultimately set out strict duties that I regard as applying not only to others but also to myself.

This is a crucial point that some of Gewirth's critics seem to have missed.[23] Such a framework may still appear on the surface to possess an is-ought gap. Rights and duties appear different from other kinds of reasons and causes. But that is because the normative structure is not obvious. Nevertheless, upon careful reflection, one discovers that rights and duties and some kinds of reasons and causes emerge as what is necessary to the possibility of prospective purposive voluntary action. Thus, Gewirth solves the logical problem of how to go from an is-statement to an ought-statement that traditionally had haunted naturalistic approaches such as Aristotle's—that all persons aim at a highest good—and, arguably, Aquinas's—that the universe is purposive.[24] The two latter approaches began from some description of the world or the individual but, even aside from other difficulties because they were outside the internal conative standpoint of the agent, failed to produce a moral ought.[25]

At this point, the reader may ask how a judge should handle philosophical objections to Gewirth's theory. Most philosophical theories, especially most ethical theories, Gewirth's being no exception, have had their share of critics. What is the obligation of a judge confronted by criticisms? Clearly, the judge should consider the objections, no doubt raised by the litigating attorneys, and to the extent that the court finds them persuasive, act accordingly.

Herein lies the real question: If the theory is subject to criticism, what hope is there that a judge's choice will ever be more than ad hoc? The answer relates to the internal perspective of the judge with its underlying pragmatism. As the judge expands the conceptual framework from which the court attempts to resolve the case, more solutions and more questions arise. At some point, the judge will decide that the solutions are decisive of the current problem and the questions unrelated to the issue at hand. For example, if the judge decides the case based on natural law, the interpretation may reflect a level of consistency with the way the judge decided other cases, but the objections may be more related to metaphysical or interpretative points. Here the judge finds, in light of current information, the best theory for deciding the case. This narrowing of the question, then, allows the judge to stop further analysis at the point where a solution seems evident. If this also means that in very hard cases, the judge has to become even stronger than Dworkin's judge Hercules, so be it. Still, it is not in every case that a judge will become a Hercules. More important, a judge will need to recognize the conditions under which to make the transformation. In this, the attorneys will help the judge by the questions they raise in resolving the case. Thus, for every case, there is a sense in which the court's decision, although presumably attempting to do justice, implicates the practice of law as a whole.

From Political Morality to Law

Thus far I have been considering how a judge might go about expanding the court's conceptual framework to decide a very hard case. But what happens if I reverse the process, that is, if I go to particular legal solutions, starting from some broad theory of political morality in general? Here, I take note of a claim made by John McDowell that there is no hard and fast distinction one can draw between internal and external reasons.[26] My claim is that in law, both internal and external reasons have relevance. What constitutes whether a reason is internal or external is determined by the perspective from which the particular legal issue is being approached. If the judge finds that the traditional sources of law provide only conflicting principles or principles that will lead to an unjust result, she has an internal reason, in terms of having a duty to decide the case, for moving to a higher level of analysis. Once having made that jump, however, she will need to rely on the broader principles of interpretation at the higher level to justify a decision. Since justifying a decision means justifying the law being applied, as well as the judge's interpretation of it, the reasons here can be said to be external. This reverse in direction begins when the judge, after exploring the broader framework, comes back to justify the law the court will adopt in terms of that framework. The effect of this shift in direction is to take us out of the judge's internal point of view and to place us in the same external point of view as that of the political philosopher. The only difference is that the judge is probably navigating a shorter course through the different levels of analysis than the political philosopher, who is seeking to justify the whole legal system. Moreover, with the shift in direction from internal to external comes a corresponding change in methodology. The pragmatism needed to justify going from a narrower conceptual framework to a broader one gives way to a deductive methodology as befits a philosophical approach. Let us then consider further the implications of this reverse in the language game we have been playing. Bearing in mind Davidson's contention that it is incoherent to talk about conceptual *schemes* and unschematized content, we begin by returning to the problem of the skeptic. Only now we give up our previous distinction between external (metaphysical) skepticism and internal (interpretative) skepticism. From now on, for our purposes, internal skepticism questions the epistemic move from narrow to broad conceptual frameworks; external skepticism questions the opposite justificatory move.

To restate the external skeptic's position: we cannot discover moral principles objectively in the way we discover physical principles, such as the law of gravity, objectively. The view is that any legal theory that attempts to ground law in a theory of morality, or morality in something broader, cannot provide a determinative basis for legal obligation. Gewirth has argued that a determinative basis for moral principles can be found in a theory of human action that any moral theory must presuppose. Accordingly, if Gewirth is correct, a connection of his theory to the law might also defeat the external skeptic's position with regard to morally justified—duty imposing—legal principles. The manner by which this occurs is analogous to the way traditional natural law theory attempts to defeat the skeptic. There the idea is to join legal theory to a view in the purposive nature of the universe. The major difference is that this new understanding avoids many problems confronted by traditional natural law theory by finding in the normative structure of action a more certain connection to purpose-fulfillment (see chapter 2).[27] The strategy is to show that a similar objective foundation in a theory of human action, as grounds Gewirth's theory of morality, also grounds a theory of just law. After showing this, we can find points of intersection where law and morality coincide and, thus, where the duty to obey law becomes manifest because the law is just. At that juncture, we will see morality as embedded in a justified conception of law as protecting rights or specific duties. Deryck Beyleveld and Roger Brownsword make just this argument.

Following Lon Fuller, Beyleveld and Brownsword advance an ahistorical, abstract understanding of morality, law, and politics, which does not mean they do not admit a historical and social understanding of these phenomena. The difference is that the latter would work for these authors only partially, depending upon how close it resembled what would be instituted by the PGC. They adopt the view that the field of law is essentially "the enterprise of subjecting human conduct to the governance of rules."[28] They further argue "that the *Legal Enterprise* can only be conceived in terms of the employment of moral reason."[29] The argument that these authors label "transcendental essentialism" shows that the category of moral reason is necessary if we are to have empirical knowledge of the law.[30] In broad outlines, their argument goes as follows: "(1) The *Legal Enterprise* and knowledge of it involves action. (2) The concept of an action commits an agent, logically, to the acceptance of a supreme moral principle, the 'PGC.' (3) Phenomena of the *Legal Enterprise* can only be properly characterized by judging their moral statuses in relation to the PGC."[31] Beyleveld and Brownsword are careful to note that even if the objectivist and absolutist character of the PGC were found to be in error, their argument would still hold against the positivist thesis of the separation of law from morality. In that instance, one would construe the PGC as relativist and nonabsolute. Again, this is true only if we understand the legal enterprise as "subjecting human conduct to the governance of rules."

More particularly, Beyleveld and Brownsword's argument begins by noting that persons have "real" interests that can be analyzed in terms of coherence with reciprocity. The latter is where moral interests arise.[32] A problem of social order occurs when personal interests conflict. An essential human nature also exists defined by "the powers, capacities, properties, etc., which we may suppose any human being to have if knowledge of human action is to be possible."[33] Law treated as a solution to the problem of social order presupposes an ideal-typical case that becomes a means for judging whether the environment of rules is morally legitimate. Their argument, in summary:

> (1) The *Legal Enterprise* can only be explained in terms of a particular model which defines it. The model is a constellation of conditions and interests which we may refer to as "the human social condition under a

> problem of social order." This model may be thought of as being bounded, on one side, by a perfectly consensual model in which personal interests and facts of human finitude are absent and, on the other side, by a perfectly coercive model in which moral interests are missing. The perfectly consensual model is incompatible with the nature of the *Legal Enterprise* because this presupposes a problem of social order which is inconceivable without facts of human finitude and personal interests. The purely coercive model is incompatible with the *Legal Enterprise* because the possibility of knowledge of *social* phenomena, and thus of knowledge of phenomena constituting the *Legal Enterprise*, presuppose the possibility of moral interests—specifically interests specified by the PGC. (2) The model of the human social condition under a problem of social order manifests an ideal-typical case in which all interests are idealistically transformed by relations of consistency with the PGC. Only in this case can coherent reasons for action be given. Such reasons are based upon real interests which provide self-sufficient explanations of actions guided by them. In non-ideal-typical cases all real interests are present, but awareness of some real interests or the ability to act on the basis of real interests is missing. In general, departures from the ideal-typical case are to be explained by citing causal mechanisms which explain why essential human nature is not manifest in action. The ideal-typical case, and the ethical ideal which it grounds, is thus a necessary yardstick for ethical evaluation, description, and explanation of activities which constitute the *Legal Enterprise*.[34]

Thus, according to these natural law thinkers, "A legal order is a moral order."[35] This means that all purposive human action and social relationships can be seen in the light of the moral right to enforce legal rules or principle through negative sanctions.

The idea is not too different from what Jürgen Habermas believes is the function of law, provided we interpret the area of general normative agreement to be determined by the PGC. This is evident from William Rehg's interpretation of Habermas's writings:

> Modern law is meant to solve social coordination problems that arise . . . where, on the one hand, societal pluralization has fragmented shared identities and eroded the substantive lifeworld resources for consensus and, on the other, functional demands of material reproduction call for an increasing number of areas in which individuals are left free to pursue

> their own ends according to the dictates of purposive rationality. The solution is to confine the need for agreement to general norms that demarcate and regulate areas of free choice. Hence the dual character of law: on the one hand, legal rights and statutes must provide something like a stable social environment in which persons can form their own identities as members of different traditions and can strategically pursue their own interests as individuals; on the other hand, these laws must issue from a discursive process that makes them rationally acceptable for persons oriented toward reaching an understanding on the basis of validity claims.[36]

"A Law is defined as a rule which there is a moral right to posit for attempted enforcement."[37] This point can thus be analyzed:

> (i) A rule is a statement of a norm. A norm is a prescription of behaviour which is thereby made obligatory, permitted, or authorized (or the converse of these). . . .
> (ii) Any means whatsoever by which attempts may be made to channel behaviour to conform with norms may be considered to be attempts to exert power. . . . Law only exists where it is obligatory to obey rules; and only if negative sanctions may be employed in attempts to enforce rules may conformity be considered to be obligatory. . . .
> (iii) The moral legitimacy of positing rules for attempted enforcement, a moral right to posit such rules, is subject to two principal conditions: (a) the rules must be posited by an authorized source. (b) the norms posited must not require immoral behaviour.[38]

Although the PGC provides a direct means for deciding which rules are optional, obligatory, or prohibited, it cannot decide among the possible optional but incompatible rules which to allow and not to allow. To avoid this problem, the PGC provides rules for delegating authority to persons or bodies that are to decide such questions in a morally satisfactory way.

> (iv) A legal order is to be distinguished from an attempted legal order. A legal order posits laws and its attempt to enforce them are morally legitimate in terms of criteria for act moral rights. An attempted legal order is guided by the ideal that the positing and enforcement of rules ought to be legitimate according to the criteria for act moral rights but may fail in various ways to achieve legitimacy in these terms.[39]

"Variation in the normative content (the laws) of a legal order is consistent with the view that all questions of moral validity are to be decided in relation to the PGC."[40] The source of the variation may be "contingent [factual] circumstances in which the PGC is applied" or "moral optionality which is permitted by the PGC."[41] An example of the former would be the case were we to question whether the PGC protects a right to provide solely for one's own health care according to one's means. Here we would need to know if there is available to society's members sufficient resources to meet basic health care needs. An example of the latter would be a rule determining which side of the street a person should drive upon. There is no moral requirement to drive either on the left or the right. There is a moral requirement to decide the issue to avoid accidents.

"If an attempt to enforce rules is to be morally legitimate then attempted enforcement must be accompanied by a number of other activities or functions: namely, the positing of laws, the determination of law-infractions, the adjudication of guilt or innocence and the application of the law in disputes between individuals."[42] The voluntary choices of individuals or their representatives must be the basis for the positing of laws. By "voluntary" I do not mean to exclude that some choices of law may be required by the PGC if free action among persons occurs. Laws against murder would be one such example. In this sense, laws must serve the common good in the sense of the well-being of everyone. The adjudication of guilt or innocence in a criminal proceeding must ensure due process. Further, the application of the law in civil disputes must be fair and nondiscriminatory. These activities or functions, in effect, define a developed legal system that can make new laws and change old ones. If the legal system is to be morally justified, each of these functions and activities must be justified by the PGC. Together, they must represent all the morally relevant teleological and deontological concerns the PGC stands for in respect to legal institutions.

Finally, as readers will recall from my discussion of the positivists, "legal orders are differentiated according to the types of procedures which are employed for positing rules, and for carrying out other legal functions."[43] These differentiations may encompass the creation of ad hoc or standing procedures for resolving disputes that can be impersonal, when no human agency is involved (for example, competing in a game of chance, such as the drawing of lots), or personal, where a human agency is involved (for example, competing in a game of skill, such as playing chess). In the case where the procedure chosen is personal, we might distinguish between internal-first-person and internal-third-person delegations, between those situations where the agents are just the parties to the dispute following previously agreed-upon rules from the situation where they bring in a third party to decide the dispute, as in naming an arbitrator. In the latter case, the delegation may be diffuse or follow a division of labor, depending on whether there is a need for special training or expertise. If there is such a need, the division of labor may be occasional, part time, or professional, full time. Moreover, in all cases of personal delegations, the power delegated may be direct or indirect, depending on whether there is a power to subdelegate and whether the parties have exercised the power. U.S. federal courts, for example, can delegate some of their functions and responsibilities to trustees, who hold hearings and make factual determinations in cases. These means are possible within the context of rule-governed activities that the PGC would justify.

From the discussion thus far, Beyleveld and Brownsword specify "what law *essentially is*."[44] That specification is as an ontology of orders that provides "the central, focal, ideal-typical case of the Legal Enterprise and its rules."[45] The ontology is a set of categories made up of "positive law" and "nonpositive law," depending on whether there is an actual attempt to exercise morally legitimate power.[46] It also sets forth categories of "ideal law" and "nonideal law," depending on whether there are practical constraints on the possibility of achieving what the PGC requires. Finally, the ontology distinguishes "necessary law" and "optional law," depending on whether the PGC requires a certain exercise of power or merely allows (through delegation) possible exercises.[47] These categories in their various possible combinations apply both at the noninstitutional—informal—and institutional social levels. In the latter application, they include formalized relationships defining public and private associations, governmental institutions, and transnational institutions. The PGC justifies these relationships as more suited to protecting basic rights and prospective purposive action in contexts where impartiality, resource availability, and procedural fairness are necessary.

Here I would note, should there still be any question, that the PGC requires every agent necessarily to admit on pain of contradiction that they have certain rights if they are to do any action for any purpose they regard as good. Those rights are to freedom and well-being. The necessity for this admission does not mean that other agents should not question whether some actions are truly voluntary and purposive. For instance, feminists sometimes question the voluntariness of women who submit to the privacy of a male's bedroom.[48] Marxists question the purposiveness of workers who submit to the exploitation of capitalists. What these persons are saying is that "true" voluntary and purposive behavior may not be involved and that this must be taken into account when deciding whether such behavior ought to be permitted by law.

But the problem with this criticism is that the persons referred to are normal adults who usually believe that their actions are voluntary and purposive. In such circumstances, it is too easy to allow the state, as a coercive body, to interfere with individual human freedom. Surely, the argument made by these thinkers is more compelling when directed to the state to help educate people as to how the influences of roles and the problem of exploitation might affect them. It is also more compelling when based on solid evidence of the individual's will having been overcome. Ultimately, then, it must be up to individuals to decide whether they are really being coerced and when enough is enough. And it is up to the collective to agree or disagree with that decision when, in the context of a lawsuit, damages have to be paid or a prison term has to be imposed. Otherwise, the concept of agency is itself being denied and along with it our individual status as persons who can think and act for ourselves; it begins to sound as if we were under the spell of a Pavlovian bell.

A related argument concerns the PGC's protection of freedom and well-being. Here the question is what must the state respect about me if I, as an individual agent, am to remain an agent, not to have my agency reduced (my nonsubtractive rights denied), and to have my agency enhanced where possible (my additive rights respected). If the PGC protects agency, then it must protect the conditions under which my agency is not only protected but also brought to fruition. Along with life, physical integrity, and mental equilibrium, this means I must be protected in relation to other sorts of serious harms I might incur when being lied to, having my property stolen, or having promises broken. It also means that I am provided with adequate food, health care, and education to continue to develop as an agent, at least where I do not have these resources through no fault of my own and there are no comparable costs to others to whom I or the state may also have duties. How exactly to balance these issues may be a legitimate area of debate among economists, social scientists, and the public at large, but balance them we must. So long as there is an honest controversy over these issues, there is the possibility that the generic rights are being denied.

We often use the word "law" in contexts where we report other people's views about what the laws are, or to refer to different moral theories that may produce different ontologies of law, or simply dogmatically or critically, depending on how open-minded we are.[49] Sometimes our usage reflects different conceptual theories about the nature of law. Other times, it reflects a secondary sense in which we mean to refer to features in common with what we take to be truly law or to specify different ways in which legal phenomena fail to be law.[50] In either case, we should now be inclined to speak of such usages as involving, at most, only partial legality.

Beyleveld and Brownsword clearly have an ontology of preference. They believe in an ontology that finds the only legitimate basis of law, and, therefore, the only basis for law, to be in the exercise of morally legitimate power—natural law.[51] Natural here is understood as the conditions that define voluntary, purposive action. Moreover, the PGC can provide the objective and absolute ethical foundation from a non-first-person external point of view for an ontology capturing the essence of law at the point where one recognizes that he can step outside the dialectically necessary method and assert the PGC assertorically (see chapter 2).

Up to this point, I have not addressed any of the various criticisms leveled at Gewirth's theory,[52] because Gewirth responds to them elsewhere.[53] Moreover, they are not central to providing a metatheory of law that can reconcile Dworkin's internal view with Gewirth's external view. However, one criticism goes directly to the issue of how well-suited Gewirth's theory is as a theory of natural law. Because that issue directly implicates my discussion of real law I shall respond to it.

Relying on the work of Alasdair MacIntyre, Russell Hittinger argues that "Gewirth's theory is a statement of what I have called in another essay 'minimalist natural law.' It conceives of natural principles of justice in terms of the minimal conditions of agency quite apart from religious or philosophical conceptions of a unified end to human action (MacIntyre's second stage), and apart from membership in a tradition of discourse which teaches one how to think about human actions (the third stage)."[54] Hittinger concludes that Gewirth is unable to provide for "the emergence or even the desirability of these institutions which make such a theory a necessity"; "the detailed patterns of practical reasoning that mediate the generic goods (as first principles) and concrete issues, legal contests, etc."; or "how any of us will, in a positive sense, use our freedom."[55] In short, although Gewirth's theory may be valuable to "the problems endemic to modern liberal societies," historical influences also limit its applicability to only those pluralistic political and legal institutions that "require a style of theorizing . . . in which a natural law of rights traces out the bare consensus needed for an *ordo juris*."[56] I shall address each of Hittinger's three criticisms in turn.

The claim that Gewirth's theory is unable to provide for the very institutions that make his theory a necessity confuses a question of intellectual history with one of philosophical evaluation. People do not live in a vacuum and are thus no doubt affected by surrounding social circumstances, influences, and beliefs. How else could one account for Aquinas's natural law position if not for the fact that the people of his day believed that God had purposely constructed the universe? Quite apart from what may have been the sociopsychological cause of Aquinas's thinking is the question of whether his view was correct. That question has to do with the logic of the argument and the evidence that supports it. I have already noted several serious problems with Aquinas's approach. The same is not true of Gewirth.

Although the circumstances of moral thinking in the latter part of the twentieth century may have drawn our attention to the voluntary and purposive nature of individual human actions, nevertheless, it follows independently that human action is the root of morality. Analogously, in this period we have unpacked from the notion of an atom the idea that quarks exist. Presumably, if these particles do exist, they existed at the time of Aristotle. So the question is not what caused Gewirth to discover in action the generic features he found, but whether he was right in what he discovered.

Here we begin with the fact that every moral theory, despite when it was constructed, must be concerned with regulating human behavior. This is how we recognize a moral theory from another sort of theory. Even theories of virtue have this element as a means to the development of certain character goals. Consequently, if Gewirth is correct in revealing voluntariness and purposiveness to be the generic features of human action, the fact that at a particular moment of history sociopsychological forces may have conspired to help him is irrelevant. As for the desirability of rights to freedom and well-being, again, if Gewirth was correct about the starting point, it seems that the rest of his deduction follows straightforwardly.

Hittinger's second problem concerns why only freedom and well-being are the generic features of action. Why not other features, as might define a society that sought to promote particular virtues in the hope of developing in its members a certain character? Gewirth provides the answer directly:

> Consider, for example, the saint or hero who subordinates or even sacrifices his own goods to those of other persons. "I'll go as a hostage instead of you"; "You shall have the last seat in the lifeboat rather than I." Here insofar as the saint and his recipients are prospective purposive agents and he grounds his judgments on this quality, he may be thought to be contradicting himself. . . . But such inconsistency, with its accompanying actions, is surely not immoral; on the contrary, it represents the highest form of supererogatory morality.[57]

On the other hand,

> The saint or hero is not saying that in acting as he does he acts in accord with his recipients' generic rights. It is indeed the case that he does not violate their generic rights and in this sense he acts in accord with them; but he also acts beyond what their rights require of him, which is why his action is supererogatory. . . . The case of the saint or hero is thus different from that where a person can save someone else's life at no risk of his own. . . . His self-sacrifice is an act of grace on his part, but not of strict duty, unlike what is required by the PGC and its derived rules and judgments.[58]

Putting the point another way, there may be a whole host of moral qualities worthy of both protection and encouragement above and beyond freedom and well-being. Protecting and encouraging these "secondary qualities" need not be inconsistent with protecting and promoting freedom and well-being. Indeed, the PGC would require that they not be inconsistent. In the preceding passage, the saint risks his own life not to attack, but to protect the freedom and well-being of her recipients. Since morality primarily involves interpersonal conduct and only secondarily inner personal conduct, this choice by the saint is not inconsistent with the PGC. Even if one believes that the primary point of morality is to make a virtuous person, at some level, the notion of virtue will have to include how well one treats others. Human beings do not live in isolation from their fellows, and morality, by definition, does not concern itself strictly with self-interested action even when the interest is to make oneself a morally better person. Gewirth's theory simply states what the basic constraints must be for any interpersonal theory of morality that might also encourage virtuous behavior: that is, that we are free to help one other, even at the cost of our own lives, provided we do not violate the equivalent rights of others.

Hittinger's third complaint is that Gewirth's approach works only for "a pluralist society that needs above all else to reach guaranteed standards of rule-abidingness."[59] Here again, Hittinger is incorrectly suggesting that Gewirth would try to place some bar on the possibility that human agents could set higher standards for themselves to achieve a personal or social level of fulfillment. The fact that agents may do this, or even be encouraged to do this, does not become entangled in the idea that there are also strict duties behind some character traits one might seek to develop. It just means that in moral psychology, there may be more at stake than merely following rules. According to Gewirth,

> It is one thing to have a duty to try to develop a virtue; it is another to have a duty to act from virtue. Moral virtues are not the same thing as morally right actions; they are deep-seated traits of character whereby persons not only do what is morally right in the sense of obligatory but do it habitually, with knowledge that it is right and because it is right. This "because" refers to the choice and motivation of the agent. In certain cases, from circumstances beyond his control a virtuous person may fail to do what is right; but he at least conscientiously tries. The concept of virtue includes the concept of related action: the courageous person tends to perform courageous actions, the just person just actions, and so forth. The virtue adds to the action not only the dispositional regularity of habitualness but also the "internal" aspects of knowledge, choice, and motive or reason in the sense of ground. Persons can be praised or blamed not only for their actions but also for having or not having relevant motives.[60]

Thus have we now discovered a basis for real law. It is revealed when a judge, after having appealed to a wider conceptual framework of natural law to decide a case, reverses the process and asks why the decision is justified. Never does the judge reach beyond the Davidsonian limit of language and beliefs, but neither is it necessary to do so. The judge has access to a theory of political morality in general as a basis to decide very hard cases. The conception of law as the regulation of social behavior presupposes this theory. The judge can decide very hard cases and still be assured of having a well-grounded rationale in a theory of action that provides a determinative basis for the decision.

CHAPTER SIX

Difficult Cases

Let us now take up the question I asked at the outset of this book: How is a judge to decide a very hard case, a case in which the applicable principles of law are internally inconsistent or challenge the prevailing political morality? Here, "prevailing" is understood to mean a framework of principles and rules that is (or, at least, for a long time has been) thought to be just within a society. The prevailing political morality, of course, may fall into question if the people making up the society are beginning to doubt its values. (Recall that very hard cases differ from hard cases in which a judge merely has no fixed legal rule to apply.) Relying on the metatheory developed in chapter 3, I shall now offer an answer to this question. In doing so, I shall make use of a Gewirthian natural law approach to resolving three very hard cases and a Dworkinian constructivist approach to resolving two hard cases. The choice of approach follows the argument in the metatheory for how a judge should decide difficult cases: by determining the level of abstraction needed and then by acting in accord with the court's institutional political responsibility to do justice. The cases chosen represent ideas that have had significant impact on subsequent constitutional decisions, and, no doubt, will continue to do so. One could find recent cases to fit the paradigm as well.

The U.S. Supreme Court decided these five cases on constitutional grounds. They were each problematic, although for different reasons. The first and third are hard cases; the second, fourth, and fifth are very hard cases. In *Bowers v. Hardwick*,[1] the first case to be taken up, the Court upheld a state sodomy statute that prohibited adult consensual homosexual activity in private. The problem with this case was its inconsistency with earlier privacy cases, which meant it was within the prevailing political morality available to the Court to resolve, though it failed to do so. In the second case, the infamous *Dred Scott v. Sanford*[2] decision, the Court upheld a federal law requiring free states to return escaped slaves back to their masters before the beginning of the Civil War. At the time, the society's political morality on the question of slavery was in a shambles; one segment of the society adamantly opposed slavery, another segment adamantly supported it, and still another wanted only to preserve the Union. The third case, *Roe v. Wade*,[3] first recognized a woman's federal constitutional right to have an abortion. The case was problematic at a higher theoretical level because traditional natural law theory provides no consistent position about the moral status of the unborn, and the theory the Court adopted to decide the case—privacy—presupposed an answer to the personhood question. The fourth case, *Lochner v. New York*,[4] struck down a New York statute that limited the number of hours per week bakers could work. *Lochner* represented the developing libertarian views of the post–Civil War era but later became problematic when the proponents of the New Deal egalitarian policies of Franklin D. Roosevelt refused to accept as just the ad hoc economics of libertarianism. The final case, *Plessy v. Ferguson*,[5] allowed for separation of public facilities based on race, provided roughly equal facilities were made available. *Brown v. Board of Education*[6] effectively overruled *Plessy* on the arguably natural law ground that separate but equal was neither equal nor constitutional.

The choice to focus on U.S. constitutional law cases is related to my own familiarity and to the breadth of their impact on that society's institutions. The points made are general and should apply to the political and legal institutions of any society that seeks to do justice, allowing for morally optional differences in institutional structures. Regardless of how any particular society may divide its institutional functions, provided one of its unassailable goals is to do justice, the principles that govern application of the metatheory will apply in that society. As for the choice of these cases, *Dred Scott*, *Lochner*, and *Plessy* are ideal for natural law analysis; *Hardwick* and *Roe* better fit a constructivist analysis. As for the order of discussion, I attempt to place side by side hard cases against very hard cases to show their related differences in respect to levels of abstraction; I also treat *Hardwick* ahead of *Roe* because the theory of privacy *Hardwick* refused to apply was much more straightforward than it was when applied in *Roe*, where the all-important question concerned the personhood of the unborn fetus. In other words, *Roe* reached the issue of privacy only because the Court judged that the unborn was not a person for purposes of constitutional protection. Otherwise, the order of the cases is chronological.

The reader should not misunderstand the inclusion here of just these cases. The point is not merely to attack or to seek reversal of these previous Court decisions. The adoption of the Thirteenth Amendment ending slavery effectively rendered moot *Dred Scott*. *Hardwick* should be reversed because it unjustly burdens the civil rights of gays and lesbians. It does this by denying them basic privacy protection and by marginalizing them in respect to other issues such as military service, marriage, and adoption. If legislatures can restrict adult consensual homosexual activity under the guise of sodomy statutes, courts are reluctant to afford other protections that address the legal status of gay persons. The legal community today deeply regrets *Lochner*, and it is without precedential value. Finally, *Brown* in effect corrected the injustice of *Plessy*. Therefore, the main reason for looking at these cases, besides their historical significance, is to see how the metatheory I have developed might be used to understand past cases and to resolve interesting and controversial future cases. In this sense, the point is to show an educational connection brought about by a theory that relates law to morality.

Privacy, Sodomy, and Society's Political Morality

In *Bowers v. Hardwick*, the Supreme Court upheld the constitutionality of a Georgia sodomy statute that prohibited same-sex sexual activity between consenting adults even in one's home.[7] The Court's rationale was that the constitutional right to privacy that developed in the line of cases from *Griswold v. Connecticut*[8] (which struck down a Connecticut statute that prohibited married persons from using contraceptives or receiving advice as to their use) to *Roe v. Wade*[9] (which struck down a Texas statute prohibiting abortions) did not cover two adult gay persons choosing to have sex in the privacy of one of their homes. The Court never even reached the issue of whether another right or a compelling state interest outweighed the claimed right to privacy. The Court reasoned that the issue was strictly one of scope or coverage and that the line of cases previously developed protected procreation and marital intimacy. For reasons I have developed in my book *The Right to Privacy*, it is now time for the Court to overturn that decision.[10]

Recapping that earlier book, I presented a general foundation for a constitutional right to privacy based in autonomy. Historically, legal privacy developed separately in the Fourth Amendment, tort, and constitutional areas of the law. Of course, Fourth Amendment privacy is also constitutional. The distinction here is meant to separate the very old—going back to Magna Carta—area of recognized state limitations on the gathering of information of a crime from the modern question of whether the state is limited in which individual liberties it can prohibit. In the Fourth Amendment area, the intersubjective test of having a reasonable expectation that something is private is now the key; in the tort area, it is not being placed in a false light or having embarrassing facts revealed about oneself, not having one's seclusion or solitude invaded, and not having one's likeness used for commercial purposes without one's consent.[11] Legal privacy in the Fourth Amendment and tort areas encompasses primarily the selective disclosure of information in the form of protections on one's home, person, papers, and effects against unwanted intrusions by both the state and other citizens. In contrast, constitutional privacy involves the right to make certain sorts of intimate decisions—to take specific actions such as having an abortion—which the *Hardwick* court tried to limit to marital intimacy and procreative choice. The first question, then, is, on what basis are the courts justified in treating some information, states of affairs, and especially *action* as falling under the rubric privacy?

Surprisingly, an analysis of the cases themselves provides the answer by revealing two features they share in common. First, they involve instances of negative freedom, in the sense of the self-to-be-let-alone. Second, they involve the notion of self-regardingness, in the sense that no one else's interest is involved other than the actor's.[12] Here it might be argued that there are different plausible ways to characterize what these cases stand for and that the way one chooses implicates one's own descriptive and prescriptive worldview. Still, that does not mean that the choice of characterization is ad hoc. To the contrary, if legal privacy has already been recognized by the courts as indicated in many cases, and if the privacy determination in those cases can be justified on the basis of a theory of autonomy, then the fact that one tries to understand exactly what the courts saw or should have seen as the salient privacy aspect of these cases is certainly not arbitrary. It is just a means, and not necessarily the only one, to tease out the answer to when autonomy may be implicated in some future case. Together, the two descriptions give rise to a definition of privacy that both describes self-regarding acts and shows how convention aids recognition of privacy claims to information and states of affairs.[13]

Only the former was at stake in *Hardwick*, and to show how it operates in that case I begin by defining a private act: "An action is self-regarding (private) with respect to a group of other actors if and only if the consequences of the act impinge in the first instance on the basic interests of the actor and not on the interest of the specified class of actors."[14] Built into the definition is the recognition that privacy is a *relational* concept, although it is not *relative* in respect to its meaning. The relational aspect identifies the group membership of the one who is the object of the claim. Thus, a person's sexual activities may be private to certain family members but not private to her physician; whether the same person will come into an inheritance may be private with respect to the physician but not private regarding these same family members.

What prevents the definition from being relative is the specification of what it means for an "act to impinge in the first instance." Clearly, an act can impinge on the interests of another for no other reason than that the other knows the society allows such acts and this causes the person psychological or moral outrage. To prevent this problem from destroying any possibility of there existing private acts, the theory specifies the only circumstance under which an action can impinge in the first instance on the interests of another. It is where the mere description of the action, without the inclusion of any additional facts or causal theories, suggests a conflict. This specification, in turn, requires a corresponding limitation on the word "interest." This is necessary to avoid the possibility that too broad a concept of interest may undo what we have achieved by the restriction in the first instance. Thus, the performance of an action must not impinge the basic interests of freedom and well-being. All other interests are derivative, combining a basic interest with some conception about facts or social conventions.

The basic interest in freedom includes expression, privacy, thought, and worship; in well-being it includes health, physical integrity, and mental equilibrium. Education and marriage are examples of derivative interests. The former is derivative of the basic interest in well-being combined with the factual conception that education will advance one's well-being. The latter is derivative of the basic interest in freedom combined with the social convention of marriage. Notably, when a basic interest conflicts with an action, no privacy exists by definition. But when a derivative interest conflicts with an action, a court must decide whether it is more important to protect privacy or the other interest.

Going back to *Hardwick* and the problem of adult consensual homosexual activity in the home, clearly a privacy interest is involved. There is nothing in the description of the action that on its face impinges on the basic interests of any other person. Thus if privacy is to be limited in such a case, it must be because the state has a more compelling derivative interest to protect than protecting individual privacy. Indeed, it was the Court's failure to recognize just this point, that the concept of privacy encompasses all self-regarding acts, which led it to draw the hasty conclusion that adult consensual homosexual activity in the home was not even within the coverage of the right.

Still, one might want to question why a court should be concerned with protecting private acts at all. Is it not because such acts involve no harm, at least not to any nonconsenting third persons, and the criminal law exists to prevent harm? This is what Joel Feinberg thinks.[15] Of course, not all commentators agree that self-regarding acts are necessarily nonharmful.[16] Moreover, just because private acts fit a definition that is consistent with the general type of cases the courts have previously protected does not mean—except, perhaps, for reasons of consistency or stare decisis—that courts should continue to afford such protection. Here is where autonomy comes in.

If autonomy in the sense of self-rule is a value, presumably those instances of autonomy that involve no conflict with another's basic interests should be an idealization of this value. If the claimed private acts are truly self-regarding, their claim to protection should go undisturbed. To put the point another way, the reasons that would normally incline us to restrict autonomy, though we otherwise value it in order to avoid infringing upon someone's basic interests, are out of place where true instances of privacy are at stake. This raises the further question, given the possibility of derivative interests: How should we deal with a conflict of privacy that involves derivative interests? To answer this question, we need to find a common denominator between privacy and the other interests with which it may conflict.

I have argued that the right to privacy delineates a realm of self-regarding acts, and I have shown how these acts connect to what I mean by autonomy as a value.[17] That same autonomy justification also justifies the creation of democratic institutions and the recognition of many other active rights, besides privacy, such as rights that protect persons in their various activities, including freedom of speech, press, worship, and assembly. It also justifies the state in not treating privacy as the sole or most important value if doing so would harm important derivative interests. Seen in this way, protecting autonomy provides the common denominator for deciding cases in which the state claims a compelling interest to restrict privacy.[18] Incidentally, maximizing autonomy in general provides a common denominator that can resolve privacy conflicts involving other active rights, like freedom of the press, but this leads to another issue unrelated to the present concern.[19] When does the state have a compelling interest?

The state has a compelling interest that overrides individual privacy when the interest it is seeking to protect is more important to the protection of autonomy in general than protecting individual privacy. By more important, I mean that the interest is more essential to protecting self-rule than protecting individual privacy. Preventing a person who carries a contagious disease that is transmitted by an airborne virus from privately going whereever he wants is one example of such a compelling state interest. In this situation, privacy does not drop out of the picture but remains as a background right, regulating just how far the state can go to preserve its interest. Thus, we apply the rule that the maximum intrusion on privacy is the minimum necessary for the state to achieve its interests.[20] The rule protects autonomy against overly broad intrusions on privacy. For instance, in the case of AIDS, where the danger mostly can be alleviated by proper education and the use of condoms, state quarantining of individuals who tested positive for the AIDS virus would be unjustified.

In *Hardwick*, the Court never reached the question of compelling state interest, however, because it misunderstood the coverage of the right. Nevertheless, one might ask, hypothetically, how should the Court have decided this question? Four concerns present themselves as possible candidates for a compelling state interest. Each involves prohibiting sodomy. The first prohibits sodomy to protect the participants against harm, the second to prevent the spread of AIDS and other sexually transmitted diseases, the third to uphold a certain view of public morality, and the fourth to protect the institution of marriage. Since I have responded to each of these issues in detail in *The Right to Privacy*, I shall offer only a cursory response here.[21]

Regarding the first issue, allowing adult consensual homosexual activity in private places, just as allowing adult consensual heterosexual activity, implies no presumption of harm, nor does it prevent the state from taking lesser intrusive actions through the criminal and tort law to protect participants. Second, proper education and the taking of reasonable precautions during sexual activities can prevent the spread of AIDS and other sexually transmitted diseases. Moreover, such approaches avoid the need for extreme curtailments on liberty. Third, when a narrower view of public morality restricts self-regarding acts, it undermines the human freedom that is essential to individual autonomy, for it prevents persons from figuring out for themselves what is in their own interests even when there exists no comparable harm to others. Fourth, coercive measures do not serve the institution of marriage; possibly such measures induce a level of resentment and distrust against the institution among people who would not choose traditional marriage but for lack of other legitimate sexual outlets, feel trapped into doing so.[22]

This brings us to two questions: What is autonomy? Why would a court be justified in treating autonomy as a value? I have been assuming a defined notion of autonomy that carries privacy, but now I shall examine this assumption.

Autonomy means self-rule. At the most basic level, self-rule is manifest by free participation in activities that set their own rules. This is the area where issues of privacy arise when the question is whether one's action intrudes on another's interest within the rules of the given society.[23] At the next level, what might be considered a metaprivacy level, protection of autonomy means that the rules of the activity are not designed to burden unnecessarily the possibility of autonomous action. Here, the main consideration is what protects autonomy in general. Laws prohibiting adult consensual heterosexual or homosexual sodomy are good examples of rules that unnecessarily burden the possibility of autonomous actions. For even when such laws are only sporadically enforced, they promote a background moral climate that allows other forms of discrimination against the people who would participate in these activities.[24] At the highest level, promotion of maximal autonomy adjudicates cases involving conflicts of rights to produce the greatest amount of autonomy for everyone.[25] Though my definition of a private act rides on what I mean by autonomy and is consistent with the case law before *Hardwick*,[26] recognition of the right to privacy is predicated on autonomy being a reason for and an end of democratic institutions.[27] Why is this the case?[28] Political morality provides the answer.

Political morality shows that Western democracy is justified, among other ways, by a principle of self-rule. This principle in turn presupposes a priori that the individual is free to engage in self-regarding—private—acts. It also takes as a reason for and an end of democratic institutions the right of citizens to vote their own interests. This latter right "presupposes that the individual is free to vote" and, more important, "free to discover his or her interests compatible with a like freedom for all."[29] When treated as an end of democratic institutions, this latter right requires the protection of privacy of information and states of affairs a posteriori as a way to discover one's own interests. Moreover, it also ensures protecting private acts, given the psychological tendency of individuals to be chilled in what they do by what others know about it.[30] In this, too, democracy is protected by giving people the private space within which they can figure out their real interests. Thus, "providing for the discovery of one's own interests is the only aspect of autonomy that one must value to formulate a general right to privacy."[31]

In the United States, the Ninth Amendment states: "The enumeration in the Constitution of certain rights, shall not be construed to deny or disparage others retained by the people."[32] Clearly, the principle embodied in the amendment provides a helpful conduit between autonomy as a background political value of the society and the right to privacy as a fundamental constitutional right deserving of governmental protection.[33] Of course, one might want to push the point by asking how a court should decide a case in which the society's political morality is inconsistent in that it is unable to provide a determination of competing values. In that instance, a court would have to look for a more general justification of autonomy based on a still higher level of political morality. Here, a Gewirthian natural law approach, insofar as it is able to resolve conflicts without presupposing an obviously value-laden framework, will be more helpful than the democratic liberalism of a John Rawls. Rawls's view works only up to the point where it can resolve conflicts over autonomy because individual comprehensive doctrines allow for compromise.[34] As Richard Posner has noted, "The values that all reasonable rational people in our society endorse make too thin a gruel to resolve the difficult cases."[35] In contrast, Alan Gewirth's approach starts out only with what it means to be an agent and the rules of inductive and deductive reasoning. Therefore, Gewirth's system can resolve even fundamental ideological conflicts, provided the parties are rational and willing to admit that their views must presuppose both human action and the idea of persons as agents.

In *Hardwick*, the Court erred in failing to guarantee the protection of privacy and the promotion of autonomy to every citizen of the United States regardless of their sexual orientation.[36] This error is particularly noteworthy because a consistent interpretation of the prevailing political morality suggests that the Court should have decided the other way. But it did not.

Instead, the Court in its majority opinion, through Justice Byron White, refused to articulate the political morality that underscored the long line of constitutional privacy cases beginning with *Griswold v. Connecticut:*

> Accepting the decisions in these cases and the above description of them, we think it evident that none of the rights announced in these cases bears any resemblance to the claimed constitutional right of homosexuals to engage in acts of sodomy that is asserted in this case. No connection between family, marriage or procreation on the one hand and homosexual activity on the other has been demonstrated, either by the Court of Appeals or the respondent. Moreover, any claim that these cases stand for the proposition that any kind of private sexual conduct

> between consenting adults is constitutionally insulated from state proscription is unsupportable.[37]

Clearly, Justice White did not see or want to see the inconsistency of the Court's position with that of the cases he was interpreting. *Eisenstadt v. Baird*,[38] which is in this line of cases, held that a state could not prohibit distribution of contraceptives to unmarried persons. *Carey v. Population Services International*[39] held that a state could not criminalize contraceptive sales to minors. *Roe v. Wade*[40] guaranteed a woman's right to an abortion. The Court's majority opinion ignored the possibility that these cases, along with the form of government under which it was operating, might define some underlying political morality, such as the protection of autonomy in general.[41] Instead, the Court treated the cases inconsistently and too superficially as supporting family, marriage, or procreation. The Court did not appear to consider that a better approach to uniting these cases might exist that would also justify democracy in the limited government sense we think of today.

What was really going on in *Hardwick*? Perhaps Chief Justice Warren Burger's concurring opinion captures more of the underlying prejudice that was really at stake in both the majority's opinion and in his concurring opinion than any claim about consistency. In the chief justice's words, "To hold that the act of homosexual sodomy is somehow protected as a fundamental right would be to cast aside a millennia [*sic*] of moral teaching."[42]

Slavery and Natural Law

In a review of Robert M. Cover's book *Justice Accused*, Ronald Dworkin asks why so many antislavery judges decided lawsuits favoring slavery in the years before the American Civil War.[43] The lawsuits arose from a set of enactments adopted by the U.S. Congress in 1793 known as the Fugitive Slave Acts. Under the enactments, runaway slaves "who had escaped to a free state might be arrested by a slave-catcher without a warrant, brought before federal officials, and then returned to [their] masters."[44] Following Cover, Dworkin says that these

> anti-slavery judges suffered not from too much formalism but from too little. They looked not to the technical language [which might have given them some leeway] but to the purpose of the provisions they were

called upon to interpret. They understood the constitutional provision and the Congressional statutes were designed to appease the South and preserve the Union, and they cut through any number of narrowly legalistic and verbal arguments, which would have justified decisions for slaves, to promote that purpose.[45]

According to Dworkin's interpretation of Cover, these judges were legal positivists who saw their institutional role "to advance whatever politics the superior institutions—the Constitutional Convention and the Congress—had set in train, and not to attempt to interfere with these policies no matter how wrong they seemed."[46]

For his part, Dworkin offers a different explanation. The judges had a choice. They could defend the legislative and constitutional policy—the original Constitution recognized slavery[47]—or they could defend human rights. Since the days of John Marshall, the Supreme Court in particular had sought "to protect the rights of individuals" by limiting the "power of the state."[48] Moreover, the public in many states where these judges sat opposed the Fugitive Slave Acts. Nevertheless, the judges sought to promote the constitutional and legislative policy because they "could not easily accept that the judicial branch should be institutionally committed to one side or another of [a national crisis so potentially violent that it might end in war]."[49] Dworkin's proffered solution to the judge's moral dilemma was to follow

> the general principles of justice and fairness that these statutes and rules, taken together, presuppose by way of implicit justification. . . . The general structure of the American Constitution presupposed a conception of individual freedom antagonistic to slavery, a conception of procedural justice that condemned the procedures established by the Fugitive Slave Acts, and a conception of federalism inconsistent with the idea that the State of Massachusetts had no power to supervise the capture of men and women within its territory.[50]

Dworkin, however, says little about how the original Constitution provides a ground for Congress to adopt the Fugitive Slave Acts.[51]

J. L. Mackie has challenged this formulation of Dworkin's internal political morality, sometimes called "the third theory of law," to distinguish it from natural law and positivism. Mackie adopts Dworkin's view of interpreting statutes to provide a coherent fit to the settled law; he then subverts Dworkin's view by using it to reach an immoral result. For instance, Mackie takes exception to Dworkin's claim that the "Fugitive Slave Acts 'left open many questions of procedure, particularly about the power of the free states themselves to impose restrictions on the process in the interests of the alleged slave.'"[52] According to Mackie:

> The judges held that these restrictions were overruled by the federal laws, and this seems to follow from a straightforward interpretation of Article VI of the United States Constitution: "This Constitution and the laws of the United States which shall be made in pursuance thereof . . . shall be the supreme law of the land; and the judges in every State shall be bound thereby, anything in the constitution or laws of the State notwithstanding."[53]

As for any due process challenge to the constitutionality of the acts, Mackie notes that the proceedings the acts established were only preliminary: "The legal issue about the fugitive's status was still to be decided in the state from which he had come, and that, surely, was where witnesses to his identity and status would be available."[54]

Even if the law was unsettled and the judges involved adopted Dworkin's approach, it does not follow that the conclusions they would reach would be any different from the conclusions they did reach. Again, citing Mackie: Dworkin's "rights thesis, like the natural law doctrine that it in some ways resembles, is a two-edged weapon. It is particularly risky for an opponent of slavery and of racial discrimination to appeal to states' rights within a federal system."[55]

Interestingly, both Mackie and Dworkin believe that had the judges relied on natural law they "might have refused to enforce the Fugitive Slave Acts."[56] Mackie contends that "the judges would have held that even if the Acts were settled law in the sense of being unambiguous and regularly enacted statutes, they were not genuine law because they violated principles of justice and natural right which were prior to any manmade system of law."[57] Dworkin says,

> Some lawyers thought that this body of natural law was superior to any positive law, so that the pro-slavery provisions of the Constitution and the Fugitive Slave Acts, which violated the natural rights of man to be free, were invalid as a matter of law.
>
> Others thought that natural law acted, not as a test of positive law in this way, but as a reserve body of law available to fill in the gaps when

> positive law was incomplete or unclear. They agreed that the reserve of natural law required a liberal rather than a pro-slavery interpretation of the unclear constitutional and statutory provisions.[58]

However, is it historically true that everyone who claimed to follow some form of natural law position have been against slavery? Aristotle, for example, thought some people lacked the fullness of deliberative reason and thus were natural slaves.[59] Moreover, the early history of the United States reflects several compromises by natural law/natural rights thinkers, like Thomas Jefferson, who allowed slavery to exist in southern states to create and preserve the nation. To put the point directly,

> It is one thing to claim that an ideal legislator ought to be committed to justice and the public good in his/her acts of legislation. But it may be the case both that human legislators are not unanimous in their moral opinions, and all the more that citizens subject to the law are not completely or at all in agreement with each other or with any of the legislators. . . .
>
> A classic example is provided by the framing of the Constitution of the United States in 1787. The framers found it necessary to compromise on the issue of slavery, and subsequently judges who themselves held slavery to be abhorrent and unjust nevertheless held also that the duties of their constitutional station required them to administer faithfully the laws regarding slavery.[60]

Given that historically even natural law theorists have not been in complete agreement on the question of slavery, what is it that makes the issue today more resolvable from a moral point of view? The answer is that Gewirth has provided us with a better theory from which to work.[61] Though not without its detractors, the theory is nevertheless able to provide a determinative answer to this important question by showing how support for slavery implies a logical contradiction in the concept of agency itself, assuming, of course, that slaves too are agents. But, given that the definition of agency is being able, at least prospectively, to engage in voluntary purposive behavior, there is no reason not to recognize this status as applying to slaves. Consequently,

> It follows that such a rule as (3) "All persons of black ancestry ought to be enslaved" is directly refutable through the PGC. A person who accepts such a rule necessarily contradicts himself. This self-contradiction is not contingent on his also accepting such a judgment as (4) "I, if I should

> turn out to have black ancestry, ought not to be enslaved." Rather, acceptance of (3) by any agent necessarily condemns him to self-contradiction because (3) is inconsistent with (5) "All prospective purposive agents have the generic rights"; and every agent logically must accept (5).[62]

Gewirth's view provides a determinative answer to the question of slavery. Even so, two more questions arise. First, what is the relevance of a theory that made its debut in 1978 to solving a problem that occurred over one hundred years earlier? Second, given that there is much debate among philosophers about how determinative Gewirth's conclusions are, how should a court treat the debate? A third question concerning whether the slave is a person in the relevant sense of being an agent requires a theory of agency. I address this in the context of abortion and will leave it to the reader to draw the parallel to the slave situation.

In response to the first question, we might begin with an analogy. Six hundred years ago, many people, including many who were well-educated, believed that the world was flat; this was the dominant theory of the time. Still, it was not the only theory known. Since the days of the ancient astronomers, the theory had existed that the world might be round. The latter, though not the dominant theory, was consistent with the observation that the hulls of ships sailing past the horizon disappear before the tops of the masts. Moreover, the latter theory was correct, although its final proof had to await the outcome of Magellan's round-the-world voyage. Nevertheless, as the age of exploration continued, beginning with Columbus's voyage to the New World, it became more believable to hold to the view that the world was round and less believable to hold the contrary view.

In the period just before the Civil War, it was reasonable to believe that Africans brought to this country were not naturally set to be slaves. The abolition movement was gaining strength, and one hundred years earlier, the Declaration of Independence had proclaimed, "All men are created equal." Even the provisions in the Constitution allowing slavery were just political compromises to keep northern and southern states together in forming the Union. Of course, none of this provides any definite proof that slavery was wrong, but it does strongly question the legitimacy of the practice. Admittedly, some of the reasons offered against slavery at the time were economic; others were moral. All supported the idea that one needed to move beyond the prevailing political morality to decide the issue. In short, the courts needed a wider conceptual framework in which to view the question, and they had access to natural law theories that could have provided this framework. Their refusal to reach these theories explains why even the people of their day found the decisions to be so unjust.

In response to the second question, a critic should ask whether Gewirth's theory provides a coherent and more satisfactory explanation than any of its competitors as to what moral duties there are. By satisfactory, I mean that the theory should be able to provide conclusions from premises that are consistent with most of our noncontroversial moral intuitions. It does not mean that there is no room for interpretation, or there probably would be no controversy to start with. In appealing to more highly ordered premises we move up the ladder of abstraction to more general moral principles upon which we hope to find common ground. If the theory satisfies this condition, then judges should pay attention to it even if all may not agree. Of course, if the theory proves false, then at most that would be a reason for judges to look elsewhere in deciding this and other very hard cases; it would not be a reason for abandoning the search. But no one has shown Gewirth's theory to be false, and there are good reasons that follow from our general understanding of moral action and agency for thinking it may be true. Consequently, the determination of whether to apply the theory should be based on how well the premises satisfy both our general understanding of moral agency and fit at least our noncontroversial moral intuitions as compared to all other relevant theories.

Abortion and the Internal Point of View

In 1973 the U.S. Supreme Court rendered its most controversial recent decision when it decided *Roe v. Wade*.[63] The case involved the issue of whether a woman had a constitutional privacy right to have an abortion despite a state law prohibiting abortions unless necessary to save the life of the mother. "Abortion" here means the termination of the life and the continued development of the fetus. In *Roe*, the Court, per Justice Harry Blackmun, held that the "right to privacy, whether it be founded in the Fourteenth Amendment's concept of ordered liberty and restrictions upon state action, as we feel it is, or, as the District Court determined, in the Ninth Amendment's reservation of rights to the people, is broad enough to encompass a woman's decision whether or not to terminate her pregnancy."[64] The case remains controversial for several reasons, foremost among them concerning the status of the unborn. Are the unborn to be treated as persons possessing rights, including the right to life, that the courts should be protecting? The answer is not obvious, and there is much debate over the topic.

Traditional natural law theory finds abortion to be immoral, as the Catholic Church's opposition to abortion shows. This follows from Aquinas's idea that the first requirement of all nature is to continue in existence. Not every natural law thinker follows this traditional view, however. Alan Gewirth, for example, offers an important argument for instances when abortion is morally legitimate. Gewirth's argument makes use of the PGC and another principle, the Principle of Proportionality.[65] It provides: "When some quality Q justifies having certain rights R, and the possession of Q varies in degree in the respect that is relevant to Q's justifying the having of R, the degree to which R is had is proportional to or varies with the degree to which Q is had."[66]

According to Gewirth, the PGC and the Principle of Proportionality together point to the conditions that justify abortion by setting out the appropriate boundaries of the mother's generic rights.

> The justifying criteria for having the generic rights is that one is a prospective purposive agent who has purposes he wants to fulfill. When someone is less than a full-fledged prospective agent, his generic rights are proportional to the degree to which he approaches having the generic abilities constitutive of such agency, and the reason for this proportionality is found in the relation between having the rights and having the generic abilities required for acting with a view to purpose-fulfillment. The fetus, of course, lacks the abilities, except in remotely potential form. In addition, it also lacks any purposes of even the most rudimentary sort, because of its lack of any physically separate existence and of even an initial acquisition of memories. Hence its generic rights, by comparison with the rights of the mother, are minimal.[67]

It is important to note exactly what Gewirth means by the generic abilities. He does not mean that one agent might possess more rights to freedom and well-being than another perhaps because the agent has more purposes either through being smarter or more experienced. Such criteria as intelligence or experience would impose additional requirements for the claiming of rights beyond the mere fact that one is a prospective purposive agent. The theory rules out such criteria as overbroad. Although there may be degrees of becoming a prospective purposive agent, there are no degrees of being such an agent. Once one is a prospective purposive agent, one has the rights in full. For Gewirth, then, the abilities that must be present for rights to exist are just the abilities necessary to define one as a prospective purposive agent.

These abilities are voluntariness—controlling one's actions by one's unforced choice with knowledge of relevant circumstances—and purposiveness—having some purposes or goals (the number does not matter) that one wants to fulfill. In prospective purposive agents, these two abilities are present, even when the agents are asleep. In contrast, the fetus is more like the raw materials entering an automobile manufacturing plant. As we would say of these materials that they are not yet automobiles, we would say of the fetus that it is not yet an agent. Again, the situation is different where persons are asleep or in temporary comas; they have the requisite abilities, although they are not being presently exercised. They are like the automobiles that are not being operated or are in need of minor tune-ups or the addition of gasoline to be able to function. In these instances we would not say that the automobiles do not exist, just that they are not currently operating. The fetus does not have the requisite abilities; it lacks no specific part. Its overall development is not yet capable of voluntary purposive action. Consequently, it does not have the same generic rights to freedom and well-being as every other agent does.

Returning to the question of abortion:

> It must also be recognized in accordance with the Principle of Proportionality, that the justification of abortion and hence of abrogating the fetus' generic rights may vary in degree. To begin with, . . . the fetus approaches having the generic rights to the extent to which it approaches having the generic practical abilities and corresponding purposes and desires. Hence, a six-month fetus has the right to well-being to a greater degree than a three-month fetus, and the latter more than a four-week fetus, and so forth, so that there is correspondingly less justification for abortion the greater the approach to maturation.[68]

This situation is analogous to a seventeen-year-old's claim to the school district to be provided a civics lesson before obtaining the age of voting. It is a stronger claim than a similar one made by a sixteen-year-old, a fifteen-year-old, and so on. Furthermore, Gewirth points out that much depends upon the nature of the conflict between the mother's rights and those of the fetus:

> The conflict involves that the mother's generic rights to the use of the abilities required for purpose-fulfillment are threatened by the fetus being carried to term. With regard to well-being the threat may be the mother's

> death, or some diminution of physical or mental health, or lesser but still sizable losses. With regard to freedom, the threat may be a continuation of the kind of severe violence or coercion that occurs when impregnation is due to rape or seduction or other causes beyond the mother's ability to control. In all such cases, abortion is justified regardless of the fetus' stage of development. For the mother, as a purposive agent, already has the generic practical abilities and the purposes to which these are directed, and their being lost, endangered, or attacked for the sake of the fetus would involve that the generic rights of someone who has them in full would be drastically subordinated to a minimal possessor of these rights. . . .
>
> In cases where the threat to the mother's rights is less severe, the justification of abortion is correspondingly less, and the fetus' stage of development becomes a more relevant consideration. Here, however, it is also important to consider the relation between the mother's generic rights and the prospects for the fetus' development of the generic abilities required for purpose-fulfillment. As we have seen, if there is no conflict of rights, then the fetus, because of its human potentialities, has such right to well-being as is required for developing its potentialities for growth toward purpose-fulfillment. But the prospect for fulfilling this right are often meager when the mother's physical, psychological, or social circumstances render her unable or unwilling to give her baby the nurturing care it needs. In such cases the mother's rights to freedom and well-being are threatened and with them also the aforementioned right of the fetus.
>
> Where the prospects of fulfilling the latter right are poor, this fact, together with the fetus' lack of practical abilities and purposes, may also justify abortion.[69]

Such considerations would not even begin to justify infanticide since presumably the newborn would be placed for adoption, given to a relative or friend, or placed in a foster home. More important, it would possess strong rights with no comparable conflict with any rights of the mother.

Gewirth's view of natural law/natural rights, then, would resolve at least some moral questions that underlie court restrictions on the state's power to restrict abortions. Why, then, is there so much controversy? Not everyone in society knows Gewirth's theory, yet alone shares his moral outlook, even though his view on reflection might resolve the issue. More important, given that as one moves to broader levels of analysis one incurs new controversies, a court, if it can consistently decide a case within the prevailing political morality, is bound to do so. In the slavery cases, recall that society's political morality was highly inconsistent, often depending on where one resided, and, even if one resided in a free state, the reasons were not only moral but often economic. Consequently, appeal to a higher level of political morality was both necessary and appropriate if justice was to be done. On the abortion question, however, it is just the higher level of political morality that seems most in dispute.[70] Therefore, if there is a less controversial way—all ways will be controversial—for resolving the problem, a court is obligated to take that route, at least until the deeper solution can attract a wider consensus. After all, courts are supposed to decide cases from the inside out, that is, beginning with the narrowest conceptual framework and expanding only when necessary to avoid inconsistency and to do justice. This approach is necessary to prevent judges from imposing their own idiosyncratic points of view on society. Given, then, that judges are to decide cases from the inside out, how should a court decide the question of state restrictions on abortion? Two approaches present themselves: one procedural, the other interpretative.

On the procedural side, we note that courts deal with questions about abortion in the context of issues of personal privacy. Here, the question is whether abortion is a self-regarding act. To answer this question, we have to know the sense in which we think of an act as self-regarding. As I have already argued,[71] self-regardingness is not affecting another's basic interest in freedom and well-being. A minimal requirement for suggesting that another's interest is involved is the presence of prospective interests in freedom and well-being. In other words, as with Gewirth's view, one would have to show that the fetus is a prospective purposive agent:

> Were the fetus shown to be a person (in the sense of possessing those attributes that would make it an agent), then clearly no claim to privacy between the mother and the fetus would be plausible. The plausibility of the claim, under our privacy definition, depends on being able to describe the action of the mother without describing it as an impingement on the basic interests of the fetus. Abortion, connoting the death of the fetus, prevents the possibility of such a description. Consequently, were the fetus shown to be a person, there would be no problem from the standpoint of privacy . . . with the state restricting abortions.
>
> Still, it may be argued that given the gravity of the possible interest involved, it is wrong to place the burden of proving the fetus is a person on those who would seek to restrict abortions. It should be placed instead on those who would seek to allow choice. Indeed, this argument would

> seem persuasive if it were as plausible to think of the fetus as a person as it is to think of it as not being a person. However, given the many views of what constitutes a person, our intuitions on the issue are not clear. Certainly, if agency is the deciding criterion, there is little reason to think of the unborn (especially at an early stage in the mother's pregnancy) as possessing the requisite voluntariness and purposiveness to be an agent. The unborn does not exhibit voluntary actions since it is living off the mother and is necessarily confined within her. Nor is there any reason to think that at an early stage in the pregnancy the fetus would possess, even remotely, any purposes that could be called its own. . . .
>
> [A]t an early stage in the pregnancy, thinking of the fetus as a person seems largely implausible. Where exactly one should draw the line seems unclear, since there is a range between plausibly believing that the fetus has rights and believing that it does not. Nevertheless, the fact that the line may be difficult to draw does not mean that the boundary does not exist. Indeed, it is with respect to just such boundary questions that those who would seek to limit a woman's right to choose an abortion should bear the burden of proving the fetus is a person.[72]

Otherwise, the point of a cutoff is where the fetus can live outside the womb—"viability." There, no comparable conflict exists between the rights of the woman and those of the fetus to justify abortion.

Ronald Dworkin suggests an alternative, interpretivist approach to how courts should decide questions of state restrictions on abortion. Dworkin claims that the question concerning whether the human fetus is a person "cannot be resolved by legal research or scientific evidence or conceptual analysis."[73]

> The key question in the debate over *Roe v. Wade* is not a metaphysical question about the concept of personhood or a theological question about whether a fetus has a soul, but a legal question about the correct interpretation of the Constitution which in our political system *must* be settled one way or the other judicially, by the Supreme Court, rather than politically. It is the question whether the fetus is a *constitutional* person, that is, a person whose rights and interests must be ranked equally important with those of other people in the scheme of individual rights the Constitution establishes.[74]

According to Dworkin, the answer to this question is that the fetus is not a constitutional person.

> The equal protection clause requires states to extend the protection of their laws against murder and assault equally to all persons, and if fetuses were constitutional persons any state legislation that discriminated against them in that respect, by permitting abortion, would be "suspect," under equal protection principles, and the Supreme Court would have an obligation to review such legislation to determine whether the state's justification for the discrimination was "compelling." . . . I stress this point because it is important to notice that those who urge the Supreme Court to leave the question of abortion to the states, to decide as their politics dictate, have in effect conceded that the fetus is *not* a constitutional person.[75]

Moreover, "[t]he principle that the fetus is not a constitutional person fits better with other parts of our law and also with our sense of how related issues would and should be decided if they arose than the rival principle that it is."[76] As Dworkin also notes,

> Even if the fetus is a human being, it is in a unique situation politically as well as biologically for a reason that could properly be thought sufficient to deny it constitutional status. The state can take action that affects it, in order to protect or advance its interests, only through its mother, and only through means that would necessarily restrict her freedom in ways no man or other woman's freedom could constitutionally be limited: by dictating her diet and other personal and intimate behaviors for example.[77]

On Dworkin's interpretivist view, the fetus is not a constitutional person. Therefore, as a matter of its legal personhood, it has no claims to rights. Does this mean a state has no duty with respect to protecting prenatal life unless there are threats to the life and the health of the mother? Dworkin does not think so. He argues that "the state has a legitimate interest in maintaining a moral environment in which decisions about life or death are taken seriously and treated as matters of moral gravity."[78] The way in which the state can legitimately recognize this interest is to place restrictions on late-stage abortions.[79]

> It is almost a universal conviction that abortion becomes steadily more problematic morally as a fetus develops toward infanthood, as the difference between pregnancy and infancy becomes more a matter of the baby's location than of its development. This widespread conviction seems odd so long as we believe that whether abortion is wrong depends

> on whether a fetus is a person from the moment of conception. But the belief is compelling once we see abortion is wrong, when it is, because it insults the sanctity of human life. The insult to that value is greater when the life destroyed is further advanced—when the creative natural and human investment in it is greater. The rare woman who has had a genuine opportunity to abort early in her pregnancy, when in almost everyone's view the insult is much less, but who decides on abortion only near the end may well be indifferent to the moral and social meaning of her act. Society has a right, if its members so decide, to protect its culture from that kind of indifference, so long as the means it chooses do not infringe the rights of pregnant women to a choice.[80]

Of course, I do not wish to suggest that all serious scholars are on the same side of this issue. R. M. Hare, for example, argues that if we apply the Golden Rule—"Do unto others as you would have them do unto you"—to the question of abortion, we arrive at the conclusion that abortion ought not to be allowed if the fetus would turn out to be someone who would be glad to be alive:

> If we are glad that nobody terminated the pregnancy that resulted in our birth, then we are enjoined not, *ceteris paribus*, to terminate any pregnancy which will result in the birth of a person having a life like ours. . . . The "universalizability" of moral judgments, which is one of the logical bases of the Golden Rule, requires us to make the same moral judgment about qualitatively identical cases, and about cases which are *relevantly* similar. Since no cases in this area are going to be qualitatively *identical*, we shall have to rely on relevant similarity. Without raising a very large topic in moral philosophy, we can perhaps avoid the difficulty by pointing out that the relevant respects here are going to be those about our life which make us glad that we were born. These can be stated in a general enough way to cover all those persons who are, or who are going to be or would be, glad that they were born.[81]

The argument clearly raises a number of questions, including whether there would be any cutoff to when a prebirth entity or even potential entity has a right to be born. For example, does the argument work to end contraception? Would it also end even the rhythm method of contraception? Might there be a claim for egg and sperm to be united in a situation where this was not likely? Hare seems to be willing to admit that contraception may be wrong, at least in cases where the future of the fetus will not be miserable and, possibly, for reasons having to do with the well-being of the mother.[82] Still, one might want to question whether predictions about the fetus's future are even tenable.

A somewhat related theory by Don Marquis argues that abortion is immoral because it prevents the possibility of the preborn from having a valuable future like ours.[83] Here the point is to show "only that abortion is prima facie wrong, not that it is wrong in any and all circumstances."[84] The argument is interesting in that it provides another attempt to unlock the intuition behind why killing is wrong. But, like Hare's view, Marquis's view too raises the problem of where to draw the line. Unlike Hare, Marquis says we draw the line where something, presumably the fertilized egg, is not present. But why there rather than some other place? Marquis attempts to answer this question by noting that it would be difficult, if not impossible, to know which of the millions of sperm will unite with a single ovum. But this does not give an answer to why it is permissible to prevent any uniting at all.[85] Gewirth's system is better on this issue because in discussing what is present he is able to distinguish a prospective purposive agent from a potential agent. Thus, he provides a basis for weighing an actual harm to a full-fledged agent (the mother) against a still speculative harm to a potential agent (the fetus).

I should mention the position taken by Joel Feinberg, which is not an argument against abortion but tells us what the criteria are for justifying abortion in light of our deeper concern to protect human agency. According to Feinberg,

> The characteristics that confer common sense personhood are not arbitrary bases for rights and duties, such as race, sex or species membership; rather they are traits that make sense out of rights and duties and without which these moral attributes would have no point or function. It is because people are conscious; have a sense of their personal identities; have plans, goals, and projects; experience emotions; are liable to pain, anxieties, and frustrations; can reason and bargain, and so on—it is because of these attributes that people have values and interests, desires and expectations of their own, including a stake in their own futures, and a personal well-being of a sort we cannot ascribe to unconscious or nonrational beings. Because of their developed capacities they can assume duties and responsibilities and can have and make claims on one another. Only because of their sense of self, their life plans, their value

hierarchies, and their stakes in their own futures can they be ascribed fundamental rights. There is nothing arbitrary about these linkages.[86]

Feinberg's position does escape the cutoff difficulties associated with the views of Hare and Marquis by having consciousness provide the distinguishing feature for when abortion is permissible. But, in a more fundamental way, Feinberg's view seems to presuppose an agency model. The description of what he takes to be consciousness, in particular having a stake in one's own future, seems to be very close to what Gewirth means by purposiveness. Moreover, the fact that conscious persons can reason and bargain to avoid certain undesirable outcomes suggests voluntariness. Thus I do not see much difference between what Feinberg is asserting here, other than that perhaps he provides more of the psychological background to our moral rights claims, from what Gewirth is saying. Both views focus on the way action and morality go together better than either the views of Hare or Marquis. Feinberg's view comes a little closer to Dworkin's at the point where we consider third-party reactions to abortion. Because a human fetus bears human resemblance, many people are profoundly offended to see it destroyed. Still, the same might be said of desecrating a new corpse. Yet we would not say that the corpse had a right to life. Instead, we would make laws against desecrating corpses.[87] This solution may not carry over to abortion, however, because there the harm to the woman who is forced to carry the fetus to term may outweigh any offense to others.

In deciding whether it is Aquinas, Dworkin, Feinberg, Gewirth, Hare, Marquis, Samar, or anyone else who provides the best approach to the question of abortion, a court should begin its analysis by asking which method offers the most persuasive argument that simultaneously justifies its responsibility to decide cases justly. Moreover, a court should begin its analysis from inside the traditional legal point of view. Only if that point of view proves inadequate (because it cannot provide a consistent set of principles) or unjust (under a broader theory of political morality) may the court move to a wider conceptual framework for deciding the case. Along the way, Dworkin and Samar provide intermediate approaches, while Aquinas, Gewirth, Feinberg, Hare, and Marquis provide alternative natural law positions. The rationale the court ultimately follows may not provide an absolutely certain basis for its decision, but this is acceptable if the interpretation rendered is the best that one can hope for, given the information available. After all, law will sometimes be virtual even when it appears reasonable.

Lochner *and the Court's Failure to Do Justice*

In 1905 the U.S. Supreme Court decided *Lochner v. New York*, a case involving a New York maximum-hour law that limited the number of hours a baker could work to sixty per week.[88] In finding unconstitutional the New York law, the Court ushered in a new era of constitutional libertarian jurisprudence that would last until 1937 and be responsible for striking down many state labor laws attempting to regulate employer/employee relations. In *Lochner*, the Court reached its decision by declaring that the liberty protected by the due process clause of the Fourteenth Amendment included the right to contract in general and the right to buy and sell one's labor power in particular. The decision is interesting because, among other reasons, it represented a change in the Court's previous position that the Civil War amendments created no "new nationalism, libertarianism or egalitarianism beyond the context of race relations."[89] In the earlier *Slaughterhouse Cases*, for example, the Court refused the invitation of white butchers in Louisiana to use the Fourteenth Amendment to strike down a state law that monopolized the slaughterhouse industry.[90] Today, the legal community widely regrets the *Lochner* decision, although not because the Court interpreted the Fourteenth Amendment more broadly than the intent of its drafters.

Bruce Ackerman suggests a reason that today's lawyers still widely regret the decision. According to Ackerman, *Lochner* and its protégés up to 1937 were out of step with decisions after that date. The difference was that until 1937, the Court was unwilling to allow states or the federal government to regulate conditions involving the workplace except where, under the state's police power, it was necessary to protect public morality, minors or wards of the state, or the health and safety of the citizenry. The result of this attitude was that several early pieces of federal New Deal legislation—alleged to reinvigorate the country and put America back to work after the 1929 depression—failed to pass constitutional muster. By 1937, however, a sizable majority of the American public was in disagreement with the Court's position on these issues. As a result, there was an attempt in Congress to pass legislation to increase the size of the Court to twelve members, over the usual nine, which would have allowed Franklin Roosevelt to appoint, or pack, the Court with supporters of his New Deal views. The resulting political controversy that these events brought forward led the Court to reconsider its previously held constitutional position. The Court remained at nine members but with a new constitutional philosophy as to what constituted legitimate state regulation of the economy.

Thus, it happens that the year 1937 spelled the downfall for *Lochner* and the cases that followed it. It was in that year that the Court decided *West Coast Hotel v. Parish*, a case involving a state minimum-wage law for women.[91] In holding the statute constitutional, the Court said, "the exploitation of a class of workers who are in an unequal position with respect to bargaining power and are thus relatively defenseless against the denial of a living wage . . . casts a direct burden for their support on the community. What these workers lose in wages the taxpayers are called upon to pay. . . . The community is not bound to provide what is in effect a subsidy for unconscionable employers."[92] Of historical note, one justice who participated in the *Lochner* hearing but dissented from the majority's opinion seems to have anticipated the direction in which the country was eventually to move. Justice Oliver Wendell Holmes in that noteworthy dissent stated, "I think that the word liberty in the Fourteenth Amendment is perverted when it is held to prevent the natural outcome of a dominant opinion, unless it can be said that a rational and fair man necessarily would admit that the statute proposed would infringe fundamental principles as they have been understood by the traditions of our people and our law."[93]

The change in direction caused by *West Coast Hotel* marked another change. Previously, the Court had held in *Swift v. Tyson* that the federal courts were not bound in diversity cases—cases between citizens of different states—to the common law of the states in which they sat.[94] This decision allowed for the development of the so-called federal common law. Federal common law encouraged laissez-faire and the avoidance of unfavorable state court rulings affecting commerce. According to Cass Sunstein, this period of development came under attack during the depression when the legal community came to see *Swift* as no longer providing either "a neutral or necessarily desirable method of social regulation."[95] It is probably no coincidence that in 1938 *Erie Railroad Co. v. Tompkins*[96] overruled *Swift* professedly on the ground that the Constitution guarantees "state rather than federal regulation of intrastate commerce transactions."[97]

The contemporary fallout from the Court's seemingly radical change in position has led constitutional scholars into a kind of schizophrenic understanding of this period. As Ackerman explains:

> If a modern lawyer seriously entertained the possibility that *Lochner* was legally plausible when it was decided in 1905, the prevailing myth about the New Deal prevents her from treating the holding in the legally detached way she deals with *Dred Scott*. Since the New Deal myth of

> rediscovery tells her that nothing fundamentally new was created in the 1930s, she cannot rid today's Americans of the ghost of *Lochner* in the same way that she deals with *Dred Scott*—by pointing to a subsequent period of constitutional creativity that repudiated the old case's justifying principles. Instead, when it comes to *Lochner*, the official story of our past leads us to narrow our choice to two extreme alternatives [assuming stare decisis]: either *Lochner* was wrong in 1905 and the modern activist state is constitutionally legitimate or it was right and the modern activist state is unconstitutional.[98]

Another approach suggested by Mort Horwitz does not seek to justify the *Lochner* decision but to treat it in terms of politics and to show how events surrounding the decision brought the political reality of the court into the limelight.

> The emergence of industrial society thus meant not only that redistributive motives would inevitably be activated by the reality of an increasingly unequal society. It also meant that the relatively fixed common law categories on which the police power doctrines had been erected would fall apart, as any categorical distinction between health of a worker and the conditions of industrial life became ever more difficult to maintain. As these traditional categories of police power doctrine dissolved, every exercise of the police power could suddenly be seen as disguising redistributive motives, for, indeed, every exercise of the police power had always been capable of being characterized as confiscation or redistribution. Only the common law foundations of police power doctrine had obscured this challenge. By representing the intellectual inquiry as one of deciding whether the challenged regulation was really within the police power and then limiting that category to standard common nuisances, judges traditionally had been able to avoid the charge that they were engaged in the political task of choosing which regulations to approve. But once the problems generated by industrial society undermined the ability of courts to continue to offer traditional definitions of the category of health, safety and morals, the inherently redistributive potential of the police power emerged with a vengeance.[99]

Ackerman's own way of handling the problem is to draw a distinction among three different periods of American history, which he interprets as creating essentially different republics.[100] The first republic arose, according to Ackerman, with the birth of the Constitution and the creation of federalism. It lasted until the period of Reconstruction following the Civil War. At that point a new period began, with the adoption of the Thirteenth, Fourteenth, and Fifteenth Amendments, which Ackerman labels the "middle republic." According to him, this was the period when a libertarian guarantee to all citizens of the rights to own property and to do what they want with their labor power would replace the old federalism of limited federal powers and state's rights. At first the rights applied only in the context of race relations, reflecting the history behind the amendments' adoptions. But over time, the rights became more general as they receded into the background of the American constitutional order. Only a limited police power of the state would confine the later rights, which is what the Court tried to do in *Lochner*. Being afraid that the police power might be used whenever the legislature wanted to redistribute wealth, the Court narrowed the legitimate scope of the power to "an inherent category of things that affected health."[101] Although "'it may be true' that the trade of a baker is more unhealthy than any other occupation, . . . 'there can be no doubt that the trade of a baker, *in and of itself*, is not an unhealthy one to the degree' that would justify regulation."[102] The third republic, which began in 1937, changed again the climate of American constitutional jurisprudence. This time the change did not protect property rights from intrusions by the state. The state could now affect private economic relations for the sake of giving everyone a fair share of, or at least a fair opportunity at, the economic pie. This latter egalitarian or so-called "welfare" period is the one we are in currently.

According to Ackerman, each of these three republics represented a fundamental shift in the way the American people viewed their government. Each involved a constitutional change, although the last one was undertaken without use of the amendment process. The changes brought about were also different in terms of both their pervasiveness and importance to the American public from the more mundane day-to-day changes reflected in the development of legislation. Ackerman calls this "dualism." Through it he can explain the events that hastened in the Court's 1937 constitutional reconsideration without having to appeal to the formality of the constitutional amendment process. He is also able to cure the schizophrenia that today's constitutional scholars experience over the *Lochner* period, for, given the informal way in which the constitutional order was altered beginning in 1937, one is now no longer forced to choose, assuming one believes in stare decisis, between upholding *Lochner* or upholding the New Deal.

Of course, to the Court of the third republic, New Deal legislation meant that it had to reinterpret the second republic's view that the Fourteenth Amendment's equal protection clause guaranteed "to each person" the right "to own private property and contract freely concerning its use."[103] The way in which the Court came to this reinterpretation has been a most interesting topic of modern constitutional jurisprudence, which Ackerman explains. In *U.S. v. Carolene Products Co.*, the Court in 1938 upheld the federal Filled Milk Act that prohibited transportation in interstate commerce of milk, cream, or skimmed milk, but not butter or margarine, that contained fat or oil other than milk fat.[104] The statement was an obvious concession by Congress to the interests of dairy farmers. In the famous footnote four of that case, the Court first proposed reading the Bill of Rights as containing "specific provision[s]," as opposed to a more general restriction on governmental actions. As such, the courts were now to pay attention to the fact that the word "property" appears in the Bill of Rights only twice and the word "contract" not at all. (The right to contract is protected in the original Constitution, no doubt because the framers thought it was too important to await adoption of the Bill of Rights.) The effect of this change was to limit these economic provisions to a role no more significant than other provisions of the Bill of Rights, which concern the establishment of religion and the free exercise thereof, freedom of speech and the press, the right of association and petition, and unreasonable searches and seizures. Moreover, as Ackerman notes, the footnote proposes

> a new area of life as the centerpiece of egalitarian concern. This is the structure of politics. While politics was always important, its significance had been enormously enhanced within the modern activist state. No longer did constitutional principles enshrining limited government and the protection of property constrain the ability of politically dominant groups to reallocate resources in their favor. Instead, politics would be the central strategic forum in the post–New Deal system. If individuals and groups were to protect and further their interests, they would have no choice but to participate actively in the ongoing political life of state and nation.[105]

Ultimately, this amounted to a decision by the Court to change directions without a wholesale abandonment of the principles of the previous period. Property and contract would remain as protected categories but in a much more limited way. Speech, press, worship, association, and criminal procedure would take on more protection. Activist government would become the order of the day, and reasonable regulations would be enforced. Perhaps it was not fortuitous that a precedent case decided just the year before *Carolene Products* anticipated much of this new rhetoric. In *Palko v. Connecticut*, the Court disclaimed the general right to review the acts of other branches of government but stated it would selectively incorporate against the states aspects of the Bill of Rights previously applied only against the federal government.[106] This "incorporation doctrine" held that certain rights such as speech, press, assembly, and so on were "implicit in the concept of ordered liberty" under the Fourteenth Amendment and, thus, applicable against the states because they were "so rooted in the traditions and conscience of our people as to be fundamental."[107]

On first reading, Ackerman's explanation of how the third republic came about makes sense, and it may be historically correct. From a deeper philosophical view, however, the approach raises an unsettling question. As Richard Posner states it, Ackerman

> does not explain *why* we should bestow legitimacy on revolutionary excitement. Suppose that in some future period of economic crisis, akin to that which spawned the New Deal, a Hitler-style demagogue is elected President and persuades Congress to enact plainly unconstitutional statutes sweeping away basic civil liberties. The courts duly invalidate these statutes, but the demagogue is reelected on the crest of a wave of public indignation at judicial obstructionism and within a few years is able to pack the courts with judges who share his views and uphold his laws. The sequence would for Ackerman create a constitutional revolution that the next generation of judges would be *legally* obligated to preserve—even though it entailed their disregarding the written Constitution, which had never been amended—until another constitutional revolution erupted. Why would one want to encourage judges to behave in this way by telling them that otherwise they would be acting lawlessly?[108]

The problem Posner is pointing to is that the normative legitimacy of the Court's 1937 shift toward an activist state cannot be justified on political or historical grounds. This would be true even if a formal amendment process had been involved. Presumably, the same crests of public indignation over judicial obstructionism, which Posner's example raises, could also produce a constitutional amendment that does away with many basic civil liberties. If so, it would be just as wrong. The problem is not with method but with the nature of the alleged justification being offered. Justice requires more than even supermajority rule.

Ronald Dworkin argues that the problem in *Lochner* was not with the Court's subsequent 1937 turnabout; it was *Lochner* itself. Accordingly, his justice Hercules, if faced with the *Lochner* set of facts, would have refused

> to substitute his judgment for that of the legislature when he believed the issue in play is primarily one of policy rather than principle, when the argument is about the best strategies for achieving the overall collective interest through goals like prosperity or the eradication of poverty or the right balance between economy and conservation. He would not have joined the *Lochner* majority, for example, because he would have rejected the principle of liberty the Supreme Court cited in the case as plainly inconsistent with American practice and anyway wrong and would have refused to reexamine the New York legislature's judgment on the issues of policy that then remained.[109]

Dworkin's distinction between policy and principle works to escape from under *Lochner* only if the right to contract, including the right to purchase and sell one's labor power, is a matter of policy and not of principle. Egalitarian liberals believe this, but libertarians, like the majority in *Lochner*, do not. So the choice Dworkin believes Hercules should make seems arbitrary even at the level of the society's current political morality. The problem here is different from the choice of terms and assignment of technical meanings to words like "action" and "agent" in Gewirth's system. What differentiates the two is Gewirth's choice to select, as his starting point, concepts that any theory of morality—egalitarian, libertarian, and so forth—must presuppose. This he does by a combination of both empirical investigation and conceptual analysis. On the empirical side, Gewirth identifies what kinds of moral precepts—oughts, duties, obligations, rights—have been set forth in moral discourses, including various features of human behavior with which these precepts are concerned. This was followed on the conceptual side by an analysis of what was involved in such precepts and the nature of action as circumscribed by them.[110] The lack of specific cultural determinants is the result of allowing only what is logically necessary and not contingent on the revealing of these concepts. If this means Gewirth is invoking a broader ideological framework that presupposes reason and the possibility of human voluntary action, then, as I explained earlier in reference to various postmodern challenges to reason as such, this may be what is necessary if moral discourse is to have any meaning at all. How, then, should we resolve the question of the legitimacy of the *Lochner* position?

Cass Sunstein offers a promising approach:

> The defect of the *Lochner* period can be understood in three different but clearly related ways. In its narrowest form, the problem was the decision to take market ordering under common law standards as the baseline from which to decide constitutional cases. More broadly, the *Lochner* Court regarded consideration of the plight of the disadvantaged as impermissible partisanship; it was insufficiently public or general and not neutral at all.
>
> More broadly still, the Court took as neutral and inviolate a system that was legally constructed and that did not have a strong claim as a matter of justice. One cannot treat as a taking from A to B a decision to transfer resources to which A had no entitlement in the first place. The whole notion of a "taking" depends on a belief in a right to the property in question. Once the common law itself was seen to allocate entitlements and wealth, and the allocation seemed controversial, a decision to generate a new pattern of distribution could not be for that reason impermissible.[111]

Sunstein goes on to argue that the status quo neutrality of pre–New Deal constitutionalism "took as natural and prepolitical systems that in fact were created by law and controversial and indefensible from the standpoint of justice."[112] We do not uncover the mistake in *Lochner* when we analyze the case in terms of the government's role in limiting voluntary choices or even in terms of the Court's commitment to free markets. We uncover the mistake when we analyze the case to reveal the Court's failure to reveal the challenge to justice that accompanied taking the legal/economic status quo as neutral and prepolitical. In effect, the Court's mistake was to limit its analysis of the issues raised in *Lochner* to conform to a view of the Fourteenth Amendment that presupposed "the freedom of master and employé to contract with each other in relation to their employment,"[113] unless certain very narrowly circumscribed limitations applied relating to the police power of the state.

Given that the Court in *Lochner* took property rights as its starting point for the sense of liberty it was concerned about, the question arises of how else the Court might have decided the case. To begin with, the Court should have asked itself why protecting property rights would protect liberty. It should also have asked whether liberty was the only value the Fourteenth Amendment protected. Recall that the amendment also provides guarantees of due process and equal protection, which suggests an egalitarian concern for the well-being of persons in addition to liberty. Considering the *Lochner* statute's obvious concern with the difference in bargaining position between the bakers and their employers, the Court erred by not at least considering whether it would better serve liberty and well-being to side with the bakers in this instance. The Court thus should have questioned what liberty and the other provisions of the Fourteenth Amendment were aiming at. Following Gewirth,

> Social rules are dynamically-instrumentally justified when they serve to remove or at least reduce this inequality of effective rights. In their bearing on the distribution of wealth, the aim of these rules is for the most part meliorative rather than conservative or revolutionary. As such, they fall between two extremes. A certain libertarian extreme would defend the existing distribution of wealth insofar as it has resulted from voluntary or contractual arrangements that ensue on an initial, presumably just acquisition. The other, egalitarian extreme proposes a drastic redistribution to be guided solely by the aim of maximally benefiting those who are least advantaged. The former extreme does not recognize the independent right to well-being, including additive goods, on the part of those whose initial position in life subjects them to serious disadvantages. The latter extreme does not recognize the independent right to freedom as applied in the production of valued commodities and the consequent earning of income. . . .
>
> In contrast to these extremes, the PGC recognizes the claims of both freedom and well-being. The aim of the social rules it justifies dynamically-instrumentally is neither to distribute or redistribute wealth with no regard for contribution or effort nor to maintain the existing distribution unchanged while ignoring the disadvantages that unfavorable economic and social backgrounds impose on persons' capabilities for attaining additive and even basic well-being. Rather, the aim of the PGC's social rules, in their bearing on economic distribution, is the double one of permitting the free exertion of productive effort to recap its rewards and of providing compensating goods to those who are disadvantaged in the ways indicated above.[114]

Gewirth's approach, which recognizes the need to moderate the opposite extreme positions of egalitarian liberalism and libertarianism, was available to the *Lochner* Court. The view that liberty is meaningless unless one can effectively act under it, is not new. The idea of maximizing liberty in general presupposes a mutual concern for well-being as well as for freedom. More important, this idea was implicit in the legislative intent behind the statute the Court was considering. Therefore, the Court's failure honestly to treat this question is where, subsequent history aside, the normative legitimacy of its pre-1937 decisions breaks down. The problem was not simply that the Court's decision misunderstood its own responsibility by not reaching to a higher level of analysis; the problem was that in its interpretation of the law, the Court had an opportunity to do justice and failed to do it.

Plessy, Brown, *and the Social Construction of the "Natural"*

After *Dred Scott*, probably the most vilified Supreme Court decision is *Plessy v. Ferguson*.[115] The case concerned a Louisiana statute that required railroad companies to offer "equal but separate accommodations for the white and colored races."[116] Plessy, who claimed to be seven-eighths Caucasian, was arrested after he refused to vacate a seat in a coach assigned to whites. His case challenged the constitutionality of the statute on grounds that separate facilities denied him the Fourteenth Amendment's guarantee of equal protection of the laws. The Supreme Court disagreed. Writing for a majority of the Court, Justice Henry B. Brown, whose last name ironically would spell the downfall of *Plessy*, stated, "The object of the amendment was undoubtedly to enforce the absolute equality of the two races before the law, but *in the nature of things* it could not have been intended to abolish distinctions based upon color, or to enforce social, as distinguished from political, equality, or a commingling of the two races upon terms unsatisfactory to either."[117]

A key to the opinion is the distinction Justice Brown drew between "'civil' and 'political' equality on the one hand and 'social' equality on the other."[118] Cass Sunstein has noted that the Court was in effect saying that social equalities are prepolitical and not themselves the result of law.[119] As the Court put it, "If the two races are to meet upon terms of social equality, it must be the result of natural affinities, a mutual appreciation of each other's merits, and a voluntary consent of individuals. . . . Legislation is powerless to eradicate racial instincts, or to abolish distinctions based upon physical differences."[120] This view belies the fact that the statute in *Plessy* did not leave the races free to meet voluntarily but mandated forced segregation as a matter of law. Justice Brown's failure to recognize how Louisiana's statute helped to create the very differences the Court was relying on to justify it anticipated a similar mistake the Court made in 1905 regarding the economic status quo in *Lochner*.

A similar response is available to another argument essential to the *Plessy* decision, where the Court stated, "We consider the underlying fallacy of the plaintiff's argument to consist in the assumption that the enforced separation of the two races stamps the colored race with a badge of inferiority. If this is to be so, it is not by reason of anything found in the act, but solely because the colored race choses [*sic*] to put that construction upon it."[121] Like *Lochner, Plessy* reflects a kind of limited natural law thinking. As Sunstein points out, *Plessy* deepened "the claim that the common law of tort, contract, and property could be seen as a kind of natural state. The *Plessy* court took the view one step further. It saw legislation requiring separation as a mere reflection of social customs and practices, rather than as something that helped create these practices."[122] Still, the mention of social customs and practices raises the question of whether what was at stake for the Court was a natural law position at all.

No doubt for the Court and many members of the society, the views expressed in *Plessy* followed a kind of natural law.[123] Perhaps a better reading of the Court's position—better in the sense that, at the time, society's political institutions seemed indifferent to the problem of justice for African Americans—would base it on the prevailing political morality of the society. Dworkin's own writings on *Plessy* are less focused on the then-prevailing political morality of the society. Instead, he concerns himself with the political morality of the society fifty years later when the Court decided *Brown v. Board of Education*.[124]

In *Brown*, the Court had the opportunity to right the damage caused by its earlier decision in *Plessy*. *Brown* involved a challenge to the laws of several states that required separate educational facilities for black and white children.[125] In Richard Posner's view, the challenge went to "whether racial segregation of public facilities in the South was intended or likely to keep blacks in their traditionally subordinate position."[126] Chief Justice Earl Warren, writing for the Court, chose to narrow the issue, however, probably to gain unanimous consent for his opinion, to the consequences of separate but equal education on "the educational attainments and psychological well-being of blacks."[127] This meant bringing in social science data to attest to the effects of segregation on public school children.

> Today, education is perhaps the most important function of state and local governments. Compulsory school attendance laws and the great expenditures for education both demonstrate our recognition of the importance of education to our democratic society. It is required in the performance

> of our most basic public responsibilities, even service in the armed forces. It is the very foundation of good citizenship. Today it is a principal instrument in awakening the child to cultural values, in preparing him for later professional training, and in helping him to adjust normally to his environment. In these days, it is doubtful that any child may reasonably be expected to succeed in life if he is denied the opportunity of an education. Such an opportunity, where the state has undertaken to provide it, is a right which must be made available to all on equal terms.[128]

Warren makes the Court's sole focus the psychological effects of *Plessy*'s "separate but equal" doctrine on public education in contemporary society. Doing so allows him to be able to provide a reason for interpreting the Fourteenth Amendment as more inclusive than its original framers may have intended.

> An additional reason for the inclusive nature of the Amendment's history, with respect to segregated schools is the status of public education at the time. In the South, the movement toward free common schools, supported by general taxation, had not yet taken hold. . . . Even in the North, the conditions of public education did not approximate those existing today. . . . [C]ompulsory school attendance was virtually unknown. As a consequence, it is not surprising that there should be so little history of the Fourteenth Amendment relating to its intended effect on public education.[129]

Bruce Ackerman interprets this language as an attempt to set up a confrontation between *Brown* and Justice Brown. Quoting *Brown*, Ackerman remarks that subsequently "[t]he state, not the children must bear responsibility for the fact that school segregation 'generates a feeling of inferiority as to their status in a way unlikely ever to be undone. . . . Any language in *Plessy v. Ferguson* contrary to this finding is rejected.'"[130] Sunstein describes this confrontation as "so completely" collapsing the world of segregation as to make the very idea of such "a voluntary and law-free sphere of society seem nearly unintelligible."[131] And Dworkin describes it as the likely result of what Justice Hercules would decide if the *Brown* case confronted his court.

> He knows that the congressmen who proposed the Fourteenth Amendment had a different view, which they declared in official legislative history. But . . . , he does not believe that this much matters now. It cannot

> be evidence of any deep and dominant contemporary opinion to which he must refer, as one aspect or dimension of interpretation, for reasons of fairness. The old legislative history is no longer the act of a nation personified declaring some contemporary public purpose. Nor is this the kind of issue in which it is more important that institutional practice be settled than that it be settled in the right way. The Court had already, in earlier cases, given people reason to doubt that established patterns of racial distinction would be protected much longer. The plaintiff schoolchildren are being cheated of what their Constitution, properly interpreted, defines as independent and equal standing in the republic; this is an insult that must be recognized and removed. So if *Plessy* is really precedent against integration, it must be overruled now. Everything conspires toward the same decision. Racially segregated public schools do not treat black children as equals under any competent interpretation of the rights the Fourteenth Amendment deploys in the name of racial equality, and official segregation is therefore unconstitutional.[132]

These commentators recognize the need to unveil the concept of the natural that the *Plessy* Court had taken for granted. For Ackerman and Sunstein, this meant seeing the natural as a social and legal construction. For Dworkin it meant seeing the Court as finally ready—in part because of decisions that arose after *Plessy*—critically to reassess what it had previously done; this was the most telling aspect in the *Brown* decision. Still, these critics are pointing out that the choice of which question to ask controls the answer given. So more important than their differences was the question the *Brown* Court asked: Was racial segregation of the public schools just? Obviously, the political morality of the society would take a long time to begin to answer that question. The subsequent difficulty of society's institutions to desegregate the schools, including busing to achieve racial integration, confirms this.

With *Brown*, the Court asked and answered this question through empirical social science statistics. The data showed that "separate but equal" was not equal, allowing the Court, then, to draw the conclusion that it was unconstitutional.[133] The evidence showed that segregation had created a sense of inferiority and diminished learning among African Americans.[134] Otherwise, the Court's decision was not remarkable either as to its rhetoric or subtlety. Herbert Wechsler, for example, criticized the *Brown* opinion for not providing a neutral principle of sufficient generality upon which the Court could have rendered its decision.[135] Sunstein has objected to this criticism on the ground that the neutrality that Wechsler is talking about "disregards the historical context and unequal backdrop, that is, the system of racial subordination" in this country.[136] Still, the question remains: Was there a more highly ordered moral principle on which the Court could have decided the case?

One answer is to consider the role of agency in the recognition of fundamental rights, as Alan Gewirth describes it. Assume an agent contends

> that he has the generic rights not simply qua prospective purposive agent but only because and insofar as he has certain more specific characteristics that pertain only to some partial group short of all prospective purposive agents. The favored characteristics may be those of belonging to some particular race, religion, nation, or economic class, or they may be such characteristics as a certain high level of intelligence or benevolence or having a certain kind of knowledge or purpose. Hence, the agent would be logically committed through the principle of universality to holding only that the members of this particular group have the generic rights.
>
> To this contention the [Argument from the Sufficiency of Agency] furnishes an adequate reply. Even if the agent were to lack these favored characteristics, he would still hold that he has the generic rights, since it is necessarily true of every agent that he implicitly claims the generic rights for himself on the ground of their necessity for his purposive pursuits. Hence, the sufficient reason for which he claims the rights must abduce simply the characteristic of being a prospective purposive agent, so that he must admit that all other prospective purposive agents also have these rights.[137]

In *Brown*, the social science data that the Court examined clearly showed the impairment of the self-esteem of African-American children attending racially segregated schools when compared to white children. Moreover, the Court noted that everyone would gain from a more diverse student body. Juxtaposing these empirical facts against the Argument from the Sufficiency of Agency, the conclusion follows:

> Each person must refrain from feeling or exhibiting contempt toward others; persons must not be insulted, belittled, or patronized, nor must they be discriminated against on grounds of race, religion, [gender, sexual orientation,] or nationality. Put positively, the duties of such respect require that persons have toward one another an attitude of mutual

> acceptance and toleration, including acquiescence in diversity so long as this falls within the limits set by the PGC's duties regarding basic and nonsubtractive goods.[138]

The claim is that not only do individuals have moral duties. When broadened to take justificatory account of the social role of institutions, including courts, society also has a duty to promote prospective purposive agency and not to tolerate those conditions that prevent persons from achieving their full potential through no fault of their own. In *Brown*, the Court recognized this duty even if it was not eloquent in its reasoning. Its interpretation of the Fourteenth Amendment clearly reflects the importance of education to self-esteem and the corresponding moral duty of the state, when providing educational facilities, to provide those facilities to all citizens on "equal terms."

Brown overrules *Plessy*. In rhetoric, it overrules *Plessy* only to the extent that *Plessy* is inconsistent with *Brown*. In fact, it overrules *Plessy* through the cases that followed *Brown*, which invalidated state laws requiring "the segregation of beaches, golf courses, parks, buses and other noneducational facilities."[139] Yet even with these changes, it was not until after Congress and the executive branch became involved in 1964 that widespread desegregation occurred.[140] If there is a moral here, it is that protecting fundamental rights cannot be left to the exclusive control of any one branch of government no matter how just that branch of government may appear. As Alexander Bickel has noted, "The [U.S. Supreme] Court commands no significant police power of its own" and, therefore, has to rely on the enthusiasm of the executive to carry out its orders; thus on difficult issues such as the segregation cases placed before it, the Court will place itself in the position of engaging in a "continual colloquy with the political institutions, leaving it to them to tell the Court what expedients of accommodation and compromise" they will accept.[141] The courts in other societies may not command any more power than the U.S. Supreme Court and may command less. Nor is the problem solved by an institutional commitment to neutrality. A decision that adopts a morally suspect and potentially harmful concept of neutrality as its worldview cannot resolve any debate over how fundamental rights are applied. Thus, the moral duty to protect human rights by law must be the political responsibility of all agencies and branches of government consigned with the tasks of making, interpreting, and enforcing the law. Moreover, it must be the responsibility of all citizens, qua moral agents, to participate in the political process to ensure that these rights are protected. As prospective purposive agents, all persons have the obligation to ensure the generic rights of their fellows through an institutional process that can best protect generic rights in the long run. This is one of the positive duties the PGC imposes on citizens in a democracy. It follows from the fact that in claiming the basic rights to freedom and well-being, every citizen stands in the same shoes as every other citizen. Thus, in claiming rights for oneself, one must equally claim them for others similarly situated. Where this duty is not followed or followed only half-heartedly, the protection of fundamental rights is in serious question.[142] This is made evident by yet another infamous case that ignored this responsibility, this time regarding civil liberties rather than civil rights. The distinction is the difference between freedom and equality.

In 1944, the Supreme Court decided *Korematsu v. United States*.[143] The case involved a World War II military exclusion order that barred American citizens of Japanese descent from remaining on the West Coast. At the time, the United States, along with many countries, was at war with Japan, Germany, and Italy. The alleged purpose of the order was to protect against espionage and sabotage. Korematsu, a citizen of California and a resident of San Leandro, "was convicted in federal district court for remaining . . . in the state whereof he is a citizen, near the place where he was born, and where all of his life he had lived."[144] There was no question about Korematsu's loyalty, nor was there any evidence that he was other than a law-abiding citizen except for the matter in question. Moreover, it was clear to the Court that the order was directed to "curtail the civil rights of a single racial group."[145] There had been no similar effort to isolate German Americans or Italian Americans, and the Court had no basis for holding that Japanese Americans posed any greater threat to the security of the United States than any other citizen group whose members shared a common ancestry with nations the country was at war with, currently. Indeed, the Court implied as much when it applied a "rigid scrutiny" test to determine the order's legitimacy. Under the test, the state had to show a compelling interest before it could continue the relocation. The nature of this compelling interest, however, seems highly suspect, and the Court's application of it questionably sincere, given that the Court upheld the constitutionality of the exclusion order merely as one of many "hardships [that] are part of war."[146]

The case clearly exposes a particular prejudice against and fear of Japanese Americans that existed at the time. More to the point, it is a case where the Court backs away from its traditional function of constitutional review to affirm a claim to military necessity in a time of great fear and national crisis. And the Court's decision is not explainable in terms of its post–New

Deal willingness to defer to other branches of government on questions of regulation. The case clearly runs contrary to the one area that the Court had stated it would continue to protect, the basic liberty rights provided for in the Bill of Rights.[147] Thus the case is dangerous to civil liberties because fear and a national crisis may breed a sense of paranoia so deep that questionable claims to military or police necessity will be allowed to seduce those very civil liberties that are then most in need of protection.

In 1944 the Court was willing to suspend these basic civil liberties for an entire class of citizens because of a national fear and paranoia, just as it had done a generation before because of a fear of interracial commingling and a mistaken view of the natural. If there is a warning here, it is that the protection of civil liberties is most fragile when left solely to the determination of a political morality that in times of crisis may be misaligned from what it is in times of peace. It is in times of crisis when decisions affecting human rights will need to be made, and even well-intentioned persons may misconstrue their responsibilities about what these decisions ought to be. This suggests that we should not wait until a crisis develops to find out how our institutions will operate. Especially in times of reasonable calm, citizens need to recognize their political responsibility, at least in situations involving difficult cases, to demand from their political and judicial leaders a broad-based moral justification for their actions. This is necessary so that in times of crisis a sense of that responsibility will already be present both in the citizenry and in the institutions themselves.

In sum, society's institutions need tools by which to evaluate their own decisions and those of their fellow institutions. Such tools should include, but are not limited to, the kinds of analyses I have suggested. Education is necessary to discover one's political responsibilities. Character in officeholders helps to ensure the carrying out of responsibilities. Most essential are after-the-fact reviews of their decisions, like in *Brown* and with the critics of *Korematsu*, to discover errors and to avoid making similar mistakes in the future. "It is perfectly true, as philosophers say, that life must be understood backwards. But they forget the other proposition, that it is lived forwards."[148] Only under conditions of ongoing critical reassessment of the way government operates might a reasonable expectation develop that, when in future cases our rights are most in need of protection, our institutions will be up to the task of protecting them.

CHAPTER SEVEN

Legal Education

I engage in the risky business of politics in this chapter by formally stepping into the ring of one of the most serious and divisive debates ever to hit the legal academy, at least in the United States. It is the debate over formalism and foundationalism in legal education, and it is formidable.[1] On the one hand, there is the formalist/foundationalist position. Its goal is to ground every legal decision in some recognized legal doctrine either by what the doctrine says or by what the legislature or Founders may have had in mind when adopting the doctrine. Novel court-created doctrines are not looked upon favorably by holders of this view, especially if the decisions depart from what the original intent had been. Some traditional natural law principles may be accepted, however, provided the law is otherwise unclear and it is reasonable to assume that those who framed the law upheld these doctrines. As a consequence, many less sympathetic thinkers view the formalist/foundationalist position merely as an effort to "preserve" various hierarchial power structures from attacks that are claimed to be flippant, lightheaded, and out of step with the political morality of the society, even though many other scholars have seriously questioned the moral legitimacy of that system.

On the other hand, there is the equally controversial instrumentalist/nonfoundationalist position. That view holds that legal doctrine is devoid of any ultimate rational foundation, that it exists strictly to serve the goals or interests of the dominant power elite at a given time. Thus, the view challenges traditional legal values, rules, principles, hierarchial structures, and even the methods of legal reasoning as serving only the interests of the people who have the greatest power in the society. Both of these views concern the way law is actually taught in law schools, with students playing the role of pawns on a chessboard of different approaches to legal education over which they have little power and even less understanding. Both of these views overstate their cases against the other as if only two positions were possible. Thus, the situation is damaging not because it forces the students to choose between maintaining the status quo or yielding to nihilism but because it fails to afford them any choice other than what these two approaches represent. Indeed, the problem with legal education, as I am describing it, is the implicit, sometimes explicit, assumption that one position must be all right or all wrong with nothing in between. It is the politics in the way the views are presented rather than the politics professors may want to affect that is the most challenging aspect of this problem on both theoretical and pedagogical grounds.

Theoretically, the two views do not allow for an understanding of the deep normative structure that lies behind legal decisionmaking. I have argued that this structure is presented in a metatheory that consists of a hierarchy of consecutively wider conceptual frameworks. Such a metatheory allows at every stage of legal decisionmaking, legislative or judicial, an inquiry into the legitimacy of the decisions made at all prior stages. But it also allows that sometimes we will not reach the highest or any particular intermediate stage because no issue is present. Even if we did reach that highest stage, where I have suggested Alan Gewirth's natural law/natural rights system resides, there is the cutoff to coherence, as there is nowhere else to go. Still, even with these restrictions built in, there would remain a far greater understanding of legal decisionmaking in adopting this approach than that which the two views would permit. Pedagogically, allowing students to look for the middle ground between the status quo and nihilism helps them to discover for themselves what they really believe about the legal system's legitimacy, about the legitimacy of particular laws, and about the political structures that govern the society as a whole. Not to allow this process to occur is to do more than evade an issue that John Stuart Mill so eloquently referred to when he described the role of a free marketplace of ideas in the search for truth.[2] It is also to suggest in an insidious way the idea that truth is always a matter of choice between opposites, even when the issue is not one of logical bifurcation.

Beyond these considerations there are also the harms, both moral and intellectual, that accompany a too-narrow view of law. On the moral side, society as a whole suffers whenever mere preservation of a particular hierarchy or service to a favored group is allowed to dominate all responsibilities or duties to other people, including those with whom we may sometimes disagree. Those responsibilities and duties cannot be adequately confined to some conditioned response imposed on us by law professors, regardless of political bias. But neither are they to be ignored because the system provides no just solution for them. On the intellectual side, law students, the legal profession, and society suffer if, as a result of this process, they come away thinking that nothing is true or false, right or wrong. All judgments are equally valid, no matter what their basis in the evidence. All behavior is acceptable if it supports a favored position or unacceptable merely because there exists some force in society that prevents us from engaging in it. In short, all becomes politics, including our occasional benighted altruistic concerns.

If the situation that I have described exists and is as influential as I have made it out to be, at least potentially, then the problem of what to do about law school education would seem to be the problem of holding too narrow an understanding of what law and legal education should be about. Even if the difficulty is more benign than what I am suggesting here, it is certainly important enough to pay attention to. For the sake of the education of the next generation of lawyers, judges, legislators, academics, and others who may seek a legal education, it is necessary to ensure that what they are taught maximizes rather than limits their understanding of the nature of law. If there is the possibility of an approach to law that is not confined to having to choose between preserving the status quo on the one side or denying all objectivity on the other, then there is an improvement. Such an approach will presumably adopt the best of both worlds, leaving behind the worst.

A Brief Word About Terminology

I shall be using "traditionalism" and "legal constructivism" to refer to two distinct factions that exist in various American law schools and, presumably, in other places as well. The factions are identified not by their substantive political opinions, although often the traditionalists are on the political right and constructivists are on the political left. Rather, the factions are identified according to whether they are rigidly formalist and naively foundationalist or instrumentalist and nonfoundationalist.

The traditionalists follow a theory of judicial decisionmaking that generally allows them to decide cases under some established category, regardless of whether the underlying value assumptions are still thought legitimate.[3] They also tend to follow the method of legal education begun by Christopher Columbus Langdell at the Harvard Law School in 1870 in which the case method was first introduced into legal education.[4] The idea behind that method was to find within each case the foundational principle or rule that the court relied upon to decide it. Once that principle or rule was found, it could be used to decide other cases and to predict what courts would do in the future. Followers of this view include natural law/natural rights traditionalists such as John Finnis and some positivists/majoritarians such as Robert Bork. The legal constructivists take the opposite stand. They adopt theories that suggest that some legal concepts may have outlived their usefulness and apply those theories to case law. And they view supposedly neutral rules and principles to favor individuals with greater social or economic power. Legal realists, critical legal studies followers, one-dimensional feminists, and critical race theorists are examples of this view. These latter groups are outgrowths of the legal realist movement and, in particular, of Oliver Wendell Holmes's influential *Common Law*.[5]

There is an inevitable artificiality in drawing such a tight distinction. Not every law professor fits on one side or the other. My purpose in drawing this distinction, then, is just to define the extremes and not to suggest that everyone need fall in one or the other category. Nor do I mean to suggest that one can decide which category a person falls into merely by knowing his substantive political views on particular legal doctrines such as the First Amendment or privacy or even what kinds of courses he teaches. Less to either extreme but still inside this dichotomy are the views of such scholars as Richard Posner, Cass Sunstein, myself, and a number of others. Still, the value of drawing a tight distinction is that it allows us to fit a potentially wide range of theories, including the metatheory I have been urging, within a spectrum of current views on legal education. Thus, my position can now be seen as one where formalist concerns yield to instrumental concerns until one reaches the appropriate level of abstraction. At that point, an objective (in my sense, intersubjective) foundation exists for decisions that are to be made at the earlier level. Put another way, grounding law in a hierarchy of normative considerations terminating only in rational purposive action while also defending reason against poststructuralist attacks suggests methodological conservatism and epistemic foundationalism. On the other hand, challenging the received political morality when it recognizes rights whose only or seemingly primary effect is to preserve the status quo makes the view substantively liberal and, at least in a limited way, instrumental. But this should become clearer once I illustrate more particularly what I mean by traditionalism and legal constructivism and, then, compare it to my own vision.

Traditionalism

I shall deal with two prominent conservative legal thinkers, Robert Bork, a kind of majoritarian/positivist, and John Finnis, a natural law/natural rights thinker. My reason for focusing on these two persons and, in particular, treating them against a backdrop of gay rights issues is to show how having an unexamined position on a set of controversial topics likely to affect people's lives is intellectually unhealthy and morally dangerous. More generally, it is to show how too rigid a formalism or too naive a foundationalism often means that justice will not be given by the legal system to people who most need it. Since some law courses teach formalism and foundationalism under the guise of such doctrines as original intent and strict constructionism, I see this issue as directly related to a critique of current legal education. This point is of course generalizable beyond gay issues to other matters, some of which I have already discussed, and may even apply to other, less controversial, political views. And it is not just a criticism of the right. Moderates and liberals too will often show a lack of appreciation for questioning their deep assumptions about law, political morality, and society's institutions in contexts where these assumptions are at stake. This is particularly true when the left adopts the all-too-easy approach of saying everything is a social/legal construction.

RIGID FORMALISM

I begin with a discussion from a recent book by Robert Bork, treating it under the heading of traditionalism to illustrate how a search for an original intention to a constitutional text or a legislative enactment—as is sometimes taught in law schools—can be quite limiting when it is the only method taught, even though it may possess the pretense of an objectivist bent. More particularly, in *Slouching Towards Gomorrah: Modern Liberalism and American Decline*,[6] Bork disdains much about current American political institutions and especially the U.S. Supreme Court, largely because the Court has not followed this approach. Bork's position is that the Supreme Court today caters to a left-wing intellectual elite from whom the justices gain respectability in the same way that the Court at the turn of the century catered to business persons.[7] Bork's solution is to adopt a constitutional amendment that would allow the Congress to overturn Supreme Court decisions when they seem out of touch with the mainstream political ideology of the society.[8] In particular, Bork wants to undo the Court's efforts in securing individual rights protections in the areas of sexuality, rap lyrics, and pornography—by which he means sex displays rather than, as in the feminist view, attacks on or subordination of women—because he sees them as hedonistic.[9] He also wants to attack the Court's previous attempts to secure social and economic equality through affirmative action, which he sees as undemocratic.[10]

No doubt these issues raise troubling and difficult questions for balancing individualism and the social welfare, especially when our conceptions of these ideas are set out within different ideological frameworks. No doubt it would be beneficial for the political branches, the legislature and the executive, to address some of these difficulties, provided they could do it in more than a benign, compromising manner and provided they would simply not reaffirm the dominant ideology of the moment. But exactly how this could come about, given the inherent political nature of these institutions, is difficult to imagine. For example, should different views about these concerns be addressed through education, censorship, or more discussion? This in itself is a matter of much debate. These debates do not occur in more popular settings, in part, because the distribution of power in America often reflects itself in a status quo ideology that has little or no reason to examine its own assumptions. It thus does not encourage deeper levels of reflection, which explains why mainstream America may not be sympathetic to some issues that so-called left-wing intellectuals seem concerned about or that the right calls to our attention.

In this regard, intellectuals, the theater community, Hollywood (when it is not solely out for the buck), and the mainstream media may provide a valuable democratic forum in which to counter our lack of self-conscious awareness on these issues. The recent movie *Dead Man Walking*[11] and the relatively recent film *Long Time Companion*[12] exemplify two efforts in which the motion picture industry did a good job in this respect. Moreover, these issues do not always get the attention they deserve because people wear a multiple number of hats—parent, lover, worker, citizen, and so on—in their daily lives and as a consequence may be paying inadequate attention to their equally important role as citizens. When that happens and, especially, when good arguments are present to suggest that fundamental rights of individual liberty and social equality are involved, justice requires that something be done.

In American society we provide the courts with the power to decide these issues subject to certain controls by the other branches of government or constitutional amendment by the people. The courts are subject to majoritarian controls not only by the possibility of the Congress changing the number of judges and justices who sit on the Supreme Court (packing) but by the Congress determining the appellate jurisdiction of that Court and the salaries of all federal judges.[13] An institution with these safeguards of moderation may be ideally situated to put some brakes on the ideological bias and prejudice of the political branches that would otherwise have no limitations in American political life. Arguably, this effort to control the ultimate power of the courts would make unnecessary and unbalanced Bork's suggestion of giving Congress the power to overrule the courts, including the Supreme Court. At the same time, allowing the courts to moderate the influence of passive majoritarian tyranny is as much at the foundation of the idea of judicial review as the desire to control active majoritarian tyranny is at the foundation of the separation of powers doctrine.[14] What is unfortunate about rigid formalists such as Bork is that their very rigidity does not allow them to appreciate how these delicate balances can serve important democratic ends. The Supreme Court's decision in *Romer v. Evans*,[15] and Bork's criticisms of it, illustrate what I have in mind.

In that case, the Court overturned a Colorado state constitutional amendment that would have prohibited local municipalities and the state legislature from giving gay or lesbian persons quota preferences or protected status from sexual orientation discrimination on the basis that it violated the Fourteenth Amendment guarantee to equal protection of laws.[16] Prior to the case coming before the Court, the cities of Aspen, Boulder, and Denver passed nondiscrimination ordinances, and other municipalities were believed likely to follow suit. The state of Colorado sought to prevent this from happening and to reverse what had happened by passing a state constitutional amendment that made such enactments illegal. The Supreme Court's rationale in striking down the Colorado amendment was that passage of the provision had been motivated by "animus" and that the persons affected would be unable to do anything about it unless they could win statewide elections. Gays, lesbians, and bisexuals are sometimes effective in preventing discrimination at the local level. With that avenue closed to them, the Court reasoned, gays, lesbians, and bisexuals were being denied true equal protection of the laws as guaranteed to everyone under the Fourteenth Amendment. The decision meant that the state and its municipalities were again free to pass nondiscrimination legislation if they thought it appropriate to do so. According to Bork, this decision was wrong, even though it would not require the state or its municipalities to do anything, because the state had a basis in morality for passage of the amendment and nothing in the federal Constitution or in the Fourteenth Amendment prevents this action by the state:

> There is no logical or constitutional foundation for the majority's decision in *Romer v. Evans*. The decision is an unsupported victory for homosexual activists, with whom the Court evidently sympathizes. As Justice Scalia said in dissent, the Colorado constitutional provision was merely a "rather modest attempt by seemingly tolerant Coloradans to preserve traditional sexual mores through the use of laws."[17]

Bork fails to see how much his own thinking is based on unjustified assumptions about the rule of law, constitutional theory, political morality, and politics—his own ideological commitments. This is made evident when one looks carefully at exactly what the Court said in *Romer.* "It is not within our constitutional tradition to enact laws of this sort," that is, laws that place heavy barriers in the way of persons who seek the assistance of government. Was the Court here really operating illegitimately, or was it coming to grips with the essence of its legitimacy, at least with respect to this problem? How should we interpret the Court's statement here? Is there not an issue of constitutional doctrine or moral theory to be fleshed out when government seeks to shut itself off from the needs of a group of its own citizens? Should not the responsibility of government be to keep itself available to respond to the needs of all citizens? Even when such availability is restricted, as it is, for instance, when the First Amendment restricts government's power to regulate speech, is not that to ensure among other things the protection of democracy and the search for truth?[18] Is Bork right in the way he characterizes the issue here? How about the question of morality? What should courts consider with respect to this question? Bork and Scalia suggest that it is a legitimate governmental purpose "to preserve traditional sexual mores." But why should this be so, especially where the activity is privately performed between consenting adults and society is engaged in a debate over whether these activities are immoral?[19] Even if Bork believes judges should not play the role of legislators, it would seem he should provide some deeper moral reason for his position, particularly when such a fundamental right as the First Amendment right of petition is being narrowed.[20]

As for the question of politics, Bork's argument assumes contradictory positions. On the one hand, he supports Scalia's dissent, but Scalia's dissent states, somewhat questionably, that "because those who engage in homosexual conduct tend to reside in disproportionate numbers in certain communities, . . . have high disposable income, . . . and of course care about homosexual rights issues much more ardently than the public at large, they possess political power much greater than their numbers, both locally and statewide."[21] On the other hand, Bork is willing to entertain that gays may not possess enough power to change the Colorado constitution; indeed, that is his whole reason for saying that the majority of Coloradans need not have to give in to these activists.[22] Thus it would seem, relying on Bork's approach, that if a government wanted to diminish the influence of a group of its citizens, one legal way to do so would be to offset their ability to gather public support by widening the audience to whom they must appeal. This, for Bork, would seem to be a legitimate mark of constitutional majoritarianism. Yet he offers no principle, including a principle of majority rule, for why this should be the case. It seems to be a matter of wanting one's own side to win. If Bork's position is that the Constitution recognizes states to have authority over municipalities, then he needs to state the theoretical grounds for that recognition so that one can determine whether they apply in a context where the actions of the state are effectively cutting off the voice of a significant segment of the community. This is particularly problematic in a democracy since presumably allowing small groups to influence narrow parts of society broadens rather than narrows citizen participation in government without corresponding harm to wider interests. If the claim is that wider interests are harmed when morality is denied—like allowing slavery in a new territory—then the claim needs to be supported by moral arguments rather than moral biases, which, given the background autonomy principles that justify democracy, are unlikely to succeed (see chapter 6).

I do not want to overplay the influence of Bork on traditionalism, but his refusal to examine his own positions critically comes up repeatedly. (Yet he is not alone in this tradition in his refusal.) In another passage, Bork discusses the federal government's response to a Hawaii lawsuit that may require the state of Hawaii to recognize same-sex marriages under its state constitution. Bork's concern is that other states might then be forced, under the "full faith and credit" clause of the federal Constitution, to grant legal recognition to same-sex marriages entered into in Hawaii. In *Baehr v. Levin*,[23] the Supreme Court of Hawaii held that the state constitution's equal protection guarantee would not permit restricting marriage to a man and a woman without the state's first showing a compelling interest. Assuming the state fails to do this, as it now appears likely, it will be reasonable to expect that other states will be asked to recognize Hawaii's same-sex marriages under Article 4 of the federal Constitution, which requires each state to give "full faith and credit" to the laws and judicial decisions of another state.[24] The second sentence of that provision, however, states that "Congress may by general laws proscribe the Manner in which such Acts . . . shall be proved, and the Effect thereof."[25] Bork has suggested that one approach to offsetting the full faith and credit requirement in this context would be for the federal government to enact—which indeed it now has enacted—the Defense of Marriage Act (DOMA).[26] That act provides that no state or the federal government will be bound by a Hawaii same-sex marriage for purposes of entitlements or recognition. Bork has no problem with DOMA's attempt to undermine the impact of Hawaii's potential action on other states' laws because he believes that such legislation would protect the family as the basic unit of society.[27] This view, even more than the fact that most Americans have not accepted same-sex marriage, seems to be at the core of his concerns. The legal and personal problems that gays and lesbians encounter when they are denied what in the heterosexual context the Supreme Court has held to be a fundamental right,[28] including the right to make health and property decisions for a seriously ill spouse, are not considered. Instead, Bork cites *Bowers v. Hardwick*,[29] the Supreme Court decision that upheld, as no violation of privacy, a Georgia sodomy statute that made adult consensual homosexual activity in the home a criminal offense. Chiding the dissent in that case, Bork disdains the possibility that rights may be protected "not because they contribute in some direct and material way to the public welfare, but because they form so central a part of an individual's life."[30] Bork fails to show, of course, why a male/female married couple should be the basic unit of society or why same-sex marriages cannot contribute in a direct and material way to the public welfare. Surely, same-sex marriages could provide an additional place for adoption of unwanted children, a chance for the personal and emotional growth of the participants, and an opportunity for stereotypes and misconceptions to be exposed. All in all, Bork fails throughout his book to inquire into the meanings and sources of his own ideological assumptions. Such failure shows a questionable lack of concern, but it is particularly outrageous when those very assumptions underlie the problems one is addressing and cause other people to suffer.

In short, Bork wants it both ways. He wants the state to overrule municipalities when it comports with his ideological assumptions but not to be overruled when he disagrees with another state's or federal principles. Absent is the theoretical ground for why this should be so. In my system, that ground is provided when the courts appeal to the appropriate framework capable of resolving the issues they face.

NAIVE FOUNDATIONALISM

Another legal scholar, John Finnis, claims to start from first principles, but it is unclear that he ever examines the underlying ideology behind those principles. Accordingly, Finnis's work in the natural law area seems to ignore rather than confront the very serious objections that have been raised against this kind of theory. For example, in "Law, Morality and 'Sexual Orientation,'" Finnis draws his readers' attention to criticize the "standard European model" for regulating sexual behavior and states that under it, "the state is not authorized to and does not, make it a punishable offense for adult consenting persons to engage in private, in immoral sexual acts (for example, homosexual acts)."[31] Notice immediately the connection of immorality to all homosexual acts without so much as a footnote or an argument for why this should be so. Granted, he may discuss this issue elsewhere, and later in the essay he claims these views belong to Plato, Aristotle, Kant, and the Judeo-Christian tradition. Still, one wonders if his position does not beg a number of questions about whether a homosexual orientation is a choice and whether morality should prohibit the behavior regardless.

The preceding passage suggests a particular reliance on dogma when it serves Finnis's position. But in the very next sentence, we find the opposite dogma. "On the other hand, states do have the authority to discourage, say, homosexual conduct and 'orientation' (i.e., overtly manifested active willingness to engage in homosexual conduct)."[32] What is it that allows flagging with quotation marks the word "orientation" in the second statement quoted and in the title of the essay but not the word "immoral" in the first? The connotations of the word "orientation" as focusing on status over action are also out of step with his moral position on this matter. The failure to examine the underlying ideology of his own first principles is sharply illustrated when he states:

> Copulation of humans with animals is repudiated because it treats human sexual activity and satisfaction as something appropriately sought in a manner as divorced from the actualizing of an intelligent common good as is instinctive coupling of beasts—and so treats human bodily life, in one of its most intense activities, as appropriately lived as merely animal. The deliberative genital coupling of persons of the same sex is repudiated for a very similar reason. It is not simply that it is sterile and disposes the participants to an abdication of responsibility for the future of humankind. Nor is it simply that it cannot *really* actualize the mutual devotion that some homosexual persons hope to manifest and

> experience by it, and that it harms the personalities of its participants by its dis-integrative manipulation of different parts of their personal reality. It is also that it treats human sexual capacities in a way which is deeply hostile to the self-understanding of those members of the community who are willing to commit themselves to real marriage in the understanding that its sexual joys are not mere instruments or accomplishments to, or mere compensations for, the accomplishment of marriage's responsibilities, but rather enable the spouses to *actualize and experience* their intelligent commitment to share in those responsibilities, in that genuine self-giving.[33]

One would want to ask a number of questions concerning gay and lesbian people who live together as couples, raise families together, or care for each other until death. Yet Finnis does not explore these matters, at least not in this essay, in which he clearly intends to support a position against gay marriage.[34] Something is theoretically amiss, and that something is exhibited in a subsequent interpretation he makes of a particular passage in Plato's *Gorgias:*

> Reality is known in judgment, not in emotion, and *in reality*, whatever the generous hopes and dreams and thoughts of *giving* with which same-sex partners may surround their sexual act, these acts cannot express or do more than is expressed or done if two strangers engage in such activity to give each other pleasure, or a prostitute pleasures a client to give him pleasure in return for money, or (say) a man masturbates to give himself pleasure and a fantasy of more human relationships after a grueling day on the assembly line. This is, I believe, the substance of Plato's judgment—at the moment in the *Gorgias* which is also decisive for the moral and political philosophical critique of hedonism—that there is no important distinction in essential moral worthlessness between solitary masturbation, being sodomized as a prostitute, and being sodomized for the pleasure of it. Sexual acts cannot *in reality* be self-giving unless they are acts by which a man and a woman actualize and experience sexually the real giving of themselves to each other—in biological, affective and volitional union in mutual commitment, both open-ended and exclusive—which like Plato and Aristotle and most people we call marriage.[35]

Translators may not agree on what meaning to assign a particular idea in an ancient language even if there are generally acceptable translations of the text. For instance, a fairly standard translation of the relevant passage of the *Gorgias* that Finnis refers to presents it thus:

> SOCRATES: If it was only his head that he wanted to scratch—or can I push the question further? Think what you will answer, Callicles, if anyone should ask all the questions that naturally follow. And as a climax of all such cases, the life of a catamite—is not that shocking and shameful and miserable? Will you dare to say that such people are happy, if they have what they desire in abundance?
>
> CALLICLES: Are you not ashamed Socrates to drag our discussions into such topics?
>
> SOCRATES: Is it I who do this my nobel friend, or the man who says it unequivocally that pleasure, whatever its nature, is the key to happiness, and does not distinguish between pleasures good and evil? . . . But my good sir, consider whether pleasures so indiscriminate can after all be the good. For if it is so, then the many shocking things we just now hinted at must evidently result, and many others too.[36]

John Boswell has noted that the word "catamite" comes from the word "catamitus" and "is supposedly derived from 'Γανυμήδης' the name of the Greek youth raped by Zeus."[37] If Boswell's view is correct, then the passage may have a very different interpretation than the one Finnis assigns to it. Martha Nussbaum offers still another account, actually somewhat related to Boswell's comment. Nussbaum's account renders the word "catamite" as "male prostitute" and, in particular, one who chooses habitual passivity. "In fact, Callicles is depicted as having a young boyfriend of his own," about which Socrates expresses no view.[38] My point here is not to get into the subtleties of translation, on which I am not qualified to speak. Nor is it to examine Finnis's first principles solely in terms of their consequences for homosexuality. My claim is that even our understanding of law may involve unexamined ideological assumptions about what purpose the law is to serve. For example, should law preserve gender roles, and are laws against homosexuality designed with this purpose in mind?[39] Also, I suggest that one must be careful when employing modern terminology such as "homosexual," "homosexuality," and "homosexual orientation" as synonyms for what the Greeks had in mind concerning man-boy or man-man relations.[40] Certainly, much more would need to be said if one wanted to make this kind of historical comparison between ancient Greece and late twentieth-century society, but that would take us far afield from my purpose here, which is to question the way ideology sometimes obstructs good legal reasoning. In Finnis's case, his ideology may have led him to a too-easy justification for current sexual mores.

Seemingly, Cass Sunstein has this kind of problem in mind when he asks what assumptions we start with but do not question. Sunstein argues that too often "status quo neutrality disregards the fact that existing rights, and hence the status quo, are in an important sense a product of law."[41] What is accepted as natural is in fact conventional. This is important not just to understand decisions in cases but to see how attitudes are formed in legal education. For example, CLS scholar Duncan Kennedy criticizes legal education as producing a hierarchical ranking of professors and students that for future lawyers anticipates law-firm partnership tracks and the operations of the courts. Kennedy's concern is that such education serves merely as a "reproducer of hierarchy," an incubator for a certain ideology that presents "a set of political attitudes toward the economy and society in general, toward law, and toward the possibilities of life in the profession."[42] The latter may affect even those persons who do not practice law but have some involvement with the legal system. Moreover, Kennedy claims that legal education fails to provide those who will practice with the tools they need, leaving it instead up to the law firms to provide this education. In this respect, when law schools teach skills, they do so

> through class discussion of cases in which it is asserted that law emerges from a rigorous analytical procedure called legal reasoning, which is unintelligible to the lay person but somehow both explains and validates the great majority of the rules in force in our system. At the same time, the class context and the materials present every legal issue as distinct from every other—as a tub on its own bottom, so to speak—with no logic or even any reason to hope that from law study one might derive an integrating vision of what law is, how it works, or how it might be changed (other than in the incremental case by case, reformist way).
>
> Second, the teaching of skills in the mystified context of legal reasoning about utterly unconnected legal problems means that skills are taught badly, unself-consciously, to be absorbed by osmosis as one picks up the knack of "thinking like a lawyer." . . . Third, the schools teach skills in isolation from actual lawyering experience. "Legal reasoning" is sharply distinguished from practice, and one learns nothing about practice.[43]

What both of these criticisms imply about traditionalism—that is, legal education that is rigidly formalist and naively foundationist—is twofold. First is the point that the system does not question its own value assumptions but takes as a given—except, perhaps, on a low-level, incremental case-by-case level—the principle ideological commitments of individuals who stand to benefit the most by keeping the system the way it is, that is, those in current positions of power. Noam Chomsky, in talking about education in general, describes the situation:

> The less educated . . . tend to be more sophisticated and perceptive about these matters, the reason being that education is a form of indoctrination and the less educated are the less indoctrinated. Furthermore, the educated tend to be privileged and they tend to have a stake in the doctrinal system, so they naturally tend to internalize and believe it. As a result, not uncommonly and not only in the United States, you find a good deal more sophistication among people who learn about the world from their experience rather than those who learn about the world from a doctrinal framework that they are exposed to and that they are expected as part of professional obligation to propagate.[44]

Second, and this is a practical point, law schools operate more from the standpoint of creating future appellate court judges than they do from the standpoint of preparing future attorneys for practice. This serves as a means to protect the ideological superstructure because it places the greatest emphasis on how not to change things (at least not very much) and leaves it up to the law firms, who also have a stake in not changing things, to prepare lawyers who occasionally need to change things somewhat. In contrast, in Europe, legal education is directed to the education of judges through an approach that makes greater use of doctrine than our own; the practical training of lawyers is frequently handled by a required apprenticeship or further study at a litigation training institute.[45]

Legal Constructivism

I reference here a slew of legal theorists, including some CLS scholars , critical race theorists, and feminists who can be identified by the fact that they adopt an instrumentalist/nonfoundationalist view of law. I do so in reverse chronological order to the actual historical development of these groups to show, first, where some of the issues are today, and, second, how we reached this point. As it was with traditionalism, my goal here is both to give examples of the positions and to critique them where I believe they fall short. As a preface, especially since I am dealing with this development in reverse chronological order, I would draw the reader's attention to a perspective that Robin West presents in "Disciplines, Subjectivity and the Law,"[46] which I believe engages the underlying epistemological question behind much of their work.

> Given the modern and post-modern disillusionment with reason, how should we criticize or evaluate a law? How should we go about criticizing law, if not by reference to general principles derived from reason? What does it mean, given the "death of reason," to ask whether a particular law—say, a statute outlawing "surrogacy contracts," or a judicial decision requiring the busing of schoolchildren to achieve integrated schools, or a law criticizing sexual sodomy, or a constitutional provision or constitutional interpretation invalidating state statutes that criminalize abortion on demand—is a *good* law or a *bad* law, a *just* law or an *unjust* law, a moral law or an amoral law?[47]

In response to this question, West states that we should step outside the legal academy and look not to other academic disciplines but "to our sympathetic understandings both of the ideal community central to civic republicanism and the ideal individual central to liberal utilitarianism and the commitments to freedom, welfare, tolerance, nurturance, egalitarianism, individualism, and communitarianism that compete within and between them."[48] We also should rely on stories and metaphors to understand the lives of persons other than ourselves. And although we should use economics to understand some of the "invisible consequences of our policies and desires," our moral view should reach us from the heart and not from the mind.[49]

West's view is clearly impassioned and her claim is noncognitivist and far-reaching, mostly in the sense that it denies any rational moral or epistemological underpinnings for what we ultimately judge to be right. But on the same basis her view neutralizes itself as a ground for deciding conflicting choices that may arise when, for example, our concern for egalitarianism runs contrary to our concern for individualism or when our concern for individualism runs contrary to our concern for communitarianism. Such conflicts often arise and can be seen in any major election or read in almost any newspaper when issues involving freedom, welfare, and tolerance arise.[50] Of course, this presumes that the individuals trying to resolve these conflicts are not true Humeans. For if they were, then they would believe that our moral differences can be identified as conflicts over facts and not differences in sentiments. But this would be too hard a sell for most people to adopt, given that the history of the world is replete with examples where people have held quite intensely different positions.[51] Still, without rationality to adjudicate the differences in these areas, one wonders if the critics might not be right that we have only politics to determine outcomes. I hope that the approach I shall present will provide an alternative to noncognitivism by providing a means for rationally resolving these conflicts.

CRITICAL RACE THEORY'S SUBJECTIVITY

In the area of critical race theory, race is taken as the primary factor for understanding social relations as seen by a number of African-American, Asian-American, Hispanic-American, and Native-American thinkers. Almost all of these thinkers see race as a social construction but one that is particularly difficult to grasp because it is so insidiously embedded in society. For example, Derrick Bell has noted that race is behind both the conservative theories oriented toward the status quo and the liberal theories designed to combat discrimination.

> The message the formalist model conveys is that existing power relations in the real world are by definition legitimate and must go unchallenged. Equality theory also necessitates such a result. Nearly every critique the Realists launched at the formalists can be hurled at advocates of liberal civil rights theory. Precedent, rights theory, objectivity merely are formal rules that serve a correct purpose. Even in the context of equality theory, they will never vindicate the legal rights of black Americans.[52]

In general, Bell is more extreme than some of his colleagues in that he doubts "the possibility of ever eliminating the racist strain in American life."[53] (This may serve as a call to arms or it may create an overall cynicism about making any improvement at all.) More particular to the passage, however, is the way he delineates "the legal rights of black Americans" if he is not willing to adopt some form of rights theory. Without a theory of rights, how can we talk about anybody's rights in more than an ad hoc way?

Supporting Bell's position, Linda Greene writes: "I agree in principle with Bell's timely philosophy. . . . [T]he adherence to, and faith in, a system of rights without an understanding of the politization of those rights foreshadows political immobilization and impotency."[54] Patricia Williams disagrees, however. In her critique of the attack on rights, Williams "reminds us that it is not the exercise of false rights that has injured blacks, but the denial to blacks of rights extended to others."[55] In *City of Richmond v. J. A. Croson Co.*,[56] for example, the Supreme Court held unconstitutional a Richmond, Virginia, plan to set aside 30 percent of construction contracts to be given to minority contractors in a community in which minority contractors had previously received less than 1 percent of the city's construction business. The Court's position was that the set-aside violated the Fourteenth Amendment's equal protection clause because the city's rationale was based on a "sheer speculation" as to the nexus between past discrimination and current statistical disparities. Williams has noted that

> non-interpretative devices, extrinsic sources and intuitive means of reading may be the only ways to include the reality of the unwritten, unnamed, context of race. . . . The black power movement notwithstanding, I think many, many people of color still find it extremely difficult to admit, much less prove, our desire to be included in alien and hostile organizations and institutions, even when those institutions also represent economic opportunity."[57]

Charles R. Lawrence III puts it another way: "Requiring proof of conscious or intentional motivation as a prerequisite to constitutional recognition that a decision is race dependent ignores much of what we understand about how the human mind works. It also disregards both the irrationality of racism and the profound effect that the history of American race relations has had on the individual and collective unconscious."[58]

Williams believes that the way through this problem is the use of first-person narratives to illustrate the effects of racism on the human psyche. In her book, *The Alchemy of Race and Rights*, she presents a number of narratives regarding her own struggles to deal with racism as a member of a renowned university law faculty.[59] She also states that listening to different voices from their own subject-position is the way education must go in the future.[60] What conclusion, then, do we draw from this and the other passages?

Clearly, these people do not commit the same kind of mistake that I have suggested the rigid formalists/naive foundationalists commit. They do not fail to examine the underlying ideological assumptions that may be motivating the law and their own and other people's behaviors at any particular time. Nor are they unwilling to question a legal standard, including a liberal one, like equality, to see what may lie behind it. Where they do go wrong, however, is in not developing an epistemological framework that would ensure the truth of their claims. Here it might simply be that these thinkers do not want to play the truth language game. They may prefer instead to ground their positions on some other criteria such as "comprehensiveness, style, unity, honesty, aesthetic flair, strength, health or vitality" to name just a few.[61]

But these criteria, when treated as potential groundings for a system of law, are very weak. For instance, a person who thought the most important criterion was comprehensiveness would have little reason to alter her position when confronted by someone who believed that unity or honesty was the central most dominating thesis. Indeed, we see this whenever people speak of coming from different philosophical traditions as a way of justifying why their views are as good as anybody else's. It was the reason Socrates in *The Republic* tried to find common ground to adjudicate his claims with those of his opponents. The drive toward a common ground is important to offset battles over which the law would have little to say if no further evaluation were possible. These are the battles that I have called very hard cases. For example, listening to different voices is no doubt important to understanding different conceptual *frameworks*, as social scientists and anthropologists remind us. It may also be essential to the discovery of actual incidents of racism that otherwise might go unnoticed.[62] But it is also true that human beings have a tremendous ability to rationalize their own positions and not to see the context of their position as accurately as one might hope. This point comes about because different voices do not make different conceptual *schemes* when viewed from a third-party perspective. From that point of view, one has the occasion to determine which interpretation is stronger in light of the agreed-upon evidence. As an example, let me tell a story of a friend of mine on a related issue.

My friend was criticized for being a racist when as a gay, white male, he fired a straight female employee of color, in the company in which he was a manager. The basis for the firing was that the employee came into work on one occasion more than two hours late without a good reason, was given a warning, then came into work late on the next eight reporting days, finally coming in two hours late on the last day. Even so, the charge that my friend's action was racially motivated might have been justified if it were not for the fact that he hired this person along with other minorities—African Americans, Latinos, gays, and lesbians—and was, from his perspective, enforcing the same rules for everyone in the same way. Of course, the employee in question, from her perspective, did not or would not see the neutrality in which the rules were being applied. And this was not because the employee claimed to find some inherent bias in the rules themselves but because the employee thought my friend favored gay white males. What does one do with a situation where two perspectives on the same situation differ significantly, especially if one is in upper management and has to decide whether the firing was justified? Putting aside any pro-management bias, the question of the justification for the firing itself raises important factual questions. They cannot be resolved simply by appealing to either perspective but must be resolved, if at all, by appealing to objective standards of evidence to which everyone can agree. Indeed, this narrative shows, then, that without foundations in an intersubjective, and not just subjective, reality, it is too easy to fall into the trap of seeing every event from only one vantage point. This is particularly problematic because sometimes vantage points conflict as they did here and, then, the different voices have to be weighted against each other in light of what the evidence presents. Judges do this all the time and there is no way around it, short of substituting one bias for another.

In this vein, Paul Butler has suggested "that since the judicial system is doing African Americans so little good and so much harm, black jurors should practice jury nullification—acquitting a black defendant they believe to be guilty—if the crime in question is nonviolent," a *malum prohibitum* rather than a *malum in se*.[63] Granted this may not be the movement's mainstream, which is more related to remembering the history of racism in the United States and "detecting its residue in even the most neutral-seeming corners of the law."[64] But even that mainstream may, when it fails to acknowledge foundations, misconstrue the very facts before its eyes. For example, Williams describes the student evaluations she received at the end of a year of teaching law school:

> It is the end of a long academic year. I sit in my office reviewing my student evaluations of me. They are awful, and I am devastated. The substantive ones say that what I teach is "not law." The nonsubstantive evaluations are about either my personality or my physical features. I am deified, reified, and vilified in all sorts of cross-directions. I am condescending, earthy, approachable, and arrogant. Things are out of control in my classroom, and I am too much the taskmaster. I am a PNCNG (Person of No Color and No Gender) as well as too absorbed with ethnicity and social victimhood. My braids are described as being swept up over my "great bald dome of a skull," and my clothes, I am relieved to

> hear are "neat." I am obscure, challenging, lacking in intellectual rigor, and brilliant. I think in a disorganized fashion and insist that everyone thinks as I do. I appear tired all the time and talk as if I am on speed, particularly when reading from texts. My writing on the blackboard is too small.[65]

Williams goes on to describe how, when her evaluation scores were published in the school newspaper, two students came to see her.

> They think the response has to do with race and gender, and with the perceived preposterousness of the authority that I, as the first black woman ever to have taught at this particular institution, symbolically and imagistically bring to bear in and out of the classroom. Breaking out of this, they say, is something we all suffer as pawns in a hierarchy, but it is particularly aggravated in the confusing, oxymoronic hierarchic symbology of me as black female law professor. That, I tell them in a grateful swell of unscholarly emotionalism, feels like truth to me.[66]

Now, no teacher, including myself, likes to receive negative evaluations, and some of the ones Williams describes seem off the issue of education and probably expose biases and prejudices, as the two students suggest. But certainly all of them do not, and if these are the evaluations she is getting it would at least be worth her revisiting her teaching style. Why are the students feeling this way? Is the teaching style too different from what law schools generally teach, such that it needs more introduction? Is she spending enough time explaining what she is trying to do? Maybe these students need to be shown why her methods are helpful and what limitations there are. Maybe other factors need to be sorted out. In the end, Williams will have to decide either that her teaching style is correct and that the difficulties were the students' or that it could be improved in certain definite ways. But this will not be doable or, at least, not doable very well if she relies only on her own subjective perspective. Whatever her final judgment on these matters, the point is that there should be some deliberation on the issue that attempts to balance the different perspectives at stake.

My response is not to express any distaste for including the first-person perspective in legal decisionmaking, as Williams and others have suggested. Such a perspective can be useful to the social scientist or investigator in understanding how different persons or groups see themselves as well as what might motivate them to action in different situations. Leslie Espinoza, for example, sees that her expectations as a young child growing up in California were limited compared to the reality of becoming a law professor. In part, she attributes her departure from expectations as coming to understand the social construct they represent.[67] So critical race scholarship can expose not only overt forms of racism but also subtler internalized failings that such racism, even after it is formally dissolved, continues to breed. Moreover, it can provide a basis for a shared global discourse that can encompass many different views of the world. As Robert A. Williams has noted, "Pushed to the brink of extinction by the premises inherent in the European's view of the world, contemporary [Native American] tribalism recognizes the compelling necessity of articulating and defining its own vision within the global community." Still, I do want to take notice of the limitations that accompany this first-person approach. As this whole book attests, I regard that perspective as essential to the ultimate justification of morality and law. But note that this justification works only if one is prepared to take the next step, as Kant did, to finding universal concepts of the understanding. This latter is necessary to transform in a fair manner what may appear *to the individual* to be true—the reality of racism in one's own life—subjectively to what could appear *to others* of all races to be true intersubjectively, such as a standard of equality, given adequate discussion and debate. For instance, when taken to an extreme, critical race theory's effort to expose invidious racism may lead to a weakening of one of the most important tools we have to combat such racism. Mari Matsuda "argues that we should stop trying to develop speech codes that protect all kinds of speech equally—that of Nazis as much as that of pacifists—and start acknowledging that we know that racists are different."[68]

Yet how are we to judge pacifists' speech as more valuable than Nazi speech? There may be contexts where pacifists' speech could be harmful as, for example, when an enemy in a justified war is holding out for better terms in a combat situation. Moreover, are we not playing into the hands of the Nazis we so despise when we provide reasons to deny our own freedom to discuss difficult issues simply because we do not like what someone might have to say? (I am assuming we would continue restricting speech that represented "a clear and present danger" as the courts have defined that phrase, as well as "fighting words.") Choosing what can be said according to what is popular or in vogue is a dangerous precedent to be setting because it can easily backfire against groups and ideas we would most want to hear. Perhaps, some critical race theorists' view of holding a "black perspective" that can recognize racism in places where white people seldom find it can perform this Kantian task. But that would depend on whether all people could adopt this outlook at least in principle. Such a perspective, as Jerome Culp states it, "is opposed to racial oppression in the same sense that feminist means opposition to patriarchy and oppression of women."[69] Nevertheless, I doubt that this point of view would be of much help to solving the problem(s) of racism once someone chose to adopt a different view of the subject, say an Asian-American perspective or a feminist perspective. At that point the issue shifts from how the event is seen from one or the other vantage point to how the different viewpoints are to be mediated and to what action ought to be taken.

THE LIMITS OF RADICAL FEMINISM

Related to my epistemic concerns regarding critical race theory is a similar concern I have with regard to certain aspects of feminist jurisprudence as taught in law schools. Deborah Rhode describes feminist jurisprudence, at its most general level, as sharing a common goal with CLS and critical race theory: to confront established distributions of power. The methods employed to reach that goal often make use of deconstructive or narrative methodologies to expose seemingly neutral gender situations.[70] These methods are controversial in that they give rise to questions concerning the objectivity of law. They are also controversial because they treat gender as a social construct in the same way that the critical race theorists treat race as a social construct. Celina Romany describes these methods as giving "personal experience epistemological standing, offering counter narratives which serve as critiques of the values and assumptions lying beneath our social and political organization, social contract included."[71] However, at least two problems arise with respect to this approach: the first is within feminism itself and concerns claims of gender essentialism; the second concerns feminism's relationship to broad questions about truth.

With respect to the first issue, Angela Harris has argued that feminism cannot disentangle itself from "the web of race and gender—of being enmeshed always in multiple, often contradictory, discourses of sexuality and color."[72] Any attempt to do so in the name of "unmodified feminism" recreates all women "in the image of the white woman."[73] Feminism could benefit from giving up its quest for a unitary self and adopting Martha Minow's "realization that difference—and therefore identity—is always relational, not inherent."[74] The opposition to this antiessentialist critique sees this multivoiced approach as a problem of watering down the specific oppression women face based on their sex. In particular, Catharine MacKinnon writes: "To argue that oppression 'as a woman' negates rather than encompasses recognition of the oppression of women on other bases, is to say that there is no such thing as the practice of sex inequality."[75] MacKinnon's point is that to recognize and treat gender discrimination, it may first be necessary to distinguish it from other forms of discrimination both legally and morally. Only then are we in a position actually to remedy the problem. Nevertheless, the problem with both sides of this argument is that they conflate two related but distinct sets of concerns, which causes them to appear to be speaking at cross-purposes. I label these two sets of concerns substantive and strategic.

On the substantive side, all oppression by definition is immoral. This includes any discrimination based on an irrational or irrelevant premise, whether it is ultimately directed against persons because of their race, nationality, creed, gender, or sexual orientation, to name a few areas. Of course, whether a criterion is relevant or rational will involve some further discussion regarding the purpose for which the criterion is offered. I have provided elsewhere a discussion of how this issue might be resolved with regard to sexual orientation discrimination.[76] When MacKinnon says one must guard gender-based discrimination from being attenuated by too close a connection to other forms of discrimination, one faces the problem of explaining why from a moral point of view it should matter if the various forms of discrimination are lumped together. It is not like murder and theft, in which the consequences of the former are morally more serious to purposive agency than the consequences of the latter, although both are immoral. On the other side of the coin are strategic concerns. Here, it is important to ask whether politically it is better to stand united against all forms of discrimination by, let us say, developing a comprehensive statute or whether it is better to take up the issue piecemeal, one form of discrimination at a time. While I tend to prefer the former of these strategies—there is strength in numbers—I recognize that there may be strategic reasons, such as not biting off more than one can chew, for choosing the latter approach. The latter approach might be politically more obtainable in a context where, for example, some vile form of discrimination has been occurring and the public is already sensitized to the issue. In reference to strategic considerations, then, MacKinnon may be right to say, at least in some contexts, that politically to stop gender-based discrimination one has to identify it uniquely and that includes identifying those harms that are caused by it.[77] These questions would have to be worked out at the time by people involved in making these choices.

Causing the internal debate that I have referred to are substantive and strategic considerations merged under one category of essentialism. This produces or identifies gender as a more basic form of discrimination than, say, race or sexual orientation.[78] MacKinnon's concerns here seem to run opposed to the concerns of commentators who have a different set of priorities for solving social and moral issues. To put it bluntly, one may not find it much of an achievement to be freed from discrimination if it means being freed to become a white woman where one is not white and does not want to be treated as if one were white. Of course, a different problem arises with regard to why a person might want to be treated as black, white, gay, straight, male, or female. No doubt in some contexts respect for such differences adds to a cross-cultural understanding of the many ways in which peoples differ and society is distinct. Still, in other contexts and from a moral point of view, such differences may not be relevant if the matters at stake are jobs, housing, or simply being able to use public accommodations.[79]

The second issue concerns feminism's relationship to the question of truth. Margaret Jane Radin describes feminism and pragmatism as allied in the sense that their theory of "truth is inevitably plural, concrete and provisional."[80] Citing John Dewey, Radin writes, "Truth is a collection of truths; and these constituent truths are in the keeping of the best methods of inquiry and testing as to matters of fact."[81] Radin also cites William James for the point that "truth for us is simply a collective name for verification processes, just as health, wealth, strength, etc. are names for other processes connected with life, and also pursued because it pays to pursue them."[82] For Radin, then, feminism must be committed "to finding knowledge in the particulars of experience" and not in "abstract idealism, transcendence, foundationalism, and atemporal universality."[83] That is to say, feminism must find the truth in immanence, historicity, concreteness, situatedness, contextuality, embeddedness, [and] narrativity of meaning."[84] The problem with this view is that it is too limited. It is not what it includes but what it excludes that is the problem. In particular, it fails to provide the holder of the view with a way to assess her own vantage point. There is no higher platform to step onto when trying to assess the political morality of one's own society. Thus, the view cannot ensure that the injustice one is seeking to correct is a real injustice and not just the correct method of thinking and talking currently in vogue or, at least, in vogue with those with whom one identifies. If the latter had been the case before the woman's rights movement became popular, surely its greatest achievements, including the right to vote, might never have come about. Nor, again, does it help to have people disavow any interest in finding a higher platform. Regardless of what framework they start from, critical race theory, feminism, what-have-you, there will always be some other framework with which it may conflict. When that happens, the appeal to a more highly ordered position may be the only way to resolve the controversy. The possibility of widening conceptual frameworks is necessary to access not just the coherence of a given interpretation in a concrete, historically situated, social context. It is necessary to show how that interpretation might fit within a still wider understanding of what morality requires generally.

CRITICAL LEGAL STUDIES' BAR OF POLITICS

Much has been written on the critical legal studies movement, but I shall focus on the question of foundations. Joseph Singer states that CLS scholars have demonstrated three points:

> First, we have demonstrated in a variety of contexts that law varies according to time and place, and that this historical and social contingency applies to legal reasoning, legal rules, and governmental and social institutions. Second, we have shown that legal reasoning is indeterminate and contradictory. . . . Third, we have argued that law is not neutral.[85]

As a result of these claims and others like them, some scholars have charged that the CLS's theories are nihilistic, have no social vision, and offer no alternative programs or positive suggestions for the future. These charges are sometimes based on the CLS's refusal to acknowledge any but contingent foundations for law, and their refusal to recognize that existing legal doctrine can be coherently construed. But according to Singer, this does not mean that the CLS has given up all claim to what we should do or how we should live. Only the abstract moral categories are given up, not all discussion of moral and legal choices. Such discussions are subject to the proviso that they "focus on the rich context in which these problems occur."[86] For example,

> it may be useful to characterize two persons as "employer" and "employee" and to develop generalizations to describe and govern their relationships. But it is important to remember that these are real people

> that we are talking about, and when we describe them in this way for the purpose of judging what their relationships should be like, we are closing ourselves off from their actual life experiences.[87]

Of course, Singer does not say how different life experiences are, or should be, taken into account by a court when rendering a decision in a case. For that matter, he offers no criterion of relevance or materiality for what the proper description of any act should be. Few people might doubt that, where possible, courts should seek to prevent cruelty, misery, and loneliness and even to encourage democracy, but these are not the issues over which most contemporary legal thinkers debate. Remember: a benevolent despot may satisfy a number of these concerns, perhaps all of them, but at a cost of much freedom; and a minimum, free market state may avoid the freedom problem, but only by not doing much to upset the status quo.

No doubt, the problem of how to construct law or whether we should even try is deeper than what the CLS can offer in the form of a proactive, positive jurisprudence, given their position on foundations. But when some members of the CLS go further in their claim against foundations to assert that legal sentences have no ethical or institutionalized meaning, they make a bad situation worse. Drucilla Cornell argues that those "irrationalists" in the CLS

> have not only shown that rules of procedure cannot escape an appeal to an outside ethical justification. They have also shown us that the very idea of a rule as a force that pulls us down the track through each new fact situation, determining the outcome of a particular case, is false. Therefore, no line of precedent can fully determine a particular outcome in a particular case, because the rule itself is always in the process of reinterpretation as it is applied. It is interpretation that gives us the rule and not the other way around. This insight is what has come to be known as the "indeterminacy thesis," which has been mistakenly identified at times by proponents of the thesis themselves, with the proposition that there is no institutionalized meaning, no "real" intelligibility of the legal sentence. The proposition should always be understood to be that law cannot be reduced to a set of mechanical rules, a self-sufficient mechanism that pulls us down the track through each new fact situation. Law, in other words, cannot be reduced to a self-generated and self-validating set of cognitive norms. Interpretation always takes us beyond a mere appeal to the status quo.[88]

Cornell sees the central error of the irrationalists as replacing "the truth of reconciliation with the truth of castration"; this occurs when "the deconstruction of the hubris of ontology (which is meant to show the groundlessness of legal ontology) is confused with radical skepticism and with *Unsinnlösigkeit*," the claim that all legal sentences are senseless.[89] Cornell acknowledges "that without a foundationalist conception of reason in either the neo-Kantian or the Hegelian sense, the 'secularization' [by which she means the way knowledge and ideas become detached from their original sources] of the modern world will remain incomplete."[90] Put another way, "Deconstruction reminds us that the meaning of the 'ethical' is necessarily displaced into the future because the Good is not fully present to the mind."[91] Still, as things are, Cornell is willing to accept it. What she is not willing to accept is that we must give up the capacity to maintain an ethical responsibility for law and a social vision for the future just because we give up abstract moral principles.

But if the process of interpretation is the way Cornell intends this responsibility to manifest itself, she needs to explain what it would mean to have a misinterpretation, given that primary responsibility for the outcomes of cases is strictly placed in the hands of an interpreter. That is, how should we make an interpretation? Are there tools to be used for all interpretations, and if so, what are they? Without solid foundations, it will always be uncertain whether what has guided the interpreter is what ought to have guided the interpreter. Recall, with H. L. A. Hart, that Nazi judges also interpreted their laws so as "to maintain the state's tyranny effectively."[92]

Nor can we hope for a way out of this situation by claiming, as Ronald Dworkin does, that the CLS is concerned only with external skepticism or *global* internal skepticism.[93] For Dworkin, the difference between internal skepticism and global internal skepticism is the difference between being skeptical of certain claims or interpretations about law, such as the claim that law is logically connected to morality, and being skeptical of *any* effort to conceive legal doctrine as coherent, that is, not contradictory.[94] The problem is that Dworkin wants to resolve difficult interpretative questions with an appeal to the political morality of the society. Unfortunately, cases like those that arose during the period of slavery in the United States undermine any privileging of the political morality of the society to resolve questions of this sort.

These references do not show that the CLS is unconcerned with what law can do in the creation of a social vision. This criticism is too facile, focusing as it does only on the nihilistic aspect of the CLS position and failing to recognize that CLS scholars have been concerned with issues of morality in law even though they deny any claim to an absolutist set of moral principles. To the contrary, what I am most concerned about in this debate is where the limits must lie in any positive jurisprudence that the CLS can offer. The CLS is surely correct that in many cases, law reflects a political or at least an ideological response to a certain set of historical, social, and economic conditions. But this is not the end of the issue. The real issue is how to get behind these apparent facades to set out an evaluation for law in moral terms. This is particularly important when contingent foundations, as in the slavery example, are most insecure. Depending on how one answers this question will determine which legal rules and principles are recognized. For the CLS, this question is answered politically, but I find this approach far too dangerous and contingent to be the end of the matter and a beginning for legal education.

Threshing, Not Trashing

I have been arguing against pure traditionalism and pure legal constructivism in legal education, but I have also been claiming that each of these positions has something positive to offer to that education. On the side of traditionalism is the concern for foundations and the formalist claim to objectivity. On the side of legal constructivism is the willingness to unmask and evaluate the ideological underpinnings of much of what we take for granted as the neutral character of law. Contrariwise, on the traditionalist side, there is an unwillingness to question the ideological assumptions that may be motivating what its proponents take to be the law. On the constructivist side, there is the possibility of getting caught in an ideology of victimization or politics.[95] My call, therefore, is for a different approach from both of these positions, one that makes the best uses of each and limits the negative aspects of both. As I have described traditionalism as rigid formalism and naive foundationalism, I would pick the foundationalist aspect as the most important contribution to legal education. Similarly, as I have described legal constructivism as instrumentalism and nonfoundationalism, I would pick the instrumentalist aspect as its most important contribution to this area. Why these choices and not formalism or nonfoundationalism? I did not choose formalism because it becomes an end in itself rather than an end in a reasoned position. I did not choose nonfoundationalism so there would be the possibility of searching for a reasoned end. I have particular reasons in mind for the choices I did make.

LAW SCHOOL

Legal education has to focus on law as an instrument for human flourishing and as having a deep foundation in political morality. The first is necessary if law is to be more than just a tool of the most powerful voice(s) in society. The second is necessary if laws are not to be arbitrary in their aims or purposes but are to provide clear moral directions for court decisions. The reason for having political morality as the foundation is to ensure that there is a duty to obey law both by courts and the public. Law must be understood as morally justified if it is to have any claim on obedience, and law must serve a social good that morality can recognize. Even when law relates to a morality in a neutral situation, such as which side of the street to drive on, it must be taken as serving a moral purpose if it is to implant a duty of obedience. In the particular example, the purpose may be to avoid accidents and to encourage democratic processes in deciding what standards to follow. But this means morality cannot be separated from law either in the educational process or anywhere else. Hence, a legal education must include a moral education properly understood.

Now, my sense of moral education needs to be disclosed. By a moral education, I do not mean acquainting students with some set of moral principles adopted as the doctrine of a particular religious faith or secular authority merely because they have been so adopted. I mean a process of inquiry on the order of the kind performed by Socrates that requires investigation into the meaning of moral terms and the evaluation of possible justifications for moral rights. Only in this way will there be any assurance of not disguising the ideological prejudices of any group under the appearance of legal neutrality. But this also means that students, teachers, lawyers, and judges must become philosophers as well as legal practitioners or theoreticians. Moreover, it means doing both well in the sense of taking into account all relevant information, normative and empirical, including knowledge of all relevant theories, and making arguments based on that information. Martha Nussbaum makes the point:

> The typical Socratic inquiry is an examination of some concept (or concepts) that the person questioned uses all the time in his or her professional activity, but hasn't really clarified for or to himself. Legal arguments very commonly make use of concepts to the understanding of which professional philosophers have devoted a lot of effort, concepts such as justice, equality, liberty, free will, emotion, sexuality and sexual

desire, and the quality of life. Lawyers and judges frequently find themselves in the position of making theoretical claims about such matters. Judicial opinions are full of such claims. Yet the discussion rarely shows even the most elementary awareness of the rigorous work that philosophers have been doing, work that would very likely contribute to the clarification of the judge's or lawyer's own process of reasoning about these matters.[96]

What, then, should a legal education consist of if it is to be a moral education as well? As a preliminary matter, law schools and universities generally must agree upon a program of prelegal education, which does not have to be too confining but which must include study in philosophy, the social sciences, literature, and at least one hard science and mathematics. Allowance should be made for students already well into their undergraduate studies by phasing in these prerequisites over a three- to four-year period. The model I have in mind, which fits the standard liberal arts education with allowance for a major in some other area like business, is the model used for pre-med courses.[97] But, obviously, unlike pre-med courses, I want the emphasis to be on philosophical and social scientific areas of study as well as on the hard sciences. (Since hard sciences are included, the possibility of joint programs between medical and law schools should be unaffected.) This is to prepare the mind for the kinds of methodological investigations that lawyers and judges have to confront whenever traditional reasoning by analogy proves inadequate, which often happens on theoretical issues in the law, as I have pointed out. Future lawyers will also have a need for broader methodological understandings when seeking the advice and aid of expert witnesses whose core disciplines will seldom use reasoning by analogy.

Once these requirements are satisfied and students are admitted to law school, they should be required to take a general survey course in philosophy of law in their first semester of their first year, along with constitutional law, civil procedure, and legal writing. The survey course should emphasize questions and methods of conceptual and normative analyses, including articles on classical and contemporary ethics, epistemology, and language in a legal context.[98] They must examine such questions as "What is law?" "Are there legal duties?" and "How are such duties justified?" Having constitutional law taught early will provide the basis for further discussion of the role of political theory in law. One school that has a first-year program somewhat along these lines is the Illinois Institute of Technology, Chicago-Kent College of Law. Another is the University of Chicago, and there are others. The University of

California at Berkeley, for example, is known for its interdisciplinary law and social justice programs at the graduate and undergraduate levels. In addition to these requirements, the students should be acquainted with social science methods, at least at the level of being able to assimilate and understand information of legal significance that arises from these disciplines. If the students' undergraduate education was strong in this area then that may be adequate for law school.

After this initial preparation, the second semester of the first year and the entire second year and first semester of the third year can be devoted to traditional law subjects, except that now the students will be encouraged to engage in more than just reasoning by analogy. They should also question the received legal principles that the cases are said to represent in terms of a more highly ordered conceptual framework that requires the students to interweave epistemological and moral understandings of what the law is about. In other words, black-letter law courses should become a thing of the past, except perhaps at the end of their formal education when they prepare for the bar examination. The students should be shown the social, political, and economic policy concerns in almost every rule or principle of law they apply. Richard Posner has done this on the economic side in tort law.[99] Other scholars have addressed the political and social issues.[100] I merely suggest that we continue doing this in all areas of the law, using a rigorous philosophical approach along with traditional legal methods. The students should be required to consider what is happening in the law from a social and philosophical perspective that seeks to explain and justify the political and social roles and causes of the law in society. In both these respects, the students should be encouraged to go beyond the case method of education and adopt a kind of problem method. Here, the idea of a problem is treated broadly, and the cases become merely the take-off for, rather than the end of, deeper reflections on society, politics, morality, and the law.

The courses that I have suggested as preliminary to a legal education must continue to be interwoven into that education with the various legal courses that the students will undertake. Reasoning by analogy and close readings of cases and statutes will still be necessary, as the students will need that preparation for much future practice. But in addition, under the method I am suggesting, the students will become more than just practitioners of law; they will become persons capable of understanding at a fairly general level how law impacts and is structured by society and its norms. It will also provide the students with a wider breadth of arguments with which to engage the legal system and to ensure that justice is done. Including a philosophical education in the law curriculum cannot be without question, however. As Nussbaum reminds us:

> Socrates and Aristotle saw that the archenemies of good philosophy in public life are the sophists, people who by their clever glibness win attention, but whose lack of deep human engagement and rigorous self-scrutiny leads them to advance proposals that bring philosophy into discredit among practical people. We have not moved far from ancient Athens in this respect. The Sophists are still very much in evidence, and, unfortunately, a large proportion of the philosophers who are routinely read in law schools are such sophists.[101]

Nussbaum has in mind certain recent trends in continental philosophy such as deconstruction and some aspects of analytic philosophy when it also becomes jargon-laden and fails to appreciate the practical side of philosophy. Perhaps Nussbaum is too harsh in discounting these trends. Surely, if they are kept within reasonable confines—deconstruction as a third-person tool of social science and analytic philosophy adjusted to accept cross-disciplinary openness—they could add much to what we already know and hope to understand about law. But of course this presupposes that we would be able to work out specific courses that can achieve these goals.

Finally, students in the second semester of their third year in law school should be required to take a clinical practicum or internship. This is necessary for most students who anticipate actual practice, and all students would certainly gain from the real-world experience that goes along with actual practice. Here, "the workplace may be the best setting for novices to learn the skills of lawyering."[102] It is not enough to leave this practicum to second-year, summer-associate hiring, however. Unfortunately, everyone does not get the opportunity for such an experience and even, for those who do, the expectations and standards of performance may vary widely among firms. Thus, the program of internships should be operated jointly by academics and practitioners in the field, analogous to hospital internships but of shorter duration. The involvement of practitioners is needed because they know the day-to-day expectations that accompany practice; the faculty adds overall direction and consistency to the program. Such a program would also be good for those who later may want to teach law to ensure that they understand in more than just an abstract way how theory is related to practice. But such persons should also be required to prepare and write a major work in an area involving original research along the lines of a doctoral dissertation in other fields. This could be done while working or teaching but would need to be completed within a reasonable period of time. Pedagogically, this effort would prepare the future law professor for the demands of publication and the kinds of questions that are emerging in law schools today and that require an understanding of what the essence of law really is. Academically, the work should represent a serious contribution to law or legal institutions. Such a contribution is necessary to continue a high level of debate on what has always been true but in recent years has perhaps become more obvious; the relationship of law to deep concerns about morality and social obligation.

My discussion suggests that universities and law schools in particular need to encourage a certain degree of cross-disciplinary academic teaching. No longer should students of law be separated geographically from the main campus, as occurs at some schools both figuratively and actually. More important, law schools should have on their faculty specialists in philosophy and the social sciences analogous to the system of schools such as the University of Chicago that emphasize an interdisciplinary education.[103] The current curriculum should be expanded well beyond the borders that it now occupies. This does not mean giving up bar preparation but recognizing it as the least important aspect of what law schools should be doing. On that score too, the bar should be altered to reflect more than just an understanding of the rules; it should reflect a competent understanding of the practice. In this regard, a portion of the bar should be tied to the last year's internship I have described, where students are evaluated by what they can actually do in the field. And there may need to be sections for particular specialities such as criminal and civil litigation, business transactions, and public interest law, which can be taken after the first year of practice. These suggestions are tentative and subject to what I hope will be a good deal of discussion. That, more than anything else, should vastly improve our legal education and the students' abilities to engage the different kinds of frameworks that define legal reality.

I have been arguing for what I am sure some critics will want to dismiss as an approach that has never been tried before or, at least, not very well. What I am pushing for has much to do with attaining a comprehensive understanding of what law is about. But whether the criticisms come from traditionalists or legal constructivists or both, they are likely to be inadequate if they reproduce in their stead only the current status quo. There is no way of getting around it. The two alternatives of traditionalism and legal constructivism do not provide an adequate education of what law is about. There is no avoiding the reality that law structures our social environment profoundly and is just as profoundly structured by it. Every change, from abortion to gay marriage to changes in affirmative action, reflects this structuring, as well as maintaining the status quo. But there is also no turning away from the fact that we must be equally profound in the way we treat and understand these changes. To do any less is to give up on our ability to govern ourselves, not only our immediate desires but our reflective sense of what will lead to a better, more noble, and happier life. This means not removing philosophy or teaching it as outside the engagement of our practical lives. It means not teaching it as a subject separate from law but as law's foundation. As Alfred Lord Whitehead once observed, "Philosophy asks the simple question: What is it all about?" The same is true when philosophy is applied to law: What is law all about?

My argument here largely has been for the formal inclusion of philosophy in legal education. This seems to me as essential today as it was when Roscoe Pound and Wesley Newcomb Hohfeld advanced the same thesis in their teaching at Harvard Law School earlier in the twentieth century.[104] Still, many scholars will want to resist my suggestion on the ground that philosophy is unable to cut off irrationalism in the law. More to the point, they will fear that philosophy will not provide grounds for determining better or worse legal arguments, reasons, or conclusions. But I have tried to show that this so-called criticism is based on an incomplete analysis. Thus I differ from the CLS in that I do not go that further step to leaving everything to politics. This to me is like throwing out the baby with the bathwater. Answers are available, and they are available on a correspondence to the next highest framework or, if one is at the epistemic limit, coherence to what the best moral theory provides. In short, I believe one can still make good arguments for affording an intersubjective favoring of one position over another. This is what law students, lawyers, even judges need. But it is not reason *simpliciter*. Thus I agree with Bertrand Russell:

> Philosophy, though unable to tell us with certainty as to what things are, greatly increases our knowledge as to what they may be; it removes the somewhat *arrogant* dogmatism of those who have never travelled into the region of liberating doubt, and it keeps alive our sense of wonder by showing familiar things in an unfamiliar aspect.[105]

Philosophy has always been in search of the truth, whether it is epistemological truth, moral truth, or legal truth. Sometimes the truth eludes us. Today, perhaps more than ever previously thought, issues of justice are ever-present and prominent in our academic, political, and social lives. Therefore, we have even more reason to make use of this form of discourse for all that it can provide. At the very least, we should not abandon it at the very moment where we begin the education of future lawyers.

LAW PRACTICE

I should say a few words regarding the practice of law before closing this chapter. For most law students, their first real exposure to the practice of law comes either after their second year of law school, during their summer recess, or after graduation, presuming, of course, that the student is lucky enough to find a position with a law firm, a corporate legal department, a government agency, or a legal aid clinic. Whichever route opens up to them, these soon-to-be lawyers will confront a host of different and somewhat narrowing intellectual problems.

If, for example, the future lawyer joins a large law firm, she can expect to be given light assignments while preparing to sit for the bar examination. Once that is completed, however, the new associate will be assigned a fair amount of research in the first two years. (The pattern described varies according to the size of the firm.) The purpose of the research, as the partner or senior associate in charge will explain, will be to prepare memorandums for clients on actions they can legally perform or memorandums or briefs to convince a court on the way to decide a case. In most situations, there will be almost no direct client contact; the partners or senior associates in charge will keep that privilege for themselves. Thus, there develops early on, especially in the larger law firms, a distinction between what the young lawyer may have anticipated she would be doing in serving clients and what she is actually doing in providing bits and pieces of research for complicated cases with virtually no client contact. More senior associates and partners prefer not to perform basic research tasks and so fob them off on the new associates where the view is that this is the beginning of an initiation process into the firm's hierarchy. Moreover, the new associate will be expected to perform this research function solely within the confines of the law library, using only such additional materials as are provided by the trial record (if there is one), depositions, interrogatories, pleadings, and on-line legal research services.

Why do firms operate in this fashion? Aside from the fact that many of the more senior staffs do not want to perform basic research tasks, there is the view that this kind of training is necessary if the young lawyer is eventually going to be able to serve client needs. Clients are seen as customers of the firm who have either fallen into some sort of legal difficulty or want to avoid falling into difficulty. Legal practice is seen as providing these clients legal advice as to what course of action to pursue. Preventions of harm to their clients' interests and damage control are the two central focuses that most law firms adopt in their relationships to clients. They are also the two focuses of the practice that most law firms regard law schools as inadequately teaching. So they take on this responsibility themselves in the first two years with new associates.

The question arises as to whether law firms are correct in thinking they serve their clients' needs when the work they do on behalf of their clients is doctrinal research on the current state of the law. No doubt predictability is an important issue for a client, but it is too easy to believe one can predict the ultimate legal outcome of a course of action based strictly on doctrinal research. Especially in an area that is undergoing development and change, where the courts are in flux as to what the law is, it may be essential for the attorneys handling a question in this area to consider more than doctrine. They may need to take into account important philosophical, social, and economic arguments that favor one position over another, and they may need to take into account the political makeup of the court and society's position on the issue. Otherwise, the very predictability they seek may elude them. Take, for example, the recent case *Romer v. Evans*, the Colorado case in which the Supreme Court held that a state could not, as a matter of federal constitutional equal protection law, restrict itself or its municipalities from passing progay antidiscrimination legislation.[106] What was so surprising about this case was not its outcome, but the fact that the Court's majority opinion never once cited *Bowers v. Hardwick*.[107] As *Hardwick* was the infamous 1986 Supreme Court case that allowed states to adopt antigay sodomy statutes, the failure even to cite it in a case that was supporting equal protection for gays and lesbians was quite surprising. How is the decision (and it was a decision) not to cite *Hardwick* to be understood? Is it suggesting that *Hardwick* may soon be overturned? Clearly, a doctrinal analysis of the case law prior to *Romer* would not be adequate in answering this question any more than a doctrinal analysis of the cases prior to *Hardwick* could have predicted the result in that case.[108]

What then does a decision like this suggest with regard to predicting a legal outcome? It suggests that, as with law school education, law practice must take into account a broader set of considerations than those that are traditionally thought of as doctrinal. It must take into account the political makeup of the court, whether some of the judges have a particular expertise in some area, like economics, as well as the social and economic contexts in which the issue comes about.[109] Does the question involve a legal area that society is currently in doubt about? What are the philosophical arguments pro and con? In context, these are practical questions as much as they are theoretical ones, for they bear directly on serving a client's interest. In some situations, they require a lawyer to take a step away from a too-strict reliance on traditional legal doctrine and toward a more creative approach to legal understanding. Where a legal area is controversial or a particular form of analysis seems likely to persuade a court, a more creative approach may be the only path. This too is a judgment that would have to be made in consultation with the client. Law firms should give young associates more client contact so that they can appreciate just how clients make these judgments and the import that their research might have on a client's decision.

Furthermore, these considerations suggest that lawyers must not be only reactive but also proactive in regard to potential arguments that may be only dimly perceived. Who would have thought that a privacy argument tacked onto the end of a brief in *Griswold v. Connecticut* would have opened the door to the development of constitutional privacy law? Granted, there was precedent for this development, but until *Griswold* that precedent had not taken root as a constitutional doctrine.[110] Looking back, one can see how other cases at the time supported this development, but when the decision was rendered, it was clearly novel as is the Court's recent unanimous decision to allow a sitting president to be civilly sued.[111]

Some of the ideas I have discussed in regard to law firms also apply to other areas of legal practice, including work in corporate law departments, government agencies, and legal aid clinics. With these employers the problem is usually not a lack of client contact but more often than not too many cases for the lawyer to handle. As a result, there arises within the practice of law different tiers of service to clients, depending on the client's wealth. If people can afford an expensive firm, including the hiring of high-priced experts to testify on their behalf, they are likely to have more strategic options at their disposal than if they are poor and must rely on legal aid. Even government can be overburdened in serving the public interest when the number of cases assigned to a particular agency, for example, the Environmental Protection Agency, is high. In that instance, the resources that can be devoted to a single case are often low compared to the resources a private firm representing a corporate defendant can bring to the same case. In such a situation, a private firm may be able to create delays in the enforcement of a particular regulation that is in the public's interest and thereby hold off important governmental protections of the environment. Arguably, some of the current controversies surrounding the tobacco industry fit this scenario.

Clearly, these various problems do not require the same kind of solution. Nor are all of these problems confronted by every law firm, government agency, or legal aid clinic in every case. But they are present often enough. Thus, my suggestions should be understood to apply situationally, depending on the difficulties being confronted. In the case of a too-narrow form of legal research, the solution may be to expand one's perspectives to include other considerations. In this book I have provided a theoretical model for how this expansion might be undertaken. It means taking into account the political, social, economic, and philosophical issues that may be at stake in a course of action. In the situation of an overburdening caseload, the solution may be to assign greater resources, including more attorneys, to deal with the cases. Law schools each year turn out thousands of soon-to-be attorneys looking for jobs. Though a few of the lucky ones find high-paying positions, most do not. And of those who do, it is usually at the cost of selling their bodies and minds to seventy-or-more-hour workweeks. This is absurd when some lawyers scrape by at salaries of less than $20,000 per year. Moreover, because the higher salaries must ultimately be recouped as attorney fees from clients, firms that pay these salaries funnel away valuable resources that might otherwise be made available to clients who cannot afford high-priced law firms. Therefore, my suggestion is that lawyers' salaries should be curbed according to an agreed-upon formula to be developed by state bar associations.

I focus on state bar associations because they would be better able to assess the costs of living in their home state than would a national organization. The formula to be developed by the associations should have two elements. First, there should be a salary base that provides a reasonable income to meet professional and personal responsibilities, including school-loan repayments, to be worked out by the association members. Once that is set aside, any further monies should be paid either as bonuses or dividends, depending on whether it is paid to associates or equity partners, according to a formula that reflects number of years worked, competency in the performance of professional responsibilities, and new business brought into the firm. As one of the costs of doing business, the state bar should set forth guidelines for a contribution based on income produced in the previous year to be assigned to a pool where each firm shares fairly, according to its size, in furnishing legal services to the community at large. This would offset the need for legal services by persons who otherwise could not afford it. It would also acknowledge that some law firms are able to operate in the wealthier business markets that they do only because government has created laws that affect these markets. Since government regulation is at least collaterally responsible for the economic distribution of services toward wealthier clients, it is only fair that the people who benefit from these laws should make available quality legal services to all. The money assigned to the pool would be paid prior to the payment of any bonuses or dividends and should be made a tax-deductible business expense. There should also be a credit for firms that contribute services directly to low-income clients toward what their contribution would otherwise be to the pool. In this sense, the pool would become an incentive to offer legal services to everyone rather than some sort of self-imposed tax.

Moreover, the number of hours new associates should be expected to work per week should be brought closer to the national average in most fields of forty hours. And, especially with the contribution plan in place, law firms should devote more resources to pro bono cases or cases based on a sliding scale of income. The latter might be further supported by having firms join together in pooling experts for the sake of serving the public and possibly by setting limits on what they are willing to pay experts for court appearances. There would have to be a careful economic evaluation of this suggestion so as not to make it uneconomical for experts to want to testify on behalf of clients. But, here too, there may be a way for groups like the American Bar Association and the American Medical Association to work out guidelines for fees that doctors can charge, for example, and for determining their responsibility in providing a service to clients who need their testimony. Otherwise, subject to certain constitutional contract restrictions, laws might be passed to regulate fees in this area. If firms pool their economic power, these limitations might be imposed without regulations. This approach would also provide an impetus for young lawyers to be given more client contact and, at the same time, reduce some of the pressures on legal aid clinics. It could also provide a further place for the training of lawyers through the legal internship program I have suggested. Dental schools, for example, often have clinics to serve the public at a lower cost that are supervised by professors of dentistry and practitioner dentists. Some firms have already contributed their services directly to a nonprofit legal organization, the American Civil Liberties Union, and there are other examples.

All areas of legal practice should be engaged in a continuing form of legal education that includes more than just seminars on new legislation or new case developments. It must also include social and political analyses as well as philosophical inquiry and economic reforms of discussion covering areas in which lawyers practice. It must draw attention to new areas of the law where legislation is needed because the law is too thin. Lawyers practicing in a particular area should be required to sit periodically for these seminars as a criterion for renewing their licenses. This need not necessarily involve examinations, given that the area of practice itself would create an incentive to learn the material. Other commentators have made some of the suggestions I make here.[112] If these suggestions are adopted, they should not only advance the overall professionalism of lawyers but also significantly contribute to the public's respect for lawyers, which unfortunately has been declining in recent years.

CONCLUSION

I have shown in this book how a deep issue about the relation between legal and political philosophy arises from an inquiry concerning legitimate sources of law and the duty to obey law. Concerning that relation, there are both descriptive and prescriptive sides. On the descriptive side, the analysis shows how a court's dual determination, as to what constitutes an appropriate source of law and what it means to follow law, affects how it decides cases. On the prescriptive side, the analysis provides criteria for when a court, in seeking to do justice, should follow only traditional sources of law and when it should look beyond these sources: first to the political morality of the society, ultimately, to a theory of natural law/natural rights. A judge, when deciding a difficult case, should appeal to successively wider ranges of political moralities as is necessary to ensure that the decision is both determinative and just.[1] Once that is done, the judge must reverse the process so that the principles discovered at that more abstract level can be used as a ground for deciding the case at hand.

There is objectivity here in the sense that principles at a high level of abstraction are relied on to justify an interpretation of the law to a particular case. If the controversy continues up the ladder to where these principles are found, then the appeal needed to resolve it will have to move up past that level to a yet higher level. This is necessary if correspondence truth is going to decide the controversy. Eventually, we reach the Davidsonian limit beyond which there is no where else to go. At that point, the discourse that we are using to contain our conceptual framework is at its widest extent, given the interpretative nature of our language and beliefs. Consequently, our understanding of truth must alter to reflect no longer a correspondence view but a coherence view. So too must the sense of objectivity change from a position that some arguably noncontroversial higher level of abstract principles might permit to one that is intersubjectively the most coherent understanding possible, given the nature of our language and beliefs.

The deep issue is why the process works to provide a means for judicial decisionmaking. The answer is that apparently legal systems are inherently incomplete, no matter how many rules and principles they may contain. A system of rules and principles is complete in this sense if all the cases we need to decide are indeed decidable within the system. In the case of positivism, law is certainly incomplete in that the judge has discretion in how to decide a case whenever the rules of law do not provide a solution. (Positivism provides a set of primary rules governing behavior and secondary rules that determine what the primary rules are. It is incomplete whenever a court is free to exercise discretion over whether a particular behavior comes within the scope of some primary rule.[2]) In contrast, legal realism provides a complete system in the sense that every case is decidable because the law is whatever the highest court to decide says the law is. But legal realism is non-rule-governed because a judge is always free to interpret any rule or principle that comes before the court.

This brings us to legal idealism. Here, Ronald Dworkin wants to have it both ways. He wants a system that is both complete and governed by rules and principles because he wants to deny the legal critic's claim that some cases will have no right answer. But he goes about achieving this denial by bringing in the political morality of the society as a part of law. In Dworkin's view, even principles that determine how courts should interpret law must be a part of the law. Thus, Dworkin would include within law the principle that a judge should interpret any new case so as to reproduce the settled law; and where necessary, because more than one inconsistent principle might fit the settled law, he would also include the principle of making the law conform to the society's political morality. Dworkin's principle of interpretation, in effect, interprets itself. More generally, if *L* is a system of rules and principles and *I* is a principle of interpretation within *L*, then the truth of *I* will not be decidable within *L* unless *L* is circular. But that raises the question: Must *L* be circular? Under the positivist model, *L* is not circular since there is always some secondary rule—the Rule of Recognition—that is outside *L*. But under Dworkin's model, there is no outside of *L*. (*I* is a substantive principle in L and the prevailing political morality that gives it meaning is taken to be a part of *L*.) The problem here is that Dworkin does not distinguish between an internal epistemic move to obtain greater knowledge and an external justificatory move to ground one's decisions. As a result, he cannot handle cases that fundamentally challenge the legitimacy of *L*. For him, such cases raise issues that are simply out of court. But they are not outside of what a judge must decide, as witnessed by the discussion of very hard cases. These are real questions that require a theory of political morality in general to help with their resolution.

Going back to the example, if *I* is truly a principle of *L*, then the political morality that would justify *I* in *L*, which Dworkin calls "law as integrity," cannot be a part of *L*. More generally, for any *I** in *L* justified by a theory of political morality *P*, one can assert the truth of *I* in terms of *P* only provided *P* is outside *L*. To avoid the circularity problem, one moved outside *L*. Dworkin would extend *L* to include the grounds of the political morality, *L**, because he believes those grounds are part of the constitutional order defining *L*. But whenever one does this, it is necessary to recreate the possibility that there will be some case not decidable in *L**, and one recognizes that case by its trademark of calling *L** into question. In other words, one is back to the point that H. L. A. Hart makes, that the Rule of Recognition is never valid, only accepted.[3]

The metaprinciple that justifies *I* in *L* cannot itself be a member of *L*, if *L* is consistent. Moreover, one can offer no proof for *L*'s consistency internal to *L* (because the consistency of *L* would have to be judged in terms of some *P* outside of *L*). Yet, one can deny the consistency of *L* if *L* is made up of inconsistent rules or principles, as would be recognized internally by a judge. For example, if a rule in *L* provides that people drive on the left and another rule provides that they drive on the right, *L* is inconsistent, and there is no way to adjudicate the question of which side of the street to drive on. On the other hand, if *L* incorporates a rule of interpretation, such as "follow the most recent rule," the question of which side of the street to drive on may be decidable. But this then raises the further question of why follow the most recent rule as opposed, for example, to the one that was most frequently followed in the past. Here one reaches a substantive and not simply a semantical question, and it is not enough to say that a rule is a rule.

The CLS proponents were correct when they said that they could not find any basis upon which to conclude that law is consistent. They were correct because they confined themselves to the internal point of view, where proof of the consistency of law is not possible and where sometimes laws come about to fulfill policy goals of the legislature, as when it provides a bailout to a large company that employs many workers but not to a small one. Outside the internal perspective the possibility exists of finding a metatheory under which the consistency of law may be shown. But this requires a move to principles, including principles that under some circumstances might allow policy questions to dominate. The CLS criticism that challenges the determinacy of our language, logic, and moral reasonings still applies, even to external points of view. But its importance is attenuated the higher one moves up the ladder, diminishing entirely at the moment one reaches the Davidsonian limit.

Similarly, other critics of Dworkin were correct who said that no matter what political morality is included in law, there will remain some question that cannot be answered within law. This follows from the fact that a substantive principle cannot justify itself without circularity. That is, law is necessarily incomplete. The duty to obey law presupposes that the laws are both consistent and just, and there is no a priori ground for excluding a case from arising that may question the justice of the legal system. But these critics were also incorrect when they suggested that there was no way to circumvent this problem. Although it is not Dworkin's approach, appeals to a more highly ordered political morality will allow for decisions that would otherwise not be decidable within law.

Still, one might ask, continuing the same line of argument, if this conclusion does not put morality itself, in this case the theory of natural law, into doubt. Here one discovers, if the theory of natural law is sufficiently fundamental to be at the Davidsonian ceiling of meaningful inquiry, that there will be no further questions to ask by way of its justification. The Davidsonian ceiling exists at the point where any further question along the same line—in this case, justification of a norm—would require one to be able to distinguish scheme and content, something that is not possible to do. Since such a distinction is, therefore, not meaningful, correspondence concerns must collapse into coherence concerns, with the resulting splotch being a kind of moral fact and the notion of incompleteness becoming unclear. Alan Gewirth seems to recognize this aspect of his own theory when he notes that once one gets to the level of agency, any more basic concern will fall under a different modality, such as the modality of psychology or metaphysics. In other words, at the level of agency, all questions of moral justification are logically part of the normative structure of agency. In this sense, for Gewirth, the ought-statement (PGC) is truly derivable from the is-statement (defining agency) because, within the modality of ethics, the former statement is just a special way to view the latter (for an illustration of my conclusion, see Figure 3).

I make use of the term "discourse" because I see how it may illustrate much of what I have been saying up to now (see Fig. 3). By "discourse" I mean various conceptual frameworks arranged in a hierarchy from narrower to broader sets of concepts sharing a common theme.[4] Treating it in this way, one can speak of being inside a discourse as holding a kind of internal, intersubjective

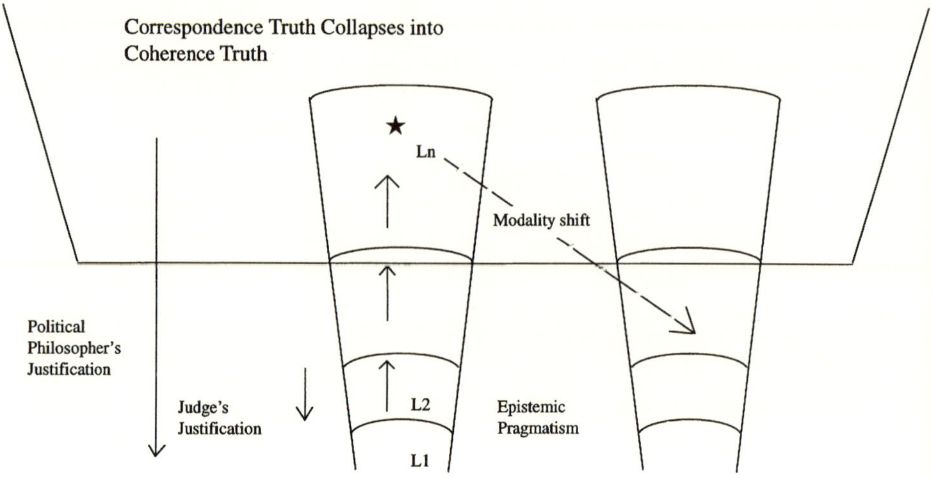

Figure 3. The political philosopher's "external" perspective of the relationships between legal and political philosophy. The two cones represent different discourses relevant to courts: the one on the left includes moral justifications for law and the legal system; the one on the right includes causal psychology. Several cones may be involved in a legal decision. The ceiling at the top represents the Davidsonian scheme/content limit. The modality line represents the shift in the type of discourse when one passes the Davidsonian limit.

point of view. Being outside a discourse, that is, conceiving several discourses, is a kind of external viewpoint relative to any particular discourse. (Here I modify my prior use of internal and external from applying to different moves between frameworks—when applied to legal decisionmaking—to affording different outlooks on the various language discourses that relate to law.) Rules of interpretation determine which frameworks are subsumed into which discourse. The rules are nothing more than a set of metathematic or interpretative concepts, which I use to assign different frameworks to different discourses. Discourse itself I treat as having the shape of a cone in order to represent the widening frameworks that define the discourse. I prefer the cone to concentric circles to capture the way more highly ordered frameworks can both critique and justify (in the preceding sense of external) decisions based on narrower frameworks. As for the frameworks that make up a cone, these are determined internally by their use in decisionmaking and externally in my new sense by their ability to add interpretative coherence or family resemblance to the rest of the discourse. In this latter sense, normative frameworks, including law when treated as a set of duties and rights, fit a normative discourse cone, and empirical frameworks, such as intention and motivation, fit an empirical (psychological) discourse cone. Thus, when viewed externally in this broader sense, each discourse displays a set of interpretative connections subsumed under a metatheoretic framework. The principles I present in chapter 3 signal the kinds of conceptual frameworks that make up the legal decisionmaking discourse cone. For example, Dworkin's idealized framework and a system of natural law/natural rights fit within a normative/choice discourse regarding the regulation of human behavior. But the causal theories known as behavioral conditioning and learning theory both fit a discourse of empirical psychology. In contrast to the role discourse plays in uniting various frameworks is the role a conceptual scheme plays in uniting many discourses. Here the difference is that no thematic relations may exist between the discourse cones being united. Empirical psychology and normative ethics are two such discourses that fit within the broad scheme of our language and beliefs, including its principles of translation, but arguably share no thematic connections. This brings me, then, to the question of discourse boundaries.

There are also two kinds of incoherence present that surround what might be called a "discourse cone" made up of different frameworks in a hierarchy of abstraction (see Fig. 3). The two kinds of incoherence are local and global. Global incoherence is the kind of incoherence that Davidson discusses when one tries to make sense of the scheme/content distinction, that is, when one talks as if one could step outside one's conceptual scheme. But there is also local incoherence. For instance, I am presented with alternative sets of unrelated concepts in terms of which I must make a choice as to how I am to interpret whatever it is that is before me. The distinction between empirical psychology and normative ethics I mentioned above presents one such example. A close analogy in the perceptual area to what I have in mind is illustrated by Ludwig Wittgenstein's famous duck-rabbit example.[5]

First, I see a duck, then I see a rabbit, then I see a duck again, then I see . . . I never see a duck-rabbit; it is simply not in my perceptual framework to have this vision. But insofar as I can jump between the two perceptions that first appear as duck, then rabbit, then duck again, I am not in the area of global perceptual failure, either. I may be stuck seeing either duck or rabbit, but I am seeing something. Law, as a broadening set of conceptual frameworks within a still broader normative discourse (the cone in Fig. 3) is like the duck vision. There is a limit at the top of the discourse, where I suggested (because of its general foundation in agency) Gewirth's arguments reside and from

Figure 4. Wittgenstein's duck-rabbit.

which there is no place higher to go within the discourse. And there may be jumps to different discourse cones that, like the rabbit vision, involve issues of causation, intention, and an entire host of factual questions that law must also be concerned with. Most important to this analysis is that there is no intermediate ground between seeing the picture as either a duck or a rabbit.

In both law and morality, the concept of action plays the conceptual equivalent of the perceptual duck-rabbit. It also helps us to understand whether one is talking about law descriptively or prescriptively. For instance, when understood in terms of Austinian—pre-Hartian—positivism, the concept of action provokes a descriptive discourse in which issues of physical and mental causation, such as intentionality, and surrounding social circumstances, help one predict what an actor is likely to do. When understood in terms of Fullerian/Dworkian/Gewirthian idealism, the concept of action invokes a prescriptive discourse in which notions of voluntariness and purposiveness are presupposed by every claim to act. Since I am primarily concerned with the way a morality of action can provide an upper bound to legal/normative discourse, I will say just a few more words on how a Gewirthian moral view might fit in here. But first I note that the two understandings can also be compared to Jürgen Habermas's idea of how different discourses relate to claims about facts and claims about norms.

> When understood by participants engaged in interaction and discourse, truth claims are claims about the objective world that all human beings share, and moral claims have to do with norms for interpersonal relationships that any autonomous adult should find rationally acceptable from the standpoint of justice and respect for persons. If such claims are valid, then any competent speaker should, under suitable conditions, be able to accept the claim on the basis of good reasons. When a claim is contested, actually bringing about such rational acceptance requires actors to shift into a *discourse* in which, the pressures of action having been more or less neutralized, they can isolate and test the disputed claim solely on the basis of arguments.[6]

Between fact and value lies a logical gap where no rule of translation exists. This point explains why traditional naturalistic attempts to try to bridge the fact/value gap have failed.[7] There is simply no place to ground the rule that would allow translation of the one into the other because of the way the concepts that define each area are parceled out. But note that it is only when trying to bridge fact and value externally that this gap appears so insurmountable. Internally, the gap is merely transient. That is to say, the normative concepts needed to resolve the problem are present in each statement of the discourse. Only the principle of translation is lacking to convert from one normative is-like statement to another normative ought-like statement. Put another way, inside the normative discourse cone, there are no pure fact-statements in the sense of strictly empirical statements, although there are statements, such as those about action, that may at first appear as if they were purely factual. From this it follows, as Gewirth believes, that the internal viewpoint, if properly construed, by his dialectically necessary method, can allow one to go from a statement of action, which is itself to be understood normatively, to a statement about rights. Action, when viewed internally, possesses the normative structure of voluntariness and purposiveness.[8]

In contrast, action, when viewed externally, is empirical and strictly causal. Here is the difference the law has traditionally recognized between intent and capacity: the first is an element of certain crimes like murder and is proved by actions and statements; the second concerns whether a person can even be a criminal as when, for example, he is found to be legally insane; it is proved by expert medical testimony based on a physical or psychological examination that determines that the person fits a certain psychological category. Thus, we see why Gewirth believes he has bridged the fact/value and is/ought gaps and why some of his critics, who fail to understand what he is doing, arrive at the opposite conclusion. Both Gewirth and they are looking at human action but from two very different vantage points. Gewirth's perspective is to look at agency as it would be understood and discussed strictly from within the internal conative standpoint of the agent. That perspective forces him to go inside the normative discourse cone where action itself is described not as a product of unintended causes, such as the insanity example, but as the outcome of chosen reasons, such as the intent example. That is why he speaks of an action as being voluntary when it is within the unforced choice of the agent.

Here, choice can be direct and occurrent, as when the agent chooses to act for some reason; dispositional, as when the agent could have chosen not to perform the action but does not make that choice; or indirect, as when the agent puts himself in a situation (for example, drunkenness), knowing that a certain action is likely to occur.[9] In some situations, both a strictly empirical and a normative description may be possible. When that happens, the choice is determined by what one hopes to accomplish by the description offered. If the law presupposes that a person can control his behavior provided that he has a coherent internal framework and no outside external forces acting on him, at least not such as would seem unregulatable by internal reasons, the normative approach will be the one chosen. Otherwise, an empirical view will be preferred.

Gewirth's agency perspective also pushes one into the first-person perspective, and that is how the is/ought gap is closed; advocacy to act for purposes one takes as good necessitates at least implicitly that the agent claim rights to the necessary conditions for action (see chapter 2). Once that is accomplished, the agent's recognition that it was only her status as an agent that led to this subjective necessity becomes transformed through universality into the intersubjective recognition that any other prospective purposive agent could make a similar claim. The agent accepts for herself duties to promote the freedom and well-being of others as the only rational conclusion to be reached given the justificatory condition. Thus, the transient gap ceases to exist at the point where, by use of the dialectically necessary method, one not only discloses the normative structure of action internally but goes on to advocate for the conditions that make such action possible. The duck-rabbit example fits in to illustrate the move to adopt the normative perspective, which I have described as preceding the move to the first-person perspective.

Habermas also recognizes what I call local incoherence. His system is based on the idea of setting up an "ideal speech situation" where all people in society dedicate themselves to truth, and the rejection of force, deception, and reliance on irrelevant emotions.[10] Here, the individual is treated not in isolation, as in Gewirth, but in conversation with another person. In this situation, participants adopt the moral point of view, that is, they "*transcend* the social and historical context of their particular form of life and particular community and adopt the perspective of *all* those possibly affected."[11] The commitments to truth and nonviolence made in the ideal speech situation, thus, define a metadiscourse, a kind of dialectic, that can encompass other discourses. Habermas believes that adopting the internal point of view "privileges practical [as distinct from speculative] discourse as the form of communication that secures the impartiality of moral judgment together with universal interchangeability of participant perspectives."[12] For instance, Habermas's view would anchor

> the legitimacy of law in a discourse that is conceptually prior to the distinction between law and morality. . . . Legitimate law must pass a discursive test that potentially engages the entire range of different types of discourse. These include not only moral and ethical discourses but also "pragmatic" discourses in which alternative strategies for achieving a given aim are assessed; in addition, insofar as an issue involves conflicting particular interests and values that do not permit consensus, a legitimate legal regulation of the issue must involve fair compromise.[13]

Habermas considers various pragmatic discourses because he does not believe that general rights adopted in the ideal speech situation will ever determine public policy. The reason is that differences of interpretation related to institutional and cultural history will always come into play in deciding particular legal norms.[14] Habermas admits that agreement may not always be forthcoming even within the internal point of view on specific legal arrangements and, consequently, regulations based on compromises may be necessary. Still, it is not clear what would ensure such compromises. For, unlike the Gewirthian first-person perspective, Habermas's internal view does not start from any subjective necessity.[15] Instead, he holds to an intersubjective, rather than to a subjective, perspective as the ground for fair compromise. The problem, of course, is that it is not obvious why people with radically different views should want to compromise inside this perspective. Even if these commitments, to the extent that they play any organizing role of their speech situation, guaranteed compromise, it is not clear where the compromise would be struck if the situation was one where the parties—as on the abortion issue—had radically opposite views.[16] How does a pro-choice person compromise with someone who believes that *any* abortions are wrong, even if it is not clear who has the better argument.[17]

Gewirth's solution to this problem is to adopt the internal first-person conative stance of the agent. Here the obligation to be reasonable comes out of the desire not to contradict oneself as a rational agent. Intersubjectivity is brought in only after the agent has realized that he has certain rights.[18] Since the ground of the agent's assertion is that he is a prospective purposive agent, any agent would come to this same conclusion qua agent applying the dialectically necessary method. Consequently, any rational agent logically must admit on pain of contradiction that he has the same rights as everyone else. In other words, no agent qua agent stands in a more privileged position with respect to his fellow agents when it comes to being a rights holder.[19] Therefore, under Gewirth's system, policy choices must be made so as to guarantee the equal rights of all. Nothing is left but the means by which these policies will bring about the ends that the PGC directs. Here, there can be legitimate differentiating grounds within the relevant empirical discourse for preferring one approach to another for guaranteeing equal rights.

It might be interesting to note what would result if the internal point of view were applied to descriptive discourse and the external view to normative discourse. (My point here is to suggest that the discussion explaining Figure 3 has applications beyond the confines of legal and moral reasoning.) There are four possibilities, each of which can be tied to a particular jurisprudential and moral tradition. I have already suggested that when the internal perspective is put on normative discourse, we gain a set of moral laws that from our view appear universal. The natural law/natural rights tradition and Dworkian idealism are the jurisprudential equivalents. When the internal perspective is applied to descriptive discourses, we have a worldview, be it, for example, the view of science or religion.[20] Such a worldview is critiqueable but only by appeal to a more highly ordered framework of concepts within the same discourse cone. Because of localized incoherence, the truth of the worldview cannot be determined outside a discourse cone. Thus, when the internal perspective is applied to descriptive discourses with respect to law, we have a socio-psychology of law as illustrated by the positions of Marxism and feminism. In contrast, when the external view is applied to descriptive discourse we have conceptual relativism or, in law, legal realism and the CLS movement. Likewise, when the external view is applied to normative discourse, we have moral relativism or positivism. Finally, it should be noted that Gewirth's delving into the normative structure of agency and selection of only those features of voluntariness and purposiveness that all moral theories presume allows him to derive not just an ought from an is but an ought that applies universally within normative discourse and not just to particular cases.

Let us consider one final question. How should legal education proceed, given the close connection between legal and political philosophy? The answer is to teach law students how to read and understand legal-philosophical texts, especially texts that attempt to justify and explain legal principles and principles of justice. Further, they must be taught how to make sense of political-philosophical arguments that account for the obligation to obey law. This is especially true in preparing students to meet situations where fundamental rights, as typify much of constitutional law, are at stake. Moreover, even in other areas of the law, the policy interests may not be well articulated, the rights not always well defined or well grounded, and the precedents, to the extent that they even exist, contradictory or contrary to basic principles of justice. We need to be assured that our future policymakers, whether they are lawyers, politicians, judges, or other governmental or private-sector decisionmakers, understand the full breadth of their political responsibilities. They need to be trained in techniques of conceptual and normative analyses so that they are prepared to face the difficult intellectual challenges involved both in clarifying a concept and justifying a right.

Recent additions to law school curriculums of justice courses and courses in jurisprudence represent an important step in this direction. Still, more needs to be done. First, these courses might be made part of a standard law school curriculum. Second, existing courses in more traditional areas should be supplemented with exercises requiring conceptual and normative analyses to accompany reasoning by analogy and statutory interpretation. In courses such as contracts, property, torts, criminal law, corporations, labor relations, and so forth, the economic, moral, or political underpinning must not be presumed, as if it were outside the realm of what a lawyer should be concerned with. Instead, these issues must be confronted with the full panoply of arguments available. In this regard, I take heed of a point made by Martha Nussbaum concerning the dilemma a law professor faces when preparing students for the practice of law:

> I am sure that it is a terrible question for the law professor whether to encourage in students habits of thought that the legal profession on the outside will stamp out, crush, extirpate. On the other hand, it seems to me that judges and legal thinkers could do with a bit more wonder of the Socratic sort: not unguided free play of the faculties, but a concerted rigorous inquiry into the subtleties of some foundational issue, informed by the relevant empirical information. I also think, with Socrates, that this sort of thinking is a good thing for human beings in general. So I am willing to say, let the law students learn to wonder, and then perhaps, wherever they are, they will feel the pressure of a Socratic question arising up to annoy them as they are trying to be simple.[21]

The pain of our moral fraility is not caused, as some left-wing social constructivists would have it, by belief in universal moral objectivity or moral realism. It is caused, as many right-wing realists would have it, by belief in our own infallibility. We must never be afraid to speak what we believe or to make moral judgments when necessary, based on our best reasonings, in the hope of either changing the minds of others, simply doing what is right, or getting a clearer vision of our own positions. But we must never be so arrogant in our own viewpoints to believe we could not be mistaken. That is the deep lesson of both our moral and legal reasonings and hopefully the goal of a truly fulfilled life. I hope this book makes a contribution to this moral development in legal education, in addition to providing a deep understanding of judicial decisionmaking and a recommendation for deciding very hard cases.

NOTES

Preface

1. Ronald Dworkin, *Taking Rights Seriously* (Cambridge, Mass.: Harvard University Press, 1977).

2. See, e.g., Ronald Dworkin, *Law's Empire* (Cambridge, Mass.: Harvard University Press, 1986), pp. 260–63.

3. Andrew Altman, "Legal Realism, Critical Legal Studies, and Dworkin," *Philosophy and Public Affairs* 15 (1986): 205–36.

4. Duncan Kennedy, "Form and Substance in Private Law Adjudication," *Harvard Law Review* 89 (1976): 1685, 1777.

5. See J. L. Mackie, "The Third Theory of Law," *Philosophy and Public Affairs* 7 (1977): 9–10 (arguing that Dworkin's internal approach to political morality is ultimately subjective).

6. But see Ronald Dworkin, "Pragmatism, Right Answers, and True Banality," in *Pragmatism in Law and Society*, ed. Michael Brint and William Weaver (Boulder, Colo.: Westview Press, 1991), p. 362, in which Dworkin argues that even Richard Rorty's pragmatism cannot occupy a unique external point of view to law.

7. H. L. A. Hart treats this problem with the use of a distinction between secondary rules (rules that govern lawmaking, such as the legislation that Congress passes and the president signs) and the Rule of Recognition. In essence, the Rule of Recognition is a secondary rule, but unlike other secondary rules, it has the unique status of not being valid in terms of any more basic rule; it is merely accepted by the institutions of the society in which it operates (H. L. A. Hart, *The Concept of Law* [Oxford: Clarendon Press, 1961], pp. 77–79, 105–6).

8. See Alan Hunt, "The Critique of Law: What Is 'Critical' About Critical Legal Theory?" in *Critical Legal Studies*, ed. Peter Fitzpatrick and Alan Hunt (New York: Blackwell, 1987), p. 10.

9. I have in mind here H. L. A. Hart's idea of secondary rules, John L. Austin's idea of law as a command backed by a sanction, and Robert Bork's idea of original intent.

10. Two examples include Lon Fuller and Ronald M. Dworkin.

11. H. L. A. Hart, for example, thought that fidelity to law was part of the internal point of view because there was no necessary logical connection between law and morality; Ronald M. Dworkin thought that moral principles were part of law because attempts to respond to external skepticism only led to incoherence. See H. L. A. Hart, *The Con-*

cept of Law, 2d ed. (Oxford: Clarendon Press, 1994), pp. 254–59 (discussing the internal and external view of rules and how Hart's account differs from Dworkin's).

12. See Neil MacCormick, *H. L. A. Hart* (Stanford, Calif.: Stanford University Press, 1981), pp. 43–44 (classifying a quasi-external, "hermeneutic," point of view).

13. The idea is that one could not even talk about law and morality if each of these systems truly represented a separate conceptual scheme. See Donald Davidson, "On the Very Idea of a Conceptual Scheme," in *Inquiries into Truth and Interpretation* (Oxford: Oxford University Press, 1984), pp. 183–98.

14. See Kip S. Thorne, *Black Holes and Time Warps: Einstein's Outrageous Legacy* (New York: Norton, 1994), pp. 438–45.

15. See Dworkin, *Law's Empire*, note 2.

Introduction

1. H. L. A. Hart, *The Concept of Law* (New York: Oxford University Press, 1961), p. 246 n. page 98.

2. See ibid. (showing how actual legal practice blurs the distinction between historical or causal sources and legal or formal ones).

3. See Ronald Dworkin, *Law's Empire* (Cambridge, Mass.: Harvard University Press, 1986), pp. 257–58.

4. See ibid., pp. 128–29, 255–56.

5. See ibid., pp. 99–101.

6. See ibid., pp. 101–2; see also Lon Fuller, *The Morality of Law*, rev. ed. (New Haven: Yale University Press, 1978).

7. See Dworkin, *Law's Empire*, note 3, pp. 254–55; see also Ronald Dworkin, "Is There Really No Right Answer in Hard Cases?" in *A Matter of Principle* (Cambridge, Mass.: Harvard University Press, 1985), p. 119.

8. See Dworkin, *Law's Empire*, note 3, pp. 271–74; see also Andrew Altman, "Legal Realism, Critical Legal Studies, and Dworkin," *Philosophy and Public Affairs* 15 (1986).

9. See Dworkin, *Law's Empire*, note 3, pp. 152–53.

10. See Raymond Belliotti, *Justifying Law: The Debate over Foundations, Goals and Methods* (Philadelphia: Temple University Press, 1992), pp. 159–61, 203–7.

11. See Dworkin, *Law's Empire*, note 3, pp. 75–76.

12. See ibid., pp. 80–81.

13. This question represents the metaethical debate currently existing between cultural relativists and absolutists.

14. See Dworkin, *Law's Empire*, note 3, p. 255.

Chapter 1. Sources of Law

1. H. L. A. Hart, *The Concept of Law* (New York: Oxford University Press, 1961), pp. 13–14.

2. Plato, *Republic*, in *Plato: The Collected Dialogues Including the Letters*, ed. Edith Hamilton and Huntington Cairns (Princeton: Princeton University Press, 1961), bk. 4, p. 433a.

3. Aristotle, *Nicomachean Ethics*, in *The Basic Works of Aristotle*, ed. Richard McKeon (New York: Random House, 1941), bk. 5, p. 1129b6-30.

4. Thomas Aquinas, "Concerning the Nature of Law," in *Summa Theologica, The Basic Writings of Saint Thomas Aquinas*, ed. A. Pegis, 2 vols. (New York: Random House, 1945), 2: 743.

5. Ibid.

6. Ibid., p. 744.

7. Ibid.

8. Ibid., p. 746.

9. Ibid.

10. Ibid.

11. Ibid., p. 747.

12. Ibid.

13. Ibid.

14. Ibid., p. 748.

15. Ibid., pp. 752–53.

16. See ibid., p. 750.

17. See ibid.

18. Aristotle, *Nicomachean Ethics*, note 3, bk. 1, p. 1095a15.

19. Quantum mechanics teaches, for instance, that one cannot measure the exact position and momentum of an electron simultaneously because the very process of looking involves putting energy into the system that, in turn, affects the outcome. We can hope to know only what the probability is that, at a given moment, the electron will be at a certain position or have a certain momentum. This understanding of probability is different from the usual understanding that reflects simply a lack of information regarding the salient factors affecting a system. The same is not the case in quantum mechanics. There we are barred from ever having all the information about a system that would allow us to make the hoped-for determinations.

20. See Aquinas, "Concerning the Nature of Law," note 4, p. 750.

21. See ibid.

22. See ibid.

23. See ibid.

24. See ibid.

25. See ibid.

26. See ibid.

27. Ronald Dworkin, "Justice for Clarence Thomas," *New York Review of Books*, November 7, 1991, 41, 44, col. 4.

28. See ibid.

29. See ibid.

30. Raymond Belliotti, *Justifying Law: The Debate over Foundations, Goals and Methods* (Philadelphia: Temple University Press, 1992), p. 32 (citing Michael Moore, "A Natural Law Theory of Interpretation," *Southern California Law Review* 58 [1985]: 279). Moreover, Moore believes that his view is a natural law position because (a) it affirms a moral reality from which we can generate right answers to normative questions, and (b) it requires us, when deciding cases, to follow intrepretative premises derived from that morality.

31. *Dred Scott v. Sanford*, 60 U.S. (19 How.) 393 (1857).

32. *Plessy v. Ferguson*, 163 U.S. 537 (1896).

33. *Bowers v. Hardwick*, 478 U.S. 186 (1986).

34. See Janet Shibley Hyde, *Understanding Human Sexuality*, 3d ed. (New York: McGraw-Hill, 1986), p. 20.

35. See Aquinas, "Concerning the Nature of Law," note 4, p. 785.

36. See ibid. Two qualifying principles are often used to avoid such problems, forfeiture of life and double effect. However, forfeiture of life, which allows the death penalty for one who threatens the life of another, still violates natural law's absolute proscription against taking a life. Double effect, which says that some actions have both good and bad consequences, requires that the bad consequence (death) not be the cause of the good consequence (punishing the evildoer), which it is in this case. Therefore, neither solves the problem. See C. E. Harris, Jr., *Applying Moral Theories*, 3d ed. (Belmont, Calif.: Wadsworth, 1997), pp. 104–5, 121.

37. See Belliotti, *Justifying Law*, note 30, p. 31.

38. John Austin, *Lectures on Jurisprudence*, ed. R. Campbell, 4th ed. (London: John Murray, 1873), Lecture 1, pp. 88–89.

39. Ibid., p. 89.

40. Ibid., p. 91.

41. Ibid., Lecture 6, p. 226.

42. Ibid., p. 227.

43. J. Feinberg and H. Gross, eds., *Philosophy of Law*, 4th ed. (Belmont, Calif.: Wadsworth, 1991), p. 4.

44. Ibid.

45. Ibid.

46. Ibid.

47. Ibid.

48. Ibid.

49. John Chipman Gray, *The Nature and Sources of the Law*, 2d ed. (Boston: Beacon Press, 1963), p. 104, and see Oliver Wendell Holmes, "The Path of the Law," *Harvard Law Review* 10 (1897): 457, 458.

50. Gray, *Nature and Sources of Law*, note 49, p. 100.

51. Andrew Altman, "Legal Realism, Critical Legal Studies and Dworkin," *Philosophy and Public Affairs* 15 (1986): 205–36.

52. Karl Llewellyn, "Some Realism About Realism," *Harvard Law Review* 44 (1931): 1222, 1252 (challenging Jerome Frank's claim that rules and precedents lack authority).

53. See Belliotti, *Justifying Law*, note 30, pp. 166–67. But see Mort J. Horwitz, *The Transformation of American Law, 1870–1960: The Crisis of Legal Orthodoxy* (New York: Oxford University Press, 1992), p. 271 (questioning whether the field of law and economics is a true heir of the legal realist movement).

54. Thomas C. Grey, "Holmes and Legal Pragmatism," *Stanford Law Review* 41 (1989): 787, 848, 854–55.

55. Feinberg and Gross, eds., *Philosophy of Law*, 3d ed., note 4, p. 6.

56. Ibid.

57. See Belliotti, *Justifying Law*, note 30, pp. 187–89 (classifying the various positions that have defined the CLS movement).

58. See ibid., pp. 203–7.

59. See ibid., pp. 159–61.

60. Central to the CLS position is the denial of objective human goods. Roberto Unger claims this is necessary if the significance of human choice as an expression of one's personality is not to be reduced to "the passive acceptance or rejection of independent truths" (*Knowledge and Politics* [New York: Free Press, 1975], p. 77).

61. Andrew Altman, "Legal Realism, Critical Legal Studies, and Dworkin," note 51, p. 222.

62. See John Finnis, "Natural Law and Legal Reasoning" in *Natural Law Theory: Contemporary Essays*, ed. Robert P. George (Oxford: Clarendon Press, 1992), p. 136 (arguing that "it is the diversity of *rationally* appealing human goods which makes free choice both possible and frequently necessary").

63. Hart, *Concept of Law*, note 1, p. 80.

64. Ibid., p. 86.

65. See ibid., pp. 92–93.

66. U.S. Constitution, Article 1, section 7.

67. Ibid.

68. Hart, *Concept of Law*, note 1, pp. 57, 105–6.

69. See H. L. A. Hart, "Positivism and the Separation of Law and Morals," *Harvard Law Review* 71 (1958): 593, 622–24.

70. See Lon Fuller, "Positivism and Fidelity to Law," *Harvard Law Review* 71 (1958): 644–45; see also *The Morality of Law*, rev. ed. (New Haven: Yale University Press, 1969), p. 38–39.

71. Ibid.

72. See Margaret Jane Radin, "Reconsidering the Rule of Law," *Boston University Law Review* 69 (1989): 781, 807–10 (arguing that a broad reading of Wittgenstein makes the rule of law contingent on "surrounding social activities and understandings").

73. See Belliotti, *Justifying Law*, note 30, p. 75.

74. Ronald Dworkin, "The Model of Rules," *University of Chicago Law Review* 35 (1967): 23, 25.

75. Ibid., pp. 23, 27.

76. See ibid., p. 29.

77. See ibid., p. 27.

78. See ibid., p. 34.

79. See ibid., pp. 35–36.

80. See ibid., p. 36.

81. Ibid., p. 38.

82. See ibid., p. 45.

83. Ronald Dworkin, "Hard Cases," *Harvard Law Review* 88 (1975): 1064.

84. Ibid., p. 1065.

85. See ibid., p. 1078.

86. See ibid., p. 1084.

87. See ibid., p. 1085.

88. Ronald Dworkin, *A Matter of Principle* (Cambridge, Mass.: Harvard University Press, 1985), p. 143.

89. Ibid., pp. 143–44.

90. See ibid., pp. 161–62.

91. Dworkin, "Hard Cases," note 83, p. 1083.

92. Ronald Dworkin, *Law's Empire* (Cambridge, Mass.: Harvard University Press, 1986), p. 225.

93. See ibid., pp. 65–66.

94. Ibid., p. 229.

95. Ibid., pp. 252–53.

96. See J. L. Mackie, "The Third Theory of Law," *Philosophy and Public Affairs* 7 (1977): 3–16.

97. See ibid., p. 9.

98. Ibid., p. 16.

99. Joseph Raz, "The Relevance of Coherence," *Boston University Law Review* 72 (1992): 303.

100. David Kairys, introduction to *The Politics of Law: A Progressive Critique*, ed. D. Kairys, 2d ed. (New York: Pantheon Books, 1990), pp. 7–8; but see Lawrence Solum, "On the Indeterminacy Crisis: Critiquing Critical Dogma," *University of Chicago Law Review* 54 (1987): 462 (claiming that CLS overstates its case against Dworkin when it argues indeterminacy as opposed to underdeterminacy). From a point of view based in economics, "Kenneth Arrow showed that when institutions make decisions, by majority vote, they will generate logically inconsistent results unless the voters have very similar orderings of preferences" (Frank H. Easterbrook, "Stability and Reliability in Judicial Decisions," *Cornell Law Review* 73 [1988]: 425).

101. Dworkin, *Law's Empire*, note 92, pp. 266–70.

102. This point is effectively made by Douglas Litowitz in response to Dworkin's claim that law as integrity can find a right answer in almost every case. Considering the case of *McLoughlin v. O'Brian*, 1 App. Cas. 410 (1983), in which a mother sought damages for negligent infliction of emotional distress arising from seeing injured family members in a hospital following an automobile accident, Litowitz argues: "In cases like this, Dworkin is stuck in the position of holding either of the following absurd positions: (i) the best decision (a public liability fund) is not really the best decision because it has no precedent; or (ii) since the seemingly best decision would destroy reasonable expectations, it cannot in fact be the best decision. The problem here is one of circularity: the right answer is defined as the one Hercules would reach, and any alternative answer that seems better is not really better, because it is not reached using the Herculean process. There is no way to break out of the hermeneutic circle to ensure that Hercules' decision is correct from the outside, in addition to being internally consistent" ("Dworkin and Critical Legal Studies on Right Answers and Conceptual Holism," *Legal Studies Forum* 18 [1994]: 153–54.

103. David Ingram, *Reason, History and Politics* (Albany: SUNY Press, 1995), p. 254.

104. See D. Caudill and S. Gold, eds., *Radical Philosophy of Law: Contemporary Challenges to Mainstream Legal Theory and Practice* (Atlantic Highlands, N.J.: Humanities Press, 1995).

105. From a comment by Raymond Belliotti to a draft manuscript of this book.

106. See Karl Marx, "Alienated Labor" from the *First Manuscript*, in *Karl Marx: Early Writings*, trans. T. B. Bottomore (New York: McGraw-Hill, 1963), pp. 120–34; see also Raymond Belliotti, "The Legacy of Marxist Jurisprudence," in Caudill and Gold, eds., *Radical Philosophy of Law*, note 104, pp. 3–4.

107. See Belliotti, "Legacy of Marxist Jurisprudence," note 104, p. 4.

108. Ibid., pp. 5–6 (citing Richard Schmitt, *Introduction to Marx and Engles: A Critical Reconstruction* [Boulder, Colo.: Westview Press, 1987], p. 30).

109. Ibid., pp. 8–9.

110. Ibid., pp. 7–10.

111. See John Stuart Mill, *On Liberty* (New York: Penguin Classics, 1988), pp. 115–16; see also chapter 2.

112. Belliotti, "Legacy of Marxist Jurisprudence," note 104, p. 24.

113. Horwitz, *Transformation of American Law,* note 53, p. 271.

114. Belliotti, "Legacy of Marxist Jurisprudence," note 104, pp. 25–26 (citing Catharine MacKinnon, *Feminism Unmodified: Discourses on Life and Law* [Cambridge, Mass.: Harvard University Press, 1987], p. 34).

115. Ibid., p. 27.

116. Ibid., p. 29 (citing Mari J. Matsuda, Charles Lawrence, Richard Delgado, and Kimberle Williams Crenshaw, *Words that Wound: Critical Race Theory, Assaultive Speech and the First Amendment* [Boulder, Colo.: Westview Press, 1993], p. 6).

117. See, e.g., Richard Posner, *Economic Analysis of Law,* 4th ed. (Boston: Little, Brown, 1992), sec. 1.2, pp. 12–15.

118. See Jeremy Bentham, *The Works of Jeremy Bentham,* ed. Sir John Bowring, 11 vols. (New York: Russell and Russell, 1962), 3: 483–91; 5: 235–37.

119. See Alan Gewirth, *Reason and Morality* (Chicago: University of Chicago Press, 1978), p. 55.

120. See Richard Posner, *The Problems of Jurisprudence* (Cambridge, Mass.: Harvard University Press, 1990), pp. 356–57.

121. In the area of democratic theory, for example, an analogous phenomenon has occurred. Joseph Schumpeter describes this phenomenon in terms of two different concepts of democracy. Under the classic doctrine, "The democratic method is that institutional arrangement for arriving at political decisions which realizes the common good by making the people itself decide issues through the election of individuals who are to assemble in order to carry out its will." Under his "alternative" doctrine, "The democratic method is that institutional arrangement for arriving at political decisions in which individuals acquire the power to decide by means of a competitive struggle for the people's vote" (Schumpeter, "Two Concepts of Democracy," in *Political Philosophy,* ed. Anthony Quinton, *Oxford Readings in Philosophy* [New York: Oxford University Press, 1967], pp. 153, 173–74). Clearly both phenomena describe situations in which questions about the common good—whether it is even discoverable—reign supreme. For a different approach to democratic decisionmaking that focuses on the influences of small groups rather than of large movements, see generally Robert A. Dahl, *A Preface to Democratic Theory* (Chicago: University of Chicago Press, 1956).

122. Sidney A. Shapiro, "Keeping the Baby and Throwing Out the Bathwater: Justice Breyer's Critique of Regulation," *Administrative Law Journal of American University* 8 (1995):721, 725–26 (citing Stephen Breyer, *Regulation and Its Reform* [Cambridge, Mass.: Harvard University Press, 1982]); for a discussion of market failures, see Cass Sunstein, *After the Rights Revolution: Reconceiving the Regulatory State* (Cambridge, Mass.: Harvard University Press, 1990), pp. 48–55.

123. See Sunstein, *After the Rights Revolution,* note 122, p. 69.

124. For a discussion with several examples of noneconomic norms, see ibid., pp. 57–69.

125. See Shapiro, "Keeping the Baby," note 122, p. 721.

126. Ibid.

127. Ibid., p. 722.

128. See Mancur Olson, *The Logic of Collective Action: Public Goods and the Theory of Groups* (Cambridge, Mass.: Harvard University Press, 1971), pp. 43–52.

129. Daniel A. Farber and Philip P. Frickey, *Law and Public Choice: A Critical Introduction* (Chicago: University of Chicago Press, 1991), p. 24.

130. See ibid., pp. 38–39.

131. See, generally, Kenneth Arrow, *Social Choice and Individual Values*, 2d ed. (New Haven: Yale University Press, 1963). Arrow showed that no method of combining individual preferences can guarantee either minimum rationality (if society prefers X to Y and Y to Z, then it prefers X to Z) or the Pareto standard (if one person prefers X over Y and no one else has a preference, then society prefers X over Y). For example, "Suppose that three legislators must vote on where to locate a new federal facility, and that the preferences are as follows: *Legislator 1* prefers Texas to Illinois, and Illinois to Florida; *Legislator 2* prefers Illinois to Florida, and Florida to Texas; *Legislator 3* prefers Florida to Texas, and Texas to Illinois. Now, suppose they first decide between Texas and Illinois, with the winner to be paired against Florida. Legislators 1 and 3 prefer Texas, so it wins the first round. One [*sic*] the second round, legislators 2 and 3 combine to pick Florida over Texas, so the choice is Florida. Does the choice of Florida represent the 'majority will'? No, because two of the three legislators actually prefer Illinois to Florida! In fact, unless procedural rules restrict how many motions can be made, the voting would continue forever. On a majority vote, Illinois loses to Texas, which then loses to Florida—but Florida loses to Illinois, so we are right back where we started! The legislators are trapped in a revolving door with no exit" (Farber and Frickey, *Law and Public Choice*, note 129, pp. 38–39).

132. See Brian Barry, "Justice and the Common Good," *Analysis* 21 (1960–1961): 86.

133. See, e.g., Richard Posner, "The Concept of Corrective Justice in Recent Theories of Tort Law," *Journal of Legal Studies* 10 (1981): 206.

134. See John Rawls, "Two Concepts of Rules," *Philosophical Review* 64 (1955): 6.

135. *Lochner v. New York*, 198 U.S. 45 (1905) (holding unconstitutional a New York labor reform law setting the maximum number of hours bakers could work).

136. See Ludwig von Wittgenstein, *Philosophical Investigations: The English Text of the Third Edition*, ed. G. E. M. Anscombe, 3d ed. (New York: Macmillan, 1958), p. 32e, no. 67.

Chapter 2. The Duty to Obey Law

1. See A. J. Simmons, *Moral Principles and Political Obligations* (Princeton: Princeton University Press, 1979), p. 23 (discussing the distinction between our "'obligation to obey the law,' which is a *moral* requirement, and our 'legal obligations,' which are not").

2. An argument by Niklas Luhmann attempts analytically to define law as a closed system independent of all other systems, including politics; see "Operational Closure and Structural Coupling: The Differentiation of the Legal System," *Cardozo Law Review* 13

(1992): 1419, 1436–37. See also Niklas Luhmann, "Law as a Social System," *Northwestern University Law Review* 83 (1989): 136, 137 n. 2 (defining an "autopoietic" system as one that constructs itself by interaction of its parts). Richard Münch challenges this conclusion on the ground that when we talk about human actors, they "*really* observe and operate according to the 'codes' of a plurality of systems which are kept analytically separate by the theorist" ("Autopoiesis by Definition," *Cardozo Law Review* 13 (1992): 1463, 1467–68).

3. Joel Feinberg, "Civil Disobedience in the Modern World," *Humanities in Society* 2, 1 (1979): 37; reprinted in *Philosophy of Law,* 5th ed., ed. Joel Feinberg and Hyman Gross (Belmont, Calif.: Wadsworth, 1995), p. 125.

4. Ibid.

5. In Anthony D'Amato, "On the Connection Between Law and Justice," *University of California Davis Law Review* 26 (1993): 527, we find a situation where a law that conforms to Aquinas's definition—the traffic rule against crossing the double line—leads to the unnecessary killing of a child crossing the street against the light. In this case, crossing the double line would have endangered no one and saved the child's life. The point is that facts sometimes lead us to reconsider our duty to obey a "just" law, especially where no harm other than the mere breach of a law will result and an important good will be served.

6. See Lon Fuller, *The Morality of Law,* rev. ed. (New Haven: Yale University Press, 1978), p. 78.

7. John Finnis, *Natural Law and Natural Rights* (Oxford: Clarendon Press, 1980), pp. 276–77.

8. Ibid., p. 155.

9. For an interesting critique on the use of the "common good" in defining "democracy," see Joseph Schumpeter, "Two Concepts of Democracy," in *Political Philosophy*, ed. Anthony Quinton, *Oxford Readings in Philosophy* (New York: Oxford University Press, 1967), pp. 154–56.

10. Russell Hardin, "My University's Yacht: Morality and the Rule of Law," in *The Rule of Law,* NOMOS 34 (1994): 222.

11. See Feinberg, "Civil Disobedience in the Modern World," 37–60.

12. On morality's requirement to act *from* duty as opposed to acting *in accord* with duty, see Immanuel Kant, *Foundations of the Metaphysics of Morals*, trans. Lewis White Beck (Indianapolis: Bobbs-Merrill, 1981), pp. 13–14.

13. On the necessity of presupposing freedom to have the moral law, see ibid., p. 13.

14. See John Rawls, "Two Concepts of Rules," *Philosophical Review* 64 (1955): 6.

15. See Baron de Montesquieu, *Selected Political Writings*, trans. Melvin Richter (Indianapolis: Hackett, 1990), pp. 182–92. In this selection from *The Spirit of the Laws* (1748), Montesquieu was influenced by the English constitution; an early title to this excerpt was "The Principles of Political Liberty as Found in the Constitution of England" (p. 271 n. 7).

16. Ibid., pp. 173–76.

17. Rawls, "Two Concepts of Rules," pp. 3–13.

18. *Sindell v. Abbott Laboratories*, 26 Cal. 3d 588, 607 P. 2d 924, 163 Cal. Rptr. 132 (1980).

19. See, e.g., *Federalist* no. 47, James Madison, in *The Federalist Papers* (New York: New

American Library, 1961), arguing for adoption of the U.S. Constitution because it would provide for a separation of powers as a means to avoid tyranny, and *Federalist* no. 51, James Madison, arguing for adoption of the U.S. Constitution on the ground that it provides for federalism as a means to ensure a meaningful though not overpowering central government.

20. Richard Rorty believes that democracy does not need an ahistorical justification, that loyalty to our own society is justification enough (see *Objectivity, Relativism and Truth: Philosophical Papers*, 2 vols. (New York: Cambridge University Press, 1991), 1: 199).

21. Alan Gewirth, introduction to *Political Philosophy*, ed. A. Gewirth (New York: Macmillan, 1965), p. 1.

22. Ibid., p. 2.

23. Ibid.

24. C. G. Prado, *Starting with Foucault: An Introduction to Genealogy* (Boulder, Colo.: Westview Press, 1995), p. 160 (citing Michael Foucault, "The Subject and Power," Afterword to Hubert Dreyfus and Paul Rabinow, *Michael Foucault: Beyond Structuralism and Hermeneutics* [Brighton, Sussex: Harvester Press, 1983], p. 209, and Foucault, *The History of Sexuality*, vol. 1, trans. Robert Hurley [New York: Vintage, 1980], p. 10).

25. Friedrich Nietzsche, *Beyond Good and Evil: Prelude to a Philosophy of the Future*, trans. Walter Kaufmann (New York: Vintage, 1966), p. 98.

26. Gewirth, ed., *Political Philosophy*, note 21, p. 4.

27. Ibid., p. 5.

28. Ibid.

29. Ibid.

30. See ibid.; see also Thomas Hobbes, *Leviathan, with Selected Variants from the Latin Edition of 1668*, ed. E. Curley (Indianapolis: Hackett, 1994), chap. 11, no. 2; chap. 13, no. 3; and chap. 14, no. 4.

31. See H. J. McCloskey, "A Non-Utilitarian Approach to Punishment," *Inquiry* 8 (1965): 249, 256.

32. Plato, *Republic*, in *Plato: The Collected Dialogues Including the Letters*, ed. Edith Hamilton and Huntington Cairns (Princeton: Princeton University Press, 1961), bk. 1, p. 331c.

33. Gewirth, ed., *Political Philosophy*, note 21, p. 9; see also Thomas Aquinas, "Concerning the Nature of Law," in *Summa Theologicia, The Basic Writings of Saint Thomas Aquinas*, ed. A. Pegis, 2 vols. (New York: Random House, 1945), 2: 774.

34. Gewirth, ed., *Political Philosophy*, note 21, p. 9.

35. In G. W. F. Hegel, *Philosophy of Right*, trans. T. M. Knox (Chicago: Encyclopedia Britannica, 1942), p. 13, Hegel states that "the Owl of Minerva spreads its wings only with the falling of dusk," by which he means that only after society exists do we question what would an ideal society be like.

36. Gewirth, ed., *Political Philosophy*, note 21, p. 9.

37. Ibid.

38. See ibid., p. 10.

39. Ibid., p. 12; see Hegel, *Philosophy of Right*, note 35, nos. 187, 188; see also Karl Marx and Friederich Engles, *The Communist Manifesto* (1888), reprinted in *Basic Writings on Politics and Philosophy*, ed. L. Feuer (Garden City, N.Y.: Doubleday, 1959), p. 29.

40. Gewirth, ed., *Political Philosophy*, note 21, p. 13; see John Stuart Mill, *On Liberty*, ed. Gertrude Himmelfarb (New York: Penguin, 1982), chap. 1.

41. Gewirth, ed., *Political Philosophy*, note 21, pp. 13–14.

42. Ibid., p. 14; see Jean-Jacques Rousseau, *The Social Contract and Discourse on the Origin of Inequality*, ed. L. Crocker (New York: Pocket Books, 1989), bk. 1, pp. 22–23.

43. This classic statement of the prisoner's dilemma shows how lack of cooperative behavior leads to a worse result than would otherwise be the case if everyone cooperated. Recall that two prisoners are kept separate and told that each is about to squeal on the other. The police have said they will offer the first to confess and to implicate the other five years and will seek ten years for the other. If neither cooperates, both stand to get two years. If both talk, they each get ten years. Since no communication is permitted between the prisoners and each prisoner wants to protect his or her own interest, there is an incentive to talk even though this is not the best choice in terms of their individual self-interests.

44. Gewirth, ed., *Political Philosophy*, note 21, p. 15; see John Locke, *The Second Treatise of Government*, ed. T. P. Pearson (Indianapolis: Bobbs-Merrill, 1952), nos. 25 and 27; Immanuel Kant, *The Metaphysics of Morals*, trans. M. Gregor (New York: Cambridge University Press, 1991), pp. 63–64.

45. Gewirth, ed., *Political Philosophy*, note 21, p. 15.

46. Ibid., p. 16.

47. Ibid.; see Robert Nozick, *Anarchy, State and Utopia* (New York: Basic Books, 1974), ch. 7.

48. Gewirth, ed., *Political Philosophy*, note 21, pp. 16–17.

49. Ibid., p. 17; see Jeremy Bentham, *Principles of Morals and Legislation* (New York: Hafner Press, 1948), p. 125 n. 2.

50. Gewirth, ed., *Political Philosophy*, note 21, p. 17.

51. Ibid., p. 18.

52. Ibid.

53. Ibid.

54. Ibid.; see Hobbes, *Leviathan*, note 30, chap. 8.

55. Gewirth, ed., *Political Philosophy*, note 21, p. 18; see Locke, *Second Treatise of Government*, note 44, no. 27.

56. Alexander Bickel has noted two traditions he sees as describing Western political thought: contractarian, which he takes to be liberal, and Whig, which he takes to be conservative. The essential difference is that contractarian thought allows for the discovery of natural rights, as in Rawls's theory, for example; Whig thought sees rights as set by culture, not exceedingly different from contemporary communitarians. See Bickel, *The Morality of Consent* (New Haven: Yale University Press, 1975), pp. 3–4. Indeed, Bickel favors the latter arguably on the ground that what is given by government can be taken away by government (pp. 53–54). In this he is right if the relationship between citizen and society is treated noncontractually. Bickel fails to see, however, that the Whig tradition succumbs to a different criticism, especially in a pluralistic society where toleration for a minority group may be necessary for stability even though it may vary, depending on what political view is in vogue. This suggests that neither of these two views is adequate to guarantee fundamental rights.

57. Gewirth, ed., *Political Philosophy*, note 21, p. 18; see Kant, *Foundations of the Metaphysics of Morals*, p. 66.

58. Gewirth, ed., *Political Philosophy*, note 21, p. 19.

59. Ibid.; compare Hobbes, *Leviathan*, note 30, chap. 17, with Locke, *Second Treatise of Government*, note 44, no. 149.

60. Gewirth, ed., *Political Philosophy,* note 21, p. 19; see Rousseau, *Social Contract and Discourse on the Origin of Inequality,* note 42, bk. 1, pp. 38–41.

61. Gewirth, ed., *Political Philosophy,* note 21, p. 19.

62. Ibid., pp. 19–20; see Locke, *Second Treatise of Government,* note 44, no. 119.

63. Gewirth, ed., *Political Philosophy,* note 21, p. 20.

64. Ibid.; see Locke, *Second Treatise of Government,* note 44, no. 96.

65. Gewirth, ed., *Political Philosophy,* note 21, p. 20.

66. Ibid., p. 21.

67. Ibid.; see Plato, *Republic,* bk. 5, pt. 7.

68. Gewirth, ed., *Political Philosophy,* note 21, p. 22; Aristotle, *Nicomachean Ethics,* in *The Basic Works of Aristotle,* ed. Richard McKeon (New York: Random House, 1941), bk. 5, p. 1129b6–30.

69. Gewirth, ed., *Political Philosophy,* note 21, p. 23; see Aristotle, *Nicomachean Ethics,* note 68, bk. 5, p. 1131a22–b14.

70. Gewirth, ed., *Political Philosophy,* note 21, p. 23.

71. Ibid.; see Aristotle, *Nicomachean Ethics,* note 68, bk. 5, p. 1131a22–b14.

72. Gewirth, ed., *Political Philosophy,* note 21, p. 23.

73. Ibid., p. 24; compare Hobbes, *Leviathan,* note 30, chap. 21, with Locke, *Second Treatise of Government,* note 44, no. 149.

74. Gewirth, ed., *Political Philosophy,* note 21, p. 24; compare Jeremy Bentham, "A Fragment on Government," in *The Works of Jeremy Bentham,* ed. J. Bowring, 11 vols. (New York: Russell and Russell, 1962), 1: 287, no. 20, with James Mill, *Political Writings,* ed. T. Ball (New York: Cambridge University Press, 1992), p. 4, and J. S. Mill, *On Liberty,* note 40, chap. 3.

75. Gewirth, ed., *Political Philosophy,* note 21, p. 24; see Rousseau, *The Social Contract and Discourse on the Origin of Inequality,* note 42, chap. 2.

76. Gewirth, ed., *Political Philosophy,* note 21, p. 24; see Hegel, *Philosophy of Right,* note 35, no. 279.

77. Gewirth, ed., *Political Philosophy,* note 21, p. 25.

78. Ibid.

79. Ibid.

80. Ibid., p. 36.

81. Ibid.

82. Ibid., p. 27; see also Joel Feinberg, *Harm to Others,* vol. 1, *The Moral Limits of the Criminal Law* (New York: Oxford University Press, 1984), pp. 31–36.

83. Gewirth, ed., *Political Philosophy,* note 21, p. 27; see, e.g., Catharine A. MacKinnon, *Only Words* (Cambridge: Harvard University Press, 1993), arguing for restrictions on pornography on the ground that it harms women and children: "If there is anything that only pornography can say, that is exactly the measure of the harm that only pornography can do" (p. 22); Catharine A. MacKinnon and Ronald Dworkin, "Pornography: An Exchange," *New York Review of Books* 41 (1994): 47, debating whether pornography should be protected speech; Irving Kristol, "Pornography, Obscenity, and the Case for Censorship," *New York Times Magazine,* March 28, 1971, arguing that obscenity debases civilized society; Vincent J. Samar, "A Moral Justification for Gay and Lesbian Civil Rights Legislation," *Journal of Homosexuality* 27, 3/4 (1994): 147, arguing on behalf of civil rights protections in housing, employment, and public accommodations for gay and lesbian people.

84. See Gewirth, ed., *Political Philosophy*, note 21, p. 27.

85. Ibid.

86. Ibid.

87. Ibid., p. 29.

88. Ibid.

89. Ibid.

90. Nozick, *Anarchy, State and Utopia*, note 47, pp. 174–82.

91. Locke, *Second Treatise on Government*, note 44, no. 27.

92. Ibid., no. 26.

93. See Nozick, *Anarchy, State and Utopia*, note 47, pp. 26–30.

94. For instance, Frank I. Michelman discusses how U.S. Supreme Court Justice William J. Brennan Jr.'s egalitarian, multiculturalist constitutional-legal doctrine forced an "elusive and ever-contestable" distinction "between (i) proper governmental defense of a particular conception of liberal social structure and (ii) illicit governmental imposition of one or another partisan ideology" (Michelman, "Super Liberal: Romance, Community, and Tradition in William J. Brennan, Jr.'s Constitutional Thought," *Virginia Law Review* 77 [1991]: 1261, 1261–1263).

95. Gewirth, ed., *Political Philosophy*, note 21, p. 3.

96. Daniel Brudney, "Hypothetical Consent and Moral Force," *Law and Philosophy* 10 (1991): 235.

97. Ibid.

98. Ibid., pp. 243–44.

99. Ibid., p. 249.

100. Ibid., pp. 249–50 n. 18.

101. John Rawls, *Political Liberalism* (New York: Columbia University Press, 1993), p. 24.

102. Brudney, "Hypothetical Consent and Moral Force," note 96, p. 253.

103. Rawls, *Political Liberalism*, note 101, p. 19. This latter point is particularly important since *Political Liberalism* differs from Rawls's earlier work, *A Theory of Justice* (Cambridge, Mass.: Harvard University Press, 1971), in that he no longer makes a presumption that members of a democratic society should share comprehensive religious, philosophical, or moral doctrines (see Vincent J. Samar, "Just Society: A Review of John Rawls's *Political Liberalism*," *Business Ethics* 22, 1 (1995): 629.

104. Brudney, "Hypothetical Consent and Moral Force," p. 253.

105. Rawls, *Political Liberalism*, note 101, secs. 9, 13.

106. Ibid., pp. 353–55; see Cass Sunstein, *Democracy and the Problem of Free Speech* (New York: Free Press, 1993), chap. 8; see also *Federalist* no. 70 (Alexander Hamilton).

107. Samar, "Just Society," note 103, p. 637 (citing John Rawls, *Political Liberalism*, note 101, p. 206).

108. Rawls, *Theory of Justice*, note 103.

109. Alan Gewirth, *Reason and Morality* (Chicago: University of Chicago Press, 1978), pp. 20, 108.

110. Samar, "Just Society," note 103, p. 630.

111. Gewirth, *Reason and Morality*, note 109, p. 108.

112. Samar, "Just Society," note 103, p. 632.

113. Gewirth, *Reason and Morality*, note 109, p. 20.

114. Samar, "Just Society," note 103, p. 629.

115. See, generally, Michael J. Sandel, *Liberalism and the Limits of Justice* (New York: Cambridge University Press, 1982), who raises questions throughout the work about Rawls's seeming metaphysical conception of persons.

116. See Samar, "Just Society," note 103, p. 630.

117. Gewirth, *Reason and Morality*, note 109, p. 361.

118. Samar, "Just Society," note 103, p. 636.

119. Jürgen Habermas, *Between Facts and Norms: Contributions to a Discourse Theory of Law and Democracy*, trans. William Rehg (Cambridge, Mass.: MIT Press, 1996), p. 63.

120. Alan Gewirth, "The Basis and Content of Human Rights," *Georgia Law Review* 13 (1979): 1149; see Gewirth, *Reason and Morality*, note 109, chap. 2, for a thoroughgoing examination of the derivation of the Principle of Generic Consistency (PGC). As this aspect of my work is primarily geared to justifying a system of political responsibility, I will focus on the article "The Basis and Content of Human Rights." However, it should be noted that these issues are also taken up in *Reason and Morality*.

121. Gewirth, "Basis and Content of Human Rights," note 120, pp. 1148–49.

122. Ibid., p. 1149.

123. Ibid.

124. Ibid., pp. 1150–51.

125. Ibid., p. 1152.

126. Ibid..

127. See ibid.

128. Ibid.

129. See Michael Walzer, *Spheres of Justice: A Defense of Pluralism and Equality* (New York: Basic Books, 1983), p. 313.

130. See Gewirth, "Basis and Content of Human Rights," note 120, p. 1152.

131. Ibid., pp. 1153–54.

132. Ibid., p. 1154.

133. Ibid., p. 1155.

134. Wesley Hohfeld has distinguished four different uses of the term "right" by how they relate to their correlatives. Claim rights, as one type, are distinguished by the existence of a correlative duty associated with them. Duties arising out of promising come about because of claim rights. Liberty rights or "privileges," such as the right to pick up ten dollars lying in the gutter, are generally not correlated with any duty. Powers, as for example in the power of the legislature to make the laws, are correlated with liabilities by all those subject to the laws. Finally, immunities, as for instance the Fifth Amendment's immunity against self-incrimination, are correlated with disabilities that apply when the state tries to coerce a confession. See Hohfeld, *Fundamental Legal Conceptions*, ed. Walter W. Cook (Westport, Conn.: Greenwood Press, 1964), pp. 35–64. Gewirth makes use of Hohfeld's first two senses of the word "right" when describing what the PGC protects (see *Reason and Morality*, note 109, pp. 67–68).

135. Rehg, introduction to Habermas, *Between Facts and Norms*, p. xxvii. Responding to how a society can hold together where religious ties no longer bind and the people have begun to develop very different worldviews, Habermas states that "the core of modern law consists of private rights that mark out the legitimate scope of individual liberties and are thus tailored to the strategic pursuit of private interests" (p. 27).

136. Ibid., p. xxvii.

137. See Gewirth, "Basis and Content of Human Rights," note 120, p. 1164; see also Gewirth, *Reason and Morality*, note 109, pp. 308–9.

138. See Gewirth, "Basis and Content of Human Rights," note 120, p. 1164; see also Gewirth, *Reason and Morality*, note 109, p. 292.

139. Habermas, too, finds a need for a system of rights, which he divides into five categories. The first three categories are the negative rights that guarantee private memberships, due-process, and individual choice and autonomy. The next two are positive rights to political participation and to social welfare. For Habermas, as for Gewirth, both sets of rights—negative and positive—are essential to respecting the whole person. In this, he is able to draw together the liberal-civic republican split that is illustrated between Rawls and Sandel. See Rehg, introduction, to Habermas, *Between Facts and Norms*, note 119, p. xxvii.

140. See Alan Gewirth, *The Community of Rights* (Chicago: University of Chicago Press, 1996), p. 352, arguing that the PGC's protection of the generic rights to freedom and well-being requires a "supportive" state in which government acts to ensure that all persons have available to them the necessary conditions for action and generally successful action. Gewirth has in mind the formation of an economic constitution that would guarantee the positive side of the basic rights supplemented by legislation, which would then implement the constitutional provisions in particular institutional practices.

141. Cass Sunstein, "On Legal Theory and Legal Practice," *Theory and Practice*, ed. I. Shapiro and J. DeCew, NOMOS 37 (1995): 281.

142. Cass Sunstein, "Commentary on Analogical Reasoning," *Harvard Law Review* 106 (1993): 741, 784–85; see also Cass Sunstein, *Legal Reasoning and Political Conflict* (New York: Oxford University Press, 1996), p. 68.

143. Sunstein, "Commentary on Analogical Reasoning," note 142, p. 785.

144. Ibid., p. 782.

145. Ibid.

146. Ibid.

147. Ibid., pp. 782–83.

148. *Winterbottom v. Wright*, 10 Meeson & Welsby 109, 152 Eng. Rep. 402 (1842).

149. *Thomas v. Winchester*, 6 N.Y. 397 (1852).

150. *MacPherson v. Buick Motor Company*, 217 N.Y. 382, 111 N.E. 1050 (1916).

151. See Edward H. Levi, *Introduction to Legal Reasoning* (Chicago: University of Chicago Press, 1949), pp. 20–21.

152. The point here is that law is not self-evaluating. To the extent that the case before the court is calling into question the legitimacy of the applicable law, one needs a theory of political morality. See Richard H. Fallon, Jr., "'The Rule of Law' as a Concept in Constitutional Discourse," *Columbia Law Review* 97 (1997): 1–56.

Chapter 3. Metatheory

1. Plato, *Republic*, in *Plato: The Collected Dialogues Including the Letters*, ed. Edith Hamilton and Huntington Cairns (Princeton: Princeton University Press, 1961), bk. 1, p. 331e.

2. Aristotle, *Nicomachean Ethics*, in *The Basic Works of Aristotle*, ed. Richard McKeon (New York: Random House, 1941), bk. 5, p. ii12. See also Richard Posner, "The Concept

of Corrective Justice in Recent Theories of Tort Law," *Journal of Legal Studies* 10, 1(1981): 187–206 (arguing for an updated Aristotelian concept of corrective justice in today's tort law).

3. See *Coker v. Georgia*, 433 U.S. 584 (1977), in which the Supreme Court held that assigning the death penalty for a rape that did not result in the victim's death was cruel and unusual punishment under the Fifth Amendment.

4. Sometimes sexual orientation discrimination is circumvented by the high price of maintaining an appearance of being straight, with the denial which that implies. See Vincent J. Samar, "A Moral Justification for Gay and Lesbian Civil Rights Legislation," *Journal of Homosexuality* 3/4 (1994): 168–69.

5. Aristotle, *Nicomachean Ethics*, note 2, bk. 8, pp. ix2–x3, and *Politics*, note 2, bk. 3, pp. 1282b15–83a23, bk 4, pp. 1289b26–90a28.

6. Brian Barry, "Justice and the Common Good," *Analysis* 21 (1960–61): 86, 86–90, reprinted in *Political Philosophy*, ed. A. Quinton, *Oxford Readings in Philosophy* (New York: Oxford University Press, 1967), p. 191 (subsequent citations from *Political Philosophy*).

7. John Rawls, *A Theory of Justice* (Cambridge: Harvard University Press, 1971), p. 5.

8. Robert Nozick, *Anarchy, State and Utopia* (New York: Basic Books, 1974), pp. 150–53.

9. In fairness, it should be noted that Nozick has disavowed his libertarian view as "seriously inadequate" and has suggested that he no longer should be pigeonholed as a "libertarian." See Nozick, *The Examined Life: Philosophical Meditations* (New York: Touchstone, 1989), p. 17.

10. Alan Gewirth, *Reason and Morality* (Chicago: University of Chicago Press, 1978), p. 205.

11. Here I would note a distinction Gewirth makes among actual, prospective, and potential agents. Actual agents are currently engaged in voluntary purposive behavior. Prospective agents have the capacity to engage in such behavior, although they are not currently so engaged. A person who is asleep is a prospective agent. The capacities are in place, but they are not engaged in voluntary purposive action. Potential agents, like the unborn fetus, very young children, and persons with serious mental challenges, do not have the abilities to engage in voluntary purposive behavior, although in the case of the fetus and the young child, they are in the process of developing these capacities. For this reason, potential agents possess the generic rights only to the degree to which they can actually engage in voluntary purposive behavior. Consequently, only actual and prospective agents have a full-fledged claim to the generic rights. See Alan Gewirth, *Reason and Morality*, note 10, p. 141.

12. For a discussion of the strengths and weaknesses of institutions in tragic choice situations, see Guido Calabresi and Phillip Bobbitt, *Tragic Choices: The Conflicts Society Confronts in the Allocation of Tragically Scarce Resources* (New York: Norton, 1978).

13. I owe this solution to a paper about Gewirth's system written by Bruce Barton, when he was a graduate student at the University of Chicago.

14. See Peter Singer, "Rich and Poor," *Practical Ethics* (Cambridge, Eng.: Cambridge University Press, 1979), pp. 158–81.

15. See Alan Gewirth, "Starvation and Human Rights," in *Human Rights* (Chicago: University of Chicago Press, 1982), pp. 197–217.

16. Gewirth, *Reason and Morality*, note 10, p. 294.

17. In the United States the Congress determines the size of the federal courts, including the Supreme Court. See John E. Nowak and Ronald D. Rotunda, *Constitutional Law*, 4th ed., Hornbook series (Minneapolis: West Publishing Company, 1991), sec. 2.6.

18. Brian Barry describes this way of talking as an application of Rousseau's idea of the "general will." The idea is that a common interest can be found in a society he would today call heterogeneous, where each person is equally affected by the policy adopted. Barry applies this notion to a large, complex, modern nation-state where individual and group interests differ by adopting the metaphor that one of the many hats a citizen wears is "member of the public (see Barry, "Public Interest," *Aristotelian Society*, suppl. vol. 38 (1964): 1–18).

19. For a brief comment on this issue, see Jean-Jacques Rousseau, *The Social Contract and Discourse on the Origin of Inequality*, ed. Lester G. Crocker (New York: Washington Square Press, 1967), p. 114.

20. Other roles for the judge, not discussed in the text, include supporting the legal system, ensuring that the laws are interpreted to best serve a legitimate legislative purpose, ensuring the integrity of the courts, aiding in dispute resolution, and so on.

21. See Ronald Dworkin, "The Model of Rules," *University of Chicago Law Review* 35 (1967): 23.

22. See ibid., pp. 26–27.

23. Some commentators distinguish metarules and metalegal frameworks. In the former category, one example taken from law and economics is Posner's idea of wealth maximization. Jonathan R. Macey, "The Internal and External Costs and Benefits of Stare Decisis," *Chicago-Kent Law Review* 65 (1989): 104. "The label 'meta-legal framework' refers to the nonconscious assumptions and beliefs about law, legal institutions, and [the judge's] task as a member of the legal profession, that inform an individual's perceptions and analyses of legal problems." Donna A. Boswell, Comment, "The Parameters of Federal Common Law: The Case of Time Limitations on Federal Causes of Action," *University of Pennsylvania Law Review* 136 (1988): 1447, 1469. In such a framework, the articulation of rights may require consistency with other principles making up a "comprehensive political system" and an equal distribution. H. William Fischer, "Dworkin's Right Answer Thesis: A Statistical Regression Coherence Model," *Iowa Law Review* 73 (1987): 162. The different commentators "implicitly believe that we can determine the value of a rule within the system [of law] by resort to a metasystem"; the difference lies "over what that metasystem should look like" (Stuart Banner, "Please Don't Read the Title," *Ohio Law Journal* 50 (1989): 243, 249–50) and whether it is internal or external to the legal system. See Jean R. Sternlight, "Symbiotic Legal Theory and Legal Practice: Advocating a Common Sense Jurisprudence of Law and Practical Applications," *University of Miami Law Review* 50 (1996): 707, 710 n. 10.

24. At least in the area of individual rights guarantees, many constitutional scholars believe that there is a need for an "extra constitutional" normative theory. See Peter M. Shane, "Conventionalism in Constitutional Interpretation and the Place of Administrative Agencies," *American University Law Review* 36 (1987): 578. However, not everyone follows this view. See, e.g., Phillip Bobbitt, *Constitutional Interpretation* (Cambridge, Mass: Basil Blackwell, 1991), pp. 13–22 (arguing that a constitutional decision is justified only to the extent that it relies on one of the six modalities of recognized constitutional argument—historical, textual, structural, doctrinal, prudential, or ethical). One reason seems

to be that until now, such theories have produced only "more open-ended complexity" (Peter H. Schuck, "Legal Complexity: Some Causes, Consequences and Cures," *Duke Law Journal* 42 [1992]: 10).

25. The incommensurability problem I am referring to here is that one cannot move between the internal and external perspectives by any set of logical moves originating inside the internal perspective because it is just that perspective that is called into question by the very need for such a move. One must appeal, therefore, to a metaperspective that oversteps both the internal and the external.

26. Here I would note that Peter Winch believes that the internal point of view privileges the rationalizations of those participating in the process (see "Authority," in Quinton, ed., *Political Philosophy*, note 6, pp. 97–111).

27. See, e.g., Michael Perry, *The Constitution in the Courts: Law or Politics* (New York: Oxford University Press, 1994), chaps. 2–5; Cass Sunstein, *The Partial Constitution* (Cambridge, Mass.: Harvard University Press, 1993), appendix A, pp. 235–38.

28. *Ratio essendi* asks what is the reason for being.

29. *Ratio cognoscendi* asks how do we know.

30. But see Richard Delgado, ed., *Critical Race Theory: The Cutting Edge* (Philadelphia: Temple University Press, 1995), p. xiv (arguing that African Americans view U.S. society as fundamentally racist).

31. See Joel Feinberg, "Civil Disobedience in the Modern World," *Humanities in Society* 2 (1979): 37–60 (arguing that in a society that views itself as nearly just there is a high probability of conformance between what the law requires and what morality requires).

32. P. H. Partridge has argued that a reason for the seeming decline of political theory in recent years is the shift in interest, approach, and emphasis that has accompanied an ideological consensus over the legally established organizations, allocation of political rights and powers, and objectives and justifications of policy (see "Politics, Philosophy, Ideology," *Political Studies* 9 (1961): 217).

33. Ronald Dworkin, *Law's Empire* (Cambridge, Mass.: Harvard University Press, 1986), pp. 14–16.

34. Joel Feinberg asks whether a prima facie obligation (PFO) to obey law is either a self-evident proposition of morality or one that derives from other more basic moral PFOs. In both instances, he concludes that a PFO to obey law cannot be found (see "Civil Disobedience in the Modern World," note 31, 37–60).

35. See William Lee Miller, *Arguing About Slavery: The Great Battle in the United States Congress* (New York: Alfred A. Knopf, 1995), pp. 22–24 (arguing that in the period prior to the American Civil War there was a strong feeling developing in the country that ownership of human beings is contrary to American republicanism, American civil liberties, and American representative government).

36. John Rawls, *Political Liberalism* (New York: Columbia University Press, 1993), pp. 15–22.

37. See Dworkin, *Law's Empire*, note 33, pp. 199–202.

38. Here I take note of a point that Cass Sunstein makes when he says that the U.S. Supreme Court's big decisions about abstract principle are aberrations, that usually the Court tries to decide cases particularly without taking sides on more abstract principles. This notion of resolving cases on narrow grounds Sunstein describes as the Court's par-

ticular jurisprudence, by which he means to compare it with the more general theoretical approaches of people such as Ronald Dworkin and Richard Posner. See Sunstein, *Legal Reasoning and Political Conflict* (New York: Oxford University Press, 1996), pp. 35–38; cf. Ronald Dworkin, *Freedom's Law: The Moral Reading of the American Constitution* (Cambridge, Mass.: Harvard University Press, 1996), pp. 1–12 (arguing that the Bill of Rights contains general moral principles of liberty, equality, and dignity and that judges must interpret those general principles to decide constitutional cases).

39. I owe this example to a comment Raymond Belliotti raised about an earlier draft of this work.

40. The justification for this point is developed by Alan Gewirth in *The Community of Rights* (Chicago: University of Chicago Press, 1996), pp. 38–44.

41. See John Rawls, "Two Concepts of Rules," *Philosophical Review* 64 (1955): 6.

42. From the standpoint of a judge operating within a legal system, Raymond Belliotti suggests that a coherence method of moral reason in legal reasoning can provide (1) a limited justification for a moral code and the moral judgments emanating from it; (2) a suitable moral code to serve as background morality for Dworkin's theory; (3) no clear present claim to the discovery of objective moral truths; and (4) more than a merely conventionalist account of background morality. See Belliotti, "Toward a Theory of Judicial Decisionmaking: A Synthesis of Ideologist Jurisprudence and Doctrinalism," *Catholic University Law Review* 28 (1983): 245. In contrast to Belliotti's suggestion, I claim that once a judge reaches a question of political morality, she is no longer operating *within* a particular legal tradition but is at the point of justifying the system itself, including her obligation to follow the law. At this point, the judge, depending on whether the society's political morality is itself controversial, may be in the position of having to compare competing theories of political morality on the basis of metaethical considerations. Such is how a judge would go about resolving what I call very hard cases. The issue results from the fact that the judge's obligation to follow the law originates not in legal philosophy (as I have used that phrase) but in a notion of political responsibility that must be part and parcel of an overall justification of the legal system.

43. The standard Marxist approach is not to treat such issues prescriptively but descriptively as part of the current state of historical materialism, although some scholars disagree. See Louis Althusser, *For Marx*, trans. Ben Brewster (New York: Pantheon Books, 1969), pp. 51–52 (noting how some scholars view Marx's early work to embody an ethical theory). Consequently, the theory has little persuasive force when brought up against such normative approaches as Alan Gewirth's, which do not presuppose any economic mode of production.

44. See Gewirth, *Community of Rights*, note 40, chap. 5.

45. David Hume, for example, argues that human beings are both determined and free in the choices they make. The sense in which they are determined is that their choices result from their own motives and character. The sense in which they are free is the degree to which their choices arise from their own deliberations. See Hume, *An Enquiry Concerning Human Understanding; A Letter from a Gentleman to His Friend in Edinburgh*, ed. Eric Steinberg (Indianapolis: Hackett, 1977), pp. 53–69; see also Donald Davidson, "Freedom to Act," in *Essays on Actions and Events* (Oxford: Clarendon Press, 1980) pp. 74–81 (arguing that "we cannot hope to define or analyse freedom to act in terms of concepts that fully identify the causal conditions of intentional action" [p. 81]).

46. See Douglas Litowitz, "Dworkin and Critical Legal Studies on Right Answers and Conceptual Holism," *Legal Studies Forum* 18 (1994): 135–36.

47. See Duncan Kennedy, "Form and Substance in Private Law Adjudication," *Harvard Law Review* 89 (1976): 1776.

48. For an excellent discussion of how a popular president and strongly supportive Congress can work together to bring about higher lawmaking outside the constitutional amendment process, see Bruce Ackerman, *Foundations*, vol. 1, *We the People* (Cambridge, Mass.: Harvard University Press, 1991), p. 268.

49. In the history of the Supreme Court certain cases have drawn the Court's reputation into serious doubt. The infamous 1857 *Dred Scott* case (*Dred Scott v. Sanford*, 60 U.S. [19 How.] 393) is one of these. In the 1930s, the Court struck down as unconstitutional a number of pieces of New Deal legislation, following the oft-cited *Lochner v. New York*, 198 U.S. 45 (1905) (holding unconstitutional a New York law forbidding bakeries from hiring bakers to work more than sixty hours per week). These decisions placed the Court at odds with a fundamental shift in American public opinion about the role of government in securing people's lives (see Ackerman, *Foundations*, note 48, p. 268). Proposals began to be discussed seriously about increasing the number of sitting justices so as to allow President Franklin D. Roosevelt to appoint to the bench judges more sympathetic to this newly popular philosophy about the role of government. The net effect of this so-called attempt to pack the Court was no doubt the basis for the Court's turnabout in finding New Deal legislation constitutional. As a well-known adage of the day put it, "A switch in time saved nine."

50. Sunstein, *Partial Constitution*, note 27.

51. Ibid., pp. 101–2.

52. Robert Bork, *The Tempting of America: The Political Seduction of the Law* (New York: Free Press, 1990).

53. John Hart Ely, *Democracy and Distrust: A Theory of Judicial Review* (Cambridge: Harvard University Press, 1980).

54. This is why Ely argues that it was wrong for the Court in *Griswold v. Connecticut*, 381 U.S. 479 (1965), to protect the right of married people to use contraceptives as a matter of personal privacy but that it was right for the Court in *Reynolds v. Sims*, 377 U.S. 533 (1964), to protect the doctrine of one man/one vote (see Ely, *Democracy and Distrust*, note 53, pp.120–21, 221 n. 4).

55. Frederick Shauer, "Easy Cases," *Southern California Law Review* 58 (1985): 399, 401–2, 429–30.

56. Richard Rorty, *Objectivity, Relativism, and Truth: Philosophical Papers*, 2 vols. (New York: Cambridge University Press, 1991), 1: 208.

57. Ibid., p. 95.

58. Ibid., p. 96.

59. Sunstein, *Partial Constitution*, note 27, p. 114. Compare Robert Cover, "Violence and the Word," *Yale Law Journal* 95 (1986): 1601, 1602n.2, 1605 (who makes the conventionalist argument) with Mari Matsuda, "Interpreting Rights: An Essay for Robert Cover," *Yale Law Journal* 96 (1987): 1860, 1910 (who criticizes Cover's view that rights rhetoric serves the exercise of state authority and notes how such rhetoric is often used to constrain state power by those who lack it).

60. Sunstein, *Partial Constitution*, note 27, p. 114.

61. John Rawls, "The Definition of Civil Disobedience," in *A Theory of Justice*, note 7, p. 373.

62. Richard Posner, *Overcoming Law* (Cambridge, Mass.: Harvard University Press, 1995), p. 316.

63. Herbert Kohl describes postmodernism as growing "out of disillusionment with modernism's failure to produce a perfect, rational, planned, and compassionate world. . . . Postmodernism replaces modernism's utopian faith in technology and [economic] planning [à la Marxism] with an ironic, self-mocking, and somewhat detached attitude toward culture and progress. Some writers and critical thinkers associated with postmodernism are Jean Beaudnard, Julia Kristera, Umberto Eco, and J. F. Lyotard." In making a comparison, Kohl comments that "poststructuralism encompasses a number of contemporary theories of criticism that attempt to undermine structuralist interpretations. They deny that a fitted structure underlying and determining the nature of a text or a social phenomenon exists. Deconstructionist, Marxist, . . . and feminist theories of criticism are considered poststructuralist." The main theorists of poststructuralism are Jacques Derrida and Jacques Lacan. See Kohl, *From Archetype to Zeitgeist: Powerful Ideals for Powerful Thinking* (Boston: Little, Brown, 1992), pp. 119–20, 133–34.

64. Richard Rorty distinguishes himself from J. F. Lyotard over how gradually politically conscious postmodern intellectuals should forgo their faith in the Enlightenment (Rorty, *Objectivity, Relativism and Truth*, note 56, pp. 221–22).

65. Hilary Putman claims that Wittgenstein did not believe that truth had to be relativized to a set of beliefs. Anyone who thought it must fails to distinguish "between *being right* and *thinking he is right*, between *asserting* or *thinking*, on the one hand, and *making noises* . . . on the other." For such a person, "no distinction is possible between thinking one's thought is about something and actually thinking about that thing." Consequently, "to hold such a view," Putman says, is for Wittgenstein "to commit a sort of mental suicide" (see Putman, *Reason, Truth and History* [New York: Cambridge University Press, 1981], pp. 121–24, emphasis in original). See also Thomas Nagel, *The View from Nowhere* (New York: Oxford University Press, 1986), p. 106.

66. See, e.g., Francis J. Mootz III, "The New Legal Hermeneutics," *Vanderbilt Law Review* 47 (1994): 115.

67. See, e.g., Dennis M. Patterson, "Law's Pragmatism: Law as Practice and Narrative," *Virginia Law Review* 76 (1990): 937.

68. See, e.g., Allan C. Hutchinson, "Identity Crisis: The Politics of Interpretation," *New England Law Review* 26 (1992): 1173.

69. See, e.g., Stanley Fish, "Liberalism Doesn't Exist," *Duke Law Journal* (1987): 997.

70. See Peter C. Schanck, "Understanding Postmodern Thought and Its Implications for Statutory Interpretation," *South California Law Review* 65 (1992): 2505, 2508–9.

71. See Rorty, *Objectivity, Relativism and Truth*, note 56, pp. 40, 85.

72. This question is raised in R. Hayman Jr. and N. Levit, eds., *Jurisprudence: Contemporary Readings, Problems, and Narratives* (St. Paul, Minn.: West Publishing Company, 1995), p. 508 (citing David Harvey, *The Condition of Postmodernity: An Enquiry into the Origins of Cultural Change* [Cambridge, Mass.: Blackwell, 1989], p. 116).

73. Gewirth, *Reason and Morality*, note 10, p. 23.

74. See, e.g., "Interviews with Jacques Derrida *et al.*," in *Criticism in Society*, ed. Imre Salusinnzky (New York: Methuen and Company, 1987); Harvey, *Condition of Postmoder-*

nity, note 72, p. 56; and Jean-François Lyotard, *The Postmodern Condition: A Report on Knowledge* (Minneapolis: University of Minnesota Press, 1984), pp. 64–65.

75. See Jürgen Habermas, "Modernity—An Incomplete Project," in *Anti-Aesthetic: Essays on Postmodern Culture*, ed. Hal Foster (Port Townsend, Wash.: Bay Press, 1983).

76. Ross C. Murfin, "Deconstruction and *Wuthering Heights*," in *Wuthering Heights: Case Studies in Contemporary Criticism*, ed. Ross C. Murfin (Boston: St. Martin's Press, 1992), p. 360. Historically, deconstruction came about in response to European structuralism, a movement that may have been a reaction to modernism's "alienation and despair" (p. 363). In particular, French philosopher Jacques Derrida challenged the claim of members of this movement that there existed laws governing all forms of human signification, from road signs to articles of clothing to works of literature, that could provide a key to understanding "everything from an African village to a Greek myth to Rousseau's *Confessions*" (p. 363). For instance, Claude Lévi-Strauss, a structuralist anthropologist, had thought that in the world's myths were "basic plot elements" that might be part of "one great myth being written by the collective human mind" (p. 363). Exactly how this would come about is beyond the scope of this book.

77. Ibid., p. 360.

78. See Martha Minow and Elizabeth Spelman, "In Context," *Southern California Law Review* 63 (1990): 1628.

79. See, e.g., Kim Lane Scheppele, "The Reasonable Woman," in *The Responsive Community: Rights and Responsibilities* 1 (1991): 36.

80. See, e.g., Catharine MacKinnon, "*Roe v. Wade*: A Study in Male Ideology," in *Abortion: Moral and Legal Perspectives*, ed. Jay L. Garfield and Patricia Hennessey (Amherst: University of Massachusetts Press, 1984), pp. 45–54.

81. See, e.g., Catharine MacKinnon, "Pornography: On Morality and Politics," in *Toward a Feminist Theory of the State* (Cambridge, Mass.: Harvard University Press, 1989), pp. 195–214; Andrea Dworkin and Catharine MacKinnon, *Pornography and Civil Rights: A New Day for Woman's Equality* (Minneapolis: Organizing Against Pornography [734 East Lake Street 55407], 1988).

82. See, e.g., Margaret Jane Radin and Frank Michelman, "Pragmatist and Poststructuralist Critical Legal Practice," *University of Pennsylvania Law Review* 139 (1991): 1043, and Hutchinson, "Identity Crisis," pp. 1174–75.

83. See, e.g., Guyora Binder, "What's Left?" *Texas Law Review* 69 (1991): 1985, and Catherine A. MacKinnon, "From Theory to Practice, or What Is a White Woman Anyway?" *Yale Journal of Law and Feminism* 4 (1991): 13, 13–14.

84. See Iris Marton Young, *Justice and the Politics of Difference* (Princeton: Princeton University Press, 1990), p. 232; contra J. M. Balkin, "Tradition, Betrayal and the Politics of Deconstruction," *Cardozo Law Review* 11 (1990): 1613, 1629–30.

85. This is similar to a point Michael Sandel makes in *Liberalism and the Limits of Justice* (New York: Cambridge University Press, 1982), p. 149, when he criticizes rights-based theories of justice as providing too abstract a conception of the moral agent.

86. I attribute this phrasing to a critique by Raymond Belliotti of an earlier draft of this book.

87. Howard Kahane and Paul Tidman have noted that "one way to resolve semantic paradoxes is to distinguish between *levels of language*, that is, between languages that are used to talk about nonlinguistic things and those used to talk about other languages. A

language used to talk about some other language is considered to be on a higher level than the language talked about, so that sentences asserting the truth or falsity of a given sentence must be placed in a language at least one level higher than the given sentence. For instance, the sentence "The sentence 'Art is tall' is true" must be placed in a language one level higher than the language in which the sentence 'Art is tall' occurs." See Kahane and Tidman, *Logic and Philosophy: A Modern Introduction*, 7th ed. (Belmont: Wadsworth, 1995), p. 227 (citing Bertrand Russell, introduction to Ludwig Wittgenstein's *Tractatus Logico-Philosophicus* [New York: Hartcourt Brace, 1922], p. 23, and Alfred Tarski, "Semantic Conception of Truth," *Philosophy and Phenomenological Research*, vol. 4 [1994], pp. 341–75).

88. The point is that in a two-valued logic, there is only A or not-A. As long as we hold to this dichotomy, which comes from Aristotle's *On Interpretation*, in *The Basic Works of Aristotle*, ed. Richard McKeon (New York: Random House, 1941), 17b25, we have nowhere else to go. On the other hand, if we were to give up the principle of excluded middle and adopt a view associated more with Eastern mysticism and with Buddhism in particular, then we might find that there would be no paradox. See Bart Kosko, *Fuzzy Thinking: The New Science of Fuzzy Logic* (New York: Hyperion, 1993), pp. 69–70; see also Stanley Rosen, *The Limits of Analysis* (New York: Basic Books, 1929), pp. 199–200. Sometimes our concepts and understandings would be constructions; sometimes they would not be. The determining factor would be where they fell on a line between constructed and not constructed, because natural language sentences allow for interpretation. Only when the two positions fall exactly midway between their oppositions need we be concerned that we cannot say anything meaningful about them but must adopt a bifurcated interpretation altogether (see Kosko, *Fuzzy Thinking*, pp. 101–3). In any case, one might define a line as going between natural law and positivism. The two systems seem to be contradictory, but from the standpoint of the metatheory I have proposed, one can meaningfully identify a midpoint between the two to meet the needs of some judicial cases. Dworkin's sense of (society's) political morality fits in here. Having it both ways will not be of much help, however, unless one has a mitigating concept, such as society, in which to reinterpret the terms being opposed to avoid a true contradiction from occurring.

89. See, e.g., Steven D. Hales and Robert C. Welshon, "Truth, Paradox, and Nietzschean Perspectivism," *History of Philosophy Quarterly* 11 (1994): 101, 108–11 (offering a Nietzschean-like argument for escaping the paradox of saying perspectivism is absolutely true. The argument interprets perspectivism so as to allow for some statements to be true in all perspectives—such as the statement that "perspectivism is true"—while other statements are not true in every perspective—such as "John is standing to my right").

90. John Lechte, "Derrida," in *Fifty Key Contemporary Thinkers: From Structuralism to Postmodernity* (New York: Routledge, 1994), p. 107. Also, given the epistemic nature of the claims that some postmodernists ascribe to deconstruction, it is unlikely that the theory will ever be able to stand alone without background constraints.

91. See Immanuel Kant, *Foundations of the Metaphysics of Morals*, trans. Lewis W. Beck (Indianapolis: Bobbs-Merrill, 1959), sec. 3.

92. Terry Godlove, *Religion, Interpretation and Diversity of Belief* (New York: Cambridge University Press, 1989), p. 95.

Chapter 4. Virtual Law

1. See John Rawls, *Political Liberalism* (New York: Columbia University Press, 1993), pp. 156–58 (arguing for the possibility of stable democratic institutions over time despite an inconsistent background set of individually held comprehensive religious, philosophical, or moral doctrines). But see Vincent J. Samar, "Just Society: A Review of John Rawls's *Political Liberalism*," *Business Ethics* 22, 1 (1995): 635–36 (arguing that even in working democracies sometimes background, incommensurable, comprehensive doctrines prevent the possibility of consensus).

2. Note that Neil MacCormick teases out some different senses of the notions of internal and external in his *H. L. A. Hart* (Stanford, Calif.: Stanford University Press, 1981), pp. 43–44.

3. H. L. A. Hart, *The Concept of Law* (New York: Oxford University Press, 1961), pp. 86–88.

4. H. L. A. Hart, "Positivism and the Separation of Law and Morals," *Harvard Law Review* 71 (1958): 612.

5. Ibid., p. 623. Note also that Hart's treatment of law as a scheme of *general* rules means that law must follow the principle of procedural justice of treating like cases alike. But here he recognizes that meeting this condition would not prevent the creation of "laws which were hideously oppressive, and might deny to a vast rightless slave population the minimum benefits of protection from violence and theft" (p. 624). The problem is how to determine whether two cases are alike. Without a theory of rights or some other substantive basis, this problem cannot be solved.

6. See Rawls, *Political Liberalism*, note 1, pp. 103–7.

7. Ronald Dworkin, *A Matter of Principle* (Cambridge, Mass.: Harvard University Press, 1985), p. 174.

8. Ronald Dworkin, *Law's Empire* (Cambridge, Mass.: Harvard University Press, 1986), pp. 79–80.

9. Ibid., p. 86.

10. Alan Gewirth, *Reason and Morality* (Chicago: University of Chicago Press, 1978), p. 362.

11. Terry F. Godlove, *Religion, Interpretation and Diversity of Belief: The Framework Model from Kant to Durkheim to Davidson* (New York: Cambridge University Press, 1989), p. 1.

12. Willard van Orman Quine writes: "As an empiricist I continue to think of the conceptual scheme of science as a tool, ultimately, for predicting future experience in the light of past experience. Physical objects are conceptually imported into the situation as convenient intermediaries—not by definition in terms of experience, but simply as irreducible posits comparable, epistemologically, to the gods of Homer. For my part I do, qua lay physicist, believe in physical objects and not in Homer's gods; and I consider it a scientific error to believe otherwise. But in point of epistemological footing the physical objects and the gods differ only in degree and not in kind. Both sorts of entities enter our conception only as cultural posits. The myth of physical objects is epistemologically superior to most in that it has proved more efficacious than other myths as a device for working a manageable structure into the flux of experience" ("Two Dogmas of Empiricism," in *From a Logical Point of View* [Cambridge, Mass.: Harvard University Press, 1961], p. 44).

13. Godlove, *Religion, Interpretation and Diversity of Belief*, note 11, p. 2. Godlove argues that one reason why this form of conceptual relativism has become so prevalent among many mainstream academics has to do with a misreading of Kant by scholars such as Richard Rorty, F. W. J. Schelling, and Emile Durkheim. According to Godlove, these authors read Kant so as to allow for a distinction between the receptivity of incoming neutral content and organizing conceptual scheme. Godlove cites Rorty, for instance, who wants to attack Kant on this point: "It occurs to us as it did to Hegel, that these all important a priori concepts, those which determine what our experiences or our morals will be, might have been different. Men of the Golden Age, or inhabitants of the Fortunate Isles, or the mad, might shape intuitions that are our common property in different modes and might thus be conscious of a different 'world'" (p. 9) (citing Richard Rorty, "World Well Lost," in *Consequences of Pragmatism* [Minneapolis: University of Minnesota Press, 1982], p. 3). In contrast, Godlove quotes Schelling, who praises Kant: "Kant believed himself to have traversed and exhausted the entire realm of human faculties and knowledge. . . . Closer observation reveals that only just those concepts were included that were given in the contingent world view of the time" (p. 12) (citing Alan White, *Schelling: An Introduction to the System of Freedom* [New Haven: Yale University Press, 1983], p. 158). Durkheim, who sees Kant's transcendentalism as "unscientific" and "mystical," tries to break through the forms of receptivity and the rules of judgment by scientific sociological explanations (p. 13). These approaches, Godlove believes, misconstrue the point of view from which Kant's argument must be assessed if true necessity is to be extracted, namely, the first-person point of view: "In what sense are our forms of receptivity and categories 'subjectively held'? I think the answer turns on whether Kant has shown that both arise spontaneously, without our choice, and, more radically, without antecedent determinants. On this, the Kantian view, they are necessary for the possibility of any experience whatever; we must apply them, and only then recognize that we do so. If so, then any true account of our transcendental disposition must begin with and remain within experience itself. Our categories and forms of receptivity (whatever they may be) cannot be assigned causes which are themselves locatable within the empirical world for they are valid a priori," absolutely independent of all experience. They are, rather "self-thought [*selbstgedachte*] first principles a priori of our knowledge" (p. 32) (citing Immanuel Kant, *Critique of Pure Reason*, trans. Norman Kemp Smith [New York: Harper and Row, 1960], pp. 13, 167).

14. Dworkin, *Matter of Principle*, note 7, p. 172.

15. See Robert Bork, *The Tempting of America: The Political Seduction of the Law* (New York: Free Press, 1990), chaps. 6 and 7.

16. Dworkin, *Law's Empire*, note 8, pp. 79–80.

17. Ibid.

18. Ibid., p. 86.

19. Ibid., p. 174.

20. Donald Davidson, "Paradoxes of Irrationality," in *Philosophical Essays on Freud*, ed. R. Wollheim and J. Hopkins (New York: Cambridge University Press, 1982), pp. 302–3.

21. William Rehg, introduction to Jürgen Habermas, *Between Facts and Norms: Contributions to a Discourse Theory of Law and Democracy*, trans. Rehg (Cambridge, Mass.: MIT Press, 1996), p. xlv: "Habermas's approach goes beyond semantic and syntactic analyses of meaning and grammar to examine the general structures that enable competent speakers

actually to engage in successful interaction, which involves more than simply knowing how to form grammatical sentences. Specifically, competent speakers know how to base their interactions on validity claims that their hearers will accept or that could, if necessary, be redeemed with good reasons. As already mentioned, this involves a tension between facticity and validity insofar as a claim to validity raised here and now, and perhaps justified according to local standards, ultimately points beyond a particular community. At least this is the case with truth claims and moral claims."

22. Ibid., p. xvi.

23. Donald Davidson, "Thought and Talk," in *Inquiries into Truth and Interpretation* (Oxford: Clarendon Press, 1984), p. 158.

24. Ibid., p. 168.

25. Pierre Schlag, "Missing Pieces: A Cognitive Approach to Law," *Texas Law Review* 67 (1989): 1195, 1211.

26. Ibid., p. 1213.

27. Ibid., pp. 1219–20. Here we have a postmodernist attempt to refute even those philosophers of nothingness such as Jean-Paul Sartre, as opposed to philosophers of being, whom modernists and postmodernists identify with the Enlightenment.

28. The problem might be put whether to interpret the self as an ego or a being, a thing a priori or a thing constructed. Even Nietzsche hesitates to say whether the self is properly cast as an ego or as a being and, indeed, there are passages in his writings that give credence to both interpretations. See, e.g., Stanley Corngold, "The Question of the Self in Nietzsche During the Axial Period (1882–1888)," in *Why Nietzsche Now?* ed. Daniel O'Hara (Bloomington: Indiana University Press, 1981), pp. 56–57.

29. A famous illustration of a persuasive appeal that is not an argument is René Descartes's cogito, ergo sum ("I think, therefore, I am"). Here, despite the use of the term "therefore," Descartes is not making an argument, for he offers no major premise such as "All that thinks, exists." His position is meant to appeal to our intuitions. But Descartes does not leave the matter with this "self-evident" assertion of the existence of the ego, mind as opposed to body. He also tries to *argue* for the existence of the mind and bodies in the world from our clear and distinct ideas. Descartes does so by first defining clear ideas to include only the logically necessary parts of the idea, for example, shape but not color; and second by showing how these parts connect to distinguish one idea from another. According to Descartes, all our clear and distinct ideas are true (that is, reflect what is in the world) because a beneficent God guarantees them. The latter claim is shown by a series of causal and ontological arguments from our clear and distinct idea of God. As every philosophy student knows, this approach forces Descartes into a "Cartesian" circular argument. See René Descartes, *Discourse on the Method* (1637), pt. iv, and *Meditations on First Philosophy* (1641), meditation 2 (which does not actually use the phrase cogito, ergo sum), in *Discourse on Method;* and *Meditations on First Philosophy*, 3d ed., trans. Donald A. Cress (Indianapolis: Hackett, 1993).

30. Donald Davidson, "On the Very Idea of a Conceptual Scheme," in *Inquiries*, note 23, p. 197.

31. Ibid., p. 198.

32. See, e.g., Gerald Torres and Kathryn Milun, "Translating *Yonnondio* by Precedent and Evidence: *The Mashpee Indian Case*," *Duke Law Journal* (1990): 625, 637–42.

33. See David Hume, *An Inquiry Concerning Human Understanding; A Letter from a*

Gentleman to His Friend in Edinburgh and Hume's Abstract of A Treatise of Human Nature, ed. Eric Steinberg, 2d ed. (Indianapolis: Hackett, 1977), p. 14.

34. See Immanuel Kant, *Critique of Pure Reason*, trans. Norman K. Smith (New York: St. Martin's Press, 1965), p. 113.

35. Donald Davidson, "The Method of Truth in Metaphysics," in *Inquiries*, note 23, p. 200.

36. J. Hillis Miller, "Dismembering and Disremembering in Nietzsche's 'On Truth and Lies in a Nonmoral Sense,'" in O'Hara, ed., *Why Nietzsche Now?* note 28, p. 49. The basis for the claim that is being associated with Nietzsche here is put in terms of a coin of metal stamped with some image. The author is trying to show that "The failure in parallelism [between the coin and reality] arises from the fact that the image of the removal of the illusory image revealing the bare metal has the form of a figure of unveiling. The bare metal seems to be what is really 'there,' the substantial truth beneath. Thinking of it this way depends on forgetting that actually the bare metal stands for the false world of concepts, of figures which are no longer recognized as figures. To see the bare metal as truth one has to forget the forgetting, or to forget once more." (p. 49). But this is exactly Davidson's point, that we can never get out from under our conceptual scheme or know anything about it as a whole. The most we can hope for is to broaden our narrower conceptual frameworks to the point where we reach an intersubjective understanding of all that we can know.

37. Davidson, "Method of Truth in Metaphysics," note 23, p. 200.

38. Ibid., p. 201.

39. The quote is from a comment by Raymond Belliotti on an earlier draft of this book.

40. Godlove, *Religion, Interpretation and Diversity of Belief*, note 11, p. 115 (citing Carol Rovane, "The Metaphysics of Interpretation," in *Truth and Interpretation: Perspectives on the Philosophy of Donald Davidson*, ed. Ernest Le Pore [Oxford: Basil Blackwell, 1986], p. 426).

41. Richard Rorty, *Objectivity, Relativism and Truth: Philosophical Papers, 2 vols*. (Cambridge, Eng.: Cambridge University Press, 1991), 1: 241 (quoting Hilary Putman, "On Truth," *in How Many Questions*, ed. L. S. Cauman et al. [Indianapolis: Hackett, 1983], p. 44).

42. Ibid., p. 142.

43. See Davidson, "On the Very Idea of a Conceptual Scheme," note 23, p. 198.

44. Ibid.

45. I do not mean to suggest that large-scale paradigm changes do not occur in politics as well as in other fields like science. But even in science, where in the twentieth century we have seen a good example of a paradigm change with the development of general relativity and quantum mechanics, there is still the need to relate these ideas to previous experiments and modes of thinking that we believe tell us something about the nature of our universe. There is in science, after all, no effort to give up the notion of observation or symmetry even if particular theories are eroded. To the contrary, they may be eroded because of observation. For a discussion of large and small changes in scientific understanding, see Thomas Kuhn, *The Structure of Scientific Revolutions*, 2d ed. (Chicago: University of Chicago Press, 1970).

46. Cass Sunstein, "On Legal Theory and Legal Practice," in *Theory and Practice*, *NOMOS* 37 (1995): 271–72.

47. Interestingly, no less than the poet T. S. Eliot has thought that "the greatest weak-

ness of Pragmatism is that it ends by being of no use to anybody" (Eliot, "Francis Herbert Bradley," in *Selected Prose of T. S. Eliot*, ed. Frank Kermode [Orlando, Fla.: Hartcourt, 1975], pp. 196, 204).

48. See Thomas C. Grey, "Holmes and Legal Pragmatism," *Stanford Law Review* 41 (1989): 789–91.

49. See Richard Posner, *Overcoming Law* (Cambridge, Mass.: Harvard University Press, 1995), p. 4.

50. See Richard Posner, "The Jurisprudence of Skepticism," *Michigan Law Review* 86 (1988): 827, 866–67.

51. See Margaret Jane Radin, "Reconstructing the Rule of Law," *Boston University Law Review* 69 (1989): 781, 807–10.

52. See Posner, *Overcoming Law*, note 49, p. 5.

53. Posner describes Donald Davidson as one of the "heros of pragmatism" (ibid., p. 8).

Chapter 5. Real Law

1. For the distinction between correspondence and coherence truth and a critical evaluation of the latter, see Bertrand Russell, *The Problems of Philosophy* (New York: Oxford University Press, 1959), pp. 121–23.

2. Ronald Dworkin, *A Matter of Principle* (Cambridge, Mass.: Harvard University Press, 1985).

3. Ibid., pp. 134–36.

4. Willard van Orman Quine, "Two Dogmas of Empiricism," in *From a Logical Point of View* (Cambridge: Harvard University Press, 1961) claims that "a boundary between analytic and synthetic statements simply has not been drawn. That there is such a distinction to be drawn at all is an unempirical dogma of empiricists, a metaphysical article of faith" (p. 37). He continues: "My present suggestion is that it is nonsense, and the root of much nonsense, to speak of a linguistic component and a factual component in the truth of any individual statement. Taken collectively, science has its double dependence upon language and experience; but this duality is not significantly traceable into statements of science taken one by one. . . . The totality of our so-called knowledge or beliefs, from the most casual matters of geography and history to the profoundest law of atomic physics or even of pure mathematics and logic is a man-made fabric which impinges on experience only along the edges. . . . But the total field is so underdetermined by its boundary conditions, experience, that there is much latitude of choice as to what statements to reevaluate in light of any single contrary experience. . . . In repudiating such a boundary I espouse a more thorough pragmatism. Each man is given a scientific heritage plus a continuing barrage of sensory stimulation; and the considerations which guide him in warping his scientific heritage to fit his continuing sensory promptings are, where rational, pragmatic" (pp. 42–43, 46).

5. "Leibniz held that 'always, in every true affirmative proposition, necessary or contingent, universal or particular, the concept of the predicate is in a sense included in that of the subject,' and was for a time inclined to believe that all true propositions could be reduced to identities. In about 1686 he came to hold that, for contingent truths, 'the reduction proceeds to infinity and is never terminated'" (see G. W. Leibniz, *New Essays*

on Human Understanding, trans. and ed. Peter Remnant and Jonathan Bennett [New York: Cambridge University Press, 1981], pp. xxiv–xxv) (citing various authors [I have omitted] for the quoted statements). Alan Gewirth contends that Leibniz's latter position allowed him to believe that the mind of God held analytic truths (unpublished comment). Saul Kripke has written: "An analytic truth is one which depends on meanings in the strict sense and therefore is necessary as well as *a priori*. If statements whose *a priori* truth is known via the fixing of a reference are counted as analytic, then some analytic truths are contingent" (*Naming and Necessity* [Cambridge: Harvard University Press, 1980], p. 122 n. 63).

6. Howard Kahane and Paul Tidman, *Logic and Philosophy: A Modern Introduction*, 7th ed. (Belmont, Calif.: Wadsworth, 1990), pp. 430–31.

7. Donald Davidson, "True to the Facts," in *Inquiries into Truth and Interpretation* (Oxford: Oxford University Press, 1984), p. 47.

8. Richard Rorty, *Objectivity, Relativism and Truth: Philosophical Papers*, 2 vols. (Cambridge, Eng.: Cambridge University Press, 1991), 1: 137.

9. Ibid., p. 138 (quoting from Donald Davidson, "A Coherence Theory of Truth and Knowledge," in *Truth and Interpretation: Perspectives on the Philosophy of Donald Davidson*, ed. E. LePore [Oxford: Blackwell, 1986], p. 308).

10. Ibid., pp. 138–39.

11. Ibid.

12. Ronald Dworkin, *Law's Empire* (Cambridge, Mass.: Harvard University Press, 1986), p. 225.

13. See ibid., pp. 338–39.

14. See ibid., pp. 228–32, 338.

15. See Vincent J. Samar, "Just Society: A Review of John Rawls, *Political Liberalism*," *Business Ethics Quarterly* 5 (1995): 635–36 (criticizing Rawls's idea of "overriding consensus" on just this point).

16. U.S. Constitution, Article 2, section 2, paragraph 2.

17. See Mark Strasser, "Unconstitutional? Don't Ask; If It Is, Don't Tell: On Deference, Rationality and the Constitution," *University of Colorado Law Review* 66, 2 (1995): 375, 377–82.

18. See ibid. (making a strong argument for the military's inability, even under the rationality test, to justify antigay discrimination).

19. Donald Davidson, "On the Very Idea of a Conceptual Scheme," in *Inquiries*, note 7, p. 198.

20. Alan Gewirth, *Reason and Morality* (Chicago: University of Chicago Press, 1978), pp. 173–76; see also Alan Gewirth, "The Distinction Between Analytic and Synthetic Truths," *Journal of Philosophy* 50 (1953): 397 (questioning the objections raised in Quine, "Two Dogmas of Empiricism," note 4).

21. Gewirth, *Reason and Morality*, note 19, p. 363.

22. See Lon Fuller, "Positivism and Fidelity to Law: A Reply to Professor Hart," *Harvard Law Review* 71 (1958): 630, 631.

23. See, e.g., Gilbert Harman, "Justice and Moral Bargaining," *Social Philosophy and Policy* 1 (1983): 114–31, whose criticism is discussed and critiqued in Deryck Beyleveld, *The Dialectical Necessity of Morality: An Analysis and Defense of Alan Gewirth's Argument to the Principle of Generic Consistency* (Chicago: University of Chicago Press, 1991).

24. See Aristotle, *Nicomachean Ethics*, in *The Basic Works of Aristotle*, ed. Richard McKeon (New York: Random House, 1941), bk. 1, p. 1094a1–5, and my own discussion of Aquinas in chapter 1.

25. See Gewirth, *Reason and Morality*, note 20, pp. 159–61.

26. See John McDowell, "Might There Be External Reasons?" in *World, Mind and Ethics: Essays on the Ethical Philosophy of Bernard Williams*, ed. J. E. J. Althem and Ross Harrison (New York: Cambridge University Press, 1995), p. 82.

27. Gewirth's view is deontological in that he is searching for the origin of human morality in the a priori or antecedent conditions of human action. But this view is also in the tradition of ontological theories of natural law, such as Aquinas's, that attempt to derive ought from is. Hence, Gewirth's views are distinguishable from the theories of Germain Grisez, John Finnis, Joseph Boyle, William May, and Patricia Lee, among others. See Robert P. George, "Natural Law and Human Nature," in *Natural Law Theory: Contemporary Essays* (Oxford: Clarendon Press, 1992), pp. 31–32.

28. Deryck Beyleveld and Roger Brownsword, *Law as a Moral Judgment* (London: Sweet and Maxwell, 1986) (citing Lon Fuller, *The Morality of Law* [New Haven: Yale University Press, 1969], p. 96), p. 2.

29. Ibid., pp. 32–33.

30. Ibid., p. 32.

31. Ibid., p. 33.

32. Ibid., p. 147.

33. Ibid., p. 148 n. 26: "Contingent human nature refers to the manifestation of essential human nature in its interaction with forces which are not essential aspects of human nature."

34. Ibid., pp. 149–50.

35. Ibid., p. 159.

36. William Rehg, introduction to Jürgen Habermas, *Between Facts and Norms: Contributions to a Discourse Theory of Law and Democracy*, trans. Rehg (Cambridge, Mass.: MIT Press, 1996), p. xix. It is important to note that Habermas believes that "the constitutional state represents the crucial set of legal institutions and mechanisms that govern the conversion of the citizenry's communicative power into efficacious and legitimate administrative activity: law 'represents . . . the medium for transforming communicative power into administrative power.'" (p. xxvii).

37. Beyleveld and Brownsword, *Law as Moral Judgment*, note 28, p. 160.

38. Ibid.

39. Ibid., p. 161.

40. Ibid., p. 162.

41. Ibid.

42. Ibid.

43. Ibid.

44. Ibid., p. 213.

45. Ibid.

46. Ibid.

47. Ibid.

48. See Catharine MacKinnon, "*Roe v. Wade:* A Study in Male Ideology," in *Abortion: Moral and Legal Perspectives*, ed. Jay L. Garfield and Patricia Hennessey (Amherst:

University of Michigan Press, 1984), pp. 45–54 (arguing that in a society where women do not control access to their sexuality because of a pervasive male ideology, giving to women the promise of sex with men on the same terms as it is given to men, namely without consequences, is to facilitate women's heterosexual availability and to free male sexual aggression).

49. See Beyleveld and Brownsword, *Law as Moral Judgment*, note 28, pp. 214–16.

50. Ibid., p. 216.

51. Interestingly, a careful review of the history of cases decided by the U.S. Supreme Court indicates that during its first three decades of existence, the Court never upheld a law as grounded in the Constitution that was contrary to natural law. Suzanna Sherry, "The Founders' Unwritten Constitution," *University of Chicago Law Review* 54 (1987): 1127, 1167.

52. See E. Regis Jr., ed., *Gewirth's Ethical Rationalism* (Chicago: University of Chicago Press, 1984) (containing a collection of critical essays on Gewirth's theory and a response to critics by Gewirth).

53. See, generally, Beyleveld, *Dialectical Necessity of Morality*, note 23 (arguing that Gewirth's theory is essentially correct and showing where many individual critics go astray).

54. Russell Hittinger, "Natural Law and Virtue," in *Natural Law Theory*, note 27, p. 52 (relying on Alasdair MacIntyre, *After Virtue*, 2d ed. [Notre Dame, Ind.: University of Notre Dame Press, 1984]).

55. Ibid., pp. 55–56.

56. Ibid., pp. 56, 63.

57. Gewirth, *Reason and Morality*, note 20, p. 188.

58. Ibid., p. 189.

59. Hittinger, "Natural Law and Virtue," note 27, p. 55.

60. Gewirth, *Reason and Morality*, note 20, p. 332.

Chapter 6. Difficult Cases

1. *Bowers v. Hardwick*, 478 U.S. 186 (1986).

2. *Dred Scott v. Sanford*, 60 U.S. (19 How.) 393 (1857).

3. *Roe v. Wade*, 410 U.S. 113 (1973).

4. *Lochner v. New York*, 198 U.S. 45 (1905).

5. *Plessy v. Ferguson*, 163 U.S. 537 (1896).

6. *Brown v. Board of Education*, 347 U.S. 483 (1954).

7. *Bowers v. Hardwick*, 478 U.S. 186 (1986).

8. *Griswold v. Connecticut*, 381 U.S. 479 (1965).

9. *Roe v. Wade*, 410 U.S. 113 (1973).

10. See, generally, Vincent J. Samar, *The Right to Privacy: Gays, Lesbians and the Constitution* (Philadelphia: Temple University Press, 1991).

11. It should be noted that proving the tort requires a high standard of evidence when the plaintiff is a public official or a public figure. This is to protect First Amendment claims to freedom of speech and press. As such, the standard that applies is that the plaintiff must prove actual malice, that is, that the defendant knew the statement was false or was in reckless disregard of its truth (see *Time v. Hill*, 385 U.S. 374 [1967]).

12. For the view that the right to privacy should be focused on the corporal body of the individual as opposed to being focused on self-regarding acts, see Kendall Thomas, "Beyond the Privacy Principle," *Columbia Law Review* 92 (1992): 1431. I reject a related view that defines privacy as control over access to the self and limitation of access to oneself (see Samar, *Right to Privacy*, note 10, pp. 56–57.

13. See Samar, *Right to Privacy*, note 10, pp. 62–76.

14. Ibid., p. 68.

15. See Joel Feinberg, *Harm to Others*, vol. 1, *The Moral Limits of the Criminal Law* (New York: Oxford University Press, 1984), p. 11.

16. See ibid., p. 13.

17. See Samar, *Right to Privacy*, note 10, p. 89.

18. See ibid., pp. 103–17, 140–42.

19. See ibid.

20. See ibid., pp. 113, 142.

21. See ibid., pp. 167–72.

22. Indeed, the inverse argument works to support gay and lesbian marriage. To encourage people who are gay or lesbian to follow norms of monogamy and fidelity, the legal definition of marriage should be extended to include same-sex marriage.

23. See Feinberg, *Harm to Others*, note 15, pp. 86–87, 88.

24. The U.S. Army has cited the Supreme Court's allowance of state sodomy laws prohibiting homosexuality in arguing that discharging gays and lesbians from the services would not violate due process. The U.S. Supreme Court has not yet ruled on this issue. See *Walkins v. United States Army*, 875 F. 2d 699, 717 (9th Cir. 1989), *cert. denied*, 498 U.S. 957 (1990).

25. See Samar, *Right to Privacy*, note 10, pp. 104–12.

26. See ibid. pp. 62–68.

27. Ibid., p. 90.

28. Ibid., pp. 86, 205–7.

29. Ibid., p. 91.

30. Ibid., p. 94.

31. Ibid., p. 207.

32. U.S. Constitution, Amendment 9.

33. John Hart Ely does not believe that one can justify on constitutional grounds a general right to privacy, although he does believe that the Constitution centrally protects the democratic principles of participation and representation. From these some privacy protections may emerge. See Ely, *Democracy and Distrust: A Theory of Judicial Review* (Cambridge, Mass.: Harvard University Press, 1980), pp. 36–38. Robert Bork agrees that some forms of privacy—such as the general prohibition against warrantless searches—are founded in the Constitution but believes that no right comparable to the autonomy-based right alleged to apply in *Bowers v. Hardwick*, 478 U.S. 186 (1986), exists under the Constitution. See Bork, *The Tempting of America: The Political Seduction of the Law* (New York: Free Press, 1990), pp. 117–20.

34. See Samar, *Right to Privacy*, note 10, pp. 205–7.

35. Richard Posner, *Overcoming Law* (Cambridge, Mass.: Harvard University Press, 1995), p. 197.

36. Jed Rubenfeld, "The Right of Privacy," *Harvard Law Review* 102 (1989): 737,

804–5, has argued for an affirmative or teleological approach to understanding privacy law as opposed to the more traditional deontological approach. Privacy "does not exist because individuals have a sphere of 'private' life with which the state has nothing to do. . . . The right to privacy exists because democracy must impose limits on the extent of control and direction that the state exercises over the day-to-day conduct of individual lives." In effect, the right to privacy exists to prevent the state from making the identities that form our lives. Because autonomy provides an end of democratic institutions, Rubenfeld has understood this aspect of privacy law well. But he is too restrictive when he denies the deontological aspect of privacy because the autonomy privacy protects is not only an end of democratic institutions but also a justification for such institutions. It is the negative freedom associated with being left alone that makes the positive freedom of self-rule possible. In this sense, private acts provide the ideal typical case of what we would want to protect if autonomy is to be regarded as a value at all. The notion of a private act, rightly construed—so as to avoid some of the conceptual and normative problems Rubenfeld correctly refers to—means that no other basic interest is infringed. See Samar, *Right to Privacy*, note 10, pp. 65, 89.

37. *Bowers v. Hardwick*, 478 U.S. at 191.

38. *Eisenstadt v. Baird*, 405 U.S. 438 (1972).

39. *Carey v. Population Services International*, 431 U.S. 678 (1977).

40. *Roe v. Wade*, 410 U.S. 113 (1973).

41. See Morton J. Horwitz, "The Bork Nomination and American Constitutional History," *Syracuse Law Review* 39 (1988): 1029, 1033–34.

42. *Bowers v. Hardwick*, 478 U.S. at 197 (Burger, C. J. concurring).

43. Ronald Dworkin, "The Law of the Slave-Catchers: A Review of Robert M. Cover's *Justice Accused: Antislavery and the Judicial Process*," *Times Literary Supplement* (London, December 5, 1975), p. 1437.

44. Ibid. In *Law's Empire* (Cambridge, Mass.: Harvard University Press, 1986), Ronald Dworkin describes such legislation and related constitutional provisions as "checkerboard" laws that treat similar situations differently on arbitrary grounds (p. 179).

45. Dworkin, "Law of the Slave-Catchers," note 43, p. 1437.

46. Ibid.

47. U.S. Constitution, Article 4, section 2.

48. Dworkin, "Law of the Slave-Catchers," note 43, p. 1437.

49. Ibid.

50. Ibid.

51. See U.S. Constitution, Article 4, section 2.

52. J. L. Mackie, "The Third Theory of Law," *Philosophy and Public Affairs* 7, 1 (1977): 12.

53. Ibid.

54. Ibid.

55. Ibid., p. 15.

56. Ibid., p. 11.

57. Ibid., pp. 11–12.

58. Dworkin, "Law of the Slave-Catchers," note 43, p. 1437.

59. Aristotle, *Politics*, in *The Basic Works of Aristotle*, ed. Richard McKeon (New York: Random House, 1941), bk. 1.2, p. 1252a30; bk. 1.5, p. 1254b15ff.; bk. 1.13, p. 1260a12.

60. Neil MacCormick, "Natural Law and the Separation of Law and Morals," in *Natural Law Theory: Contemporary Essays*, ed. R. P. George (Oxford: Clarendon Press, 1992) (commenting on John Finnis, *Natural Law and Natural Rights* [Oxford: Clarendon Press, 1980]).

61. Michel Foucault contends that "'Truth' is linked in circular relations with systems of power which produce and sustain it. . . . [The problem is to find a means to detach] the power of truth from the forms of hegemony, social, economic and cultural, within which it operates at the present time" ("Truth and Power," in *The Foucault Review*, ed. Paul Rabinow [New York: Pantheon Books, 1984], pp. 51, 74–75). In this book, I hope I have succeeded in laying a foundation for a theory of natural law/natural rights in a Gewirthian view of morality and in a Davidsonian view of objective truth that at least avoids the obvious criticisms of cultural and conceptual relativism.

62. Alan Gewirth, *Reason and Morality* (Chicago: University of Chicago Press, 1978), p. 168.

63. *Roe v. Wade*, 410 U.S. 113 (1973).

64. Ibid., p. 153.

65. Gewirth, *Reason and Morality*, note 62, p. 142.

66. Ibid., p. 121.

67. Ibid., p. 142.

68. Ibid., p. 143.

69. Ibid., pp. 143–44.

70. Often the debate rages as a religious attack by people with a certain fundamentalist Protestant or conservative Roman Catholic bent against those individuals whom they perceive to be concerned only with what society wants as opposed to what God wants.

71. Samar, *Right to Privacy*, note 10, pp. 68–72.

72. Ibid., pp. 173–74.

73. Ronald Dworkin, "The Great Abortion Case," *New York Review of Books*, June 29, 1989, pp. 49–53.

74. Ibid.

75. Ibid., p. 50.

76. Ibid.

77. Ibid.

78. Ronald Dworkin, *Life's Dominion: An Argument about Abortion, Euthanasia, and Individual Freedom* (New York: Alfred A. Knopf, 1993), p. 168.

79. *Roe v. Wade* put into effect a trimester system in which the state was barred from prohibiting abortions in the first trimester, could limit them only for the sake of protecting maternal life in the second trimester, but could restrict them for the sake of protecting fetal life in the third trimester. Since *Roe* the Supreme Court has decided *Planned Parenthood of Southeastern Pennsylvania v. Casey*, 505 U.S. 833 (1992). That case reaffirmed *Roe*'s basic holding that a woman has a constitutional right to an abortion but substituted for the trimester system the test that any state regulation on abortion must not create an "undue burden" on a woman's right to choose by placing "substantial obstacles" in the way of her choice. In effect, the Court sought under this new approach to take itself out of having to regulate when abortions might take place.

80. Dworkin, *Life's Dominion*, note 78, p. 170.

81. R. M. Hare, "Abortion and the Golden Rule," *Philosophy and Public Affairs* 4

(1975): 201, 208–9. Contrast R. M. Hare, "A Kantian Approach to Abortion," *Social Theory and Practice* 15 (1989): 1 (offering a Kantian argument against abortion), with R. B. Brandt, "Hare on Abortion," *Social Theory and Practice* 15 (1989): 15 (responding to Hare's Kantian argument), and R. M. Hare, "Abortion: Reply to Brandt," in that journal, p. 25 (replying to Brandt's response).

82. Hare, "Abortion and the Golden Rule," pp. 213–14.

83. Don Marquis, "Why Abortion Is Immoral," *Journal of Philosophy* 4 (1989): 183.

84. Ibid., p. 194.

85. See ibid., pp. 201–2.

86. Joel Feinberg, "Abortion," in *Matters of Life and Death: New Introductory Essays in Moral Philosophy*, ed. Tom Regan (New York: Random House, 1986), p. 270.

87. For a discussion of this point, see Joel Feinberg, *Offense to Others*, vol. 2, *The Moral Limits of the Criminal Law*, 4 vols. (New York: Oxford University Press, 1985), 2: 56–57.

88. *Lochner v. New York*, 198 U.S. 45 (1905).

89. Bruce Ackerman, *Foundations*, vol. 1, *We the People* (Cambridge, Mass.: Harvard University Press, 1991), p. 115.

90. *Slaughterhouse Cases*, 83 U.S. (16 Wall.) 36, 67 (1873).

91. *West Coast Hotel v. Parish*, 300 U.S. 379 (1937).

92. Ibid., p.399.

93. *Lochner v. New York*, 198 U.S. at 76 (Holmes, J. dissenting).

94. *Swift v. Tyson*, 41 U.S. (16 Pet.) 1 (1842).

95. Cass Sunstein, *The Partial Constitution* (Cambridge, Mass.: Harvard University Press, 1993), p. 55.

96. *Erie Railroad Co. v. Tompkins*, 304 U.S. 64 (1938).

97. Sunstein, *Partial Constitution*, note 95, p. 363 n. 33.

98. Ackerman, *Foundations*, note 89, pp. 65–66.

99. Mort J. Horwitz, *The Transformation of American Law, 1870–1960: The Crisis of Legal Orthodoxy* (New York: Oxford University Press, 1992), p. 30.

100. See Ackerman, *Foundations*, note 89, pp. 58ff.

101. Horwitz, *Transformation of American Law, 1870–1960*, note 98, p. 30.

102. Ibid. (citing *Lochner v. New York*, 198 U.S. at 59).

103. Ibid., p. 128.

104. *United States v. Carolene Products Co.*, 304 U.S. 144 (1938).

105. Ackerman, *Foundations*, note 89, pp. 128–29.

106. *Plako v. Connecticut*, 302 U.S. 319 (1937).

107. Ibid., p. 325.

108. Posner, *Overcoming Law*, note 35, p. 219.

109. Dworkin, *Law's Empire*, note 44, p. 398.

110. Gewirth, *Reason and Morality*, note 62, p. 172.

111. Sunstein, *Partial Constitution*, note 95, p. 61.

112. Ibid., p. 67.

113. *Lochner v. New York*, 198 U.S. at 64.

114. Gewirth, *Reason and Morality*, note 62, pp. 312–13. Compare John Rawls, *A Theory of Justice* (Cambridge, Mass.: Harvard University Press, 1971) (reflecting a strong egalitarian approach to distributive justice), with Robert Nozick, *Anarchy, State and*

Utopia (New York: Basic Books, 1974) (arguing for a libertarian, nonpatterned approach to justice based on historical acquisition and transfers of property).

115. *Plessy v. Ferguson*, 163 U.S. 537 (1896).

116. Ibid., p. 540.

117. Ibid., p. 544 (emphasis added).

118. Sunstein, *Partial Constitution*, note 95, p. 42.

119. Ibid., p. 43.

120. *Plessy v. Ferguson*, 163 U.S. at 551.

121. Ibid.

122. Sunstein, *Partial Constitution*, note 95, p. 43.

123. See William Graham Sumner, *Folkways* (Boston: Gina and Company, 1906), p. 285 (arguing that clinical investigations showed a lower cranial capacity for Negroes that was "ineradicable by laws and the schemes of well-meaning reformers"), cited in Richard Kluger, *Simple Justice: The History of Brown v. Board of Education and Black America's Struggle for Equality* (New York: Alfred A. Knopf, 1976), chap. 13 (providing a thorough analysis of the development and downfall of racist theories following *Plessy*).

124. *Brown v. Board of Education*, 347 U.S. 483 (1954).

125. The principle case was brought by a group of African-American children in Topeka, Kansas. However, it was consolidated with similar cases brought against school districts in South Carolina, Virginia, and Delaware.

126. Posner, *Overcoming Law*, note 35, p. 72.

127. Ibid.

128. *Brown v. Board of Education*, 347 U.S. at 493.

129. Ibid., pp. 489–90.

130. Ackerman, *Foundations*, note 89, p. 150 (citing *Brown v. Board of Education*, 347 U.S. at 494–95).

131. Sunstein, *Partial Constitution*, note 95, pp. 44–45.

132. Dworkin, *Law's Empire*, note 44, pp. 388–89.

133. Robert Bork agrees with the *Brown* decision despite his otherwise strong adherence to original intention (see *Tempting of America*, note 33, p. 82). Richard Posner explains this shift in position as the only way out of having the courts monitor segregated schools to ensure that "they are physically equal" (see Posner, *Overcoming Law*, note 35, p. 248).

134. Kluger, *Simple Justice*, note 123, p. 705.

135. Herbert Wechsler, "Toward Neutral Principles of Constitutional Law," *Harvard Law Review* 73 (1959): 1, 31–35.

136. Sunstein, *Partial Constitution*, note 95, p. 76.

137. Gewirth, *Reason and Morality*, note 62, p. 119.

138. Ibid., p. 242.

139. Posner, *Overcoming Law*, note 35, p. 225.

140. Sunstein, *Partial Constitution*, note 95, p. 146.

141. See Alexander M. Bickel, *The Least Dangerous Branch: The Supreme Court at the Bar of Politics*, 2d ed. (New Haven: Yale University Press, 1962), pp. 252–54.

142. Alexander Bickel emphasizes this point by noting that "the Court has ways of persuading before it attempts to coerce, and that, over time, sustained opinion running counter to the Court's constitutional law can achieve its nullification, directly or by desuetude. It may further be that if the process is properly carried out, an aspect of the

current—not only the timeless, mystic—popular will finds expression in constitutional adjudication" (see ibid., p. 28).

143. *Korematsu v. United States*, 323 U.S. 214 (1944).

144. Ibid., p. 243 (Jackson, J., dissenting).

145. Ibid., p. 216.

146. Ibid., p. 219.

147. Ibid., pp. 234–35 (Murphy, J., dissenting) (arguing that this order was an obvious racial discrimination in violation of the equal protection clause of the Fifth Amendment); see also *United States v. Carolene Products Co.*, 304 U.S. 144, 152–53 n. 4 (1938).

148. Robert Solomon, ed., *Existentialism* (New York: Random House, 1974), p. 8 (citing Søren Kierkegaard, *Journals* [New York: Oxford University Press, 1938]).

Chapter 7. Legal Education

1. See Gary Minda, "Jurisprudence at Century's End," *Journal of Legal Education* 43 (1993): 27, 28; see also Heather MacDonald, "Law School Humbug," *City Journal* (Autumn 1995): 46 and accompanying letters.

2. John Stuart Mill, *On Liberty* (New York: Penguin, 1988), pp. 115–16.

3. See Steven M. Quevedo, "Formalist and Instrumentalist Legal Reasoning and Legal Theory," *California Law Review* 73 (1985): 147–50.

4. See Eugene Wambaugh, "Professor Langdell—A View of His Career," *Nation*, July 12, 1906.

5. Arguably, *The Common Law* was published in partial response to the approaches of Langdell and others who saw the law as embodying a justified set of principles. For Holmes, "The moral language in which many familiar rules of law are spoken is an inheritance from the primitive illusion of animism" (Oliver Wendell Holmes, *The Common Law*, ed. Mark DeWolfe Howe [Boston: Little, Brown, 1963], p. xxiii).

6. Robert Bork, *Slouching Towards Gomorrah: Modern Liberalism and American Decline* (New York: Regan Books, 1996).

7. See ibid., p. 97 (claiming that many of the judges and justices who are appointed to the courts are or are influenced by left-wing intellectuals); see also Lehrer News Hour, Gergen interview with Robert Bork, PBS, show no. 5696, Channel 11 (Chicago), November 11, 1996.

8. Bork, *Slouching Towards Gomorrah*, note 6, p. 319.

9. Ibid., p. 133.

10. Ibid., pp. 106–7.

11. *Dead Man Walking*, Polygram Filmed Entertainment (1996).

12. *Long Time Companion*, Samuel Goldwyn Co. (1990).

13. U.S. Constitution, Article 3, sections 1 and 3.

14. In *Marbury v. Madison*, 5 U.S. (1 Cranch) 137, 163 (1803), the U.S. Supreme Court case that first annunciated the doctrine of judicial review of the acts of Congress, Chief Justice John Marshall stated: "The very essence of civil liberty certainly consists in the right of every individual to claim the protection of the laws, whenever he receives an injury. One of the first duties of government is to afford that protection."

15. *Romer v. Evans*, 106 S. Ct. 1620 (1996).

16. U.S. Constitution, Amendment 14.

17. Bork, *Slouching Towards Gomorrah*, note 6, p. 114 (citing *Romer v. Evans*, 116 S. Ct. at 1629 [Scalia, J., dissenting]).

18. See Fredrick Schauer, *Free Speech: A Philosophical Enquiry* (New York: Cambridge University Press, 1982), pp. 15–46.

19. See Vincent J. Samar, *The Right to Privacy: Gays, Lesbians and the Constitution* (Philadelphia: Temple University Press, 1991) pp. 167–72 (on the illegitimacy of sodomy statutes).

20. U.S. Constitution, Amendment 1.

21. *Romer v. Evans*, 106 S. Ct. at 1634 (Scalia, J., dissenting). See also Bork, *Slouching Towards Gomorrah*, note 6, p. 114.

22. Ibid., p. 113.

23. *Baehr v. Levin*, 74 Haw. 530, 580, 852 P. 2d 44, 67 (1993).

24. U.S. Constitution, Article 4.

25. Ibid.

26. See Defense of Marriage Act (DOMA), Pub. L. 104–199,— Stat.—(1996).

27. See Robert Bork, *Slouching Towards Gomorrah*, note 6, p. 112.

28. *Lovings v. Virginia*, 388 U.S. 1, 12 (1967) (striking down a Virginia law prohibiting interracial marriage).

29. *Bowers v. Hardwick*, 478 U.S. 186 (1986).

30. Bork, *Slouching Towards Gomorrah*, note 6, p. 104. In contrast to Bork's view, it was found in the study of a small village in southern Italy, by the Research Center in Economic Development and Cultural Change at the University of Chicago, that "the extreme poverty and backwardness" could "be explained largely (but not entirely) by the inability of the villagers to act together for their common good or, indeed, for any end transcending the immediate material interests of the nuclear family." See Edward C. Banfield, *The Moral Basis of a Backward Society* (New York: Free Press, 1958), p. 10.

31. John Finnis, "Law, Morality and 'Sexual Orientation,'" *Notre Dame Law Review* 69 (1994): 1049.

32. Ibid.

33. Ibid., p. 1069.

34. As I do not want to be accused of the same overly hasty generalizations that I accuse Finnis of making, let me say from the outset that I think Finnis has failed to examine those positions that are most controversial in his views. His homonegativity simply does not seem justified. This is particularly unsettling given the incident I will describe in note 38 as his dispute with Martha Nussbaum. Still, I am willing to entertain the possibility that his positions, though arguably mistaken, may simply reflect the too-limited view of moral foundations often associated with natural law theories. For more on the distinction between homonegativity and homophobia as an explanation of antigay sentiment, see Henry E. Adams, Lester W. Wright Jr., and Bethany A. Lohr, "Is Homophobia Associated with Homosexual Arousal?" *Journal of Abnormal Psychology* 105 (1996): 440.

35. Finnis, "Law, Morality and 'Sexual Orientation,'" p. 1067 (citing Plato, *Gorgias*, in *Collected Dialogues*, trans. W. D. Woodhead, ed. Edith Hamilton and Huntington Cairns (Princeton: Princeton University Press, 1961), 494e1–5, 495b3).

36. Plato, *Gorgias*, 494e1–5, 495b3.

37. John Boswell, *Christianity, Social Tolerance and Homosexuality: Gay People in Western Europe from the Beginning of the Christian Era to the Fourteenth Century* (Chicago: University of Chicago Press, 1980), p. 79 n. 87.

38. Martha C. Nussbaum, "Platonic Love and Colorado Law: The Relevance of Ancient Greek Norms to Modern Sexual Controversies," *Virginia Law Review* 80 (1994): 1515, 1563. This essay and Finnis's essay were both drafted, at least in part, to dispute testimony given by Nussbaum at the *Romer v. Evans* trial on behalf of the persons seeking to overturn the amendment. Finnis also testified, although on behalf of the state. The dispute arose over whether the moral proscription of homosexual acts is based solely on religion or if it had other origins. The question was prompted to avoid a legal judgment possibly being based on a religious standard. After Nussbaum's testimony, Finnis challenged her for failing to inform the court as to whether the lexicon she was relying on to translate the ancient Greek had been updated and that she herself had often made use of the update. In response, Nussbaum argued that the two lexicons serve different purposes. Although a later edition might provide more useful findings on the use of a word, it also might be more biased if subsequent uses come about against a different moral backdrop.

39. See David E. Greenberg, *The Construction of Homosexuality* (Chicago: University of Chicago Press, 1988), p. 149 (discussing the disdain for passivity in ancient Greece), and p. 432 (concluding that the medical model shows "that a homosexual object choice did not necessarily imply an unconventional gender identity").

40. See K. J. Dover, *Greek Homosexuality* (Cambridge, Mass.: Harvard University Press, 1989), p. 17 (arguing against mistranslations by taking words that had a particular meaning at one time or are ambiguous in one language out of their context).

41. Cass R. Sunstein, *The Partial Constitution* (Cambridge, Mass.: Harvard University Press, 1993), p. 4.

42. Duncan Kennedy, "Legal Education as Training for Hierarchy," in *The Politics of Law: A Progressive Critique*, ed. David Kairys, rev. ed. (New York: Pantheon Books, 1990), p. 42.

43. Ibid., p. 43.

44. Noam Chomsky, *Language and Politics* (New York: Basic Books, 1988), p. 708; see also Donaldo Macedo, "Literacy for Stupidification: The Pedagogy of Big Lies," in *Multicultural Education: Critical Pedagogy and the Politics of Difference*, ed. Christine E. Sleeter and Peter L. McLaren (Albany: SUNY, 1995), p. 71.

45. See Jean R. Sternlight, "Symbiotic Legal Theory and Legal Practice: Advocating a Common Sense Jurisprudence of Law and Practical Applications," *University of Miami Law Review* 50 (1996): 707, 720 n. 59; see also Warren E. Burger, "The Special Skills of Advocacy: Are Specialized Training and Certification of Advocates Essential to Our System of Justice?" *Fordham Law Review* 42 (1973): 227, 240.

46. Robin West, "Disciplines, Subjectivity and the Law," in *The Fate of Law*, ed. Austin Sarat and Thomas R. Kearns, *The Amherst Series in Law, Jurisprudence and Social Thought* (Ann Arbor: University of Michigan Press, 1991), p. 119.

47. Ibid.

48. Ibid., pp. 156–57.

49. Ibid., p. 157.

50. Here we run into the standard dilemma that results from the apparent conflict between choosing liberty and equality when there is no more highly ordered moral prin-

ciple to appeal to. See, e.g., E. F. Carritt, "Liberty and Equality," in *Political Philosophy*, ed. Anthony Quinton, *Oxford Readings in Philosophy* (New York: Oxford University Press, 1967), pp. 127ff.

51. See David Hume, *An Enquiry Concerning the Principles of Morals* (LaSalle, Ill.: Open Court, 1966), pp. 110, 125–26. But see Alan Gewirth, *Reason and Morality* (Chicago: University of Chicago Press, 1978), p. 6 (noting the limitation of thinking our sentiments are universal).

52. Derrick Bell, "Racial Realism," *Connecticut Law Review* 24 (1992): 363, 376.

53. Larissa MacFarquhar, "The Color of the Law: Critical Race Theorists Have Developed Subtle Insights into Race and Power in America. But Do They Have Anything to Contribute to the Law?" *Lingua franca: The Review of Academic Life* (July/August 1996): 40, 47.

54. Linda S. Greene, "Civil Rights at the Millennium—A Response to Bell's Call for Racial Realism," *Connecticut Law Review* 24 (1992): 499, 500.

55. john a. powell (author's style), "Racial Realism or Racial Despair?" *Connecticut Law Review* 24 (1992): 533, 543 (citing Patricia Williams, "The Obliging Shell: An Internal Essay on Formal Equal Opportunity," *Michigan Law Review* 87 [1989]: 2128).

56. *City of Richmond v. J. A. Croson Co.*, 488 U.S. 469 (1989).

57. Williams, "Obliging Shell," note 55, p. 2139.

58. Charles R. Lawrence III, "The Id, the Ego and Equal Protection: Reckoning with Unconscious Racism," *Stanford Law Review* 39 (1987): 317, 323.

59. Patricia Williams, *Alchemy of Race and Rights: Diary of a Law Professor* (Cambridge, Mass.: Harvard University Press, 1991).

60. Barbara Johnson describes what Williams is doing here not as "a 'kind of confessional attitudinizing'" but as a relocation of Descartes's doubting subject into "the framework of historical, legal, and corporeal intersubjectivity." For more on this point, see Barbara Johnson, "The Alchemy of Style and Law," in *The Rhetoric of Law*, ed. Austin Sarat and Thomas R. Kearns, *The Amherst Series in Law, Jurisprudence and Social Thought* (Ann Arbor: University of Michigan Press, 1996), pp. 270–74 (citing Gayatri Spivak, "A Response to 'The Difference Within: Feminism and Critical Theory,'" in *The Difference Within: Feminism and Critical Theory*, ed. Elizabeth Meese and Alice Parker [Amsterdam: John Benjamins, 1989], p. 208); see also Williams, *Alchemy of Race and Rights*, note 55, p. 3.

61. I am indebted to Raymond Belliotti for making this point.

62. Recent news reports of alleged racial discrimination at the Texico Company provide illustrations of first-person accounts in this area. See Lehrer News Hour, "Alleged Racism at Texico," PBS, show no. 5697, Channel 11 (Chicago), November 12, 1996.

63. MacFarquhar, "Color of the Law," note 53, p. 44 (referencing an article by Paul Butler, "Racially Based Jury Nullification: Black Power in the Criminal Justice System," *Yale Law Journal* 105 [1995]: 677).

64. Ibid.

65. Williams, *Alchemy of Race and Rights*, note 55, p. 95.

66. Ibid., p. 97.

67. See Leslie G. Espinoza, "Masks and Other Disguises: Exposing Legal Academia," *Harvard Law Review* 103 (1990): 1878.

68. Quoted in MacFarquhar, "Color of the Law," note 53, p. 43.

69. Ibid., p. 47.

70. See Deborah Rhode, "Feminist Critical Theories," *Stanford Law Review* 42 (1990): 617, 619.

71. Celina Romany, "Ain't I a Feminist?" *Yale Journal of Law and Feminism* 4 (1991): 23, 24.

72. Angela P. Harris, "Race and Essentialism in Feminist Legal Theory," *Stanford Law Review* 42 (1990): 581, 604.

73. Ibid., p. 601 (referencing Catharine MacKinnon, *Feminism Unmodified: Discourses on Life and Law* [Cambridge, Mass.: Harvard University Press, 1987]).

74. Ibid., p. 610 (citing Martha Minow, "Forward: Justice Engendered," in "The Supreme Court 1986 Term," *Harvard Law Review* 101 [1987]: 10, 34–38).

75. Catharine MacKinnon, "From Practice to Theory, or What is a White Woman Anyway?" *Yale Journal of Law and Feminism* 4 (1991): 13, 20.

76. See Vincent J. Samar, "A Moral Justification for Gay and Lesbian Civil Rights Legislation," *Journal of Homosexuality* 27 (1994): 147, 151.

77. By analogy, Patricia A. Cain points out the many ways in which the social and legal experiences of gays and lesbians differ from those of heterosexual men and women (see "Litigating for Lesbian and Gay Rights: A Legal History," *Virginia Law Review* 79 (1993): 1551. Presumably, the same could be said of the differences between men and women.

78. Ruthann Robson criticizes feminist jurisprudence for being too preoccupied with distinguishing men from women, leaving lesbians, for example, almost invisible (see *Lesbian (Out)Law: Survival Under the Rule of Law* [Ithaca, N.Y.: Firebrand Books, 1992]).

79. I mean to imply nothing here regarding the issue of affirmative action, which involves a complex set of moral and factual considerations that would need to be worked through.

80. Margaret Jane Radin, "The Pragmatist and the Feminist," *Southern California Law Review* 63 (1990): 1699, 1706.

81. Ibid. (citing John Dewey, *Experience and Nature*, 2nd ed [LaSalle, Ill.: Open Court, 1929], p. 410).

82. Ibid. (citing William James, *Pragmatism*, ed. Bruce Kuklick [Cambridge, Mass.: Hackett, 1981], p. 98).

83. Ibid., p. 1707.

84. Ibid.

85. Joseph William Singer, "The Player and the Cards: Nihilism and Legal Theory," *Yale Law Journal* 94 (1984): 156.

86. Ibid., p. 63. Others also have made a case for an attractive side to the CLS. Gerald Frug has argued, given the CLS's understanding of power relations in law, that we need to increase the power of municipalities to increase local autonomy and individual participation (see "The City as a Legal Concept," *Harvard Law Review* 93 [1980]: 1059. See also Roberto M. Unger, *Knowledge and Politics* (New York: Free Press, 1975) (arguing for an egalitarian society without social and economic hierarchies).

87. Singer, "Player and the Cards," p. 63.

88. See Drucilla Cornell, "From the Lighthouse: The Promise of Redemption and the Possibility of Legal Interpretation," *Cardozo Law Review* 11 (1990): 1687, 1699.

89. Ibid., pp. 1700, 1690. Cornell argues that the central error of the "irrationalists" at a CLS conference was their failure to distinguish *Grundlosigkeit* (groundlessness) from *Unsinnlosigkeit* (senselessness).

90. Ibid., p. 1706.

91. Ibid., p. 1714.

92. H. L. A. Hart, "Positivism and the Separation of Law and Morals," *Harvard Law Review* 71 (1958): 593, 613.

93. See Ronald Dworkin, *Law's Empire* (Cambridge, Mass.: Harvard University Press, 1986), p. 272.

94. Ibid., p. 79; see also Owen M. Fiss, "The Death of the Law?" *Cornell Law Review* 72 (1986): 1 (who holds a view similar to Dworkin's about CLS).

95. See Dinesh D'Souza, *Illiberal Education: The Politics of Race and Sex on Campus* (New York: Vintage Books, 1992), p. 18.

96. Martha Nussbaum, "The Use and Abuse of Philosophy in Legal Education," *Stanford Law Review* 45 (1993): 1627, 1630.

97. A good example of such a model is the Law, Jurisprudence and Social Thought Program at Amherst College. Many other schools across the country have similar programs including, to mention only a few, the University of Chicago, Berkeley, and Wesley College. The American Bar Association keeps a list and some detailed accounts on these programs for interested schools to review.

98. Richard Posner makes a similar suggestion in his proposal to include legal theory, by which he means the use of scientific and humanistic methods of inquiry in legal education. See Richard Posner, "The Decline of Law as an Autonomous Discipline," *Harvard Law Review* 100 (1987): 778.

99. See Richard Posner, *Economic Analysis of Law*, 4th ed. (Boston: Little Brown, 1992).

100. See, e.g., David Kairys, ed., *The Politics of Law: A Progressive Critique* (New York: Pantheon, 1990).

101. Nussbaum, "Use and Abuse of Philosophy," note 96, p. 1641.

102. David J. Givelber, Brook K. Baker, John McDevitt, and Robyn Miliano, "Learning through Work: An Empirical Study of Legal Internship," *Journal of Legal Education* 45 (1995): 1; see also Gary L. Blasi, "What Lawyers Know: Cognitive Science, and the Functions of Theory," *Journal of Legal Education* 45 (1995): 313, 318–19 (arguing for the use in legal problem-solving of schemas and mental models developed in other domains of intellectual inquiry).

103. Syracuse University also has interdisciplinary programs with the Maxwell School of Citizenship and Public Affairs.

104. See N. E. H. Hull, "Vital Schools of Jurisprudence: Roscoe Pound, Wesley Newcomb Hohfeld, and the Promotion of an Academic Jurisprudence Agenda, 1910–1919," *Journal of Legal Education* 45 (1995): 235.

105. Bertrand Russell, *The Problems of Philosophy* (New York: Oxford University Press, 1959), p. 157.

106. *Romer v. Evans*,—U.S.—, 116 S. Ct. 1620 (1996).

107. *Bowers v. Hardwick*, 478 U.S. 186 (1986).

108. Prior to *Bowers*, the Supreme Court had decided as a matter of federal constitutional privacy law that a state could not prohibit the use of contraceptives by two persons married (*Griswold v. Connecticut*, 381 U.S. 479 [1965]) or single (*Eisenstadt v. Baird*, 405 U.S. 438 [1972]), that it could not prohibit the sale of contraceptives to minors (*Carey v. Population Services International*, 431 U.S. 678 [1977]), and that a woman had a con-

stitutional privacy right within the first two trimesters of her pregnancy to have an abortion (*Roe v. Wade*, 410 U.S. 113 [1973]).

109. Richard Posner on the U.S. Seventh Circuit has such an expertise in economics. U.S. Supreme Court Justice Stephen Breyer has written on public choice theory versus the common good. See my discussion of economic analysis in the law in chapter 1.

110. See Samar, *Right to Privacy*, note 19, chap. 1.

111. See "Excerpts from the Supreme Court Ruling on a Lawsuit Against Clinton," *New York Times*, sec. 1, p. A12, col. 5.

111. See, e.g., Warren E. Burger, "The Special Skills of Advocacy," note 45, p. 227.

Conclusion

1. Michael R. De Paul offers a related approach to different levels of moral evaluation (see *Balance and Refinement: Beyond Coherence Methods of Moral Inquiry* [New York: Routledge, 1993], pp. 31–43).

2. H. L. A. Hart recognized the incompleteness of positivism in the second edition of *The Concept of Law* (New York: Oxford University Press, 1994), p. 252, when he wrote that "cases with open texture, that is, where the law fails to determine an answer, "are not merely 'hard cases,' controversial in the sense that reasonable and informed lawyers may disagree about which answer is legally correct, but the law in such cases is fundamentally incomplete: it provides no answer to the questions at issue in such cases."

3. See Hart, *Concept of Law* (New York: Oxford University Press, 1961), pp. 57, 105–6.

4. The idea is similar to what Wittgenstein had in mind in his treatment of language games. See Ludwig Wittgenstein, *Philosophical Investigations*, ed. G. E. M. Anscombe, 3d ed. (New York: Macmillan, 1958), nos. 65–67.

5. Ibid., p. 194e (citing Joseph Jastrow, *Fact and Fable in Psychology* [Boston: Houghton, Mifflin and Company, 1900]).

6. William Rehg, introduction to Jürgen Habermas, *Between Facts and Norms: Contributions to a Discourse Theory of Law and Democracy*, trans. Rehg (Cambridge, Mass.: MIT Press, 1996), p. xv. Rehg writes that Habermas also believes that "not all types of claims anticipate the agreement of a universal audience. . . . For example, claims about what is good for a particular group (or person), or about a particular group's authentic self-understanding, may be addressed only to the individuals concerned and those who know them well. Such discourses, which Habermas labels 'ethical,' differ in both theme and scope of audience from the 'moral' discourse concerned with universal norms of justice" (p. xv).

7. See Alan Gewirth, *Reason and Morality* (Chicago: University of Chicago Press, 1978), pp. 159–61.

8. Again, by analogy, recall David Hume's need to ground the cause/effect relationship in the mind since he had no impression for it in the world. See Hume, *An Enquiry Concerning Human Understanding; A Letter from a Gentleman to His Friend in Edinburgh and Hume's Abstract of A Treatise of Human Nature*, ed. Eric Steinberg, 2d ed. (Indianapolis: Hackett, 1977), p. 52. See Gewirth, *Reason and Morality*, chap. 2.

9. See Gewirth, *Reason and Morality*, note 6, p. 32.

10. See Jürgen Habermas, *Legitimation Crisis*, trans. Thomas McCarthy (Boston: Beacon Press, 1973), pp. 107–14.

11. Jürgen Habermas, *Justification and Application: Remarks on Discourse Ethics*, trans. Ciaran P. Cronin (Cambridge, Mass.: MIT Press, 1993), p. 24.

12. Ibid., p. 50. The appeal to an internal intersubjective point of view from which one can set forth universally valid judgments is strikingly similar to Kant's use of the transcendental table of the pure concepts of the understanding in the *Critique of Pure Reason*. It is also different from Kant's work in section 3 of the *Foundations of the Metaphysics of Morals*, where he treats the first-person self subjectively as free to give oneself the moral law.

13. Rehg, introduction, note 6, pp. xxvi–xxvii. In particular, looking at the actual language that Habermas uses, we begin where he states that "norms of action *branch out* into moral and legal rules. From a normative point of view, this corresponds to the assumption that moral and civic autonomy are co-original and can be explained with the help of a parsimonious discourse principle that merely expresses the meaning of postconventional requirements of justification. . . . Despite its normative content, it lies at a level of abstraction that is *still neutral* with respect to morality and law, for it refers to action norms in general" (p. 107). Habermas describes the discourse principle he has in mind as providing that "just those action norms are valid to which all could agree as participants in rational discourses" (p. 107). In conceiving the principle, then, "It is important that we not limit a fortiori the kinds of issues and contributions and the sorts of reasons that 'count' in each case. . . . With moral questions, humanity or a presupposed republic of world citizens constitutes the reference system for justifying regulations that lie in the equal interests of all. . . . With ethical-political questions ["ethical" here referring to group values], the form of life of the political community that is 'in each case our own' constitutes the reference system for justifying decisions that are supposed to express an authentic, collective self-understanding" (p. 108). Of course, and Habermas seems to recognize this, the key to employing these multidiscourse approaches is how we resolve conflicts between the moral and the ethical-political. On this question, Habermas writes, "Oppositions between interests require a rational balancing of competing value orientations and interest positions. Here the totality of social or subcultural groups that are directly involved constitute the reference system for negotiating compromises. Insofar as these compromises come about under fair bargaining conditions, they must be acceptable in principle to all parties, even if on the basis of respectively different reasons" (p. 108).

14. See ibid., p. 312.

15. Seyla Benhabib notes, "Although the mode of analysis defined by Gewirth as 'the dialectically necessary method' bears some affinities to the emphasis in communicative ethics on 'the performative standpoint of the agent,' there are fundamental differences. First, Gewirth proceeds from a strictly monological or self-centered (although not egotistical) point of view in constructing his dialectically necessary method, while communicative ethics proceeds from the standpoint of dialogue and constructs the standpoint of agents as members of a linguistic and social community. Second, Gewirth dissolves all 'interaction' into 'transactions' among selves, on the ground that interaction represents an 'organicist' perspective, according to which all agents are mutual recipients and agents to one another. . . . From the standpoint of communicative ethics, this dissolution into transactions is completely unacceptable, for it puts the cart before the horse" (*Critique, Norm, and Utopia: A Study of the Foundations of Critical Theory* [New York: Columbia University Press, 1986], p. 356 n. 16).

16. Habermas claims that "we may assume that the know-how informing argumenta-

tive practices represents a point of convergence where participants, however diverse their backgrounds, can at least intuitively meet in their efforts to reach an understanding. In all languages and in every language community, such concepts as truth, rationality, justification, and consensus, even if interpreted differently and applied according to different criteria, play *the same grammatical role*. At any rate, this is true for modern societies that, with positive law, secularized politics, and a principled morality, have made the shift to a postconventional level of justification and expect their members to take a reflexive attitude toward their own respective cultural traditions" (*Between Facts and Norms*, note 6, pp. 311–12. I am indebted to David Ingram for pointing this issue out to me, including Habermas's hedge on the last point.

17. See also Alan Gewirth, *The Community of Rights* (Chicago: University of Chicago Press, 1996), in which Gewirth questions Habermas's claim that we can set up an "ideal speech situation." How, for example, could we ever ascertain whether all the members of society truly have dedicated themselves to truth and the rejection of force and deception and irrelevant emotional factors? What assurance would such commitments in a speech situation afford that the members would, then, agree to the same social policies and institutions in practice? (see pp. 28–29). What we end up with is an approach akin—although at a higher level of generality—to what John Rawls offers in *Political Liberalism* (New York: Columbia University Press, 1993), in which he attempts to resolve conflicts among competing comprehensive worldviews by requiring everybody to adopt as their "political" conception of justice the notion of a fair system of social cooperation as a basis for consensus building. Habermas adopts a parsimonious discourse principle analogous to Rawls's adoption of the political conception of justice. This approach has limited utility where the issues do not allow for much middle ground (see chapter 2).

18. Seyla Benhabib notes that Alasdair MacIntyre has argued against Gewirth that "from the premise that I as a rational agent require certain conditions to be fulfilled, it can never follow that you have an *obligation* not to hinder me from enjoying these conditions. . . . Put in terms which are those of Apel and Habermas, the analysis of the rational structure of action for a single agent produces an *egological* moral theory which cannot justify intersubjective moral validity. Instead of asking what I as a rational agent can intend or will to be a universal maxim for all without contradiction, the communicative ethicist asks: what principles of action can we all recognize or agree to as being valid if we engage in practical discourse or a mutual search for justification?" "Afterword: Communicative Ethics and Current Controversies in Practical Philosophy," in *The Communicative Ethics Controversy*, ed. Seyla Benhabib and Fred Dallmayr (Cambridge, Mass.: MIT Press, 1991), p. 336 (citing Alasdair MacIntyre, *After Virtue* [Notre Dame, Ind.: University of Notre Dame Press, 1981], p. 67). For a response to the MacIntyre objection, see Deryck Beyleveld, *The Dialectical Necessity of Morality: An Analysis and Defense of Alan Gewirth's Argument to the Principle of Generic Consistency* (Chicago: University of Chicago Press, 1991), pp. 232–35; see also Alan Gewirth, "Rights and Virtues," *Review of Metaphysics* 38 (1985): 739, 747–48, esp. 748 (arguing that the universality of the concept of rights follows from the universality of human action) and the fact that the agents concerned are presumed to be rational).

19. Not discussed, as it goes to a different point, are agents who can be legitimately incarcerated under the indirect applications of the PGC because they have sought to violate other agents' rights (see chapter 2).

20. Jorge Larrain argues that the change from seeing ideology solely as "a party weapon" to seeing it as a "total conception" of the world involves discovering it as "a scientific method of research," a basis for a sociology of knowledge (see *The Concept of Ideology* [Athens: University of Georgia Press, 1979], pp. 109–10). More generally, Nelson Goodman presents a concept of mind as an instrument for producing worldviews. Following Kant, he distinguishes coherence truth from correspondence truth in the development of worldviews and then shows the importance of the former for the internal point of view (see *Ways of World Making* [Indianapolis: Hackett, 1978], pp. 124–25).

21. Martha C. Nussbaum, "The Use and Abuse of Philosophy in Legal Education," *Stanford Law Review* 45 (1993): 1627, 1640.

SELECTED BIBLIOGRAPHY

Ackerman, Bruce. *Foundations,* vol. 1, *We the People.* Cambridge, Mass.: Harvard University Press, 1991.

Althusser, Lewis. *For Marx.* Trans. Ben Brewster. New York: Pantheon Books, 1969.

Altman, Andrew. "Legal Realism, Critical Legal Studies, and Dworkin." *Philosophy and Public Affairs* 15 (1986): 205.

Aquinas, Thomas. "Concerning the Nature of Law." *Summa Theologica, The Basic Writings of Saint Thomas Aquinas,* vol. 2. Ed. A. Pegis. New York: Random House, 1945.

Aristotle. *Nicomachean Ethics.* In *The Basic Works of Aristotle,* ed. Richard McKeon. New York: Random House, 1941.

———. *On Interpretation.* In *The Basic Works of Aristotle,* ed. Richard McKeon. New York: Random House, 1941.

Arrow, Kenneth J. *Social Choice and Individual Values.* 2d ed. New Haven: Yale University Press, 1963.

Austin, John. *Lectures on Jurisprudence.* Ed. R. Campbell. 4th ed. London: John Murray, 1873.

Balkin, J. M. "Tradition, Betrayal and the Politics of Deconstruction." *Cardozo Law Review* 11 (1990): 1613–30.

Banfield, Edward C. *The Moral Basis of a Backward Society.* New York: Free Press, 1958.

Banner, Stuart. "Please Don't Read the Title." *Ohio Law Review* 50 (1989): 243.

Barry, Brian. "Justice and the Common Good." *Analysis* 21 (1960-1961): 86–90.

———. "The Public Interest." *Aristotelian Society,* suppl. vol. 38 (1964): 1–18.

Bell, Derrick. "Racial Realism." *Connecticut Law Review* 24 (1992): 363–79.

Belliotti, Raymond. *Justifying Law: The Debate over Foundations, Goals and Methods.* Philadelphia: Temple University Press, 1992.

———. "The Legacy of Marxist Jurisprudence." In *Radical Philosophy of Law: Contemporary Challenges to Mainstream Legal Theory and Practice,* ed. D. Caudill and S. Gold. Atlantic Highlands, N.J.: Humanities, 1995.

———. "Toward a Theory of Judicial Decisionmaking: A Synthesis of Ideologist Jurisprudence and Doctrinalism." *Catholic Lawyer* 28 (1983): 215–52.

Benhabib, Seyla. "Afterword: Communicative Ethics and Current Controversies in Practical Philosophy." In *The Communicative Ethics Controversy, ed.* Seyla Benhabib and Fred Dallmayr. Cambridge, Mass.: MIT Press, 1991.

———. *Critique, Norm, and Utopia: A Study of the Foundations of Critical Theory*. New York: Columbia University Press, 1986.

Bentham, Jeremy. *Principles of Morals and Legislation*. New York: Hafner Press, 1948.

———. *The Works of Jeremy Bentham*. Ed. Sir John Bowring. 11 vols. New York: Russell and Russell, 1962.

Beyleveld, Deryck. *The Dialectical Necessity of Morality: An Analysis and Defense of Alan Gewirth's Argument to the Principle of Generic Consistency*. Chicago: University of Chicago Press, 1991.

Beyleveld, Deryck, and Roger Brownsword. *Law as a Moral Judgment*. London: Sweet and Maxwell, 1986.

Bickel, Alexander M. *The Least Dangerous Branch: The Supreme Court at the Bar of Politics*. 2d ed. New Haven: Yale University Press, 1962.

———. *The Morality of Consent*. New Haven: Yale University Press, 1975.

Binder, Guyora. "What's Left?" *Texas Law Review* 69 (1991): 1985–2041.

Blasi, Gary L. "What Lawyers Know: Cognitive Science and the Functions of Theory." *Journal of Legal Education* 45 (1995): 313–97.

Bobbitt, Phillip. *Constitutional Interpretation*. Cambridge, Mass.: Basil Blackwell, 1991.

Bork, Robert. *Slouching Towards Gomorrah: Modern Liberalism and American Decline*. New York: Regan Books, 1996.

———. *The Tempting of America: The Political Seduction of the Law*. New York: Free Press, 1990.

Boswell, Donna A. Comment, "The Parameters of the Federal Common Law: The Case of Time Limitations on Federal Causes of Action." *University of Pennsylvania Law Review* 136 (1988): 1447–513.

Boswell, John. *Christianity, Social Tolerance and Homosexuality: Gay People in Western Europe from the Beginning of the Christian Era to the Fourteenth Century*. Chicago: University of Chicago Press, 1980.

Bowers v. Hardwick, 478 U.S. 186 (1986).

Brandt, R. B. "Hare on Abortion." *Social Theory and Practice* 15 (1989):15–24.

Breyer, Stephen. *Regulation and Its Reform*. Cambridge, Mass.: Harvard University Press, 1982.

Brown v. Board of Education, 347 U.S. 483 (1954).

Brudney, Daniel. "Hypothetical Consent and Moral Force." *Law and Philosophy* 10 (1991): 235–70.

Burger, Warren E. "The Special Skills of Advocacy: Are Specialized Training and Certification of Advocates Essential to Our System of Justice?" *Fordham Law Review* 42 (1973): 227–42.

Butler, Paul. "Racially Based Jury Nullification: Black Power in the Criminal Justice System." *Yale Law Journal* 105 (1995): 677–725.

Cain, Patricia A. "Litigating for Lesbian and Gay Rights: A Legal History." *Virginia Law Review* 79 (1993): 1551–1641.

Calabresi, Guido, and Phillip Bobbitt. *Tragic Choices: The Conflicts Society Confronts in the Allocation of Tragically Scarce Resources*. New York: Norton, 1978.

Carey v. Population Services International, 431 U.S. 678 (1977).

Carritt, E. F. "Liberty and Equality." In *Political Philosophy*, ed. Anthony Quinton. *Oxford Readings in Philosophy*. New York: Oxford University Press, 1967.

Caudill, D., and S. Gold, eds. *Radical Philosophy of Law: Contemporary Challenges to Mainstream Legal Theory and Practice*. Atlantic Highlands, N.J.: Humanities Press, 1995.

Chomsky, Noam. *Language and Politics*. New York: Basic Books, 1988.

City of Richmond v. J. A. Croson Co., 488 U.S. 469 (1989).

Coker v. Georgia, 433 U.S. 584 (1977).

Cornell, Drucilla. "From the Lighthouse: The Promise of Redemption and the Possibility of Legal Interpretation." *Cardozo Law Review* 11 (1990): 1687–714.

Corngold, Stanley. "The Question of the Self in Nietzsche During the Axial Period (1882-1888)." In *Why Nietzsche Now?* ed. Daniel O'Hara. Bloomington: Indiana University Press, 1981.

Cover, Robert. "Violence and the Word." *Yale Law Journal* 95 (1986): 1601–29.

Dahl, Robert. *A Preface to Democratic Theory*. Chicago: University of Chicago Press, 1956.

D'Amato, Anthony. "On the Connection Between Law and Justice." *University of California Davis Law Review* 26 (1993): 527–82.

Davidson, Donald. *Essays on Action and Events*. Oxford: Clarendon Press, 1980.

———. "Freedom to Act." In *Essays on Action and Events*. Oxford: Clarendon Press, 1980.

———. *Inquiries into Truth and Interpretation*. New York: Oxford University Press, 1984.

———. "The Method of Truth in Metaphysics." In *Inquiries into Truth and Interpretation*. New York: Oxford University Press, 1984.

———. "On the Very Idea of a Conceptual Scheme." In *Inquiries into Truth and Interpretation*. New York: Oxford University Press, 1984.

———. "Paradoxes of Irrationality." *Philosophical Essays on Freud*, ed. R. Wolheim and J. Hopkins. New York: Cambridge University Press, 1982.

———. "Thought and Talk." In *Inquiries into Truth and Interpretation*. Oxford: Clarendon Press, 1984.

———. "True to the Facts." In *Inquiries into Truth and Interpretation*. New York: Oxford University Press, 1984.

Dead Man Walking. Polygram Filmed Entertainment. 1996.

Defense of Marriage Act (DOMA). Pub. L. 104-199, 110 Stat. 2419 (1996).

Delgado, Richard, ed. *Critical Race Theory: The Cutting Edge*. Philadelphia: Temple University Press, 1995.

De Paul, Michael R. *Balance and Refinement: Beyond Coherence Methods of Moral Inquiry*. New York: Routledge, 1993.

Descartes, René. *Discourse on Method* (1637). In *Discourse on Method; and Meditations on First Philosophy*, 3d ed., trans. Donald A. Cress. Indianapolis: Hackett, 1993.

———. *Meditations on First Philosophy* (1641). In *Discourse on Method; and Meditations on First Philosophy*, 3d ed., trans. Donald A. Cress. Indianapolis: Hackett, 1993.

Dewey, John. *Experience and Nature*. 2d ed. LaSalle, Ill.: Open Court, 1929.

Dover, K. J. *Greek Homosexuality*. Cambridge, Mass.: Harvard University Press, 1989.

Dred Scott v. Sanford, 60 U.S. (19 How.) 393 (1857).

D'Souza, Dinesh. *Illiberal Education: The Politics of Race and Sex on Campus*. New York: Vintage Books, 1992.

Dworkin, Andrea, and Catharine MacKinnon. *Pornography and Civil Rights: A New Day for Woman's Equality*. Minneapolis: Organizing Against Pornography, 1998.

Dworkin, Ronald. *Freedom's Law: The Moral Reading of the American Constitution*. Cambridge, Mass.: Harvard University Press, 1996.

———. "The Great Abortion Case." *New York Review of Books*, June 29, 1989.

———. "Hard Cases." *Harvard Law Review* 88 (1975): 1057–109.

———. "Justice for Clarence Thomas." *New York Review of Books*, November 7, 1991.

———. "The Law of the Slave-Catchers: A Review of Robert M. Cover's *Justice Accused: Antislavery and the Judicial Process*." *The Times Literary Supplement*, December 5, 1975.

———. *Law's Empire*. Cambridge, Mass.: Harvard University Press, 1986.

———. *Life's Dominion: An Argument About Abortion, Euthanasia, and Individual Freedom*. New York: Alfred A. Knopf, 1993.

———. *A Matter of Principle*. Cambridge, Mass.: Harvard University Press, 1985.

———. "The Model of Rules." *University of Chicago Law Review* 35 (1967): 14–46.

———. "Pragmatism, Right Answers, and True Banality." In *Pragmatism in Law and Society*, ed. Michael Brint and William Weaver. Boulder, Colo.: Westview Press, 1991.

———. *Taking Rights Seriously*. Cambridge, Mass.: Harvard University Press, 1977.

Easterbrook, Frank H. "Stability and Reliability in Judicial Decisions." *Cornell Law Review* 73 (1988): 422–33.

Eisenstadt v. Baird, 405 U.S. 438 (1972).

Eliot, T. S. "Francis Herbert Bradley." In *Selected Prose of T. S. Eliot*, ed. Frank Kermode. London: Faber, 1975.

Ely, John Hart. *Democracy and Distrust: A Theory of Judicial Review*. Cambridge, Mass.: Harvard University Press, 1980.

Erie Railroad Co. v. Tompkins, 304 U.S. 64 (1938).

Espinoza, Leslie G. "Masks and Other Disguises: Exposing Legal Academia." *Harvard Law Review* 103 (1990): 1878–86.

Farber, Daniel A., and Philip P. Frickey. *Law and Public Choice: A Critical Introduction*. Chicago: University of Chicago Press, 1991.

The Federalist Papers. New York: New American Library, 1961.

Feinberg, Joel. "Abortion." In *Matters of Life and Death: New Introductory Essays in Moral Philosophy*, ed. Tom Regan. New York: Random House, 1986.

———. "Civil Disobedience in the Modern World." *Humanities in Society* 2 (1979): 37.

———. *Harm to Others*, vol. 1, *The Moral Limits of the Criminal Law*. New York: Oxford University Press, 1984.

———. *Offense to Others*, vol. 2, *The Moral Limits of the Criminal Law*. New York: Oxford University Press, 1985.

Feinberg, Joel, and Hyman Gross, eds. *Philosophy of Law*, 4th, 5th eds. Belmont, Calif.: Wadsworth, 1986, 1991, 1995.

Finnis, John. "Law, Morality and 'Sexual Orientation.'" *Notre Dame Law Review* 69 (1994): 1049–76.

———. "Natural Law and Legal Reasoning." In *Natural Law Theory: Contemporary Essays*, ed. Robert P. George. Oxford: Clarendon Press, 1992.

———. *Natural Law and Natural Rights*. Oxford: Clarendon Press, 1980.

Fish, Stanley. "Liberation Doesn't Exist." *Duke Law Journal* (1987): 997–1001.

Fisher, H. William. "Dworkin's Right Answer Thesis: A Statistical Regression Coherence Model, Note." *Iowa Law Review* 73 (1987): 159–81.

Foucault, Michael. *The History of Sexuality*. Trans. Robert Hurley. Vol. 1. New York: Vintage, 1980.

———. "The Subject and Power." Afterword to Hubert Dreyfus and Paul Rabinow, *Michael Foucault: Beyond Structuralism and Hermeneutics*. Brighton, Sussex: Harvester Press, 1983.

———. "Truth and Power." In *The Foucault Review*, ed. Paul Rabinow. New York: Pantheon Books, 1984.

Frug, Gerald. "The City as a Legal Concept." *Harvard Law Review* 93 (1980): 1059.

Fuller, Lon. *The Morality of Law*. Rev. ed. New Haven: Yale University Press, 1978.

———. "Positivism and Fidelity to Law: A Reply to Professor Hart." *Harvard Law Review* 71 (1958): 630–72.

George, Robert P. "Natural Law and Human Nature." In *Natural Law Theory: Contemporary Essays*, ed. Robert P. George. Oxford: Clarendon Press, 1992.

Gewirth, Alan. "The Basis and Content of Human Rights." *Georgia Law Review* 13 (1979): 1149–70.

———. *The Community of Rights*. Chicago: University of Chicago Press, 1996.

———. "The Distinction Between Analytic and Synthetic Truths." *Journal of Philosophy* 50 (1953): 397–425.

———. *Human Rights: Essays on Justification and Applications*. Chicago: University of Chicago Press, 1982.

———. *Reason and Morality*. Chicago: University of Chicago Press, 1978.

———. "Rights and Virtues." *Review of Metaphysics* 38 (1985): 739–62.

———. "Starvation and Human Rights." In *Human Rights*. Chicago: University of Chicago Press, 1982.

———, ed. *Political Philosophy*. New York: Macmillan, 1965.

Givelber, David J., Brook K. Baker, John McDevitt, and Robyn Miliano, "Learning Through Work: An Empirical Study of Legal Internship." *Journal of Legal Education* 45 (1995): 1–48.

Godlove, Terry. *Religion, Interpretation and Diversity of Belief: The Framework Model from Kant to Durkheim to Davidson*. New York: Cambridge University Press, 1989.

Goodman, Nelson. *Ways of World Making*. Indianapolis: Hackett, 1978.

Gray, John Chipman. *The Nature and Sources of the Law*. 2d ed. Boston: Beacon Press, 1963.

Greenberg, David E. *The Construction of Homosexuality*. Chicago: University of Chicago Press, 1988.

Greene, Linda S. "Civil Rights at the Millennium—A Response to Bell's Call for Racial Realism." *Connecticut Law Review* 24 (1992): 499–515.

Grey, Thomas C. "Holmes and Legal Pragmatism." *Stanford Law Review* 41 (1989): 787–870.

Griswold v. Connecticut, 381 U.S. 479 (1965).

Habermas, Jürgen. *Between Facts and Norms: Contributions to a Discourse Theory of Law and Democracy*. Trans. William Rehg. Cambridge, Mass.: MIT Press, 1996.

———. *Justification and Application: Remarks on Discourse Ethics*. Trans. Ciaran P. Cronin. Cambridge, Mass.: MIT Press, 1993.

———. *Legitimation Crisis*. Trans. Thomas McCarthy. Boston: Beacon Press, 1973.

———. "Modernity—An Incomplete Project." In *Anti-Aesthetic: Essays on Postmodern Culture*, ed. Hal Foster. Port Townsend, Wash.: Bay Press, 1983.

Hales, Steven D., and Robert C. Welshon. "Truth, Paradox, and Nietzschean Perspectivism." *History of Philosophy Quarterly* 11 (1994): 101–19.

Hardin, Russell. "My University's Yacht: Morality and the Rule of Law." *Rule of Law*, NOMOS 34 (1994): 205–27.

Hare, R. M. "Abortion and the Golden Rule." *Philosophy and Public Affairs* 4 (1975): 201–22.

———. "Abortion: Reply to Brandt." *Social Theory and Practice* 15 (1989): 25–32.

———. "A Kantian Approach to Abortion." *Social Theory and Practice* 15 (1989): 1–14.

Harman, Gilbert. "Justice and Moral Bargaining." *Social Philosophy and Policy* 1 (1983): 114–31.

Harris, Angela P. "Race and Essentialism in Feminist Legal Theory." *Stanford Law Review* 42 (1990): 581–616.

Hart, H. L. A. *The Concept of Law*. New York: Oxford University Press, 1961, 2d ed., 1994.

———. "Positivism and the Separation of Law and Morals." *Harvard Law Review* 71 (1958): 593–629.

Harvey, David. *The Condition of Postmodernity: An Inquiry into Origins of Cultural Change*. Cambridge, Mass.: Blackwell, 1989.

Hayman, R., Jr., and N. Levit, eds. *Jurisprudence: Contemporary Readings, Problems and Narratives*. St. Paul, Minn.: West Publishing Company, 1995.

Hegel, G. W. F. *Philosophy of Right*. Trans. T. M. Knox. Chicago: Encyclopedia Britannica, 1942.

Hittinger, Russell. "Natural Law and Virtue." In *Natural Law Theory: Contemporary Essays*, ed. Robert P. George. Oxford: Clarendon Press, 1992.

Hobbes, Thomas. *Leviathan with Selected Variants from the Latin Edition of 1668*. Ed. E. Curley. Indianapolis: Hackett, 1994.

Hohfeld, Wesley N. *Fundamental Legal Conceptions*. Ed. Walter W. Cook. Westport, Conn.: Greenwood Press, 1964.

Holmes, Oliver Wendell. *The Common Law*. Ed. Mark DeWolfe Howe. Boston: Little, Brown, 1963.

———. "The Path of the Law." *Harvard Law Review* 10 (1897): 457–78.

Horwitz, Morton J. "The Bork Nomination and American Constitutional History." *Syracuse Law Review* 39 (1988):1029–39.

———. *The Transformation of American Law: 1870–1960: The Crisis of Legal Orthodoxy*. New York: Oxford University Press, 1992.

Hull, N. E. H. "Vital Schools of Jurisprudence: Roscoe Pound, Wesley Newcomb Hohfeld, and the Promotion of an Academic Jurisprudence Agenda, 1910–1919." *Journal of Legal Education* 45 (1995): 235–81.

Hume, David. *An Enquiry Concerning Human Understanding; A Letter from a Gentleman to His Friend in Edinburgh and Hume's Abstract of A Treatise of Human Nature*. Ed. Eric Steinberg. 2d. ed. Indianapolis: Hackett, 1977.

———. *An Enquiry Concerning the Principles of Morals*. LaSalle, Ill.: Open Court, 1966.

Hunt, Alan. "The Critique of Law: What Is 'Critical' About Critical Legal Theory?" In *Critical Legal Studies*, ed. Peter Fitzpatrick and Alan Hunt. New York: Blackwell, 1987.

Hutchinson, Allan C. "Identity Crisis: The Politics of Interpretation." *New England Law Review* 26 (1992): 1173–219.

Hyde, Janet Shibley. *Understanding Human Sexuality*. 3d. ed. New York: McGraw-Hill, 1986.

Ingram, David. *Reason, History and Politics*. Albany: SUNY Press, 1995.

James, William. *Pragmatism*. Ed. Bruce Kuklick. Cambridge, Mass.: Hackett, 1981.

Jastrow, Joseph. *Fact and Fable in Psychology*. Boston: Houghton, Mifflin, 1900.

Johnson, Barbara. "The Alchemy of Style and Law." In *The Rhetoric of Law*, ed. Austin Sarat and Thomas R. Kearns, *The Amherst Series in Law, Jurisprudence and Social Thought*. Ann Arbor: University of Michigan Press, 1996.

Kahane, Howard, and Paul Tidman. *Logic and Philosophy: A Modern Introduction*. 7th ed. Belmont, Calif.: Wadsworth, 1995.

Kairys, David, ed. *Introduction to the Politics of Law: A Progressive Critique*. 2d ed. New York: Pantheon Books, 1990.

———. *The Politics of Law: A Progressive Critique*. 2d ed. New York: Pantheon, 1990.

Kant, Immanuel. *Critique of Pure Reason*. Trans. Norman Kemp Smith. New York: St. Martin's Press, 1965.

———. *Foundations of the Metaphysics of Morals*. Trans. Lewis White Beck. Indianapolis: Bobbs-Merrill, 1959.

———. *The Metaphysics of Morals*. Trans. M. Gregor. New York: Cambridge University Press, 1991.

———. *Prolegomena to Any Future Metaphysics*. Trans. Lewis White Beck. Indianapolis: Bobbs-Merrill, 1980.

Kennedy, Duncan. "Form and Substance in Private Law Adjudication." *Harvard Law Review* 89 (1976): 1685–778.

———. "Legal Education as Training for Hierarchy." In *The Politics of Law: A Progressive Critique*, ed. David Kairys. Rev. ed. New York: Pantheon Books, 1990.

Kierkegaard, Søren. *The Journals of Kierkegaard*. Trans. Alexander Dru. New York: Harper and Row, 1958.

Kluger, Richard. *Simple Justice: A History of Brown v. Board of Education and Black America's Struggle for Equality*. New York: Alfred A. Knopf, 1976.

Kohl, Herbert. *From Archetype to Zeitgeist: Powerful Ideals for Powerful Thinking*. Boston: Little, Brown, 1992.

Korematsu v. United States, 323 U.S. 214 (1944).

Kosko, Bart. *Fuzzy Thinking: The New Science of Fuzzy Logic*. New York: Hyperion, 1993.

Kripki, Saul. *Naming and Necessity*. Cambridge, Mass.: Harvard University Press, 1980.

Kristol, Irving. "Pornography, Obscenity, and the Case for Censorship." *New York Times Magazine*, March 28, 1971.

Kuhn, Thomas. *The Structure of Scientific Revolutions*. 2d. ed. Chicago: University of Chicago Press, 1970.

Larrain, Jorge. *The Concept of Ideology*. Athens: University of Georgia Press, 1979.

Lawrence III, Charles R. "The Id, the Ego and Equal Protection: Reckoning with Unconscious Racism." *Stanford Law Review* 39 (1987): 317–88.

Lechte, John. *Fifty Key Contemporary Thinkers: From Structuralism to Postmodernity*. New York: Routledge, 1994.

Lehrer News Hour. "Alleged Racism at Texico." PBS. Show no. 5697. Channel 11 (Chicago), November 12, 1996.

———. "Gergen Interview with Robert Bork." PBS. Show no. 5696. Channel 11 (Chicago), November 11, 1996.

Leibniz, G. W. *New Essays on Human Understanding*. Trans. and ed. Peter Remnant and Jonathan Bennett. New York: Cambridge University Press, 1981.

Levi, Edward H. *Introduction to Legal Reasoning*. Chicago: University of Chicago Press, 1949.

Litowitz, Douglas. "Dworkin and Critical Legal Studies on Right Answers and Conceptual Holism." *Legal Studies Forum* 18 (1994): 135–61.

Llewellyn, Karl. "Some Realism About Realism." *Harvard Law Review* 44 (1931): 1222–64.

Locke, John. *The Second Treatise of Government*. Ed. T. P. Pearson. Indianapolis: Bobbs-Merrill, 1952.

Lochner v. New York, 198 U.S. 45 (1905).

Long Time Companion. Samuel Goldwyn Company (1990).

Lovings v. Virginia, 388 U.S. 1 (1967).

Luhmann, Niklas. "Law as a Social System." *Northwestern University Law Review* 83 (1989): 136–50.

———. "Operational Closure and Structural Coupling: The Differentiation of the Legal System." *Cardozo Law Review* 13 (1992): 1419–41.

Lyotard, Jean-François. *The Postmodern Condition: A Report on Knowledge*. Minneapolis: University of Minnesota Press, 1984.

McCloskey, H. J. "A Non-Utilitarian Approach to Punishment." *Inquiry* 8 (1965): 249–63.

MacCormick, Neil. *H. L. A. Hart*. Stanford, Calif.: Stanford University Press, 1981.

———. "Natural Law and the Separation of Law and Morals." In *Natural Law Theory: Contemporary Essays*, ed. R. P. George. Oxford: Clarendon Press, 1992.

MacDonald, Heather. "Law School Humbug." *City Journal* (Autumn 1995): 46–59.

McDowell, John. "Might There Be External Reasons?" In *World, Mind and Ethics: Essays on the Ethical Philosophy of Bernard Williams*, ed. J. E. J. Althem and Ross Harrison. New York: Cambridge University Press, 1995.

Macedo, Donaldo. "Literacy for Stupidification: The Pedagogy of Big Lies." In *Multicultural Education: Critical Pedagogy and the Politics of Difference*, ed. Christine E. Sleeter and Peter L. McLaren. Albany: SUNY Press, 1995.

Macey, Jonathan R. "The Internal and External Costs and Benefits of Stare Decisis." *Chicago-Kent Law Review* 65 (1989): 93–113.

MacFarquhar, Larissa. "The Color of the Law: Critical Race Theorists Have Developed Subtle Insights into Race and Power in America. But Do They Have Anything to Contribute to the Law?" *Lingua franca: The Review of Academic Life* (July/August 1996): 40–47.

MacIntyre, Alasdair. *After Virtue*. Notre Dame, Ind.: University of Notre Dame Press, 1981.

Mackie, J. L. "The Third Theory of Law." *Philosophy and Public Affairs* 7 (1977): 3–16.

MacKinnon, Catharine. *Feminism Unmodified: Discourses on Life and Law*. Cambridge, Mass.: Harvard University Press, 1987.

———. "From Practice to Theory, or What Is a White Woman Anyway?" *Yale Journal of Law and Feminism* 4 (1991): 13–22.

———. *Only Words*. Cambridge, Mass.: Harvard University Press, 1993.

———. "Pornography: On Morality and Politics." In *Toward a Feminist Theory of the State*. Cambridge, Mass.: Harvard University Press, 1989.

———. "*Roe v. Wade:* A Study in Male Ideology." In *Abortion: Moral and Legal Perspectives*, ed. Jay L. Garfield and Patricia Hennessey. Amherst: University of Massachusetts Press, 1984.

MacKinnon, Catharine, and Ronald Dworkin. "Pornography: An Exchange." *New York Review of Books*, March 3, 1994.

McLoughlin v. O'Brian, 1 App. Cas. 410 (1983).

MacPherson v. Buick Motor Co., 217 N.Y. 382, 111 N.E. 1050 (1916).

Marbury v. Madison, 5 U.S. (1 Cranch) 137 (1803).

Marquis, Don. "Why Abortion Is Immoral." *Journal of Philosophy* 4 (1989): 183–202.

Marx, Karl, and Friedrich Engles. "Alienated Labor," from the *First Manuscript*. In *Karl Marx: Early Writings*, trans. T. B. Bottomore. New York: McGraw-Hill, 1963.

———. *The Communist Manifesto* (1888). In *Basic Writings on Politics and Philosophy*, ed. L. Feuer. Garden City, N.Y.: Doubleday, 1959.

Matsuda, Mari. "Interpreting Rights: An Essay for Robert Cover." *Yale Law Journal* 96 (1987): 1860–915.

Matsuda, Mari, Charles Lawrence, Richard Delgado, Kimberle Williams Crenshaw. *Words that Wound: Critical Race Theory, Assaultive Speech and the First Amendment*. Boulder, Colo.: Westview Press, 1993.

Michelman, Frank I. "Super Liberal: Romance, Community, and Tradition in William J. Brennan, Jr.'s Constitutional Thought." *Virginia Law Review* 77 (1991): 1261–332.

Mill, James. *Political Writings*. Ed. T. Ball. New York: Cambridge University Press, 1992.

Mill, John Stuart. *On Liberty*. Ed. Gertrude Himmelfarb. New York. Penguin, 1982.

Miller, J. Hillis. "Dismembering and Disremembering in Nietzsche's 'On Truth and Lies in a Nonmoral Sense.'" In *Why Nietzsche Now?* ed. Daniel O'Hara. Bloomington: Indiana University Press, 1985.

Miller, William Lee. *Arguing About Slavery: The Great Battle in the United States Congress*. New York: Alfred A. Knopf, 1995.

Minda, Gary. "Jurisprudence at Century's End." *Journal of Legal Education* 43 (1993): 27–59.

Minow, Martha. "Forward: Justice Engendered." In "The Supreme Court 1986 Term." *Harvard Law Review* 10 (1987): 10–95.

Minow, Martha, and Elizabeth Spelman. "In Context." *South California Law Review* 63 (1990): 1597–652.

de Montesquieu, Baron. *Selected Political Writings*. Trans. Melvin Richter. Indianapolis: Hackett, 1990.

Moore, Michael. "A Natural Law Theory of Interpretation." *Southern California Law Review* 58 (1985): 277–398.

Mootz III, Francis J. "The New Legal Hermeneutics." *Vanderbilt Law Review* 47 (1994): 115–43.

Münch, Richard. "Autopoiesis by Definition." *Cardozo Law Review* 13 (1992): 1463–71.

Murfin, Ross C. "Deconstruction and *Wuthering Heights*." In *Wuthering Heights: Case Studies in Contemporary Criticism*, series ed. Ross C. Murfin. Boston: St. Martin's Press, 1992.

Murphy, Timothy, ed. *Gay Ethics: Controversies in Outing, Civil Rights and Sexual Science*. New York: Haworth Press, 1994.

Nagel, Thomas. *The View from Nowhere*. New York: Oxford University Press, 1986.

Nietzsche, Friedrich. *Beyond Good and Evil: Prelude to a Philosophy of the Future*. Trans. Walter Kaufmann. New York: Vintage, 1966.

Nozick, Robert. *Anarchy, State and Utopia*. New York: Basic Books, 1974.

———. *The Examined Life: Philosophical Meditations*. New York: Touchstone, 1989.

Nowak, John E., and Ronald D. Rotunda. *Constitutional Law*. 4th ed. Hornbook Series. Minneapolis: West Publishing Company, 1991.

Nussbaum, Martha C. "Platonic Love and Colorado Law: The Relevance of Ancient Greek Norms to Modern Sexual Controversies." *Virginia Law Review* 80 (1994): 1515, 1563.

———. "The Use and Abuse of Philosophy in Legal Education." *Stanford Law Review* 45 (1993): 1627–45.

Olson, Mancur. *The Logic of Collective Action: Public Goods and the Theory of Groups*. Cambridge, Mass.: Harvard University Press, 1971.

Partridge, P. H. "Politics, Philosophy, Ideology." *Political Studies* 9 (1961): 217–35.

Patterson, Dennis M. "Law's Pragmatism: Law as Practice and Narrative." *Virginia Law Review* 76 (1990): 937–96.

Perry, Michael. *The Constitution in the Courts: Law or Politics?* New York: Oxford University Press, 1994.

Plato. *Gorgias*. In *Collected Dialogues*, trans. W. D. Woodhead, ed. Edith Hamilton and Huntington Cairns. Princeton: Princeton University Press, 1961.

———. *Republic*. In *Collected Dialogues*, trans. W. D. Woodhead, ed. Edith Hamilton and Huntington Cairns. Princeton: Princeton University Press, 1961.

Plako v. Connecticut, 302 U.S. 319 (1937).

Planned Parenthood of Southeastern Pennsylvania v. Casey, 505 U.S. 833 (1992).

Plessy v. Ferguson, 163 U.S. 537 (1896)

Posner, Richard. "The Concept of Corrective Justice in Recent Theories of Tort Law." *Journal of Legal Studies* 10, 1 (1981): 187–206.

———. "The Decline of Law as an Autonomous Discipline." *Harvard Law Review* 100 (1987): 761–80.

———. *Economic Analysis of Law*. 4th ed. Boston: Little, Brown, 1992.

———. "The Jurisprudence of Skepticism." *Michigan Law Review* 86 (1988): 827–91.

———. *Overcoming Law*. Cambridge: Mass.: Harvard University Press, 1995.

———. *The Problems of Jurisprudence*. Cambridge: Mass.: Harvard University Press, 1990.

powell, john a. (author's style.) "Racial Realism or Racial Despair?" *Connecticut Law Review* 24 (1992): 533–51.

Prado, C. G. *Starting with Foucault: An Introduction to Genealogy*. Boulder, Colo.: Westview Press, 1995.

Putman, Hilary. *Reason, Truth and History*. New York: Cambridge University Press, 1981.

Quevedo, Steven M. "Formalist and Instrumentalist Legal Reasoning and Legal Theory." *California Law Review* 73 (1985): 119.

Quine, Willard van Orman. "Two Dogmas of Empiricism." In *From a Logical Point of View*. Cambridge: Mass.: Harvard University Press, 1961.

Quinton, A., ed. *Political Philosophy: Oxford Readings in Philosophy*. New York: Oxford University Press, 1973.

Radin, Margaret Jane. "The Pragmatist and the Feminist." *Southern California Law Review* 63 (1990): 1699–1726.

———. "Reconsidering the Rule of Law." *Boston University Law Review* 69 (1989): 781–819.

Radin, Margaret Jane, and Frank Michelman. "Pragmatist and Poststructuralist Critical Legal Practice." *University of Pennsylvania Law Review* 139 (1991): 1019–58.

Rawls, John. *Political Liberalism*. New York: Columbia University Press, 1993.

———. *A Theory of Justice*. Cambridge: Mass.: Harvard University Press, 1971.

———. "Two Concepts of Rules." *Philosophical Review* 64 (1955): 3–32.

Rax, Joseph. "The Relevance of Coherence." *Boston University Law Review* 72 (1992): 273–321.

Regis, E. Jr., ed. *Gewirth's Ethical Rationalism*. Chicago: University of Chicago Press, 1984.

Rhode, Deborah. "Feminist Critical Theories." *Stanford Law Review* 42 (1990): 617–38.

Robson, Ruthann. *Lesbian (Out)Law: Survival Under the Rule of Law*. Ithaca, N.Y.: Firebrand Books, 1992.

Roe v. Wade, 410 U.S. 113 (1973).

Romany, Celina. "Ain't I a Feminist?" *Yale Journal of Law and Feminism* 4 (1991): 23–33.

Romer v. Evans, — U.S. —, 116 S. Ct. 1620 (1996).

Rorty, Richard. *Objectivity, Relativism and Truth: Philosophical Papers*. Vol. 1. New York: Cambridge University Press, 1991.

_____. "World Well Lost." In *Consequences of Pragmatism*. Minneapolis: University of Minnesota Press, 1982.

Rosen, Stanley. *The Limits of Analysis*. New York: Basic Books, 1929.

Rousseau, Jean-Jacques. *The Social Contract and Discourse on the Origin of Inequality*. Ed. L. Crocker. New York: Washington Square Press, 1967.

Rovane, Carol. "The Metaphysics of Interpretation." In *Truth and Interpretation: Perspectives on the Philosophy of Donald Davidson*, ed. Ernest Le Pore. Oxford: Basil-Blackwell, 1986.

Rubenfeld, Jed. "The Right of Privacy." *Harvard Law Review* 102 (1989): 737–807.

Russell, Bertrand. Introduction. In Ludwig Wittgenstein, *Tractatus Logico-Philosophicus*. New York: Hartcourt-Brace, 1922.

———. *The Problems of Philosophy*. New York: Oxford University Press, 1959.

Salusinnzky, Imre, ed. "Interview with Jacques Derrida, *et al.*" In *Criticism in Society*. New York: Methuen and Company, 1987.

Samar, Vincent J. "Just Society: A Review of John Rawls, *Political Liberalism*." *Business Ethics* 5 (1995): 629–45.

———. "A Moral Justification for Gay and Lesbian Civil Rights Legislation." *Journal of Homosexuality* 27 (1994): 147–78.

———. *The Right to Privacy: Gays, Lesbians and the Constitution*. Philadelphia: Temple University Press, 1991.

Sandel, Michael. *Liberalism and the Limits of Justice*. New York: Cambridge University Press, 1982.

Schanck, Peter C. "Understanding Postmodern Thought and Its Implications for Statutory Interpretation." *Southern California Law Review* 65 (1992): 2505–597.

Schauer, Frederick. "Easy Cases." *Southern California Law Review* 58 (1985): 399–400.

———. *Free Speech: A Philosophical Enquiry*. New York: Cambridge University Press, 1982.

Scheppele, Kim Lane. "The Reasonable Woman." *Responsive Community: Rights and Responsibilities* 1, 4 (1991): 36–47.

Schlag, Pierre. "Missing Pieces: A Cognitive Approach to Law." *Texas Law Review* 67 (1989): 1195–250.

Schmitt, Richard. *Introduction to Marx and Engles: A Critical Reconstruction*. Boulder, Colo.: Westview Press, 1987.

Schuck, Peter H. "Legal Complexity: Some Causes, Consequences and Cures." *Duke Law Journal* 42 (1992): 1–52.

Schumpeter, Joseph. "Two Concepts of Democracy." In *Political Philosophy*, ed. Anthony Quinton. *Oxford Readings in Philosophy*. New York: Oxford University Press, 1967.

Shane, Peter M. "Conventionalism in Constitutional Interpretation and the Place of Administrative Agencies." *American University Law Review* 36 (1987): 573–99.

Shapiro, Sidney A. "Keeping the Baby and Throwing Out the Bathwater: Justice Breyer's Critique of Regulation." *Administrative Law Journal of American University* 8 (1995): 721–34.

Sherry, Suzanna. "The Founders' Unwritten Constitution." *University of Chicago Law Review* 54 (1987): 1127–77.

Simmons, A. J. *Moral Principles and Political Obligations*. Princeton: Princeton University Press, 1979.

Sindell v. Abbott Laboratories, 26 Cal. 3d 588, 607 P. 2d 924, 163 Cal. Rptr. 132 (1980).

Singer, Joseph William. "The Player and the Cards: Nihilism and Legal Theory." *Yale Law Journal* 94 (1984): 1–70.

Singer, Peter. "Rich and Poor." In *Practical Ethics*. 2d ed. Cambridge, Eng.: Cambridge University Press, 1993.

Slaughterhouse Cases, 83 U.S. (16 Wall.) 36 (1873).

Solomon, Robert, ed. *Existentialism*. New York: Random House, 1974.

Solum, Lawrence. "On the Indeterminacy Crisis: Critiquing Critical Dogma." *University of Chicago Law Review* 54 (1987): 462–503.

Spivak, Gayatri. "A Response to 'The Difference Within: Feminism and Critical Theory.'" In *The Difference Within: Feminism and Critical Theory*, ed. Elizabeth Meese and Alice Parker. Amsterdam: John Benjamins, 1989.

Sternlight, Jean R. "Symbiotic Legal Theory and Legal Practice: Advocating a Common Sense Jurisprudence of Law and Practical Applications." *University of Miami Law Review* 50 (1996): 707–78.

Strasser, Mark. "Unconstitutional? Don't Ask; If It Is, Don't Tell: On Deference, Rationality and the Constitution." *University of Colorado Law Review* 66 (1995): 375–460.

Sumner, William Graham. *Folkways*. Boston: Gina and Company, 1906.

Sunstein, Cass. *After the Rights Revolution: Reconceiving the Regulatory State*. Cambridge, Mass.: Harvard University Press, 1990.

———. "Commentary on Analogical Reasoning." *Harvard Law Review* 106 (1993): 741–91.

———. *Democracy and the Problem of Free Speech*. New York: Free Press, 1993.

———. *Legal Reasoning and Political Conflict*. New York: Oxford University Press, 1996.

———. "On Legal Theory and Legal Practice." In *Theory and Practice*, ed. I. Shapiro and J. DeCew. NOMOS 37 (1995): 267–87.

———. *The Partial Constitution*. Cambridge, Mass.: Harvard University Press, 1993.

Swift v. Tyson, 41 U.S. (16 Pet.) 1 (1842).

Tarski, Alfred. "Semantic Conception of Truth." *Philosophy and Phenomenological Research* 4 (1944): 341–75

Thomas, Kendall. "Beyond the Privacy Principle." *Columbia Law Review* 92 (1992): 1431–516.

Thomas v. Winchester, 6 N.Y. 397 (1852).

Thorne, Kip S. *Black Holes and Time Warps: Einstein's Outrageous Legacy*. New York: Norton, 1994.

Torres, Gerald, and Kathryn Milum. "Translating *Yonnondio* by Precedent and Evidence: *The Mashpee Indian Case*," *Duke Law Journal* (1990): 625–59.

Unger, Roberto Mongabeira. *Knowledge and Politics*. New York: Free Press, 1975.

U.S. Constitution.

United States v. Carolene Products Co., 304 U.S. 144 (1938).

Walzer, Michael. *Spheres of Justice: A Defense of Pluralism and Equality*. New York: Basic Books, 1983.

Wambaugh, Eugene. "Professor Langdell—A View of His Career." *Nation*, July 12, 1906. Reprinted in *Harvard Law Review* 20 (1906): 1–4.

Wechsler, Herbert. "Toward Neutral Principles of Constitutional Law." *Harvard Law Review* 73 (1959): 1–35.

West Coast Hotel v. Parish, 300 U.S. 379 (1937).

West, Robin. "Disciplines, Subjectivity and the Law." In *The Fate of Law*, ed. Austin Sarat and Thomas R. Kearns, *The Amherst Series in Law, Jurisprudence and Social Thought*. Ann Arbor: University of Michigan Press, 1991.

White, Alan. *Schelling: An Introduction to the System of Freedom*. New Haven: Yale University Press, 1983.

Williams, Patricia. *The Alchemy of Race and Rights: Diary of a Law Professor*. Cambridge, Mass.: Harvard University Press, 1991.

———. "The Obliging Shell: An Internal Essay on Formal Equal Opportunity." *Michigan Law Review* 87 (1989): 2128–51.

Winch, Peter. "Authority." In *Political Philosophy*, ed. Anthony Quinton, *Oxford Readings in Philosophy*. Oxford: Oxford University Press, 1973.

Winterbottom v. Wright, 10 Meeson & Welsby 109, 152 Eng. Rep. 402 (1842).

Wittgenstein, Ludwig von. *Philosophical Investigations: The English Text of the Third Edition*. Ed. G. E. M. Anscombe. 3d. ed. New York: Macmillan, 1958.

Young, Iris Marton. *Justice and the Politics of Difference*. Princeton: Princeton University Press, 1990.

INDEX

Abortion, 18, 152, 154–55, 161, 266n.70
- and agency, 153–54, 156–57
- Dworkin's view, 158–59
- Feinberg's view, 161
- Gewirth's view, 154–55
- Hare's view, 159
- Marquis's view, 160
- and political morality, 155–56
- and viability, 157
- *See also Roe v. Wade*

Ackerman, Bruce, 162, 163–64
- and concept of the natural, 174
- criticism of, 167–68
- dualism, 165
- interpretation of *Brown v. Board of Education*, 173
- and the role of politics, 166, 252n.49
- three republics, 164–65, 167

Action, human, 52–53, 127, 135, 262n.27
- different descriptions of, 228
- in different discourses, concept of, 226
- dispositional versus occurrent, 227–28
- as a foundation for rights, 53
- generic features of, 52–53
- when viewed outside normative discourse, 227
- *See also* Gewirth, Alan, theory of, and agency

Agent, 64, 65, 121–22, 153–54, 156, 248n.11

AIDS, 144

Alchemy of Race and Rights, The. See Williams, Patricia

American Bar Association, 218

American Civil Liberties Union, 218

American Medical Association, 218

Analogical reasoning, 57–60, 108
- compared with political morality, 59
- and precedents, 58

Argument from the Sufficiency of Agency, 53, 175

Aristotle, 44, 62, 135, 189, 255n.88
- on distribution of power, 44
- highest good, 9–10, 125
- on slavery, 150

Arrow, Kenneth, 25, 238n.100, 240n.131

Austin, John, 15, 100
- definition of law, 12–13
- descriptive view of, 35, 92, 226
- distinguishes types of rules, 12
- use of "law," 35

Autonomy
- and democracy, 187
- as self-rule, 143, 145
- *See also* Privacy

Baehr v. Levin, 187

Barry, Brian, 249n.18

Barton, Bruce, 248n.13

Bell, Derrick, 195

Belliotti, Raymond, 19–22, 251n.42

Benhabib, Seyla, 276n.15, 277n.18
Bentham, Jeremy, 23, 37, 41–42, 44
Best ethical theory of politics, 78
  and promoting voluntary purposive action, 80
Beyleveld, Deryck, 128, 129, 130, 134
Bickel, Alexander, 176, 243n.56, 268n.142
Blackmun, Harry, 152
Bork, Robert, 82, 182, 183, 264n.33, 268n.133
  amendment allowing Congress to overturn Court decisions, 183
  concern over Hawaii allowing same-sex marriage, 187
  contradictory, 186–87
  criticisms of *Romer v. Evans*, 185
  criticisms of the Court, 183–84
  and family values, 188, 270n.30
  supports DOMA, 188
  supports Scalia's *Romer* dissent, 186
  unjustified assumptions of, 186
  wants it both ways, 188
Boswell, John, 191
Bowers v. Hardwick, 11, 138, 139, 140, 141, 142–43, 144, 145, 146–47, 188, 215
Brennan, William, 7
Breyer, Stephen, 23
Brown, Henry B., 171
Brown v. Board of Education, 139, 171, 172, 174, 178
  impairment of self-esteem, 175–76
  inclusivity of Fourteenth Amendment, 173
  overrides *Plessy v. Ferguson*, 176
  separate but equal doctrine, 173, 174
  subsequent history of, 176
  use of social science data in, 174, 175
  value of diversity, 175
Brownsword, Roger. *See* Beyleveld, Deryck
Brudney, Daniel, 47, 48
Butler, Paul, 198

Cain, Patricia A., 273n.77
Carey v. Population Services International, 147
"Catamitus," interpretations of, 191
Chomsky, Noam, 193
City of Richmond v. J. A. Croson Co., 196
Civic republican, contrasted with civic humanist, 50
Civil disobedience, 34–35. *See also* Duty to obey law
Civil liberties
  basic, 178
  citizen's responsibility to protect, 178
  versus civil rights, 177
  when most fragile, 178
Common good, 25
Common Law, The, 182, 269n.5
Communitarian. *See* Civic republican, contrasted with civic humanist
Compelling state interest test, 177. *See also* Privacy, versus a state's compelling interest
Conceptual framework, 103
  when differing from our own, 123–24
Conceptual scheme
  compared with conceptual framework, xiii (*see also* Conceptual framework)
  confines truth, 97
  described, xiii
  incoherent, 127
  and justification, xiii (*see also* Truth, coherence; Truth, correspondence)
  as providing unity and organization, 97, 256n.12
Consent, hypothetical, 47–52. *See also* Deontologist, consent-
Constitutional interpretation
  democratic process approach, 82
  original intent, 82, 183
  role of history, 83
  role of language, 83
Conventionalism, 84–85
Cornell, Drucilla, 205, 206, 273n.89
Courts. *See* Judiciary, the
Cover, Robert M., 147
Critical legal studies (CLS), x, 18, 69, 117, 193, 201, 204–7

central theme of, 22
confuses groundlessness with senselessness, 206, 273n.89
focus on content, 204
law lacks foundations, 204
law may lack meaning, 205
law reflects politics or ideology, 207
legal doctrine cannot be shown consistent, 204, 222
limited positive jurisprudence of, 205
nihilistic and without social vision, 204
only concerned with external skepticism, 206
outgrowth of legal realism, 14
and politics, x, 204, 213
and power, 27, 273n.86
See also Legal realism
Critical race theory/theorists, 69, 193, 201
basis for shared global discourse, 200
as a black perspective, 200–201
can expose subtle racism, 200, 272n.60
cannot resolve factual questions, 198
and different voices, 197, 198
do not play truth language game, 197
do not commit the traditionalist mistake, 196
first-person perspective in, 200
grounding of, 197
and jury nullification, 198
question ideological assumptions, 196
need for common ground, 197
race behind conservative and liberal theories, 195
and rationalizations, 197
rights idea creates political immobilization, 195
subjective, not intersubjective, 200–201
versus freedom of speech, 200
See also Williams, Patricia
Critical theory, 19–22. *See also* Critical legal studies
Culp, Jerome, 201

D'Amato, Anthony, 241n.5
Davidson, Donald, xv, 84, 86, 101, 103, 105, 109, 110, 137
agreement thesis, 89, 100, 101, 105
incoherent to talk about schemes, 127
outside field linguist, 105
principle of charity (*see* Davidson, Donald, agreement thesis)
relation of truth to language, 122
and the scheme/content distinction, xv, 106, 114–15, 127, 225
and truth as satisfaction, 114
truth in metaethics, 106
truth in metaphysics, 104
undermines metaphysical or scientific existence, 106
as an upper limit to inquiry, 220, 223
Dead Man Walking, 184
Deconstruction, 84
criticisms of, 85–86, 87–88, 89, 102–3
displaces the ethical, 206
must buy into a broader framework, 88, 255n.89
rise of, 254n.76
self-referential paradox in, 87–88, 254n.87, 255n.88
undermines social critique, 85
versus Davidson's agreement thesis, 89
versus Kant's moral theory, 88–89
and Western idealism, 87
Defense of Marriage Act (DOMA), 188
Democracy, 26, 38, 239n.121
deontological and teleological functions divided, 79
giving a voice, 187
justified, 55, 187
Deontological
contrasted with teleological, 40
explained, 40
Deontologist
consent-, 43
formal-, 44
natural rights, 42
Derrida, Jacques, 85, 87
Descartes, René, 258n.29
Dewey, John, 106, 203
"Disciplines, Subjectivity and the Law." *See* West, Robin

Discourse(s), 223
  and action, 227
  boundaries of, 225, 226
  consisting of higher-ordered frameworks, 224
  contrasts with conceptual scheme, 225
  external viewpoint, 223
  incoherence with respect to, 225
  internal viewpoint, 222–23, 227
  and rules of interpretation, 224, 225
  shape of a cone, 224
  types of, 225
Discrimination. *See* Critical race theory; Equal protection; Feminism
Doctrine of political responsibility, 17, 30, 47, 49–50, 55–56, 59, 62, 85
Dred Scott v. Sanford, 11, 138–39, 164, 171
Due process, 55, 149, 169–70
Duty to obey law, 30–60
  applies both to individuals and institutions, 85
  conceptions about, 61
  from the internal point of view, 34, 110 (*See also* Internal point of view)
  and justice, 2, 5
  limits civil disobedience, 85
  nature of political institution, 36
  need to unite with what law is, 68
  origin of, 31
  as a prima facie obligation, 31, 250n.34
  requires courts to do justice, 78
  role of hard cases in figuring out, xi
  weak interpretation of, 98
Dworkin, Ronald, ix, xvi, 11, 56, 57, 67, 71–72, 73, 74, 77, 81, 83, 97, 98, 99, 107, 108, 111, 116, 148, 161, 168, 174, 206, 221, 226, 265n.44. *See also* Hard cases; Legal idealism (Dworkin's theory); Political morality

Easy cases
  distinguished from hard cases, 118
  and legal obligation, xi–xii (*see also* Duty to obey law; Hard cases)
  not always clear, 82
Economic analysis, 22–26
  and economic efficiency, 22–23
  and wealth maximization, 22
  See also Public choice theory
Egalitarian liberal, 46, 170
Egoism. *See* Utilitarianism, individualist
Eisenstadt v. Baird, 147
Ely, John Hart, 82, 252n.54, 264n.33
Epistemic pragmatism. *See* Pragmatism, epistemic
Equal protection, 55, 119
  egalitarian concern, 169
  for gays and lesbians, 185
  intermediate and rationality tests, 120
  and nondiscrimination legislation, 185, 248n.4
  property rights, 166, 169
  and racial set asides, 196
  right to own property and contract, 166
  suspect classification test, 120
  See also Fourteenth Amendment; Gays and lesbians
Erie Railroad Co. v. Tompkins, 163
Espinoza, Leslie, 199–200
Ethical rationalism, 52–56. *See also* Gewirth, Alan, theory of
External point of view, 91, 99
  compared to the view of the legal philosopher, xi
  contrasted with internal point of view, 73 (*see also* Internal point of view)
  in descriptive discourses, 230
  as incoherent, 101
  in normative discourse, 230
  in judging, 127
  as justifying the duty to obey law, 4 (*see also* Duty to obey law)
  as legitimizing the legal system, 4, 72
  of political philosopher, xi, 127
  as something we can discuss, 99–100
  what Dworkin must show, 96

Fact/value distinction, 125, 227
Federalism, 37
Feinberg, Joel, 33, 143, 160–61, 250n.34

Feminism, 69, 193, 201–4
conflates substantive and strategic concerns, 202
disavows wider ordered frameworks, 203
distinguishes gender discrimination, 202
as essentialism, 201, 203
gives personal experience epistemological standing, 201
and legal realism, 14–15
and the moral point of view, 203
oppression described, 202
and power, 27
and pragmatism, 203
problem of truth, 201, 203
questionable purpose behind, 203
relation to race and other categories, 201–2, 203
strategic concerns, 202–3
substantive concerns, 202
treats gender as a social construct, 201
uses deconstruction and narratives, 201
and voluntariness, 132–33
See also Critical race theory
Finnis, John, 182, 183, 189, 270n.34, 271n.38
against gay marriage, 190
begs the question, 189
claims to start from first principles, 189
connects immorality to all homosexual acts, 189
criticizes European regulation of sexual behavior, 189
defines law, 32
describes same-sex coupling, 189–90
fails to examine own ideology, 189, 190
flags the word "orientation," 189
interpretation of Plato's *Gorgias*, 190
origin of his sexual views, 189
too easy justification for mores, 191
Fish, Stanley, 85
Formalism, 84
goal of, 179
and justice, 183
rigid, 183–88
and status quo ideology, 184
where yields to instrumentalism, 182
Foucault, Michael, 38–39, 266n.61
Foundationalism, 179
and justice, 183
naive, 189–93
where objective foundation exists, 182
Fourteenth Amendment
changing view of, 166–67
incorporation doctrine, 167
Frank, Jerome, 13, 21
Freedom and well-being, 54
and voluntariness, 133
Freud, Sigmund, 102
Frug, Gerald, 273n.86
Fugitive Slave Acts, 147, 148, 149
Fuller, Lon, 16, 32, 92, 124, 128, 226
Full faith and credit clause, 187–88

Gays and lesbians, 183, 273n.77
and discrimination, 185
legal and personal problems of, 188
and marriage, 187, 284n.22
and military service, 119–20
Gewirth, Alan, xiii, 41, 51, 64, 65, 80, 85, 125, 161, 226
on political philosophy, 38, 40
See also Political philosophy
Gewirth, Alan, theory of
and abortion, 154–55
abilities to become an agent, 153–54
and agency, 121–22, 146, 156, 175, 227, 248n.11
basic argument of, 52–54, 125
conceptual and empirical aspects in, 168
contrasted with Ronald Dworkin, xv, 95 (*see also* Dworkin, Ronald)
criticisms of, 134–37
derivation of rights, 229
first-person perspective, 228, 229
and the generic features of action, 52–53, 135
and human action, 52, 227, 262n.27 (*see also* Action, human)
infanticide, 155

Gewirth, Alan, theory of, *continued*
 internal point of view, 121, 125
 interpretation of his theory, xv
 and the is/ought problem, 125, 227
 justification for social rules, 170
 justification for morality, 52–54, 94, 277n.18
 justification for reason, 86, 102
 metaethical approach, 56
 moderates egalitarian and libertarian positions, 170
 moves from subjective to intersubjective perspective, 228, 277n.18
 as a natural law/natural rights theory, 95, 96, 121, 127, 138, 146, 180
 neutral starting point in, 168
 no degrees of being an agent, 153
 normative questions end at agency, 223, 225–26
 objective truth of theory, 122
 prescriptive side, 124
 presuppositions of, 124, 127
 principle of proportionality in, 153, 154
 principle of sufficient reason, 53
 principle of universality, 53, 228
 prospective versus potential agent, 153–54, 160
 provides fair system of law, 110, 127
 and public policy, 229–30
 relevance of history, 134–35
 on rights, 52–53
 role of truth in, 123
 as a satisfactory explanation of moral duties, 152
 and slavery, 150–51
 and strict duties, 136
 and the supportive state, 247n.140
 supreme moral principle in, 54, 121 (*see also* Principle of Generic Consistency)
 as a transcendental argument, 95
 view consistent with separate legislative and judicial functions, 66
 and virtuous behavior, 136
Godlove, Terry, 257n.13
Golden rule, 159
Goodman, Nelson, 278n.20
Gorgias (Plato), 190–91
Gray, John Chipman, 13
Greene, Linda, 195
Griswold v. Connecticut, 140, 146, 216

Habermas, Jürgen, xvi, 228, 276nn.12,16
 and the constitutional state, 262n.36
 criticism of, 229
 distinguishes ethical from moral discourse, 275n.6
 'formal-pragmatic' approach to social theory, 100–101
 and ideal speech situation, 228, 277n.17
 on law, 129, 246n.135, 276n.13
 and public policy, 229
 on Rawl's notion of impartial judgment, 52
 relationship of discourse to facts and norms, 226, 257n.21
 on rights, 247n.139
Hard cases, 16–17
 distinguished from easy cases, 118
 distinguished from very hard cases, ix, 1, 138
 See also Very hard cases
Hardin, Russell, 33
Hare, R. M., 159, 161
Harm(s), 45, 67
Harris, Angela, 201
Hart, H. L. A., 7, 15, 91, 92, 206
 law requires fidelity, 124, 234n.11
 law's connection to morality is contingent, 93
 legal obligations are internal, 93
 obliged versus having an obligation, 15
 primary versus secondary rules, 15, 92, 233n.7
 recognized incompleteness of positivism, 275n.2
 rule of recognition, 15, 222
 and sources of law, 234n.2
 view distinguished from John Austin, 92
 See also Positivism

Hegel, G. W. F., 41–42, 43, 206, 242n.35
Hittinger, Russell, 134, 135, 136
Hobbes, Thomas, 40, 41–42, 43, 44, 45, 47
Hohfeld, Wesley Newcomb, 213, 246n.134
Holmes, Oliver Wendell, 13, 14, 21, 108, 163, 182, 269n.5
Horwitz, Mort J., 21, 164
Hume, David, 41–42, 43, 45, 103, 194, 251n.45, 275n.8

Ingram, David, 276n.16
Instrumentalism, and legal doctrine, 179
Internal point of view
  cannot prove law consistent, 222
  connection with institutional facts, 72
  contrasted with external point of view, 72
  criteria for going beyond traditional sources, 76–77
  described, xiii, 90–91 (*see also* Conceptual scheme)
  in descriptive discourses, 230
  on discourse, 222–23 (*see also* Discourse)
  and easy cases, xiii–ix
  and incompleteness, 81, 90, 221
  of the judge, xiii, 61, 72 (*see also* Judiciary, the)
  in normative discourse, 230
  as a producer of virtual law, 96
  protects whom, 250n.26
  role of pragmatism in, 5
  and the society that views itself as (less) nearly just, 73, 74
  strong interpretation of, 97
  two interpretations of, 97
  and very hard cases, 73–74
  weak interpretation of (*see* Duty to obey law, weak interpretation of)
  See also External point of view; Society
Interpretation(s)
  and bright-line distinctions, 120
  selecting among, 120–21

James, William, 203
Jefferson, Thomas, 150
Johnson, Barbara, 272n.60
Judicial activist, 68, 69–70
Judicial conservative, 68, 69–70
Judicial decisionmaking, 68–71
  and abortion, 161
  approach to, 108
  compared to literary criticism, 112
  can break ideological bias, 185
  and constitutional review, 167, 177, 269n.14
  constrained, 81–82
  controls on, 89, 184–85
  difficult questions for, 90
  dynamic versus static approach to, 72, 220
  and political morality, 116, 155–56
  and popular will, 268n.142
  role of principles versus policies, 116, 168
  relevance of secondary sources to, 118
  and the role of the legal profession, 89
  power of, 184–85
  and slavery, 148
  substantive interpretations in, 120
  traditionalism in, 161–82
  and the use of coherence truth, 116
  vertical versus horizontal approaches to, 119
  when to defer to legislature, 79
  where rights conflict, 122
  who should raise issues, 119
  See also Internal point of view
Judiciary, the
  belief they live in a nearly just society, 90
  cannot reach beyond the Davidsonian limit, 137 (*see also* Davidson, Donald)
  disagreements among, xvi, 116
  duty not to act from idiosyncratic biases, 79
  duty to consider political morality, 5, 117–18

Judiciary, the, *continued*
  duty to move to broader conceptual framework, 81, 98–99
  duty to obey law, 80
  has access to political morality, 137
  in handling philosophical objections, 125–26
  the Marxist judge, 79–80
  must decide very hard cases, 221
  no duty to obey an immoral law, 79
  no power of its own, 176
  preserving the legitimacy of, 5, 76
  relation to changing maps, 8
  responsibility to do justice, 62
  role distinguished from others, 69
  role of, 3, 55, 66
  shift from internal to external viewpoint, 127
Jurisprudence, schools of, 28. *See also under specific titles*
Justice
  central to all morality (distributive), 64
  concept of versus conception of, 63
  corrective (rectificatory), 62
  corrective versus distributive, 62–63
  distinguished from common good, 25, 63
  distributive, 63, 65
  as an end of political responsibility, 62–67
  issues ever present, 213
  leaves some issues open, 65
  not always about agency, 65
  principles of, 49
  relation to fundamental rights, 84
  segregation, 174
Justice Accused. See Cover, Robert M.

Kahane, Howard, 254n.87
Kant, Immanuel, 40, 42, 43, 45, 47, 51, 87, 189, 206
  cannot know the thing in itself, 105
  distinction between self as subject and self as object, 88
  presupposes freedom, 125, 273n.89
  pure concepts of the understanding, 103, 200, 201, 257n.13
Kennedy, Duncan, 192
Knowledge, as intersubjective understanding(s), 105, 106–7. *See also* Davidson, Donald, agreement thesis
Kohl, Herbert, 253n.63
Korematsu v. United States, 177, 177–78
Kripke, Saul, 114, 260n.5

Langdell, Christopher Columbus, 181–82
Larrain, Jorge, 278n.20
Law(s), 7
  ahistorical understanding of, 128
  categories of differentiation for, 132
  coherence of, xi (*see also* Truth, coherence)
  concept of action in, 227
  in a corrupt system, 80
  definitions of, 9, 32, 130
  described, 132
  descriptive versus prescriptive, 35
  as a distinct normative practice, 28
  as encouraging technological change, 2
  foundationalism in, 182
  harms caused by too narrow a view of, 180–81
  ideological assumptions behind, 191
  institution of, 4
  instrument for human flourishing, 208
  and justice, 35
  justification for, 98, 132
  maintains existing power structures, 3
  metalegal criteria for, 1 (*see also* Metatheory)
  methodological conservatism in, 182
  and morality, 2
  nature of, 8 (*see also* Thomas Aquinas, Saint)
  neutrality of, x
  not self-regulating, 247n.152
  pedigree for, 35
  and the Principle of Generic Consistency, 128–29, 130, 132
  problem of social order in, 128
  real, 137

as the regulation of social behavior, 128, 137
relationship of truth to, 115–16
relevance of moral reason in, 128
requirements to be morally legitimate, 131
sources of, xi, 234n.2 (*see also* Hart, H. L. A., primary versus secondary rules; Traditional sources of law)
and transcendental essentialism, 128
types of procedures for positing, 131–32
uses of "law," 27, 35, 133
variation in content of, 131
See also under specific titles
"Law, Morality and Sexual Orientation." *See* Finnis, John
Law, practice of, 214–19
and attorney salaries, 217
clients seen as customers, 214–15
and continuing legal education, 218–19
different tiers of service in, 215
and doctrinal analysis in, 215
in governmental agencies, 216–17
hours worked in, 218
and market effects, 217
more young lawyer–client contact, 216, 218
and the new lawyer, 214
need to pool resources and services, 217–18
predictability not enough, 215
problem of too many cases, 216
pro bono cases, 218
providing advice and damage control, 215
sometimes requires creative approach, 215
types of research in, 217
Lawrence, Charles R., III, 196
Law schools. *See* Legal education
Laws Empire. *See* Dworkin, Ronald
Legal constructivism, 193–207
believes neutral principles are biased, 182
believes some legal concepts have outlived their usefulness, 182
has an ideology of victimization, 207
instrumental aspect most important, 207
as instrumentalism/nonfoundationalism, 181, 193, 207
no reasoned end, 207
willingness to unmask ideology, 207
Legal education
and bar examinations, 212
case method in, 181–82, 210
courses in, 209, 231
different in Europe, 193
dissertation for future law teachers, 211–12
effects nonpractitioners, 192
extremist views in, not everyone's, 182
fails to provide adequate tools, 192
and human flourishing, 208
in interdisciplinary programs, 210, 212
must include a formal practicum, 211
must include a moral education, 208
must include philosophy of law, 209, 210–11
need for continuing legal education, 218–19
needs to focus on foundations, 208
not served by traditionalism or constructivism, 212
and one's political responsibilities, 231
politics in, 180
relevance of deconstruction in, 211
relevance of social sciences to, 210
role of philosophy in, 213, 230
reproduces hierarchy, 192–93
as a search for middle ground, 180
should emphasize conceptual and normative analyses, 209, 231
should hear different voices, 196
should maximize our understanding, 181
should question received legal principles, 210
should see philosophy as law's foundation, 213
as a spectrum of viewpoints, 182

Legal education, *continued*
  should support our ability to govern ourselves, 213
  teaches reasoning by analogy, 210
  trains future appellate court judges, 193
Legal education, pre-, 274n.97
  adjustment for upper class undergraduates, 209
  subjects to be included, 209
Legal idealism (Dworkin's theory), 16–19, 27, 225
  and abortion, 157–58
  account of internal and external untenable, 107
  best constructive interpretation, 17, 93, 96, 112, 138, 206
  believes ethical statements are internal, 95, 234n.11
  challenge(s) to, 18–19, 95, 116, 148–49
  circularity in, 222
  on CLS, 206
  compared to literary criticism, 112
  and conceptual relativism, 103
  contrasts to natural law, 33
  distinguishes global internal from internal skepticism, 206
  on external skepticism, 94, 99, 127
  fails to distinguish epistemic and justificatory moves, 221
  internal skepticism, 94
  judge Hercules, 18, 78, 126, 168, 173–74, 174
  law as integrity, 4, 18–19, 222
  metaprinciple in, 222
  must fit settled law or political morality, 17, 221
  necessary connection of law to morality, 93, 234n.11
  no consistency proof for, 222
  notion of a constitutional person, 157–58
  obligation to obey law is internal, 93–94
  political morality in, ix, 56, 79, 206
  principle of interpretation in, 221
  principles versus policies, 69, 77, 118, 118–19
  and the problem of slavery, 96, 147, 148, 149, 206
  right answer in every case, 221
  rules versus principles, 16, 70, 117, 118
  separation of internal and external, 73
  treats law as a complete system, 221
  and very hard cases, 96, 221
  See also Hard cases; Internal point of view; Legal principles; Political morality
Legal orders, 131
  legal order is a moral order, 129
Legal philosophy, xii
  judge's, 68
  relationship to political philosophy, 31, 220
  See also Metatheory; Political philosophy
Legal pragmatist movement, 14
Legal principles, ix, 17, 210
Legal realism, 13–14
  non-rule-governed, 221
  and the practice of law, 2
Legal realist judge, 69. *See also* Legal realism
Legislature, function of, 55
Leibniz, G. W., 114, 260n.5
Libertarians, 45–46
  contrasted with egalitarian liberals, 46, 170
Litowitz, Douglas, 81, 238n.102
Llewellyn, Karl, 13, 14
Locke, John, 41, 42, 43, 44, 45, 47, 63
Lockner v. New York, 139, 162, 165, 168, 169, 172
Long Time Companion, 184

McDowell, John, 126
MacIntyre, Alasdair, 134
Mackie, J. L., 18, 148
MacKinnon, Catharine, 21, 202, 203, 243n.83
MacPherson v. Buick Motor Company, 59
Madison, James, 49, 241n.19
Magellan, Ferdinand, 151

Marbury v. Madison, 269n.14
Marquis, Don, 160, 161
Marshall, John, 148
Marx, Karl, xiii, 19–20, 132. *See also* Marxism
Marxism, 27, 102, 251n.43
  and critical theory, 19–21 (*see also* Critical legal studies)
  and legal realism, 14
Matsuda, Mari J., 22, 200
Matter of Principle, A. *See* Legal idealism
Metaethical, 56
  and law, 98
  presupposed by normative statements, 95
  See also Gewirth, Alan, theory of
Metatheory, 249n.23
  as the best theory of politics, 78
  as bridging internal and external theories of law, 3–4
  CLS position attenuated, 222–23
  compared to traditional sources of law, xii
  composite of legal and political philosophies, 71
  contained in super metatheory, 103
  descriptive view of, 68–72, 220
  different from Dworkin's view, 77–78
  does not always reach the highest norms, 180
  does not reduce to politics, 71
  elements of, xii
  establishes levels to evaluate legal decisionmaking, 95
  as a hierarchy of conceptual frameworks, 180
  inquires into the legitimacy of decisions, 180
  and legal decisionmaking, 108
  must avoid incommensurability, 71–72, 110, 250n.25
  need to rethink settled cases, 4
  not a substantive theory, 78
  open to outside critiques, 71
  prescriptive view of, 72–82, 108, 220
  and promoting voluntary purposive action, 80
  provides a possible consistency for law, 222
  reconciles Dworkin and Gewirth's viewpoints, xv, 134
  relation to legal theory, 28–29, 61–62
  role of, 83
  sense of objectivity in, 220
  should determine appropriate sources of law, 3
  See also Pragmatism, epistemic
Michelman, Frank I., 245n.94
Mill, James, 41–42, 44
Mill, John Stuart, 20, 41–42, 44, 180
Miller, J. Hillis, 259n.36
Minow, Martha, 201
Montesquieu, Baron de, 36, 241n.15
Moore, Michael, 236n.30. *See also* Separation of powers
Moral education, described, 208
Morality
  concerned with voluntary purposive behavior, 64
  duty of government, 79
  foundation for, 39, 64, 65
  as ground for human action, 32
  presupposition behind all theories of, 127
  similarity with scientific inquiry, 39
  See also Political morality
Münch, Richard, 241n.2
Murfin, Ross C., 254n.76

Natural, the concept of the, 11, 174
  as a social construction, 174
Natural law, 8
  and the Court, 263n.51
  and the Davidsonian limit, 223
  double effect, 236n.36
  and duty to obey law, 32
  fact/value gap, 227
  forfeiture test, 236n.36
  interpretative view of, 10–11
  objections to, 11–12
  and slavery, 150, 151
  as a source for law, 59

Natural law, *continued*
sources of, 27
theories, 41
versus socially based theories, xv
and very hard cases, xii
and war crime trials, 11
See also Thomas Aquinas, Saint
Neutrality, fundamental rights versus an institutional commitment to, 176. *See also* Sunstein, Cass, and "neutrality"
Nietzsche, Friedrich, 39, 85, 255n.89, 259n.36
on the self, 258n.28
truth as illusion, 104
will to power, 102
Ninth Amendment, 145–46
Nozick, Robert, 63
Nussbaum, Martha, 191, 208–9, 210, 231, 271n.38

Objectivity, 89, 220
Original position. *See* Rawls, John, original position of
Owl of Minerva, the, 242n.35

Partridge, P. H., 250n.32
Plako v. Connecticut, 167
Planned Parenthood of Southeastern Pennsylvania v. Casey, 266n.79
Plato, 41–42, 43, 62, 106, 189
Gorgias, 190
man-boy relations, 191
and modern terminology, 191
The Republic, 42, 100, 197
translations of, 190–91
Plessy v. Ferguson, 11, 139, 171, 172, 173, 174, 176
Political activist, 68, 70–71
Political conservative, 68–69, 70–71
Political Liberalism, 48–49, 50, 51
Political morality
compared to reasoning by analogy, 59
connection to political institutions, 56
and democracy, 145
external to legal theory, 110
foundation for, 106
in general, ix, 26
as a ground for a metatheory, xii
internal inconsistency of, x, 116
in justifying the institution of law, xii, 221–22, 251n.42
limits on society's morality, xii
need to evaluate political decisions, 178
and nonarbitrariness, 4
prevailing, 138
related to our intersubjective understandings, 106–7, 259n.46
as society's morality, ix, x, xi, 19, 138, 155, 178
universal, ix
which to choose, 121
Political philosophy, xii, 36–46
judge's, 68
central questions of, 40, 44–46
and legal philosophy, 31, 220 (*see also* Metatheory)
merging deontological and utilitarian criteria, 46, 264n.36
Political responsibility. *See* Doctrine of Political Responsibility
Positivism, 12
criticisms of, 13, 15–16
descriptive, 35, 92, 221 (*see also* Austin, John)
internal point of view, 15, 234n.11 (*see also* Internal point of view)
and justice, 256n.5
and metarules, xii
nature of law, 2
and Nazi society, 80–81, 92
separation thesis, 31, 92
See also Hart, H. L. A.
Posner, Richard, xvi, 14, 85, 87, 108, 146, 167, 172, 182, 268n.133
Postmodernism, 253nn.63,64, 257n.13
distinct strains of, 86
poststructuralism versus neopragmatism, 86–87
and reason, 84
and realism, 84
See also Poststructuralism

Poststructuralism, 102, 258nn.27,28. *See also* Deconstruction
Pound, Roscoe, 213
Prado, C. G., 38
Pragmatism, 5, 100, 103, 259n.47
  epistemic, 60, 109
  instrumental aspect of, 109, 118
  not teleological, 108–9
  root in deontological understanding, 109
Primary sources, versus secondary sources, 15, 57. *See also* Traditional sources of law
Principle of Charity. *See* Davidson, Donald, agreement thesis
Principle of Generic Consistency (PGC), 54, 132, 136, 177, 277n.19
  protects agency, 133
  See also Gewirth, Alan, theory of; Law, and the Principle of Generic Consistency
Principles versus facts, disputes about, 118. *See also* Legal idealism, principles versus policies; Legal idealism, rules versus principles
Prisoner's dilemma, 243n.43
Privacy, 18, 264n.36
  and abortion, 152, 156–57
  and action, 141, 143, 274n.108
  developed in separate areas of law, 140
  general right to, 264n.33
  must not impinge on basic interest, 142
  and public morality, 144
  as a relational concept, 142
  not relative, 142
  tort, 263n.11
  versus a state's compelling interest, 143–44
Public choice theory, 23–25
  criticisms of, 24–25
  difference between public and private interests, 24
  politics, 25
Putman, Hilary, 86, 105–6, 253n.65
Quine, Willard van Orman, 256n.12, 260n.4

Radin, Margaret Jane, 203
Ratio cognoscendi, 72, 250n.29
Ratio essendi, 72, 245n.28
Rawls, John, xiii, 41, 48, 75, 85, 146
  different functions for courts and legislatures, 36
  distinguishes concept of justice from conception, 63
  meliorates courts' doing justice, 50
  method to discover natural rights, 243n.56
  original position of, 48–49, 50
  presupposes reasonable comprehensive doctrines, 56, 245n.103
  as a top-down theory, 108
  treats person politically, not metaphysically, 51
Raz, Joseph, 18
Reagan, Ronald, 24–25
Reason(s), 84, 86, 251n.42
  as ego-centered, 102, 258n.28
  internal versus external, 126
  in law, 126–27
  practical, 107–9
  theoretical, 99–107
  See also Analogical reasoning; Gewirth, Alan, theory of, principle of sufficient reason
Reason and Morality. *See* Gewirth, Alan, theory of
Regulatory politics. *See* Public choice theory
Rehg, William, 100, 129–30, 246n.135, 257n.13, 273n.89, 276n.13
Republic, The (Plato), 42, 100, 197
Rhode, Deborah, 201
Rights
  constitutional protection of, 249n.24
  and problem of voluntariness, 132–33, 251n.45, 273n.89
  property, 165–66
  prudential, 53
  responsibility for ensuring, 176–77

Rights, *continued*
  versus civil liberties (*see* Civil liberties, basic)
  versus an institutional commitment to neutrality, 176
Right to Privacy. *See* Privacy
Rigid scrutiny test. *See* Compelling state interest test
Roe v. Wade, 139, 140, 147, 152, 266n.79
Romany, Celina, 201
Romer v. Evans, 185, 186, 215
  Scalia's dissent in, 186
Roosevelt, Franklin D., 162
Rorty, Richard, 84, 85, 106, 114, 242n.20, 253n.64, 257n.13
Rousseau, Jean-Jacques, 41–42, 43, 44, 45, 47, 87, 249n.18
Rubenfeld, Jed, 264n.36
Rule of Recognition. *See* Hart, H. L. A.
Russell, Bertrand, 213

Same-sex marriage, 187–88
  place for unwanted children, 188
Sandel, Michael, 254n.85
Sartre, Jean-Paul, 257n.13
Scalia, Antonin, 186
Schelling, Alan White, 257n.13
Schumpeter, Joseph, 238n.121
Searle, John, 100
Separation of powers, 37
Shauer, Frederick, 82
Singer, Joseph, 204, 205
Skepticism, 206
Slaughterhouse Cases, 162
Slavery, 96, 147, 155–56, 187
Slouching Towards Gomorrah. *See* Bork, Robert
Social constructionism, 97. *See also* Critical race theory; Feminism; Internal point of view, strong interpretation of; Legal constructivism
Society, 74–75
  distinction between view and being nearly just, 76
Spencer, Herbert, 45
State of nature, 42–43
Substantive principle
  provides meaning, 83
  versus semantic principle, 82
Sunstein, Cass, xv, 83, 173, 182, 250n.38
  and concept of the natural, 174
  criticism of holistic theories, 57
  describes debate over formalism in law, 84
  kinds of principles, 82
  and "neutrality," 163, 169, 171, 172, 192
  questions usefulness of external viewpoint, 107–8
  top-down versus bottom-up theories of law, 108
  view compared with other legal theorists, xv–xvi
Swift v. Tyson, 163

Tarski, Alfred, 114
Teleological, 40
Thatcher, Margaret, 24–25
Theory of Justice, *A*. *See* Rawls, John
Thomas Aquinas, Saint, 8, 41, 161
  effect of history on, 135
  first requirement of nature, 153
  law defined, 9
  natural law, 10 (*see also* Natural law)
  nature of law, 8–9, 10
  on purposiveness, 9, 125, 235n.19
  types of law, 9
  view of nature, 9–10
Thomas, Clarence, 11
Thomas v. Winchester, 58
Tidman, Paul, 254n.87
Traditionalism, 183–93
  concern for foundations, 207
  criticisms of, 192–93
  foundational aspect most important, 207
  method of decisionmaking, 181–82
  as rigid formalism/naive foundationalism, 181, 183, 207
  protects ideological superstructure, 192–93

takes formalism as an end in itself, 207
unwilling to question assumptions, 207 (*see also* Bork, Robert; Finnis, John)
versus legal constructivism, 181
See also Legal constructivism

Traditional sources of law, xii, 26, 99, 109, 110, 126, 234n.2

Truth
analytic, 113, 260nn.4,5
coherence, 111, 115
correspondence, 106, 113, 117
eludes us, 213
and Gewirth, 123
as illusion, 104, 266n.61
in law, 115–16, 118
in metaphysics, 104
more than disquotationalism, 106
notion of satisfaction, 114
as related to knowledge, 105
as related to meaningful inquiry, 104, 220
relation to experience, 113
of sentences, 122
synthetic, 113–14, 260n.4
two understandings of, 110–15
undecidable, 221, 222
See also Davidson, Donald, agreement thesis

Unger, Roberto, 237n.60

United States v. Carolene Products Co., 166

Universalizability, principle of, 53

Utilitarianism
and harm, 45
individualist, 41, 45
merit, 44
organic, 41, 42
result-, 44
rule, 41

Very hard cases, ix
differs from hard cases, 138
effect on easy cases, xiv
and internal point of view, xii (*see also* Internal point of view)
need for philosophical critique, 3
rules in, 3
use of substantive principles in, xii
See also Hard cases

Virtual Law, xiv, 96, 100

Warren, Earl, 172–73

Weber, Max, 102

Wechsler, Herbert, 174, 175

West, Robin, 194, 195

West Coast Hotel v. Parish, 163

White, Byron, 146, 147

Williams, Patricia, 195–96, 272n.60
and teaching evaluations, 198–99
use of first person narratives, 196, 199

Williams, Robert A., 200

Will to power. *See* Nietzsche, Friedrich

Winch, Peter, 250n.26

Winterbottom v. Wright, 58

Wittgenstein, Ludwig, 86, 102, 225, 253n.65
duck-rabbit, 225, 226, 228